The Myth of Middle East Exceptionalism

Contemporary Issues in the Middle East
Mehran Kamrava, *Series Editor*

For a full list of titles in this series, visit
https://press.syr.edu/supressbook-series
/contemporary-issues-in-the-middle-east/.

The Myth of Middle East Exceptionalism

Unfinished Social Movements

Edited by **Mojtaba Mahdavi**

Syracuse University Press

∞ The paper used in this publication meets the minimum requirements
of the American National Standard for Information Sciences—Permanence
of Paper for Printed Library Materials, ANSI Z39.48-1992.

For a listing of books published and distributed by Syracuse University Press,
visit https://press.syr.edu/.

ISBN: 978-0-8156-3799-8 (hardcover)
978-0-8156-3792-9 (paperback)
978-0-8156-5577-0 (e-book)

Library of Congress Cataloging-in-Publication Data

Names: Mahdavi, Mojtaba, editor.
Title: The myth of Middle East exceptionalism : unfinished social movements /
edited by Mojtaba Mahdavi.
Description: First edition. | Syracuse, New York : Syracuse University Press, 2023. |
Series: Contemporary issues in the Middle East | Includes bibliographical references and index.
Identifiers: LCCN 2022041129 (print) | LCCN 2022041130 (ebook) |
ISBN 9780815637998 (hardcover ; alk. paper) | ISBN 9780815637929 (paperback ; alk. paper) |
ISBN 9780815655770 (ebook)
Subjects: LCSH: Protest movements—Arab countries—History—21st century. |
Social movements—Middle East—History—21st century. | Democracy—Middle East—
History—21st century. | Middle East—Politics and government—21st century.
Classification: LCC JQ1850.A91 M98 2023 (print) | LCC JQ1850.A91 (ebook) |
DDC 303.48/409174927—dc23/eng/20221122
LC record available at https://lccn.loc.gov/2022041129
LC ebook record available at https://lccn.loc.gov/2022041130

Manufactured in the United States of America

For ordinary and underrepresented people of MENA,
whose struggle for social justice debunks
myth of Middle East exceptionalism
and
In memory of Mahsa (Zhina) Amini (2000–2022),
a woman and a subaltern who was murdered
by Iran's ruling Islamists

Mahsa (Zhina) Amini (2000–2022)

Contents

viii   Contents

Foreword

John L. Esposito

The world witnessed an historic series of unanticipated popular uprisings in 2011–12 by pro-democracy movements in the Arab world. Like a tsunami, they emerged as if from nowhere, toppling in rapid succession entrenched dictators and their authoritarian regimes in Tunisia, Egypt, Libya, and Yemen and demanding reforms in Morocco, Algeria, Syria, Jordan, Saudi Arabia, Kuwait, Bahrain, and Oman.

Few, either Arab and Western governments or policy makers and Middle East experts, expected that popular nonviolent uprisings by pro-democracy movements would topple the governments. The predominance of autocrats and authoritarian governments in much of the Arab world, with formidable military and security forces, had led many, including their citizens, to question whether democratic change would occur in their lifetime.

Many policy makers and experts believed that Islam and Arab culture were incompatible with democracy. The specter of new governments coming to power made many Western governments anxious as they faced unforeseen consequences and the possibility of new, more independently minded governments. Their initial response was to hesitate and equivocate in speaking out forcefully to clearly distance themselves from these authoritarian Arab regimes and to support the democratic forces. Others, such as President Nicolas Sarkozy of France and Prime Minister Silvio Berlusconi of Italy, supported Zine El Abidine Ben Ali and Muammar Qaddafi, respectively, until the very end.

The threat of global terrorism had long provided a convenient excuse for Muslim autocrats with Western support to suppress or severely restrict democratization, the rule of law, human rights, civil society, and nongovernment organizations. Autocrats warned that the promotion of a democratic process risked furthering Islamist inroads into centers of power and threatened stability, security, and Western interests.

The United States and many Western governments followed the maxim "The devil you know is better than the devil you don't" and were blinded to the empirical evidence reported by major polls such as the Gallup World Polls (2001–7) that majorities in the Muslim world wanted democratization: greater power sharing, government accountability, freedoms, human rights, and an end to corruption. Moreover, Islamists in Egypt, Jordan, Kuwait, Morocco, Turkey, Malaysia, and Indonesia had for decades participated in mainstream society through elections and had served in city and national governments (in parliaments, cabinets, and leadership positions).

The United States, driven by its national interest (access to oil, the security of Israel and other strategically important locations), had long supported and thus perpetuated "friendly" authoritarian allies. Ambassador Richard Haas, a senior State Department official during the George W. Bush administration, confirmed this policy in 2002, stating that before the invasion of Iraq, both Democratic and Republican administrations practiced "democratic exceptionalism" in the Muslim world, "subordinating democracy to other national interests such as accessing oil, containing the Soviet Union and grappling with the Arab–Israeli conflict" (Haass 2002; see also Esposito and Mogahed 2007, 58, 91).

No wonder that although there was a widespread desire for democracy, which many viewed as necessary for their progress, majorities of those polled had disagreed with the statement that "the US is serious about encouraging the establishment of democratic systems of government in this region" (Esposito and Mogahed 2007, 58).

Pro-democracy movements and demands were driven not by religion but by long-standing political and economic issues and grievances: the lack of democracy, repression, a growing gap between a wealthy minority and the poor, rampant corruption, high unemployment levels, as well as lack of opportunity and of a sense of a future for young people. Protesters wished to reclaim their pride, dignity, and control over their lives and claim the right to determine their governments and the destiny of their lives and nation, demanding more government accountability and transparency, rule of law, respect for human rights, and an end to political repression.

The Arab uprisings revealed a broad-based inclusive movement, one not led by a single individual or driven by a single secular or religious ideology. People from every walk of life, professionals and laborers, were united in a common cause. Young and old, women and men, Muslims and Christians, the poor, middle, and upper classes, Islamists and secularists joined together in Tunisia, in Egypt's Tahrir (Liberation) Square, and across much of the Arab world. Despite the dire warnings from many rulers and the fears felt by Western governments, these popular uprisings were not an attempt at an Islamist takeover but a broad-based call for reform. Their signs, slogans, and demands were not for an Islamic state or

Islamist-dominated state. Egyptians, for example, spoke of one Egypt, singing the Egyptian national anthem and waving Egyptian flags, not Islamist placards.

Though initially not among the leadership, Islamist candidates and parties swept into power in Egypt (the Muslim Brotherhood's Freedom and Justice Party and the Salafis' Noor Party, for instance) and Tunisia (Ennahda or Renaissance Party) in postuprising elections. Far from monolithic, the Muslim Brotherhood, Ennahda, and Salafis represented diverse currents: ideologically, politically, and socioeconomically. If many voted for Islamists, many others were dismayed and feared Islamist rule would lead to increased religiosity in politics.

Election results in Egypt and Tunisia were for the first time in their histories the product of a free and fair process. Many hoped that this process was a beginning—a first step on a path toward a future that they hoped would consist of free and fair elections, more political parties, more freedoms, and the evolution of democracy in a region where they had long been absent. American and European policy makers were challenged to work with Islamically oriented government leaders. New governments in both Egypt and Tunisia faced formidable challenges: not only the "deep state" made up of the military, security, judiciary, and vast bureaucracy of the former Mubarak and Ben Ali governments but also the expectations of diverse sectors of society, in particular the need to jump-start failed economies and high unemployment.

After the uprisings, the new governments of Egypt and Tunisia struggled to govern and to deal with opposition critics and movements. The lack of compromise among Egyptian political elites led to an exclusive system in which the winners exercised unchecked authority over the very foundations of their country's political and economic institutions. In contrast to Ennahda's more inclusive political process in Tunisia, the Morsi government in Egypt installed many Islamists (Muslim Brothers and Salafis) in key power positions, often to the exclusion or minimal representation of those in the April 6 movement, "secularists," and Copts. A nationwide anti-Morsi and anti-Brotherhood protest movement galvanized on June 30, 2013, around the anniversary of Mohamed Morsi's troubled first year in power. On July 3, Morsi was ousted by General Abdel Fattah al-Sisi in a military-led coup.

By 2013, the Arab Spring began to look like an Arab Winter with the restoration of authoritarianism in Egypt as well as chaos, civil war, and sectarian violence in other countries, such as Libya, Bahrain, Yemen, and Iraq. The retrenchment in the post–Arab Spring included the military-led coup and the restoration of authoritarian governance in Egypt with major support from the United Arab Emirates (UAE) and Saudi Arabia. The United States and the United Kingdom, with closer ties to authoritarian Arab allies such as Saudi Arabia and the UAE, who seek to outlaw nonviolent Islamic movements and political parties, label some groups such as the Muslim Brotherhood and its alleged affiliates at home and abroad as terrorist organizations. These policies and actions played into the hands of and contributed to the rise and support of militant jihadists such as the Islamic State of Iraq and Syria (ISIS).

The United States and Europe did not act on their stated principles and values of self-determination, government accountability, rule of law, and human rights. They accepted the restoration of authoritarianism in Egypt. Secretary of State John Kerry described Egypt as on the path to democracy, and the Obama administration and Congress approved aid packages, legitimating the widespread belief in the Arab world that the United States and the European Union have long had a double standard when it comes to the promotion and support for democratization in the Middle East.

In contrast to Egypt, Tunisia on the whole has made significant strides toward democratization. Despite strong disagreements, some violence, and politically and religiously motivated roadblocks, Tunisia's Ennahda demonstrated a commitment to national unity and to the institutional formation of a robust democracy, characterized by an inclusive constitution, a progressive electoral law, and an institutional setting that prioritizes dialogue and compromise over exclusion and partisanship.

Ennahda won a plurality in Tunisia's first free democratic elections and reached out to include secular opposition parties in the government. After its election, Ennahda backed away from pushing for the integration of Islamic law in the Constitution, and after two years in power and engaging with opposition in dialogue, it opted to step down in favor of technocratic leadership to preserve national unity. The military stayed out of direct involvement in politics, enabling political actors to negotiate a new system.

Western Foreign-Policy Response

The United States and the European Union retreated to the old Western Orientalist narrative of a Middle East exceptionalism: the Arab world and the broader Middle East are perpetually incapable of a strong institutional and democratic reformation. Regional stability and Western national interests were once again perceived as dependent on security and the combating of violent extremism rather than on democratization. This reductionist narrative ignored the domestic realities of authoritarianism in exchange for large business and military contracts from longtime Persian Gulf allies such as Saudi Arabia and the UAE.

Failure to significantly shift from policies that focus on violence and terrorism rather than on their roots causes prioritized stability and security and diverted attention from the critical need for institutional reform. Short-term securitization in the name of political stability and security ignored what major polls in Muslim countries reported regarding the people's desire for democratization, an end to dictatorship, and its replacement with representative and accountable governance and human rights—a desire reflected in the spirit and sacrifices of many participants in the Arab uprisings. This failure and prioritization reinforced anti-Westernism as well as the mantra of militant extremists that neither Arab regimes nor their Western allies will "allow" democratization; this policy can fuel greater radicalization and recruitment by terrorist organizations.

Ironically, a major Pew poll, *The World's Muslims: Religion, Politics, and Society*, reported on April 30, 2013, that most Muslims around the world expressed support for democracy and strongly rejected violence in the name of Islam (Pew Research Center 2013).

Given a choice between a leader with a strong hand and a democratic system of government, most Muslims choose democracy. In a majority of countries surveyed, at least half of Muslims say that they are concerned about religious extremism and Islamic extremist groups.

However, despite the disappointing outcome of the Arab Spring, the genie had been let out of the bottle. Despite the increasingly authoritarian nature of many Arab regimes, in the long run the democratic aspirations and conviction of many in the Arab and broader Muslim world, in particular the younger generations, will not be eradicated in the years to come. The question now is when and what forms a democratic state can and will take place in a Muslim-majority society.

References

Esposito, John L., and Dalia Mogahed. 2007. *Who Speaks for Islam? What a Billion Muslims Really Think*. New York: Gallup Press.

Haass, Richard N. 2002. "Towards Greater Democracy in the Muslim World." Remarks to the Council on Foreign Relations, Washington, DC, Dec. 4. At https://2001-2009.state.gov/s/p/rem/15686.htm.

Pew Research Center. 2013. *The World's Muslims: Religion, Politics, and Society*. Washington, DC: Pew Research Center, Apr. 30. At http://www.pewforum.org/2013/04/30/the-worlds-muslims-religion-politics-society-overview/.

Acknowledgments

The idea for this volume originated years ago when I chaired and co-organized an international interdisciplinary conference, "The Unfinished Project of the Arab Spring: Why the Middle East Exceptionalism Is Still Wrong." It took several years to put this volume together with completely revised versions of selected conference papers as well as additional chapters from invited distinguished scholars.

This edited volume would not have been completed without intellectual and financial support from several distinguished scholars, organizations, colleagues, and students. I am grateful to each of them. For the organization of the conference, we received financial support from the Social Science and Humanities Research Council of Canada, the International Development Research Center in Canada, and the Edmonton Council of Muslim Communities Chair in Islamic Studies at the University of Alberta, among others. Many thanks to my colleague and conference co-organizer, Nermin Allam, as well as to the conference coordinators, Roozbeh Safshekan, Mariam Georgis, and Emrah Keskin.

I am grateful to the anonymous readers who took the time to review the manuscript and offered constructive comments. Special thanks go to my colleague Mehran Kamrava, who included this volume in the Contemporary Issues in the Middle East series, which he edits for Syracuse University Press. I also thank the editorial team at Syracuse University Press for their support and professionalism in publishing this volume. Needless to say, I am solely responsible for any shortcomings in this work.

I thank my research assistant, Ehsan Kashfi, for his invaluable help in the preparation of this volume. The funding from the Edmonton Council of Muslim Communities Chair in Islamic Studies at the University of Alberta as well as the support and encouragement from my colleagues in the Department of Political Science helped to put this volume together.

I dedicate this volume to the unknown and underrepresented ordinary people in the Middle East and North Africa: to women, students, workers, the middle-class poor, minorities, victims of war and occupation, and all Middle Eastern and North African subalterns for their continued quest for freedom, social justice, human dignity, and recognition.

Mojtaba Mahdavi,
July 2022

The Myth of Middle East Exceptionalism

Introduction

The Myth of MENA Exceptionalism

Mojtaba Mahdavi

More than a decade after the birth of contemporary social movements in the Middle East and North Africa (MENA),[1] we may ask what these movements have achieved and how we can evaluate their lasting legacies. Iran's pro-democracy Green Movement of 2009—the first MENA *post-Islamist* mass social movement—did not achieve its political goals. The Gezi Park movement started in Turkey in 2013 but has lost its momentum largely because of President Recep Tayyip Erdoğan's iron fist. And the Arab Spring of 2010–11 remains in multiple crises: Yemen is now home to the world's worst humanitarian crisis owing to a regional proxy war; Bahrain's monarchy suppressed the popular pro-democracy movement; and the so-called humanitarian intervention—a neoliberal invasion—ruined Libya. Chief among the predicaments were the failure of Egyptian Islamism in power and the subsequent return of a military junta to power in 2013, the rise of the Islamic State of Iraq and Syria (ISIS) in Iraq and Syria in 2014, and the breakout of a proxy/civil war in Syria—marked as another major world's humanitarian crisis with mass killing of citizens and destruction of the country. In addition, the Arab secular despots such as Bashar al-Assad in Syria, General Abdel Fattah al-Sisi in Egypt, and the populist Mohammed bin Salman al Saud in Saudi Arabia are consolidating

Earlier versions of several sections of this chapter appeared in "Whither Post-Islamism: Revisiting Discourse/Movement after the Arab Spring," in *Arab Spring and the Quest for New Metaphors: Modernity, Identity, and Change*, ed. Eid Mohamed and Dalia Fahmi (New York: Palgrave Macmillan, 2019), 15–38, and "Introduction: East Meets West? The Unfinished Project of Contemporary Social Movements in the Middle East and Beyond," in "Contemporary Social Movements in the Middle East and Beyond," special issue of *Sociology of Islam* 2, nos. 3–4 (2014): 103–10.

1. It is known to the scholars of critical Middle East studies that the label "Middle East" is a British colonial invention. A more accurate name for "Middle East and North Africa" (MENA) is "West Asia and North Africa" (WANA).

their power (Mahdavi 2019, 15–17). Even the Tunisian post-Islamist democracy seems in a crisis because President Kais Saied issued an emergency rule by decree on July 25, 2021. And last but certainly not the least, the return of the Taliban to power in Afghanistan on August 15, 2021, after two decades demonstrates a profound political crisis in the MENA and Muslim contexts.

On the surface, the confluence of the global power structure and local sociopolitical conditions appear to have repressed the revolutionary spirit in MENA. In other words, the "quiet encroachments" of counterrevolutionary forces seem to have replaced hope with despair and excitement with resentment (Bayat 2013a, 2015). Such catastrophic conditions have largely contributed to the revival of an old Orientalist discourse of "Middle East exceptionalism," implying that the region's *culture* is exceptionally immune to democratic movements, values, and institutions. Even the most recent waves of mass protests in Lebanon, Algeria, Tunisia, Morocco, Sudan, Iraq, and Iran from 2017 to 2022 seem to have had little impact on the advocates and agents of a discourse of MENA exceptionalism.

In this introduction, however, I argue that, contrary to the conventional wisdom, the MENA region has experienced profound sociostructural transformations and is witnessing a "post-Islamist" social condition. MENA social movements are therefore in crisis but not dead; they are "unfinished" endeavors. The post-Islamist condition in MENA, in other words, nullifies the cultural determinism of the Orientalist myth of "MENA exceptionalism" and signifies the "unfinished" and ongoing processes of democratic social movements in the region.

This book's central argument problematizes and demystifies the many faces of the myth of "cultural exceptionalism" in the context of contemporary MENA social movements, which have been revived in the post–Arab Spring era. More specifically, the volume's central argument is presented in three parts. Inspired by a critical postcolonial/decolonial perspective, the first part places MENA in the larger global context, challenges the alleged cultural exceptionalism of the region, and sheds light on the impact of geopolitics on the current crises and how it may shape the interactions of global, regional, and local actors and factors. This part, in other words, puts culture in the larger historical and political context, critiques cultural exceptionalism, and advances the idea of a global MENA (Bayat and Herrera 2021b).

The second part focuses on the "unfinished projects" of contemporary MENA social movements and their quest for freedom, social justice, and human dignity. It examines different case studies in the Arab world and Iran to showcase the dynamism of MENA civil societies in their enduring resistance to the status quo and persistence in pushing for change. This part, in sum, challenges the myth of

MENA exceptionalism by examining specific cases of post-Islamist movements—the Arab youth, student, and other popular nonviolent movements—arguing against the alleged MENA cultural determinism/essentialism/exceptionalism.

A major pillar of the Orientalist discourse of "MENA exceptionalism" is the idea of gender passivity and women's exclusion/exceptionalism, which reduces the reality of gender injustice to some eternal and essentialized Muslim/MENA mindset. The third part takes up this challenge seriously by placing gender as an independent category of thought and action, demonstrating the presence of MENA women's movements, and providing contexts to the cases of gender injustice to debunk such simplistic, ahistorical, and culturalist assumptions. Although acknowledging the existence of gender injustice in the region, part three complicates and contextualizes the argument and demystifies the myth of MENA exceptionalism.

This edited volume, in sum, shows how a postcolonial/decolonial critique better explains the crisis of democratic social movements, the resilience of authoritarianism, and the violent religious and secular politics in the region. It reveals the simplicity and ahistorical assumptions of the Orientalist discourse of cultural exceptionalism.

The Myth of Muslim Exceptionalism

Western Orientalism suggests that the absence of democracy and the crisis of modernity in the Muslim world are owed to the "fact" of Muslim exceptionalism, wherein Islamic tradition and modernity are incompatible, and the public role of Islam inevitably results in autocracy. Modernity, rationalism, and democracy are Western in origin and uniquely suited to the Western culture, this Orientalist argument continues. According to Ernest Gellner, Muslim societies are essentially different from others in that "no secularization has taken place in the world of Islam" (1991, 2). In *Postmodernism, Reason, and Religion* (1992), Gellner argues that Islam has been exceptionally immune to the forces of secularization and that modernization has increased this immunization. Likewise, Bernard Lewis (1990) and Samuel Huntington (1996) argue that Western culture is unique and essentially differs from other civilizations in general and from Islam in particular. According to Huntington, whereas "in Islam, God is Caesar," in the West "God and Caesar, church and state, spiritual and temporal authority have been a prevailing dualism" (1996, 70). For Huntington, "the underlying problem for the West is not Islamic fundamentalism. It is Islam, a different civilization whose people are convinced of the superiority of their culture and are obsessed with the inferiority of their power" (217).

As Asef Bayat reminds us, three factors have contributed to the currency of such an "exceptionalist" view in the study of the Muslim countries. "The first is the continuing relevance of Orientalist/essentializing thought in the West"; the second is "the persistent authoritarian rule" in the Middle East supported by the West; and the third is the emergence of "Islamist movements that have often displaced socially conservative and undemocratic dispositions" (2007, 6). Likewise, José Casanova argues that for the Orientalists modernity is a "civilizational achievement of the Christian West and therefore not easily transferable to other civilizations other than through Western hegemonic imposition, or through the conversion to Western norms" (2001, 1050–51).

As such, for the Orientalists, Muslims and Islamic culture are incompatible with modernity not just because of Islamic fundamentalism but also because of what they consider the fundamental essence of Islam. Similarly, for Bernard Lewis (1988) the inevitable fusion of religion and state is something that historically and intellectually attaches to Islam. Implicit to his argument is that the "Islamic mind" and modern democracy are mutually exclusive.

In his critique of cultural essentialism, however, Nasr Hamed Abu Zeid challenges this Orientalist perception: "To speak about an 'Islamic Mind' in abstraction from all constrains of geography and history, and in isolation from the social and cultural conditioning of Islamic societies, can only lead us into unrealistic, even metaphysical, speculations." Instead, we need to "look for the root of this panic reaction," meaning "the crisis of modernization and [the] complicated relationship between the Islamic world and the West" (2002). Ibrahim Abu-Rabi' echoes Abu Zeid: "In many Muslim countries, hopes for a healthy process of modernization were dashed in the 1960s and 1970s." More specifically, "the petrodollars and the U.S. patronage made the post-colonial Muslim states more dependent on the global market and less on its people. It also released the forces of 'puritanical Islam' and 'militant Salafiyyah,' which endorse violence to eliminate the 'modern jahiliyyah' both at the local and global arenas" (2010, xvii–xviii; see also Mahdavi 2019, 17–20).

In *Islam, Authoritarianism, and Underdevelopment* (2019), Ahmet Kuru masterfully challenges the essentialist Orientalist discourse of blaming Islam as the major cause of authoritarianism and underdevelopment in Muslim societies. Grounded in a historical, sociological, and comparative study of Muslim contexts, he successfully demonstrates that the main cause of authoritarianism and underdevelopment in many Muslim-majority countries is the alliance between the religious scholars, or ulama, and state authorities. In other words, he implicitly both argues against the Islamist agenda of the Islamist state/caliphate and challenges the Orientalist discourse of Islamic exceptionalism.

Islamic Exceptionalism Reinvented?

The post–Arab Spring MENA conditions have profoundly contributed to the revival and reinvention of the discourse of Muslim/Islamic exceptionalism. For example, in *Islamic Exceptionalism* (2016), Shadi Hamid asks, "Why exactly does the Middle East suffer from a lack of legitimate order?" The MENA "legitimacy defeat," he argues, "is tied to a continued inability to reckon with Islam's relationship to the state." "Islam is different." And "Islamic exceptionalism is neither good nor bad" (6). The rationale for such a difference, Hamid argues, is that "the relationship between Islam and politics is distinctive, [and therefore] a replay of the Western model—Protestant Reformation followed by an enlightenment in which religion is gradually pushed into the private realm—is unlikely" (5).

Moreover, the dramatic rise of ISIS, Hamid argues, "is only the most striking example of how liberal determinism—the notion that history moves with intent toward a more reasonable, secular future—has failed to explain Middle East realities" (2016, 5). For Hamid, ISIS "draws on, and draws strength from, ideas that have a broad resonance among Muslim-majority populations. They may not agree with the group's interpretation of the caliphate, but the notion of a caliphate is a powerful one, even among more secular-minded Muslims" (11). He then concludes that "this is not to say that most Arabs or Muslims are Islamists. Most are not. However, one can sympathize with or support Islamist politics without being an Islamist—the phenomenon of Islamism without Islamists" (13).

Shadi Hamid's "Islamic exceptionalism" represents the emerging conventional literature in post–Arab Spring MENA, ascribing cultural exceptionalism to Islam/Muslims, underestimating the impact of geopolitics and postcolonial contexts in the current crises, and overgeneralizing the popularity of the Islamist idea of a caliphate to more than a billion Muslims on multiple continents. In his new book, *The Problem of Democracy* (2022), Hamid seems to reiterate the same discourse of "Islamic exceptionalism" under the new idea of "democratic minimalism." The book essentially suggests that Islamists' illiberal ideas may still win the popular votes in the region and that we must prioritize democracy over liberalism, or "democratic minimalism," for the MENA people. Hamid's idea of Islamic exceptionalism, in other words, symbolizes a body of the literature produced after the failure/crisis of the Arab Spring that seems to blame the Muslim public culture for this failure and thus ignores the structural and discursive transformations of the MENA societies, which were and continue to be evident in the popular slogans chanted by ordinary people in contemporary MENA social movements. For this reason, his argument is briefly problematized here to demystify the myth of

MENA/Muslim/Islamic exceptionalism in the broader public discourse and to nullify the puzzling idea of "Islamism without Islamists" in the literature.

An unintended consequence of Hamid's rationalization and theorization of "Islamic exceptionalism" and "Islamism without Islamists" is to reiterate the old Orientalist cliché of "Muslim exceptionalism." Such a problematic discourse does not capture the complex reality of the contemporary MENA region for the following reasons. First, the region does not suffer from a cultural exceptionalism; the MENA region has instead been affected by a "geopolitical exceptionalism" forged by "the tribology of geography, oil, and Israel—elements that have historically highlighted imperial dominance and international rivalry" (Bayat and Herrera 2021a, 4). The combination of these three geopolitical factors has profoundly contributed to the resilience of authoritarianism, violent religious politics, and the crisis of democratization. A postcolonial/decolonial critique reveals the simplicity and ahistorical assumptions of the Orientalist discourse of cultural exceptionalism and complicates the argument.

Second, the main slogans used by ordinary Muslims/people in the MENA streets in the Arab Spring of 2010–11, Iran's Green Movement of 2009 and post–Green Movements of 2017–22, and Turkey's Gezi Park movement of 2013 were absolutely devoid of a single reference to concepts/ideals such as the caliphate and the Islamic state. The popular quest in the Arab streets was to overthrow the dominant regime (*"Ash-sha'b yurid isqat an-nizam"* [The people want to bring down the regime])—not only the political regime but also, more importantly, as Hamid Dabashi (2012) argues, the hegemonic regime of knowledge and dominant apologetic postcolonial paradigms of pan-Arabism and other forms of state-sponsored nationalism, the outdated discourse of Third World socialism, and the exhausted *dawah* of Islamism. Equally important was the quest for *hurriyya* (freedom), *'adala ijtima'iyya* (social justice), and *karama* (dignity). Millions of ordinary people—men and women, young and old, religious and secular, Muslims and non-Muslims—chanted such popular and post-Islamist slogans in the Arab streets. Furthermore, Juan Cole reminds us that during the Tamarod (Rebellion) movement "in June 2013 some 22 million Egyptians signed a petition asking Morsi to leave office, far more than [the] 13 million who voted for him" (2014, 20). This is also true of the more recent popular demonstrations in Iran from December–January 2017–18 to November 2019, August and November 2021, and September 2022; the Lebanese protest in October 2019; the Algerian movement of 2019; the Iraqi protests of 2019–21; the Sudanese movements of 2019–21; the Tunisian protest in 2021; as well as the women's demonstration against the Taliban and the Panjshir resistance in Afghanistan in 2021. These movements and public protests have been absolutely devoid of a public quest for any form of Islamist caliphate/state. More specifically, it is important to note that the main motto of Iran's most recent democratic mass movement since September 2022—"*Zan, Zendegi, Azadi*" (Women, Life, Freedom)—clearly demonstrates people's quest for women's rights over their own bodies and rejects the Islamist patriarchal and misogynistic values. Iran's anti-Islamist movement largely led by women nullifies the ideas of "Islamic exceptionalism" and "democratic minimalism" for the MENA region.

Third, Hamid's concepts of "Islamic exceptionalism" and "Islamism without Islamists" are vague, simplistic, and essentialist. They fail to explain phenomenon such as how the American-led invasion of Iraq and the failure of postinvasion state building profoundly contributed to the rise of ISIS. Likewise, the rise of ISIS in Syria was a response to the brutality of Ba'athism in postcolonial Syria, the Assads' systemic suppression of popular movements, and the regional and global meddling to hijack the people's authentic demands for justice and dignity. The abstract idea of a caliphate in the Muslim imaginary played little role in the rise of ISIS.

Fourth, although Hamid correctly acknowledges the significance of religion for the Islamist forces, the overwhelming majority of the citizens in Muslim-majority states are not Islamist. We need to remind ourselves that Islamism is not merely a religious phenomenon and that it differs from religious fundamentalism in the Christian/Protestant tradition. If Islamism is defined by the idea of an Islamic state, then the MENA social movements have demonstrated that most ordinary people in the region do not associate themselves with Islamism. It is important to note that ordinary people in the MENA region hold different degrees of religiosity and, like other people around the world, enjoy a multiple/hybrid identity consisting of class, gender, race/ethnicity, nationality, as well as religious and nonreligious cultural traditions. It is not clear why religion—often with a very static and ahistorical notion—is defined as the only or major component of people's identity in MENA and as the most significant driving force for their sociopolitical actions. The concept of "Islamism without Islamists," in sum, suffers from a conceptual confusion.

Fifth, the post-Islamist spirit of the MENA movements categorically rejects the concept of an Islamic state but admires the public and civil role of religion (Mahdavi 2013). The state is a secular entity and cannot be Islamized. The Islamic state in theory is an oxymoron; it is, to use Wael Hallaq's (2013) concept, "the impossible state." The Islamic state, as Abdullahi an-Na'im (2008) argues, is a modern "postcolonial invention" with no divine justification in the Islamic tradition. It is a modern entity ruled by Islamist elites who act and speak on behalf of their interpretation of Islam. Talal Asad reminds us that both Orientalists and Islamists share "the idea that Islam was originally—and therefore essentially—a theocratic state." For the Islamists, "this history constitute[s] the betrayal of a sacred ideal that Muslims are required as believers to restore"; for the Orientalists, "it defines a schizophrenic compromise that has always prevented a progressive reform of Islam." The reality, however, is that the Islamic state is not that much the product of some Islamic essence as "it is the product of modern politics and the modernizing state" (1997, 190–91).

Sixth, Hamid rightly points out that liberalism as we experience it in the West will not be the future of Muslim-majority states and that "there is no particular reason why Islamic 'reform' should lead to liberalism in the way that [the] Protestant Reformation paved the way for the Enlightenment and, eventually modern liberalism" (2016, 25). What is problematic in his argument, however, is the way he explains such a difference. For Hamid, the "difference" boils down to one word: *Islam*. Because of its "fundamentally different relationship to politics," he argues, Islam has been "simply more resistant to secularization" (2016, 26). His argument resembles that of Ernest Gellner and other classical Orientalists in claiming that "no secularization has taken place in the world of Islam" (26). It thus overlooks the predicaments of autocratic secular modernization in postcolonial MENA and how it gave rise to the birth of modern Islamism. The major issue is not that secularization has not taken place in MENA and Muslim-majority contexts or that Islam has not been secularized but that the top-down and undemocratic imposition of *colonial secular modernity* has profoundly contributed to the rise of autocratic modernization, repressive nationalism, dictatorial Third World socialism, and dogmatic and reactionary Islamism.

Seventh, it is true, as Hamid argues, that "for the religious, religion can offer both meaning and legitimacy to ideas that might otherwise seem temporal and temporary. But to exclude Islam or to hope for—or, worse, impose—a top-down secularism requires yet more violence" (2016, 26). However, the characterization of Muslim-majority nations in line with Islamist and Islamic exceptionalism is problematic. Muslim societies are not peculiar or unique in their religiosity; as Bayat points out, "they should not be measured by the 'exceptionalist' yardstick of which religio-centrism is the central core" (2007, 6). Muslim societies hold hybrid identities that include various degrees of religious affiliation as well as diverse national cultures, socioeconomic structures, historical experiences, and political settings. The missing concept in Shadi Hamid's argument seems to be *post-Islamism*: a notion referring to a profound discursive and sociohistorical transformation in MENA and other Muslim-majority societies wherein neither the hegemonic universalism of colonial modernity nor a supposed cultural essentialism/particularism of Islamism captures the complexity of the region (Mahdavi 2013, 2019). Post-Islamism has emerged as a third alternative to the hegemonic voice of a singular and superior colonial/Western-centric modernity and an essentialist, nativist vision of Islamism. Such a dialogical discourse promotes a critical dialogue between tradition and modernity, faith and freedom, religiosity and rights, thus transcending false dichotomies and constructed binaries in post-colonial MENA (Bayat 2013b; Dabashi 2012; Mahdavi 2011, 2019).

The post-Islamist discourse, Bayat (2007, 2013b) reminds us, is neither anti-Islamic nor un-Islamic. In a post-Islamist condition, Islam is neither *the* solution nor *the* problem. Yet Islam actively contributes to the sociopolitical life of Muslims. Post-Islamism, contrary to the conventional liberal discourse, discards the privatization of Islam but welcomes civil/public religion at the societal level. The state, however, remains a neutral/civil, or *urfi*, entity. An-Na'im's words best represent the intellectual basis of a post-Islamist discourse: "Instead of sharp dichotomies between religion and secularism that relegate Islam to the purely personal and private domain, I call for balancing the two by separating Islam from the state and regulating the role of religion in politics" (2008, 267). Post-Islamism, in this way, echoes Jürgen Habermas's (2006) concept of "postsecularism," wherein religious and secular citizens have much to offer to one another.

Post-Islamism, in sum, is not post-*Islamic*. It is post-*Islamism*.[2] Not all Muslims, contrary to Hamid's argument, are Islamist. However, for many Muslims, Islam remains active and alive as a part of their individual and collective multiple identity. A post-Islamist polity is not a caliphate; it is a modern civil/*urfi* democracy attentive to local cultures and values, including those of Islam. Post-Islamism is a grassroots discourse—a "universalism from below" (Mahdavi 2009) that synthesizes the global and local paradigms of social justice, freedom, human rights, and Islamic values. It is a *glocal* paradigm (Mahdavi 2011, 2013, 2019, 21–25).

As mentioned earlier, the contemporary MENA social movements symbolize a post-Islamist turn in the region. There was no demand for a "religious

---

2. Post-Islamism, Asef Bayat argues, "represents both a *condition* and a *project*." It refers to a *condition* where Islamism "becomes compelled, both by its own internal contradictions and by societal pressure, to reinvent itself." It is also a *project*, "a conscious attempt to conceptualize and strategize the rationale and modalities of transcending Islamism in social, political, and intellectual domains" (2007, 18–19, emphasis in the original). Post-Islamism signifies the impact of secular exigencies on a religious discourse. Moreover, post-Islamism has been used as a historical and analytical category in reference to diverse politico-intellectual and social trends, such as various forms of Muslim reformist trends in postrevolutionary Iran; Ennahda (Hizb al-Nahda, Renaissance Party) of Tunisia; the Justice and Development Party as well as the Gezi Park movement of 2013 in Turkey; the Justice and Development Party in Morocco; Imran Khan's Movement for Justice (Tehreek-e-Insaf) in Pakistan; the many faces of civil Islam in Indonesia; and the Centre Party (Hizb al-Wasat) and the younger generation (not the old guard) of the Muslim Brotherhood in Egypt (Mahdavi 2011, 2019).

government" during the MENA mass uprisings of the early 2010s. Popular slogans in the Arab streets demanded human dignity, liberty, and social justice, not an Islamic state. The popular mode, however, was not antireligion; the Arab Spring "dearly [upheld] religion" (Bayat 2013b, 260). Furthermore, the post-Islamist mode of the Arab Spring did not reject the public role of religion; it challenged the false dichotomy of religion and secularism. It also transcended the religious–secular divide to become a social movement against authoritarianism and in the service of democratization.

In the post-Islamist climate of the Arab Spring, even the political statements of the Egyptian Muslim Brotherhood and/or its sponsored political arm, the Freedom and Justice Party (Hizb al-Hurriya wal-Adala), did not refer to the establishment of an Islamic state. The Freedom and Justice Party explicitly stated it did not wish to implement a theocracy, which is characterized by a "government of the clergy or by divine right" (Freedom and Justice Party 2011). The party's statements highlighted its attitudes toward freedom of religion, "rejecting sectarian strife" and recognizing the importance of allowing Christians to build churches. As these statements and similar statements reveal, however, shari'a remained the frame of reference. It is beyond the scope of this introduction to examine the *intellectual flaws* and *strategic mistakes* of the Muslim Brotherhood and its political arm, the Freedom and Justice Party, as well as of President Mohamed Morsi's policies in post–Arab Spring Egypt. Suffice it to say that as much as the younger generation of the party demonstrated their commitment to a post-Islamist polity, the old guards were trapped in their exclusivist and patriarchal Islamist discourse. One of the most concerning instances was arguably the Muslim Brotherhood's response to the End Violence to Women campaign. Initiated by the United Nations, the campaign sought the "elimination and prevention of all forms of violence against women and girls." The Muslim Brotherhood's response was to label this initiative as "misleading and deceptive" and as "contradicting the principles of Islam" (IkhwanWeb 2013). Among some of the main issues were "granting equal rights to homosexuals," "full equality in marriage legislation," "cancelling the need for husband's consent with regards to travel and work," and "granting rights to adulterous wives and illegitimate sons" (IkhwanWeb 2013). Those statements from the Muslim Brotherhood raised serious concern among many sectors of the public and did not represent the egalitarian and post-Islamist principles that initially inspired the Arab Spring and represented the dominant, though not the exclusive, viewpoint of the public. A much better example of an Egyptian post-Islamist party was the Center Party (Hizb al-Wasat) (al-Wasat Party 2011), which spoke clearly of equality of religion and equality for women and men. The party has been a clear example of more progressive trends within a post-Islamist turn in Egypt (Mahdavi 2019, 25–27).

But a more sophisticated post-Islamist party of the Arab Spring is Ennahda/al-Nahda, or Renaissance Party, in Tunisia. This party's statements clearly demonstrate a shift from Islamism to post-Islamism as they highlight citizens' rights—including minority rights—as well as issues of gender and religious freedom. They contain numerous "buzz phrases," such as the need for a "thriving democracy with mutual respect," the desire for a "culture of moderation," the guarantee of "equality for all citizens," and the "affirmation of political pluralism" (Ennahdha Movement 2011). Ennahda explicitly "rejected a Khomeini type revolution and viewed a civil and democratic state as compatible with the spirit of Islam" (Bayat 2013b, 261). "Religion should not be imposed," argued Rached al-Ghannouchi, the party's founder, in 2016; "all the teachings and text of religion [Islam], emphasize[] the principle of no compulsion in religion. Freedom of religion is absolutely affirmed in Islam. It is not the task of the state to impose a doctrine on the people. Its mission is to provide services to the people and maintain security" (quoted in *al-Hayat* 2016). Moreover, both Rached al-Ghannouchi and the former prime minister, Hamadi Jebali of the Ennahda, used the concept of *dowla madaniyah*, or civil state, instead of *almaniyah*, or secularism (which carries antireligious baggage) to distance the postrevolutionary Tunisian state from a religious state (Stepan 2012).

Although Ghannouchi and his party did not use the concept of secularism, his understanding of the concept is revealing: secularism in the West, he argues, is not an atheistic ideology, as some think. Secularism is the separation of functions: separation of the religious function from the political function. This does not mean that the state will be at war with religion. Rather, the state must protect all religions and stand in a highly neutral manner toward religions. Ghannouchi argues there is no necessary relationship between democracy and secularism. You can be both secular and a terrorist or a dictator; you can be both secular and democratic; you can be an Islamic and a terrorist; and you can be democratic and Muslim. The necessary and inevitable link among secularism, modernity, and democracy is an arbitrary link. Therefore, Islam and democracy, asserts Ghannouchi, are compatible, and democracy is the modern practice of the *shura*/consultation (al-Ghannouchi 2015). In fact, many Muslim democrats often point to the key Qur'anic concepts of *shura*/consultation, *ijma'*/consensus and *adala*/justice to support democracy (Mahdavi 2019, 27–28).

In an interview in 2014, Ghannouchi criticized Islamists who "chose the path of violence." They formulate their own "excessively strict interpretation of religious texts . . . aimed at monopolizing the right of explaining it, which means for those organizations that the text has one meaning only, and anybody who disagrees with their exegesis and understanding of it is a disbeliever and godless" (Noureddine 2014). Furthermore, Ghannouchi explicitly argues that "no political party can or should claim to represent religion and that the religious sphere should be managed by independent and neutral institutions, [as] religion should be nonpartisan" (al-Ghannouchi 2016). Ennahda's statements have made it clear that citizens' rights are universal regardless of their faith. Ghannouchi has explicitly argued that "his party should embrace the historic specificity that Tunisia for more than sixty years has had the Arab World's most progressive and women-friendly family code" (Stepan 2012, 94–97). This was demonstrated by the Ennahda's inclusion of women in the National Constituent Assembly of 2011–14 (Mahdavi 2019, 28–29).

As Sayida Qunissi, an Ennahda member of Parliament in Tunisia, shows, Ennahda has always considered itself "different from the Muslim Brotherhood at both the ideological and political levels." For her, the maturity of Ennahda in the public debate is evident: "It is no longer a matter of the relationship between Islam and state anymore, or traditionally 'Islamic' issues, but rather a commitment to finding solutions to corruption, economic development, social justice, and human rights" (2017, 234). Since even before the uprisings, Ennahda's philosophy was based on "unity and inclusion." More specifically, Ennahda worked with two Tunisian secular parties, the secular-liberal El Mottamar, or Congress for the Republic, and the socialist Ettakatol, or Democratic Forum for Labor and Liberties, after the Arab Spring (Qunissi 2017, 235–36). Ghannouchi and Moncef Marzouki, a secular human rights activist, have been able to work together in the postrevolutionary Tunisia. Furthermore, following the elections in 2014, Ennahda conceded its loss to the Nidaa Tounes (Call of Tunisia), a center-right secular party, and formed a coalition government with it (Mahdavi 2019, 29).

Sayida Qunissi's argument (2017, 238) clearly represents the main conclusions reached at Ennahda's Tenth Congress, held May 20–23, 2016, in which the party explicitly distanced itself from Islamism and the idea of an Islamic state, defining itself as a party of Muslim democrats. "'Muslim democrat' is the most accurate term to describe what Ennahda has been trying to accomplish since the beginning: reconciling Islam and democracy in the Arab world," states Qunissi. She continues: "When Rached Ghannouchi first used the term 'Muslim democratic,' it was an effort to help the media under[stand] the pitfalls of instantly and unanimously labeling diverse political actors as 'Islamists,' despite their differences. Highlighting the parallel with Christian Democratic parties in Europe, like Germany's Christian Democratic Union, seemed to be the easiest way to signify Ennahda as a political party bringing together both democratic principles and religious values" (2017, 237; see also Mahdavi 2019, 30).

Post-Islamist movements in post–Arab Spring MENA are certainly experiencing a setback, and Tunisia is not an exception: President Kais Saied announced the dissolution of the Parliament and government in July 2021. Nonetheless, Ennahda breaking away from Islamism and branding itself a "Muslim democratic" party was a step forward toward post-Islamism. Ghannouchi and other party leaders distanced themselves from Islamism and its central concept of an Islamic state. The call not for a religious state but for a civil state that would promote human rights and citizenship is an achievement. The party seems, however, to be falling into the trap of neoliberal elitist and ivory tower discourse, ignoring the urgent question of *social justice*. As I have argued elsewhere, democracy, particularly in the Global South, desperately needs an egalitarian pro–social justice discourse. Abstract liberal notions of rights need to be translated into tangible social justice policies. Otherwise, either secular despots or populist demagogues will use the rhetoric of social justice to mobilize the masses. The political crisis both in Ennahda and in the Tunisian government in 2021 speak to this problem (see *Middle East Monitor* 2021). Moreover, uneven development is a common problem in the MENA region, and only a grassroots egalitarian democracy can protect the social and political rights of masses, in particular the rights of the "subaltern groups," including the marginalized and ordinary people, the women and youth, and the "middle-class poor," all of whom served as the main force of the Arab Spring (Mahdavi 2017, 2019, 30; see also Bayat 2021).

In Egypt, the post-Islamist Wasat Party is small in number but could have been a source of greater inspiration for younger generations of the Muslim Brotherhood. Mohamed Morsi's strategic mistakes, the miscalculations of secular forces, and al-Sisi's coup were a setback to post-Islamism in Egypt. Nonetheless, as Juan Cole reminds us, the Egyptian Spring was a post-Islamist movement. The poem "Ana 'almani" (I Am Secular), which was posted at a young Egyptian website in April 2012, represents such a post-Islamist climate in the Egyptian civil society: "I am secular: . . . for me, religion is for God and the nation is for all" (quoted in Cole 2014, 17).

Post-Islamism in Iran is strong at the societal level but remains in a deep crisis at the political/state level. The Green Movement of 2009, the first MENA post-Islamist mass movement, did not succeed politically, but the quest for democracy remains strong socially in Iran. From 2017 to 2022, post–Green Movement Iran has witnessed multiple civil protests and social movements, demonstrating a popular post-Islamist spirit and the public's deep disenchantment with the dominant Islamist politics. As mentioned earlier, this is also evident in the latest waves of democratic movements that have mobilized women and men, young and old, the religious and the secular, lower and middle classes, and many minorities across the country in small and big cities against the ruling Islamists. The movement began after Mahsa (Zhina) Amini, a twenty-two-year-old Iranian Kurdish woman from the city of Saqez, was detained by the so-called morality police in Tehran on September 13, 2022, under the pretext of the state's forced hijab law. She lost consciousness in police custody and was pronounced dead at a Tehran hospital on September 16.[3] Her murder by police sparked nationwide and international protests not only in Kurdistan province but also in more than one hundred cities, including Tehran, Isfahan, Mashhad, Tabriz, Rasht, Gorgan, Hamadan, Shiraz, and Kerman, as well as demonstrations at a number of universities in Iran. Mahsa's death touched a nerve of anger in the country, causing people to chant, "Death to the dictator," "Women, Life, Freedom," and "Justice, Freedom, Hijab by Choice." Some women took their headscarves off in public demonstrations; others cut their hair and burned their headscarves on social media or in public to express their anger and frustration toward the state's misogynistic policies, gender apartheid, subjugation of women's bodies, and compulsory hijab. The 2022 protests were led largely by women and demonstrated the persistence of Iran's civil society in its quest for freedom, justice, and dignity. They showed the dynamics of women's and students' unfinished social movements as well as the predicament of Islamism in Iran.

Moreover, the depth and diversity of intellectual debates on the question of religion, democracy, gender, and human rights in postrevolutionary Iran are exemplary. However, as in the Tunisian case, the (neo)liberal post-Islamist discourse in Iran undermines the middle-class poor and the issue of social justice. One of the notable progressive post-Islamist discourses in postrevolutionary Iran is that of the neo-Shari'atis—a generation of Muslim scholars and activists on the left who are inspired by a new reading of 'Ali Shari'ati (1933–77), a celebrated critical postcolonial Muslim thinker. The neo-Shari'atis have attempted to produce a synthetic emancipatory discourse of "freedom, social justice and civil spirituality," proposing an alternative discourse to the hegemonic and West-centric secular modernity, Islamist essentialism, and elitist neoliberal post-Islamism (Mahdavi 2013, 2019, 30–31).

Turkey is another complex case where the Justice and Development Party (Adalet ve Kalkınma Partisi, AKP) demonstrated features of post-Islamist politics in its platform in 2002. The AKP platform has always been socially conservative and economically neoliberal. However, there has been a great setback and

---

3. According to eyewitnesses, she was beaten while inside a police van and slipped into a coma later (BBC 2022).

regression in the party's post-Islamist policies over the past decade. President Erdoğan's iron fist and authoritarianism, his "new Ottomanist" foreign policy in the region, and the suppression of the popular Gezi Park movement in 2013 were conducive to the deterioration of Turkish post-Islamism. The Gezi Park movement, in my view, is now a better representative of Turkish post-Islamism because it encompasses many diverse religious and secular dissidents in Turkey, ranging from post-Kemalists to post-Islamists, environmental activists, LGBTQ+ activists, and anticapitalist Muslims (Tugal 2016; see also Mahdavi 2019, 31).

Post-Islamism, in sum, can be applied as a label to a vast number of different sociopolitical positions, some arguably more democratic than others. Post-Islamists are a diverse combination of conservative, (neo)liberal, and progressive forces. They all believe in an active role for public religion in civil society but denounce the religious/divine state. Most post-Islamist parties are socially conservative and have adopted neoliberal economic policies. Post-Islamism is a significant paradigm shift from Islamism in the MENA region because it rejects the concept of a divine state. However, post-Islamism is not monolithic and has its own limitations and deficiencies (Mahdavi 2019, 21–32). Many contemporary post-Islamist forces, for example, have constantly undermined social elements of democracy and comprehensive social justice. Egalitarian policies prompt democratic support and mediate the impact of religiosity on democratic aspirations and orientations (Ciftci 2019, 2021). The crisis of some post-Islamist parties in post–Arab Spring MENA, in particular the predicaments in Morocco and Tunisia in 2021, speak in part to this problem.

"The Old Is Dying"! The Unfinished MENA Social Movements

The MENA social movements are experiencing a deep and profound crisis. However, such crisis is not unique to this region: "Almost all post-revolution moments are marked by an ecstatic exhilaration followed by a deep disappointment and demoralization. . . . The great revolutionary Rosa Luxemburg goes so far as to suggest that revolution is the only form of 'war' in which the ultimate victory can be prepared only by a series of defeats" (Bayat 2015). Likewise, Antonio Gramsci reminds us that such "crisis consists precisely in the fact that the old is dying and the new cannot be born; in this interregnum a great variety of morbid symptoms appear" (1971, 276).

MENA democratic forces are largely repressed, but the repressed will most likely return and recapture their social position. This is evident in the most recent waves of mass protests in Lebanon, Algeria, Tunisia, Sudan, Iraq, and Iran in 2017, 2019, 2020, 2021, and 2022 (Saab 2020). These protests demonstrate that the

MENA social movements of the 2010s are unfinished projects and never really ended. It is true that the first wave (2009–13) of the contemporary MENA movements was not quite successful. However, the region is currently experiencing the second wave (2017–22), and most likely will witness a third and more democratic waves in the future.

Although each of these uprisings is a distinctive case and represents a particular sociopolitical context, they all speak to the larger issue of an enduring quest for social justice, freedom, and human dignity. This quest will continue to generate new democratic social movements in the region. The genie is out of the bottle because the contemporary MENA social movements signify a deep-seated sociocultural and structural transformation in the region. The current crisis, argues Bayat, "is hardly a measure of popular consent or compliance. Rather, it is driven by the inner force of life itself, expressed through an urge for self-regulation; it is a technique of survival in rough times" (2015). Hence, these movements are rich with endless and open-ended possibilities; they are unfinished projects (Mahdavi 2014, 103–4).

The MENA social movements have created a historical momentum and "memories" of "extraordinary episodes"; they have generated "moral resources" that "have become part of the popular consciousness" of the young and restless generation in the region (Bayat 2015). For this generation, revolutions and social movements are unfinished projects. Many MENA societies and cultures, argues Dabashi, "are in the midst of systematic and epistemic changes, by virtue of the material forces that underlie their daily lives. False and falsifying binaries still afflict these cultures (East–West, Persian–Arab, Sunni–Shia) but the body of their seismic transmutation moves towards liberating horizons apace" (2015). Change, however, is not easy. Freedom is not free; it is costly. There are at least two major challenges ahead: regressive forces from within and meddling by external forces—that is, regional powers and the global hegemon. Despite such structural constraints, one should not underestimate the force of hope and will—the power of people's agency. Gramsci (1971) has reminded us that we need to overcome the "pessimism of the intellect" by the "optimism of the will." Such will and hope will be materialized, Bayat argues, "with [the] building [of] an 'active citizenry' endowed with the 'art of presence'; a citizenry that possesses the courage and creativity to assert collective will in spite of all odds by circumventing constraints, utilizing what is possible, and discovering new spaces within which to make themselves heard, seen, felt, and realized" (2015).

"The old order is largely back in business" in a number of MENA societies in the post–Arab Spring era. Nonetheless, "these are the old ways in new times, when the old order faces new political subjects and novel subjectivities; when the memories of sacrifice, the taste of triumph, and betrayal of aspirations are likely to turn quiet but lingering mass discontent into periodic social upheavals. These are uncharted political moments loaded with indefinite possibilities, in which meaningful social engagement would demand a creative fusion of the old and new ways of doing politics" (Bayat 2015).

"Epistemic Disobedience"?

One should not overlook the profound impact of the movements of the 2010s on postcolonial MENA societies. For some time, they brought together secular and religious individuals, Muslims and non-Muslims, men and women, the poor and the middle class. They transcended ethnic, religious, gender, class, and ideological divides in these societies. They symbolized a potential paradigm shift toward a "postideological," "postnationalist," and "post-Islamist" discourse in the region (Bayat 2013a, 2013b; Dabashi 2012; Mahdavi 2011, 2013, 2014). These movements were neither religious nor antireligious. The Islamic state/caliphate was not at the center of any popular slogan in the MENA streets. The MENA social movements symbolized a popular quest for human dignity, freedom, and social justice as well as a backlash against the neoliberal order—the Washington Consensus and the Structural Adjustment Program in the region. They also challenged the Orientalist "clash of civilizations" discourse and nullified the notion of "Middle East exceptionalism" (Mahdavi and Knight 2012b).

The MENA movements, in sum, represent a new paradigm shift from two hegemonic discourses of the post–Cold War era: Samuel Huntington's (1996) "clash of civilizations" and Francis Fukuyama's (1989) "end of history." Human dignity, freedom, and social justice are not exclusively Western civilizational achievements; they are widespread values across the West and the East—"a common theme in the streets of Tunis, Cairo, Aden, Tehran, Madrid, New York, Athens, and London" (Mahdavi 2014, 104–5; see also Mahdavi and Knight 2012a, xxi). Moreover, these social movements have revealed a systematic crisis in the neoliberal order that Fukuyama liked us to see as "the end point of mankind's ideological evolution and the universalization of Western liberal democracy as the final form of human government" (1989, 271).

MENA social movements were—and continue to be—nothing less than a warm welcome "to the End of the End of History" (Mishra 2013). They paved the path toward, to use Walter Mingolo's (2011) concept, an "epistemic disobedience." They resisted hegemonic universalism, celebrated our differences, and proposed a third alternative way to both Fukuyama's hegemonic universalism and Huntington's essentialist particularism. The third way is a radical call for "universalism from below" (Mahdavi 2013). It suggests that each culture/nation should engage in a critical dialogue with its own tradition and formulate the universal values of freedom and social justice in a local language that can be implemented through local/homegrown institutions. In other words, the third way "aspires to a different kind of universalism, one based on deliberation and contestation among diverse political entities, with the aim of reaching functional agreement on questions of global concern. This kind of universalism differs from one resulting from universal injunctions by self-assured subjects" (Grovogui 2013, 263). It is an unfinished project but signifies a new historical era toward post-Islamism in the Muslim contexts (Mahdavi 2014, 105).

The Book's Structure

A balanced collection of the work of both well-established and emerging scholars, this edited volume offers theory-oriented and case-study chapters. Inspired by critical postcolonial/decolonial studies and the interdisciplinary perspectives of social movement theories, gender studies, Islamic studies, and critical race theory, it challenges and demystifies the myth of MENA exceptionalism.

This edited volume consists of this introduction, sixteen chapters divided into three parts, as well as a foreword and an afterword by two distinguished scholars of Middle East and Islamic studies, John L. Esposito and Khaled Abou El Fadl, respectively. Part one, "Beyond the 'Middle East Exceptionalism,'" includes six chapters. In chapter 1, "Exceptions to Exceptionalisms! Or What MENA Offers to World History," Peyman Vahabzadeh provides an inversion of Giorgio Agamben's theory of exceptionalism and, by virtue of that, showcases the contributions of the grassroots social movements in MENA. The cases of Iran, Tunisia, and the Kurdish region Rojava, Vahabzadeh argues, allow us to appreciate the MENA region's contribution to a world history guided from the bottom up. In chapter 2, "Israel, Palestine, and the Politics of Race: Moving from Exceptionalism to Global Context," Abigail B. Bakan and Yasmeen Abu-Laban argue that an enduring view of Israel in the Western academy and popular imaginary is that it is a unique state in the context of the Middle East because it is the only "democracy" in the region. The chapter traces how this idea was constructed as part of US ideological hegemony in the aftermath of World War II and how it has been challenged in the face of the democratic impulses and movements associated with the Arab Spring as well as the growing global attention to the human rights abuses of Palestinians by the Israeli government. The authors utilize a racial contract framework to disrupt the mythologized exceptionalism that has attended studies of Israel. By placing Israel in international as well as comparative context, and by attending to the Palestinian voice, they highlight how power, politics, and race have been and remain critical to the study of Israel in a global context. Navid Pourmokhtari argues in chapter 3, "How Applicable Are Leading Mainstream Social Movement Theories to the MENA Region?," that the leading mainstream social movement theories fall short of explicating the phenomenon of mass mobilization in contemporary MENA societies. The chapter begins by problematizing the historical contexts from which such ethnocentric theories emerged and providing a critique of their core assumptions. It then showcases how the Western-centric theories are incapable of accounting for the specificities and complexities of the contemporary MENA social movements by highlighting the Egyptian Feminist Union movement in 1923, the Iranian Revolution of 1979, the Uprising of Dignity in Bahrain in 1994, the Iranian Green Movement of 2009, and the Arab Spring of 2010–11, among others. The chapter makes a case for a fresh approach to thinking about how in the context of the authoritarian state broad social movements can effectively contest power. In chapter 4, "China and Syria as an 'Ideological Exception'?," Juan Cole discusses whether China's Syria policy might be explained in the context of an "ideological exception": that is, Syria's state socialism, anti-imperialism, and secularism provide a particular case in a region rife with religious pro-American regimes such as Saudi Arabia. China's Syria policy, he then argues, may be explained in light of China's need for energy in the region, though radical Salafi groups in Syria are also seen as a threat to China because of their potential impact on China's 40 million Muslims. In chapter 5, "The Rise of ISIS in Postinvasion Iraq: A Manifestation of (Neo)Colonial Violence," Mariam Georgis problematizes the conventional cultural exceptionalist argument about the rise of ISIS. She demonstrates the political and strategic factors that gave rise to ISIS: the invasion of Iraq, sectarian policies, the Syrian proxy war, and regional factors, including the ideologies of Wahhabism and Salafism. The chapter suggests that ISIS and sectarian violence do not reflect the desires of ordinary people and that the initial appeal of al-Qaeda or ISIS can be truly eradicated only when the conditions of social, economic, and political marginalization and oppression that act as breeding grounds for such movements are eliminated. In "Recolonizing the Arab World?," chapter 6, Tariq Ali argues that to understand the Arab Spring and its mixed outcome, we need to situate it within the region's broader geopolitical politics and its historical and modern struggles against Western colonialism and American imperialism. In carrying out this analysis, the chapter adopts a fourfold approach. First, Ali unpacks the meaning and destructive effect of European colonialism and American imperialism on the possibilities of democratic changes in the region. Then he focuses on the spread of the counterrevolutionary jihadist forces in the Arab region and highlights the role of the United States and its allies in the development of those forces. The chapter also elucidates the spread of Islamophobia in the West and maps its influence on the politics of dissent and resistance in the MENA region.

Part two, "The Unfinished Project of the Resilient Citizenship," comprises five chapters. In chapter 7, "Arab Youth Nonmovements: Resilient Citizenship in the Middle East," Bessma Momani and Melissa Finn bring to our attention the significance of Arab youths' constant quest for democracy and progressive change. They argue that Arab youths are the agents of continuing social and cultural revolution within an important demographic of Arab societies. Michael Frishkopf and his coauthors argue in chapter 8, "What Happened to 'Songs of the New Arab Revolutions'?," that throughout the tumult of the Arab Spring music demonstrated its power to galvanize sentiment and mobilize civil society. The chapter highlights many examples of such revolutionary songs—music of and for grief and anger as well as of and for hope and empowerment. It then examines what happened to those revolutionary songs, composers, lyricists, and performers in the post–Arab Spring era. It also reflects on the limits of music's ability to be imbued with durable social meaning, revolutionary or otherwise, and the limits on its social power. In chapter 9, "The Future of Nonviolence in the Middle East: Iran and Beyond," Ramin Jahanbegloo argues that nonviolence, or the "Gandhian moment," is an emerging paradigm shift in political mentalities and practices in the MENA region, contrary to the mainstream argument about the region. Drawing from Mahatma Gandhi and Martin Luther King Jr., the chapter highlights the urgency and significance of nonviolence as a method of resistance in the current MENA social movements. In chapter 10, "The Rise and Fall of the Student Movements in Postrevolutionary Iran," Roozbeh Safshekan captures the cyclical rise and fall of the Iranian student movement as one of the most significant social agents of change in postrevolutionary Iran. The chapter offers a brief history of student activism before the Revolution of 1979, highlighting the role of university students in overthrowing the Pahlavi monarchy. It then examines the impact of subsequent political junctures on the student movement in postrevolutionary Iran: the Cultural Revolution and the Iran–Iraq War (1980–88), the Reconstruction era (1989–97), social and political liberalization during the Reform era (1997–2005), and authoritarianism during Mahmoud Ahmadinejad's presidency (2005–13) and Hassan Rouhani's presidency (2013–21). Chapter 11 by Paul S. Rowe, "Finished or Unfinished? The Uncertain Future of Christians in the Middle East," examines how despite ambivalence exhibited by established church hierarchies and elites, many Christians participated in the Egyptian and Syrian Arab Spring protests. The Arab Spring highlighted the possibility of a new pluralist form of representation, a possibility that was subsequently dashed by destabilization and crises in the post–Arab Spring era. Most Arab regimes continue to seek neomillet elite bargains with Christian leaders, bargains that gain support among Christians fearful of a return to a chaotic situation. The unfinished project of the Arab Spring, the chapter argues, is the expansion of the opportunity to organize and celebrate differences through civil activism and community engagement. The chapter surveys Christian responses to the past few years of crises to map the future representation of Christians' interests in MENA.

Part three, "Gendering the MENA Movements," includes five chapters. Chapter 12, "Toward a Democratization of Authority in Islamic Thought: Gender as a Category of Thought in Light of the Arab Spring" by amina wadud, provides a broad conceptual framework for examining the question of gender as a category of thought in the MENA and Muslim contexts. The author argues that the Arab Spring became symbolic of democratic aspirations for both Muslim-minority and Muslim-majority communities. Ironically, ISIS and the like also became symbolic of ways to resist the impact of the unfolding of those aspirations. Among the foundational ideas distinguishing these two movements are diametrically opposed notions of authority and, more specifically, of gender justice in Islam. The chapter then explores the construction of a democratic authority and gender justice in Islamic thought by focusing on the contributions of Islamic feminism to the democratization of authority and to gender equality and reciprocity in MENA and Muslim contexts. The following chapters examine the MENA movements' gender relations in Turkey, Iran, Tunisia, and Egypt. In chapter 13, "Remembering Istanbul: Women and Anarchistic-Queer Openings in a Belated Modernity," Poyraz Kolluoglu locates the Gezi events in 2013 as an example of the anticapitalist and antiglobalization struggles in a postnational solidarity era. As a nonaligned eco-protester witnessing how the first environment-centered resistance movement in Gezi Park evolved into civil disobedience, Kolluoglu approaches this phenomenon through the prism of autoethnography and offers a radical examination of the role of women and the anarchistic queer in "the Istanbul Commune of 2013 and the grassroots politics it set in motion in the following years." Victoria Tahmasebi-Birgani argues in chapter 14, "Women Continue the Unfinished Project of Liberation in the MENA Region through Online Activism," that people's physical presence in the form of street protests have subsided in the post–Arab Spring era. However, human rights advocates and women's groups have shifted their activism to the virtual space and social networking sites, or virtual "civil societies." Using a case study of Iranian women's online activism and drawing on other notable examples from women's cybernetworking in other MENA counties, Tahmasebi-Birgani argues that women are at the forefront of reconceptualizing and rewriting the unfinished project of the MENA movements in the 2010s. Women's online activism not only continually builds on the achievements of earlier popular uprisings in the region but also creatively expands on the meaning of democracy, equality, and justice for women in MENA countries. In chapter 15, "Women's Engagement in the Tunisian Revolution," building on framing theory and contentious politics literature, Nermin Allam interrogates women's collective action at the time of the Tunisian revolution to elucidate how gender featured in the framing of their participation. Allam's quantitative and qualitative analysis contributes to complicating and expanding debates on women's participation in national struggles beyond reductionist accounts that view their engagement as misguided or passive. The chapter shows that Tunisian women framed their participation around their citizenship; hence, the absence of gender issues in women's framing of their participation needs to be situated within the context of Tunisia's conventional and contentious politics. Mark Muhannad Ayyash examines the case of the Egyptian uprising in chapter 16, "The Egyptian Uprising and Sexual Violence," focusing in particular on materials from two groups, the April 6 Youth Movement and Nazra for Feminist Studies. In a way much different from superficial Orientalist analyses, he argues that these two groups presented a scathing critique of the sexual contract that underpins the authoritarian postcolonial regime. The challenge to the sexual contract is the uprising's achievements, its unfinished promise, and its major difficulty, which manifested itself in greater scope in the postrevolutionary moments—that the movement never managed to make central the question of the sexual contract during the revolutionary moment. The Egyptian military regime's ability to (re)assert itself through sexual violence and the "virginity tests" highlights the persistence of postcoloniality in the difficulty of deconstructing the sexual contract.

Last but not least, Khaled Abou El Fadl's afterword, "A Personal Retrospection on the Aborted Spring and Islamic Exceptionalism," historicizes and contextualizes the rise of the Arab Spring through a powerful and distinctive personal retrospection. It also masterfully critiques the MENA autocrats sponsored by petrodollars and Western (re)colonial policies, the opportunistic and undemocratic Saudi-backed ideology of Jami-Salafism, Islamophobia, and the very foundations of the discourse of "Islamic exceptionalism."

References

Abu-Rabi', Ibrahim. 2010. "Editor's Introduction: Islamism from the Standpoint of Critical Theory." In *The Contemporary Arab Reader on Political Islam*, edited by Ibrahim Abu-Rabi', vii–xxv. London: Pluto Press; Edmonton, Canada: Univ. of Alberta Press.

Abu Zeid, Nasr Hamed. 2002. "Heaven, Which Way?" *Al-Ahram Weekly*, no. 603 (Sept). At https://web.archive.org/web/20120816021237/http://weekly.ahram.org.eg:80/2002/603/sc16-17.htm.

Asad, Talal. 1997. "Europe against Islam: Islam in Europe." *Muslim World* 87, no. 2: 183–95. At http://dx.doi.org/10.1111/j.1478-1913.1997.tb03293.x.

Bayat, Asef. 2007. *Islam and Democracy: What Is the Real Question?* Amsterdam: Amsterdam Univ. Press.

———. 2013a. *Life as Politics: How Ordinary People Change the Middle East*. 2nd ed. Stanford, CA: Stanford Univ. Press.

———. 2013b. *Post-Islamism: The Changing Faces of Political Islam*. Oxford: Oxford Univ. Press.

———. 2015. "Revolution and Despair." *Mada Masr*, Jan. 25. At http://www.madamasr.com/opinion/revolution-and-despair.

———. 2021. *Revolutionary Life: The Everyday of the Arab Spring*. Cambridge, MA: Harvard Univ. Press.

Bayat, Asef, and Linda Herrera. 2021a. "Global Middle East." In *Global Middle East: Into the Twenty-First Century*, edited by Asef Bayat and Linda Herrera, 3–22. Oakland: Univ. of California Press.

———, eds. 2021b. *Global Middle East: Into the Twenty-First Century*. Oakland: Univ. of California Press.

BBC. 2022. "Mahsa Amini: Women Take Headscarves Off in Protest at Funeral." Sept. 17. At https://www.bbc.com/news/world-middle-east-62940907.amp.

Casanova, José. 2001. "Civil Society and Religion: Retrospective Reflections on Catholicism and Prospective Reflections on Islam." *Social Research* 68, no. 4: 1041–80.

Ciftci, Sabri. 2019. "Islam, Social Justice, and Democracy." *Religion and Politics* 12, no. 4: 549–76.

———. 2021. *Islam, Justice, and Democracy*. Philadelphia: Temple Univ. Press.

Cole, Juan. 2014. *The New Arabs: How the Millennial Generation Is Changing the Middle East*. New York: Simon & Schuster.

Dabashi, Hamid. 2012. *The Arab Spring: The End of Postcolonialism*. London: Zed Books.

———. 2015. "Revolutions without Borders." *Al-Araby*, Apr. 6. At http://www.alaraby.co.uk/english/comment/2015/4/6/revolutions-without-borders.

Ennahdha Movement. 2011. "Statute of the Renaissance Movement" (after the revised Ninth Congress). At www.ennah-dha.tn.

Freedom and Justice Party. 2011. *FJP 2011 Program on Freedoms and Political Reform*. At http://www.ponline.com/arti-cle.php?id=197.

Fukuyama, Francis. 1989. "The End of History?" *National Interest* 16:3–18.

Gellner, Ernest. 1991. "Islam and Marxism: Some Comparisons." *International Affairs* 67 (Jan.): 1–6. At http://dx.doi.org/10.2307/2621215.

———. 1992. *Postmodernism, Reason, and Religion*. London: Routledge.

Al-Ghannouchi, Rached. 2015. *Democracy and Human Rights in Islam*. Beirut, Lebanon: Arab House for Science.

———. 2016. "From Political Islam to Muslim Democracy: The Ennahda Party and the Future of Tunisia." *Foreign Affairs* 95, no. 5: 58–67.

Gramsci, Antonio. 1971. *Selections from the Prison Notebooks.* Edited by Quintin Hoare and Geoffrey Nowell-Smith. New York: International.

Grovogui, Siba N. 2013. "Postcolonialism." In *International Relations Theories: Disciplines and Diversity,* 3rd ed., edited by Tim Dunne, Milja Kurki, and Steve Smith, 247–65. Oxford: Oxford Univ. Press.

Habermas, Jürgen. 2006. "Religion in the Public Sphere." *European Journal of Philosophy* 14, no. 1: 1–25.

Hallaq, Wael. 2013. *The Impossible State: Islam, Politics, and Modernity's Moral Predicament.* New York: Columbia Univ. Press.

Hamid, Shadi. 2016. *Islamic Exceptionalism: How the Struggle over Islam Is Reshaping the World.* New York: St. Martin's Press.

———. 2022. *The Problem of Democracy: America, the Middle East, and the Rise and Fall of an Idea.* New York: Oxford Univ. Press.

Al-Hayat. 2016. "Al-Ghannouchi: Islam Is Accepting of Secularism and Freedom of Belief." May 22.

Huntington, Samuel P. 1996. *Clash of Civilizations and the Remaking of the Modern World.* New York: Simon & Schuster.

IkhwanWeb. 2013. "Muslim Brotherhood Statement Denouncing UN Women Declaration for Violating Sharia Principle." At http://www.ikhwanweb.com/article.php?id=30731.

Kuru, Ahmet T. 2019. *Islam, Authoritarianism, and Underdevelopment.* Cambridge: Cambridge Univ. Press.

Lewis, Bernard. 1988. *The Political Language of Islam.* Chicago: Univ. of Chicago Press.

———. 1990. "The Roots of Muslim Rage: Why so Many Muslims Deeply Resent the West, and Why Their Bitterness Will Not Be Easily Mollified." *Atlantic Monthly* 266, no. 3: 47–58.

Mahdavi, Mojtaba. 2009. "Universalism from Below: Muslims and Democracy in Context." *International Journal of Criminology and Sociological Theory* 2, no. 2: 276–91.

———. 2011. "Post-Islamist Trends in Post-revolutionary Iran." *Comparative Studies of South Asia, Africa, and the Middle East* 31, no. 1: 94–109.

———. 2013. "Muslims and Modernities: From Islamism to Post-Islamism?" *Religious Studies and Theology* 32, no. 1: 31–56.

———. 2014. "Introduction: East Meets West? The Unfinished Project of Contemporary Social Movements in the Middle East and Beyond." In "Contemporary Social Movements in the Middle East and Beyond," special issue of *Sociology of Islam* 2, nos. 3–4: 103–10.

———. 2017. "Iran: Multiple Sources of Grassroots Social Democracy?" In *Iran's Struggles for Social Justice: Economics, Agency, Justice, Activism,* edited by Peyman Vahabzadeh, 271–88. New York: Palgrave Macmillan.

———. 2019. "Whither Post-Islamism: Revisiting Discourse/Movement after the Arab Spring." In *Arab Spring: Modernity, Identity, and Change,* edited by Eid Mohamed and Dalia Fahmi, 15–38. New York: Palgrave Macmillan.

Mahdavi, Mojtaba, and W. Andy Knight. 2012a. Preface to *Towards the Dignity of Difference? Neither "End of History" nor "Clash of Civilizations,"* edited by Mojtaba Mahdavi and W. Andy Knight, xxi–xxv. Farnham, UK: Ashgate/Routledge.

———, eds. 2012b. *Towards the Dignity of Difference? Neither "End of History" nor "Clash of Civilizations."* Farnham, UK: Ashgate/Routledge.

Middle East Monitor. 2021. "Tunisia: Ennahda Resignations 'Not Leading to a New Party.'" Sept. 28. At https://www.middleeastmonitor.com/20210928-tunisia-ennahda -resignations-not-leading-to-a-new-party/.

Mingolo, Walter. 2011. "Epistemic Disobedience and the Colonial Option: A Manifesto." *Transmodernity: Journal of Peripheral Cultural Production of the Luso-Hispanic World* 1, no. 2: 44–66.

Mishra, Pankaj. 2013. "Welcome to the End of the End of History." *Bloomberg*, Dec. 31. At http://www.bloomberg.com/news/2013-12-31/welcome-to-the-end-of-the-end-of -history.html.

An-Na'im, Abdullahi. 2008. *Islam and the Secular State.* Cambridge, MA: Harvard Univ. Press.

Noureddine, Jebnoun. 2014. "Tunisia at the Crossroads: An Interview with Sheikh Rached al-Ghannouchi." Occasional Papers, al-Waleed Bin Talal Centre for Muslim–Christian Understanding, Georgetown Univ., Apr. At https://www.iosworld.org /download/Rachid_al-Ghannouchi.pdf.

Qunissi, Sayida. 2017. "Ennahda from Within: Islamists or 'Muslim Democrats'? In *Rethinking Political Islam*, edited by Shadi Hamid and William McCants, 230–43. New York: Oxford Univ. Press.

Saab, Jade, ed. 2020. *A Region in Revolt: Mapping the Region Uprisings in North Africa and West Asia.* Ottawa, Canada: Draja Press.

Stepan, Alfred. 2012. "Tunisia's Transition and the Twin Tolerations." *Journal of Democracy* 23, no. 2 (Apr.): 94–97. At http://dx.doi.org/10.1353/jod.2012.0034.

Tugal, Cihan. 2016. *The Fall of the Turkish Model: How the Arab Uprisings Brought Down Islamic Liberalism.* London: Verso.

Al-Wasat Party. 2011. *FAQ.* At http://www.alwasatparty.com/questions.php.

Part One

Beyond the "Middle East Exceptionalism"

1

Exceptions to Exceptionalisms! Or What MENA Offers to World History

Peyman Vahabzadeh

In the turbulent aftermath of the wave of revolutionary changes in the Middle East and North Africa (MENA) otherwise known as the Arab Spring—in particular in relation to the (continued regional) civil wars and/or the failed or unstable states in Iraq, Syria, Yemen, and Libya—imperial unilateralism and (neocolonial) "humanitarian intervention" (an Orwellian Newspeak) have once again dominated global politics in a manner "brighter than the sun," as the Arabic expression goes. The US-led military occupation of Afghanistan (2001) and Iraq (2003), in the name of fighting global terrorism, provided fertile grounds for assorted and increasingly factional jihadi resistances, thanks to the destabilization of these countries. The quick Taliban takeover of Afghanistan in August 2021, as US and North Atlantic Treaty Organization military forces withdrew and as the Afghan military disintegrated in the process, clearly proves the futility of the global "war on terror" in dismantling "extremism." The democratic movements deposing self-appointed, life-long "presidents" (read: dictators) in Tunisia, Egypt, Libya, and Yemen left a power vacuum that led either to the return of military dictatorship (Egypt) or to unmanageable mayhem and tragic civil wars (Syria, Libya, Yemen). Amid these grand disappointments, however, the Tunisian Jasmine Revolution succeeded where the other movements failed, becoming a glowing model for grassroots democratic change. The Tunisian success, of course, is relative and remains precarious, as evidenced by the 2021 political crisis and the 2022 Constitutional Referendum, and therefore the movement is in need of constant civil society vigilance. The inadvertent pioneer of the Arab Spring—a humble, grassroots, democratic, and nonviolent movement that inspired the grammar (and semiotics) of the wave of protests movements across MENA and beyond (see Dabashi 2012a, 117–37; Vahabzadeh 2014)—was Iran's Green Movement

(2009–10), a popular movement that, sad to say, eventually succumbed to clinical and brutal suppression. Against the silhouette of imperialist invasions, bombings of infrastructures, drone strikes, installment of puppet governments, the deaths of hundreds of thousands of the residents of these countries (deaths that are hardly ever reported in corporate media, let alone grieved), and the continued displacement of millions as refugees, all in the name of fighting terrorism, the shining "delayed defiance" (Dabashi 2015, 131) represented by the Arab Spring and the continued struggle of the ordinary people for political agency (Bayat 2010) afford us a paradoxical situation that is often met with schizophrenic responses, however critical such responses may be.

Theories such as Francis Fukuyama's "end of history" and Samuel Huntington's "clash of civilizations" are so conclusively discredited and outmoded nowadays (see Mahdavi and Knight 2012) that any effort to expose their imperialist bigotry and to refute their underlying assumptions seems like a futile exercise and a waste of precious ink. These and similar views are based on the long-rooted Hegelian notion of "world-history," which assumes that European civilization (extended to North America and Oceania) will lead the rest of the world onto the path of progress. This chapter takes an opposite trajectory. Here I want to offer a critique of a progressive critique of exceptionalism in the work of the arch architect of the concept, Giorgio Agamben. I wish not to challenge his theory, for I agree with its contours in general. What I problematize instead is the disturbing omission of agency in his thought in that he perceives the subject of the sovereign's exceptionalism merely as a victim. I intend to show how his theory impedes readers from seeing the immanent crack in the sovereign's exceptionalism. In spite of the critical tone of his work, I argue, Agamben objectifies the sovereign and thus cannot see that in condemning the subject to "sacrificial life," the sovereign inadvertently contributes to the constitution of new resistances against itself. In short, Agamben significantly lacks a theory of agency. In this light, I propose an *inversion* of the theory of exceptionalism, an inversion tuned to the pulse of progressive social movements. After an expository account of Agamben's theory, I offer an immanent critique of his work, following Ernesto Laclau, before turning to MENA to show precisely whence the resisting subject arises and how creative resistance enacts exceptions to sovereign exceptionalisms. With the example of creative resistance in MENA in mind, I conclude that even certain critical Western thoughts are permeated by distrust of agency and that in the world after postcoloniality many novel experiments in popular, democratic self-assertion come from the margins of what had been perceived for a long time in terms of (Hegelian, Eurocentric) world-history.

Agamben's *Homo Sacer*: Wither the Agent?

Giorgio Agamben's celebrated book *State of Exception* (2003, English translation 2005) followed an earlier publication, *Homo Sacer* (1995, English translation 1998). Both works gained enormous popularity after September 11, 2001, and the subsequent US-led campaigns in the Middle East, the regime changes in Afghanistan and Iraq, and the destabilization of other states in the region. World politics, it seemed, concretized Agamben's abstract theory.

The state of exception, Agamben remarks, constitutes a paradox because it is the legal form of what cannot have a legal form as it subjects persons to the "laws" from which sovereign power is exempted. The idea of the lawgiver standing outside the law is an old idea, going back to, among other works, Machiavelli's *The Prince* (1532) and Rousseau's *The Social Contract* (1762). Martial law, *état de siège*, war acts, and a state of emergency—nowadays implemented on the global stage by the whims of powerful states—are among the present-day legal enactments of the "state of exception," in which executive power overrides and absorbs juridical power (Agamben 2005, 19) and thus in which the rights-bearing citizen is for the duration of the state of emergency rendered the subject of sovereign power. Because the state of exception is justified based on "necessity," on the exigency of circumstance (Agamben 2005, 25), the legal exceptionalism in the state of exception remains extralegal. The paradox is that the law is fundamentally meant to serve and protect citizens through rights, but the supposed exigency or emergency that triggers the state of exception suspends the rights in the name of serving and protecting the citizens (Agamben 2005, 25). The law remains in effect but is suspended until the circumstance allows for the law's reenactment (Agamben 2005, 31). This is when pure violence, in a Benjaminian sense, reveals itself.

Because "the state of exception appears as the legal form of what cannot have its legal form" and, as such, "binds and, at the same time, abandons the living being to law" (Agamben 2005, 1), it produces the "sacrificial man." Agamben's "state of exception" dovetails with his earlier work on the *homo sacer*, a concept he owes to Walter Benjamin's "sacred man" ([1921] 1996) and Hannah Arendt's (1958) "end of rights of man." Put simply, the figure of the *homo sacer* captures the process through which the citizen, having lost basic rights, is reduced to corporeal, animal existence. The suspension of habeus corpus through the Military Commissions Act of 2006 under President George W. Bush as well as the infamous Guantánamo Bay, Abu Ghraib, and Bagram detention centers represent the deprivation of the individual's political rights, through which the individual becomes "bare naked life": a sacrificial human, reduced to "animal life" (*zoē*) as opposed to "political life" (*bios*), one whose killing educes no penalty (Agamben 1998, 71, 102). This reduction is achieved through the "ban" imposed by the sovereign: the "natural man" is *banned* from the political. The *camp* (i.e., occupied country) epitomizes the politically over-determined space in which humans are deprived of political rights, rendered *homo sacer*, and thus reduced to animal life. The *outcome* of the biopolitical machine, bare life, proves the nonrelationality of law and life (Agamben 2005, 87–88).

Agamben's binarism—that humans deprived of political rights become the sacrificial animal—is revealing. Theoretically, this binary renders the conquered and the occupied helpless victims of sovereign power with almost no political weight attached to their lives, enduring the camplike existence and awaiting the restoration of the law. Agamben acknowledges that the nonrelationality, or exteriority, of law and life "means to open a space between them for human action, which once claimed for itself the name of 'politics'" (2005, 88). Yet the legalist framework of his analysis is incapable of conceptualizing (political) agency, and the glimmer of hope is dimmed in the silhouette of a totalistic biopolitical machine. The fact that the law entails provisions for the sovereign to systematically suspend the law's application upon discretion sheds light on the nature of the law: any law is only as good as the sovereign that embodies it. *Homo sacer* remains an actless subject, which brings us to a critique of Agamben's theory.

Ernesto Laclau points out Agamben's Hobbesian concept of the sovereign and criticizes him for treating the *ban*—the imposed and arbitrary distinction between those who can participate in the political and those who cannot (and thus should be interned)—as an absolute based on two assumptions. Agamben assumes, first, that the banned person, the sacrificial (hu)man, is "dispossessed of any kind of collective identity" and, second, that "the situation of the outsider is one of radical defencelessness" (2014, 210). In contrast to Agamben, Laclau argues that the exclusion, exteriority, or *radical negativity* of the banned person on the contrary provides the condition of possibility of collective identity (2014, 211) beyond the *positivity* of the sovereign. This collective identity is achieved through a multiplicity of identities that enter into relations of equivalence against the imposed sovereign. The other name for this formation is *collective action*. That a homogeneous and fully reconciled society and thus an actless people can be achieved—in a camp, through the ban, and by virtue of the imposed state of exception sustained by force—is the sovereign's delusion as well as the philosopher's fancy. It is in this context that theory and practice meet: despite living under authoritarian states and often arbitrary decisions of their dictatorial leaders, the people of MENA, generally speaking, have never been reduced to *homo sacer* as conceptualized in Agamben's state of exception. This chapter shows that MENA constitutes an "exception" to the "state of exception."

MENA: State of Exception par Excellence

To "liberate" the peoples of Iraq and Afghanistan from the tyrannies of Saddam Hussein and the Taliban (before the recent return of the Taliban, which diminished Afghans' hopes for a future free from jihadism) and lead them to media-trumpeted democracy, the US-led coalition's exceptionalism and interventionism imposed the "state of emergency" on these occupied territories. One can see in these cases how the fundamental assumption in the conqueror's logic is similar to the assumption regarding Agamben's actless subject: the coalition's implicit expectation was that the people of these countries would stay put as nonpolitical people until further notice through the process of military occupation, regime change, and institution building—somehow wait out the perils of everyday life, shortage of basic necessities, and bloody insecurity until they reemerged as rights-bearing citizens upon the completion of the transition. They would endure all this because they love democracy! This attitude is captured in Dick Cheney's remarks in 2003: "I really do believe we will be greeted as liberators. . . . I have talked with a lot of Iraqis in the last several months myself, had them to the White House" (quoted in Dabashi 2011, 1). Exceptionalism works only if it is based on the fundamental assumption of an actless subject: that resistance, if any, will be manageable. It is this perception of the people of MENA, upheld by imperialist statespersons, Western media, and Orientalist Middle East "experts," that resonates with Agamben's concept of "sacrificial man." Neoconservative think tanks brilliantly failed to recognize that there is no actless subject and that exceptionalism's intent to rule by exclusion produces its own exceptions. In other words, it is true that the camp, or occupied country, ruled through the state of emergency reduces the rights-bearing citizens to sacrificial humans, naked life, and objects of arbitrary search and indefinite detention. But this is precisely when the prisoners in the camp and peoples of occupied states discover the power of refusal. Humans become revolutionary when they literally have nothing to lose but their chains and precisely because they have nothing but their physical, corporeal existence to fall back to and can claim their existence as refusal emerges as the most fundamental trait of human agency.

To our woe, we know that occupation also conjures up the most demonic elements. The Islamic State of Iraq and Syria (ISIS) is the latest example of how retrograde forces, which emulate sovereign power's exceptionalism instead of undermining it, can exploit instability and dismantle progressive elements people had built over decades of struggles. What I call "exceptions to exceptionalism," on the contrary, are *social forces that not only challenge but overcome* the sovereign's exclusive power to bestow or withdraw rights. Born out of the ban, these *collective actors* in fact create rights, empower citizens, and enable agency from below, regardless of the sovereign. These resisters within the camp challenge the vividly violent forms of subjection—the state of internment and suspension of rights—through the most *nonviolent forms of creative resistance*: collective action.

Exceptions to Exceptionalism!

In light of these observations, I want to assert that since 2009 MENA has offered something new to "world-history": resistance to various (perpetual) "states of emergency"—real or proximate—through creative assertion of citizenship either by "partial citizens" or by utterly rightless peoples. Although none of the cases discussed here fit the legal parameters from which Agamben's concepts are extracted, the quasi-camplike conditions created through the specter of foreign occupation, regime change, and proxy wars looming large over the region produced a certain collective psychology through shared anxiety and sense of instability among the peoples of MENA, who, contrary to the suppositions of Western think tanks and critical theorists alike, took compelling initiatives to transform the *grammar* of politics through grassroots movements. By enumerating three world-historical initiatives, I show how each movement challenged the Orientalist notion of "Muslim exceptionalism"—that Muslims are incapable of democratization (Mahdavi 2008, 157)—and how the logic of exceptionalism was nullified through creative initiatives.

Iran's Green Movement

With the critical defeat of Iranian Reformists in the 2005 presidential elections and the presidency of the radical-conservative Mahmoud Ahmadinejad, who pursued neoliberal economy through demagogical populism domestically and inflammatory, confrontational foreign-policy rhetoric internationally, Iran quickly became the target of crippling economic sanctions and the object of serious threats of occupation (like Afghanistan and Iraq) trumpeted by President Bush and his ally, Israel. The repressive measures put in place by Ahmadinejad's government and the specter of invasion and looming threat of war created a quasi–state of emergency in the country as Iranians in general and activists in particular were increasingly deprived of their rights. These conditions produced a certain collective psychology among Iranians as they perceived themselves literally to be rightless subjects. It is true that Iran's Reformists lacked powerful leadership and feared mobilization of civil society (Mahdavi 2008, 152–53), but civil society had ironically grown strong in the Reform years (1997–2005). The Islamic state holds its preservation as the utmost value. Ayatollah Ruhollah Khomeini submitted in 1989 that the protection of the state should be held as the highest priority, even at the cost of suspending shari'a, the jurisprudential foundation of the Islamic Republic (Mahdavi 2008, 145).

As is well known, the Green Movement was a grassroots protest that arose in the aftermath of the rigged presidential elections in 2009 that renewed Ahmadinejad's presidency for one more term, thus perpetuating the spectre of domestic repression and foreign occupation in the collective psyche of Iranians. They mobilized in vast numbers, especially the youth and women, to bring to power the reform-minded candidate (and former premier), Mir Hossein Mousavi. The movement eventually failed to persuade the authoritarian ruling class to submit to the will of the people. During its ten-month active life, however, it captured the world's imagination and offered an image of a gentle, resolute, peace-loving nation to the world, a portrait in contrast to the images of an Iranian militarized authoritarian state promoted by Western-corporate media. The Green Movement presented Iran's "Gandhian moment" through its decidedly Satyagraha engagement (Jahanbegloo 2010) and stood as "dignity's revolt" (Dabashi 2012a, 127; Vahabzadeh 2009a, 2009b). It showed the unmistakable character of a "civil rights movement" (Cornel West, in Dabashi 2010b). It offered a new, revolutionary consciousness and a form of citizenship and civic engagement that frightened the ruling establishment precisely because this form of democratic citizenship did not depend on sovereign prerogative. Having the living memory of the Reform era, the women and young people who manned the movement emerged as agents of change in the context of and in reaction to the inflammatory and populist policies of President Ahmadinejad, which had led both to the imposition of sanctions that were hurting the Iranian people and to repression of civil society. The elections and the possibility of a reform-minded president provided the opportunity for a genuine show of the people's power. Against the specter of imperialist occupation of the country, the Iranians showed they were capable of fighting back on their own terms.

People understood that they were allowed to mobilize politically only once every four years and to act only so that their participation would give the (mostly engineered) presidential elections an aura of legitimacy. In other words, Iranians live through every four years as mostly rightless subjects only to be allowed full political rights during an election. Zahra Rahnavard, a university professor and the wife of Mousavi (both under house arrest for years now), captured this curious institutionalized exceptionalism when she declared: "During the recent election [2009], women were treated as first-class citizens, but right after the election that status was taken away from them in a flash" (in Kalame 2010, 263–64).

The Green Movement presented the spirit of a nation as cosmopolitan, diverse, pluralistic, and peace loving. This bottom-up, grassroots movement was headless as the people mobilized not just to prop up a reform-minded candidate against a populist-conservative one but also to teach their leaders how to act, how to lead, and how to think, and in that goal they showed they had surpassed legal reformism. Neither Mousavi nor Mehdi Karoubi, the other defiant presidential candidate (who is also under house arrest, although it became less onerous once the state eased its restrictions in 2021) had any clear electoral platform, campaign plans, or means of mobilization. The people gave agendas to the candidates and mobilized on their behalf. In contrast to Iranian Reformists, who had consistently upheld an unfounded notion that reduced Iranians to Muslim identity (Mahdavi 2008, 155), Mir Hossein Mousavi clearly indicated, particularly in Declaration No. 18 (June 2010)—the "Charter of the Green Movement"—that he was gradually moving away from a monolithic and conventional understanding of the movement to a vision of Iran as the land of diversity, minorities, democratic aspirations, inalienable rights, protection of the poor, and the "global values of justice, freedom, independence, human dignity, and spirituality" (Mousavi 2010). Likewise, Rahnavard unwaveringly challenged the status quo: "[We] must still pursue our demands of freedom, ending discrimination against women and violence, and stopping polygamy," she stated (in Kalame 2010, 264). The movement not only created its leaders but also taught its leaders how to see the movement's constituency without ideological lens or dogmatic beliefs. As Hamid Dabashi averred at the time, "This movement is ahead of our inherited politics, floating ideologies or mismatched theories. We need to sit back and let this inspirational movement of a whole new generation of hope teach us courage and humility" (2010a, 25). In the aftermath of post-Islamism in Iran (Bayat 2007; Mahdavi 2013, 66), the Green Movement offered a new *grammar of collective action*. Born out of "the ban," Iranian *collective actors* offered new conceptualization of citizens' rights, empowered the people, and enabled agency from the below, regardless of the sovereign.

The "delayed defiance" (Dabashi 2015, 131) captured through the Green Movement indeed establishes an exception to both the logic of the sovereign's exceptionalism (accentuated through the threat of invasion) and Muslim exceptionalism. This is precisely why we can name the protest movement of 2009 in Iran, despite its failure to achieve any measurable results, as a world-historical contribution to a world-history that can no longer be regarded as an exclusive prerogative of European humanity.

The perception of Iranians as being rightless subjects, however, has been proven true in recent years with the brutal repression of the protest movements of the poor in December 2017–January 2018, November 2019 (fuel protests), and August 2021 (water protests) as well as with the supreme leader's intentional disregard of the dangers of the COVID pandemic, which resulted in hundreds of daily deaths of citizens. Yet even under the impossible conditions of a ravaging pandemic and brutal repression, Iranians have emerged in the public sphere to act collectively and steadfastly defy their rotten state, shouting the most subversive slogans of postrevolutionary times.

The Tunisian Jasmine Revolution

The self-immolation of the twenty-six-year-old Sidi Bouzid vendor Mohamed Bouazizi on December 17, 2010, set off the Tunisian Jasmine Revolution, led to the departure of General Zine El Abidine Ben Ali, and sparked the region's Arab Spring. Ben Ali had come to power in 1987 following a bloodless coup against President Habib Bourguiba. Ben Ali's initial relaxation regarding political parties hitherto repressed by Bourguiba, especially Islamic groups, soon turned into authoritarian rule (Tanriverdi 2011, 557). The international community remained silent about Ben Ali's prolonged dictatorship because he maintained a foreign policy of balanced relations "with Western Europe and the United States along with increasing inter-Arab cooperation" (Tanriverdi 2011, 559–60).

Upon the fall of the Ben Ali regime, the repressed political parties reemerged. Above all, the conservative party Ennahda (Harkat en-Nahda, Renaissance Party, a Muslim Brotherhood affiliate) proposed a return to the country's Arab and Islamic culture. Secular forces, on the contrary, emphasized the public sphere and individual freedoms (as well as suspension of religious limitations on freedom of expression). The Salafists, supported by the most disenfranchised sectors, also emerged (Zemni 2015, 12–13). Main secular parties included the centrist El Mottamar (Congress for the Republic) and the social democratic Ettakatol (Democratic Forum for Labor and Liberties). Islamists and secularists balanced out each other (Tanriverdi 2011, 563–64) because Tunisian civil society was more developed and pluralistic compared to other MENA countries and because of the country's long legal tradition, with Tunisia being the first Arab country to have a constitution since the nineteenth century (Pickard 2011, 640). It is true that Ben Ali's policies in previous decades had diminished the strength of civil society organizations, but civic actors were able to rebuild and redirect civil society associations more quickly and more robustly than other MENA nations could. A long legal tradition did not necessarily mean that the judicial institutions were strong enough for the new conditions or that the legal institutions operated effectively. The lack of judicial independence has indeed been a persistent issue in Tunisia. Tunisian activists continue to attend to these obstacles. The post–Ben Ali governments (January–March 2011) were manned largely by the figures of the ancién regime who unsuccessfully tried top-down reforms. The later smooth transition, however, was enabled by what one author calls "the dialectical *pas de deux*" between incremental institutional change and revolutionary street protest (Guazzone 2013, 31). One former Bourguiba minister, Béji Caïd Essebsi, led a new government in March 2011, and the High Commission for Political Reform, composed of representatives of the main political actors, was created and charged with preparing for the election of the National Constituent Assembly (Guazzone 2013, 32). The Tunisians' collective fear of the Egyptian experience was instrumental in the pas de deux approach (Guazzone 2013, 41), and the national roadmap was thus created.

Central to the success of this approach in Tunisia was the labor union tradition and its leadership of the protest culture. In particular, the General Union of Tunisian Workers (Union générale tunisienne du travail, UGTT) was able to control the balance of power between government policies and revolutionary demands. It was a key player in completing the Constituent Assembly elections in October 2011, in initiating the Council for the Protection of the Revolution, and in serving as a meeting place for all parties (Omri 2015, 22–23). During the crisis that ensued from the assassination of leftist leader Chokri Belaid in 2013 and the pressure on the Ennahda-led government to resign, it was the UGTT in combination with the Tunisian League of Human Rights, the Tunisian Order of Lawyers, and the Tunisian Union of Industry, Commerce, and Traditional Crafts—the four together known as "the Quartet"—that maintained the balance of power and managed the political crisis. The conflicting parties spoke through these unions, and it was through a UGTT initiative that the dissolution of the government and the appointment of a nonpolitical government became possible (Omri 2015, 24). The National Council for the Protection of the Revolution, established in February 2011 and given legal status in June 2012, was instrumental in the transition: it embraced twenty-eight organizations, unions, and parties, with Ennahda supporting but not joining it. "The [National Council] demanded to be seen as the sole depository of popular sovereignty and it asked to be recognized by presidential decree so that it could monitor the work of the transitional government" (Zemni 2015, 5). In the Constituent Assembly elections of October 2011, Ennahda won a majority, followed by the liberal party El Mottamar and the leftist Ettakatol (Pickard 2011, 637).

Following the Jasmine Revolution, gender activism in rural and urban areas, represented by the Ennahda and secular parties, respectively, also played an important role (Khalil 2014, 187). Women accounted for nearly a quarter (24 percent) of the Assembly's seats. Tunisian women won a symbolic victory in April 2011 with the passing of the Law of Gender Parity, which "required that the political parties registered for the October 2011 elections have equal gender representation, alternating between male and female candidates on their lists" (Khalil 2014, 194).

The long, complicated road from dictatorship to democracy in Tunisia—involving a plurality of actors, arduous processes of negotiations, and civil society mobilization—crystalized in the Constitution of October 2014. According to Marshall Mapondera's comparison of the old (1959) and new constitutions, the latter allows for wider civil and political rights, including presumption of innocence and prisoners' rights (2014, 5). "Labour rights are more explicit, wider, and [are] provided separately from other civil-political rights, such as political representation," and the new "Constitution commits to protecting various vulnerable groups, namely children, women, and the disabled. This is a welcome addition in accordance with the general traditional principles of social tolerance of the Tunisian Republic" (Mapondera 2014, 6). The 2014 Constitution curbed excessive presidential powers, limiting the presidency to two terms only and clearly demarcating the powers of the president and the prime minister. It limited the conditions for enacting a state of emergency, formally recognized women as equal and able candidates to the presidency, and announced gender as a basis for equality (Mapondera 2014, 5–6). This was, of course, before the new constitution was passed in 2022, in which presidential powers are increased, and so the social and political effects of this new constitution remain to be seen.

The Constitution of 2014 was certainly not beyond criticism, but compared to the older constitution it represents the fundamental laws of a society that has consciously and resolutely opted to emerge from the protest movement known as the Jasmine Revolution as a society that upholds the values of civic and human rights, pluralism, gender parity, organized labor, freedom of expression, and expansion of civil society. The Tunisian experience is so rich and involves so many actors that it is impossible to offer a fair picture of the long and arduous process of democratization in this MENA country. But lessons are learned. The political challenges facing the Tunisian people—in particular those posed by the Salafis, who threaten the fabric of Tunisia's fresh democracy—are not over, but the people have decided that their political system should uphold negotiation and debate against unilateralism and imposition of a state of emergency. Similarly, the Jasmine Revolution has not solved the country's economic and social problems, but by empowering civil society activism, labor unions, and diverse political parties, it has institutionalized the avenues through which popular grievances can lead to collective and political will for reforms. In short, the Tunisians have taught world-history how a diverse nation, left at the mercy of a permanent state of emergency, can reemerge as rights-bearing citizens thanks to the people's self-organizing, vigilance, and determination to negotiate their differences.

In one indication of the state of Tunisian civil society building, the Nobel Peace Prize was awarded to the Tunisian National Dialogue Quartet in 2015 for the four unions' tireless efforts in building a pluralistic civil society and dialogical democracy. Composed of the UGTT; the Tunisian Union of Industry, Trade, and Handicrafts; the Tunisian Human Rights League; and the Tunisian Order of Lawyers, the Quartet represents a new phenomenon: "Nowhere in the Arab and Muslim world, do we have such a solid and meaningful representation of the *national will* to freedom from state violence" (Dabashi 2020, 206, emphasis in original).

The Rojava Revolution

Subject to a continued policy of assimilation, the Syrian Kurds not only share a history of oppression with other Kurds in the Middle East but also have been deprived of social and political rights since the Ba'athist coup of 1963. The Ba'athist state renamed Kurdish towns and villages and resettled Arab Bedouins to police the Kurdish region in northern Syria. The creation of an Arab corridor along the Syrian–Turkish border in 1973 resulted in the forced resettlement of 150,000 Kurds without compensation. Yet even while Syria systematically ignored the Kurds' demands and repressed Kurdish protest movements, it provided space for the training camps of the Kurdistan Workers' Party (Partîya Karkerên Kurdistanê, PKK), which had launched armed struggle against the Turkish state since 1984 (Strangers in a Tangled Wilderness 2015, 7–9; White 2015, 20). Unbeknownst to Syrian policy makers, the PKK's presence—in particular after the gradual, ideological turn in the PKK by mid-1990s from Marxist-Leninist national liberation to democratic confederalism and feminism (or Jineology, the Science of Women, to be exact), which resulted in the movement seeking an autonomous confederalist Kurdistan within Turkey instead of separatism—left a lasting impression on Syrian Kurds.

The formation of the three autonomous and federative Kurdish cantons in northern and northeastern Syria in 2012 in the aftermath of the Syrian Civil War provides an example of the possibility of creating a democratic, participatory, and autonomous body politic based on the principles of social justice and human rights. Many liberals criticize this model for being authoritarian, but this very criticism shows how this experience is so novel that it confuses liberals equipped with an archaic and obsolete notion of individualism. Democratic confederalism cannot be measure by the liberal yardstick. In Rojava-ye Kurdistan, or Western Kurdistan—situated in the northeastern region of Syria, one of the most hostile lands, and caught between the pincers of the ruthless ISIS and a belligerent Turkish government—the cantons of Jazira (Cizre), Kobane, and Efrin were pioneers in creating genuine and progressive models of self-governance made up of equal representations of the two leading parties, the Kurdish National Council (Encûmena

Niştimanî ya Kurdî li Sûriyê) and the Democratic Union Party (Partiya Yekîtiya Demokrat). The canton structure of Rojava has since shifted owing to Turkish occupation of certain regions in northern Syria where the Kurds had set up their cantons. Unlike dominant Kurdish parties in Iraq and Iran that are based on tribal alliances, Syrian Kurds have been organizational and theoretical affiliates of the PKK. As the sole prisoner in an island prison since 1999, the leader of the PKK, Abdullah Öcalan, as well as the PKK leadership outside prison leaned toward democratic confederalism (see Öcalan 2011). PKK leadership and thus Syrian Kurdish leaders were influenced by the Zapatistas of Chiapas, Mexico, as well as by the American anarchist Murray Bookchin's "ecological municipalism" (Strangers in a Tangled Wilderness 2015, 22–23). Jineology, as mentioned, is another pillar in the PKK's approach. The Rojava Revolution in Syria represents the realization of these ideas.

This unique experiment takes place in an ever-shifting region because of Turkey's invasion of parts of northern Syria, the end of fighting with ISIS, the US withdrawal from the Syrian conflict, the intrigues of the Kurdistan Regional Government (Hikûmetî Herêmî Kurdistan) in North Iraq, and the consequent flux of refugees to the safe haven of the Autonomous Administration of North and East Syria (Rêveberiya Xweser a Bakur û Rojhilatê Sûriyeyê). Rojava is also under embargo by Turkey, Syria, and Iraq. The governing bodies from the top down within the autonomous cantons of Rojava require their legislative bodies to comprise at least 40 percent of either gender and fair representation of non-Kurdish minorities—Assyrians, Turkmans, Christians, Yazidis, and Arabs. The Social Contract of Rojava cantons is an exemplary document in democratic confederalism, a constitution that binds the cantons together and yet lets each canton decide what works best for it, such that higher-council decisions remain nonbinding at the local level, while the latter unwaveringly adheres to the fundamental rights of Rojava citizens. Power dwells in the grassroots, bottom-up model, conveying the will of citizens from neighborhood councils, city assemblies, provincial city and village assemblies, and the Congress (Strangers in a Tangled Wilderness 2015, 26–29; White 2015, 132). The cantons have declared religious freedom and equality of all minorities. The Fundamental Law regarding Women legalizes equal rights for women, imposes a ban on polygamy (while recognizing that achieving this ban is a long process), and upholds the right of divorce and employment for women. In fact, the Rojava Revolution has brought about women's emancipation from a deeply patriarchal culture. The Kurds believe that for women to be emancipated from patriarchy and violence, they must be present in all aspects of decision making in leadership and executive positions and in the ranks of women-only units of self-defense. The cantons have abolished capital punishment as well. A "people's economy" based on "use ownership" has been set up. Sitting on the historic "Fertile Crescent," Rojava has intentionally retained its traditional agricultural role as the breadbasket of Syria to maintain its economic importance to the country of which it remains a part, albeit in an autonomous fashion. Education is key, and Rojava's first university, the Mesopotamian Social Sciences Academy, announced its inauguration in September 2014. The lightly armed militias, the People's Protection Units and Women's Protection Units (founded in 2013), as well as the local *asayesh* (police) defend the cantons against ISIS and Turkish state incursions and terrorism. "An estimated 35%—around 15,000 fighters—are women" (Strangers in a Tangled Wilderness 2015, 56). These popular defense units proved not only obstinately unrelenting but also commendably efficient during the epic battle of Kobane against the devastating incursion of and siege by ISIS between September 2014 and January 2015. Rojava, however, has been constantly under attack by the Turkish military in the latest wave of repression of the Kurdish movement. Since September 2015, Turkey has been escalating its attacks against PKK bases of the Kurdistan Regional Government in northern Iraq and in Rojava, in particular by bombing and making military incursions into the canton of Cizre as well as by militarizing Kurdish towns and cities in Turkey. Parts of Rojava are currently under the occupation of Turkish-backed militias.

The democratic confederalism of Rojava is indeed one of the most progressive achievements of the people of the Middle East, a model that inspires the oppressed and frightens the regimes in the region. It shows that people of MENA (and elsewhere) need not have a heavy-handed state to regulate their affairs or bring them security. Rojava shows precisely how, contra Agamben, a rightless people that is reduced to an existence of prolonged internment can form a collective-inclusive identity, partake in collective action, and emerge as a new "people," rights-bearing citizens of a democratic polity that owes its guaranteed rights not to the sovereign state and the state's violent means of law enforcement or state of exception but rather to collective identity and collective action—in short, nonviolence. Like the autonomous Zapatista communities in Chiapas, Rojava cantons indeed depict world-history from below.

Conclusion

As exceptionalist Western powers continue to destabilize MENA, the expectation is that the interventionist forces behind regime changes and military occupations will meet no serious resistance, perhaps none other than fundamentalist forces. Although this may be the case more often than we would like to see, the three cases briefly discussed here, heterogeneous in nature, show how exceptions arise in distinction from the old imperialism's exceptionalism. These cases are not intended to conform to Agamben's juridical-conceptual study of *homo sacer* and state of exception. Any serious scholar knows that a lived, concrete instance is far more convoluted than theory admits. The three cases are showcased as "exceptions" to the various exercises of sovereign exceptionalisms in that the actors did not remain actless subjects and sacrificial humans. The "Muslim *homo sacer*" (Dabashi 2012b, 406), in other words, has turned out to be fictitious. These cases are indicative that the people of MENA are great teachers for those of us who not only oppose imperialist exceptionalism but also radically question the key assumptions of critical political theory. An unwavering reliance on progressive, democratic social movements in the region provides us with the guideposts for alternative social organizations and thus with potential contributions to "world-history" from outside the Eurocentric-metropolitan forgers of "world-history," according to which the rest must trail the West to gain admittance into capital H "History." From Chiapas to the World Social Forum to the Arab Spring to the Occupy movement, from Iran to Tunisia to Rojava, creative resistances by the poor and oppressed abound. This is world-history enacting itself from below.

References

Agamben, Giorgio. 1998. *Homo Sacer: Sovereign Power and Bare Life*. Translated by Daniel Heller-Roazen. Stanford, CA: Stanford Univ. Press.

———. 2005. *State of Exception*. Translated by Kevin Attell. Chicago: Chicago Univ. Press.

Arendt, Hannah. 1958. *The Origins of Totalitarianism*. Orlando, FL: Harcourt Brace.

Bayat, Asef. 2007. *Making Islam Democratic: Social Movements and the Post-Islamism Turn*. Stanford, CA: Stanford Univ. Press.

———. 2010. *Life as Politics: How Ordinary People Change the Middle East*. Stanford, CA: Stanford Univ. Press.

Benjamin, Walter. [1921] 1996. "Critique of Violence." In *Selected Writings*, vol. 1: *1913–1926*, edited by Marcus Bullock and Michael W. Jennings, 236–52. Cambridge, MA: Belknap Press of Harvard Univ. Press.

Dabashi, Hamid. 2010a. "Iran's Green Movement as a Civil Rights Movement." In *The People Reloaded: The Green Movement and the Struggle for Iran's Future*, edited by Nader Hashemi and Danny Postel, 22–25. New York: Melville House.

———. 2010b. "Iran's Greens and the American Civil Rights Movement: An Interview with Cornel West." In *The People Reloaded: The Green Movement and the Struggle for Iran's Future*, edited by Nader Hashemi and Danny Postel, 284–89. New York: Melville House.

———. 2011. *Brown Skin, White Masks*. London: Pluto Press.

———. 2012a. *The Arab Spring: The End of Postcolonialism*. London: Zed Books.

———. 2012b. "The End of the West and the Birth of the First Postcolonial Person." In *Towards the Dignity of Difference Neither "Clash of Civilizations" nor "End of History,"* edited by Mojtaba Mahdavi and W. Andy Knight, 397–406. London: Ashgate.

———. 2015. *Can Non-Europeans Think?* London: Zed Books.

———. 2020. *The Emperor Is Naked: On the Inevitable Demise of the Nation-State.* London: Zed Books.

Guazzone, Laura. 2013. "Ennahda Islamists and the Test of Government in Tunisia." *International Spectator: Italian Journal of International Affairs* 48, no. 4: 30–50.

Jahanbegloo, Ramin. 2010. "The Gandhian Moment." In *The People Reloaded: The Green Movement and the Struggle for Iran's Future*, edited by Nader Hashemi and Danny Postel, 18–21. New York: Melville House.

Kalame. 2010. "'If a Nation Wants to Change Its Destiny . . .': Zahra Rahnavard on Women's Rights and the Green Movement." In *The People Reloaded: The Green Movement and the Struggle for Iran's Future*, edited by Nader Hashemi and Danny Postel, 263–70. New York: Melville House.

Khalil, Andrea. 2014. "Tunisia's Women: Partners in Revolution." *Journal of North African Studies* 19, no. 2: 186–99.

Laclau, Ernesto. 2014. "Bare Life or Social Indeterminacy?" In *The Rhetorical Foundations of Society*, 207–20. London: Verso.

Mahdavi, Mojtaba. 2008. "Rethinking Structure and Agency in Democratization: Iranian Lessons." *International Journal of Criminology and Sociological Theory* 1, no. 2: 142–60.

———. 2013. "Muslims and Modernities: From Islamism to Post-Islamism?" *Religious Studies and Theology* 32, no. 1: 57–71.

Mahdavi, Mojtaba, and Andy Knight, eds. 2012. *Towards the Dignity of Difference? Neither "Clash of Civilizations" nor "End of History."* London: Ashgate.

Mapondera, Marshall N. 2014. "Tunisia's New Constitution: The Benchmark of Transitional Success for Post-Revolutionary African States." *Africa Law Today* 1:1–8.

Mousavi, Mir Hossein. 2010. "Bayaniyeh 18 Mir Hossein Mousavi va manshur-e Jonbesh-e Sabz" (Declaration No. 10 of Mir Hossein Mousavi and the charter of the Green Movement). At http://www.kaleme.com/1389/03/25/klm-22913/.

Öcalan, Abdullah. 2011. *Prison Writings: The PKK and the Kurdish Question in the 21st Century*. London: Transmedia.

Omri, Mohamed-Salah. 2015. "No Ordinary Union: UGTT and the Tunisian Path to Revolution and Transition." *International Journal on Strikes and Social Conflicts* 1, no. 7: 14–29.

Pickard, Duncan. 2011. "Challenges to Legitimate Governance in Post-Revolution Tunisia." *Journal of North African Studies* 16, no. 4: 637–52.

Strangers in a Tangled Wilderness. 2015. *The Rojava Revolution: A Small Key Can Open a Large Door*. N.p.: Combustion Books.

Tanriverdi, Nebahat. 2011. "Background of the Tunisian Revolution." *Alternative Politics* 3, no. 3: 547–70.

Vahabzadeh, Peyman. 2009a. "Jonbesh-e bikhoshunat jonbesh-e binefrat" (Nonviolent movement, hatred-free movement). *Shahrvand BC*, no. 1057 (Nov. 20): 6–7.

———. 2009b. "Khizesh-e vaqar" (Dignity's uprising). *Shahrvand BC*, no. 1044 (Aug. 21): 6–7.

———. 2014. "Suggestion, Translation, Transposition: Reflections on the Affinities of Movements in the Middle East and Beyond." *Sociology of Islam* 2:111–26.

White, Paul. 2015. *The PKK: Coming Down from the Mountains*. London: Zed Books.

Zemni, Sami. 2015. "The Extraordinary Politics of the Tunisian Revolution: The Process of Constitution Making." *Mediterranean Politics* 20, no. 1: 1–17.

2

Israel, Palestine, and the Politics of Race

Moving from Exceptionalism to Global Context

Abigail B. Bakan and Yasmeen Abu-Laban

The Challenge of Knowing "Race" in the Israel/Palestine Context

Although the Arab Spring beginning in 2011 ushered in a mood of optimism for the peoples and observers of the Middle East and North Africa (MENA), from the perspective of a decade later much of this hope has faded, while historic myths about the region have proved to be remarkably persistent. In particular, long-standing ideas about the region's ostensible challenges to meeting the norms of Western democracy continue to be asserted. Specifically, for comparative politics specialists, the MENA region has stood out in several ways as an area of "exceptionalism" when it comes to democracy. First, in both the Western academy and popular discourse, Arab countries have been portrayed as uniquely undemocratic, particularly in the era after September 11, 2001 (9/11). Second, the region as a whole is seen as distinctly undemocratic in contrast to other regions, such as North America and Europe. And third, Israel has been identified as an exception to the exception in its uniquely claimed democracy, in alignment with liberal democratic countries such as the United States, Canada, and France and in contrast to neighboring Arab countries.

These features have been typically on display for the MENA region through the classification system used by the influential US-based research institute Freedom

This chapter is equally and jointly written by the coauthors, and we acknowledge the support of the Social Sciences and Humanities Research Council of Canada. The chapter draws significantly from Yasmeen Abu-Laban and Abigail B. Bakan, *Israel, Palestine, and the Politics of Race: Exploring Identity and Power in a Global Context* (London: I. B. Tauris, 2020), 23–48, by permission of Bloomsbury Publishing PLC.

House, which has consistently presented the region as the least free among world regions. Most of the countries in the region are classified as "unfree" or "partly free," with the exception of Israel.[1] Indeed, the pro-Israeli state group Friends of Simon Wiesenthal Center for Holocaust Studies proclaimed that Freedom House's "report [for 2018], which evaluates the real-world rights and freedoms exercised by citizens across the world, confirms the deficits of freedom in most of the Middle East and highlights the important exceptionalism of Israel as the sole 'free' country in the area" (2019).

It is relevant to note that the Freedom House classification has generally been accepted and used by specialists in the field of comparative politics and the discipline of political science, among others (see, e.g., Diamond 2015, 141–44). In more recent updates covering the years 2019 and 2020, Freedom House upgraded Tunisia to the category of "free" alongside Israel (Freedom House 2021; Slipowitz and Hawthorne 2021). However, this shift is recent, and it fails to address the way in which Israel is a sole power controlling all territory, including the occupied Palestinian territory from the Jordan River to the Mediterranean Sea (Lustick 2019).

As comparative politics specialists attuned to critical race and feminist theories, we are particularly concerned with the propensity to understand and approach Israel as an exceptional free democratic country because this assertion ignores and distorts certain realities. For example, the exceptional placement of Israel is critically related to how Freedom House advances its understanding of Israel's governance and borders, identifying "Israel" as separate from the "unfree" territories of the "West Bank and Gaza" (Slipowitz and Hawthorne 2021). If the mainly Arab Palestinian populations of Gaza and the West Bank were to be included in the reporting of Israel, elections—and hence democracy—there would clearly stand in quite a different light. The denial of citizenship to the non-Jewish, Arab Palestinian populations, who continue to live under Israeli state control, clearly suggests challenges to the most basic democratic norms.

Our chapter is concerned with the kind of absenting of Palestine and Palestinians emblemized by discussions of Israel as a "democracy" because it is precisely this absenting that feeds into a neglect of race, racism, and power in Israel/Palestine within political science and related disciplines. Concepts such as colonialism and dispossession do explain key aspects of Israel's relationship to Palestine, but the inherent racialization of Palestinians also merits focused attention (Bhandar 2018; Wolfe 2016). Not paying attention to it is particularly problematic in the context of ongoing calls for democracy, freedom, and fairness in the MENA region

---

1. See the Freedom House website at https://freedomhouse.org.

that have been spawned by what are aptly entitled in this collection the "unfinished movements for transformation." Increased attention is merited to attend to racism and antiracism in civil societies globally (Abu-Laban and Bakan 2021) and to the ongoing struggles of Palestinians for self-rule.

Why consider race and racialization, and what does such an approach bring to our understanding of the region and its relationship to portrayals of states as "democratic" or to our understanding of social movement demands? Race is linked to colonialism, dispossession, and political responses such as nationalism or quests for self-determination, but race and racism also draw attention to a distinct element of power. This element is particularly relevant to the region where Israel was established in the wake of genocide and virulent antisemitism, or anti-Jewish racism, in Europe. It is also relevant because the Palestinian Indigenous population has been subject to dispossession and sustained racialized discourses and stereotypes that take on global dimensions and relate to power. The United Nations has recognized the right of return for Palestinians, but that right lacks enforcement because it is not backed by Israel or its powerful allies, such as the United States (Abu-Laban and Bakan 2021). An approach that recognizes critical race theory as well as the importance of states and ideology in racialization can help to address these pivotal issues.

To make the case, we take a threefold approach in this chapter. First, we consider more closely the North American (US and Canadian) traditions of academic scholarship and how contemporary understandings of race and racism have tended to ignore Israel/Palestine, even though racialized inequalities necessarily complicate discussions of democracy and democratization (Abu-Laban and Bakan 2008; Mills 1997) in what we term the "idea of Israel." Second, we provide a more detailed consideration of the deeper epistemological issues at play in what we term the "idea of Israel." And third, we discuss the epistemological issues relevant to what we refer to as the "absenting of Palestine." We argue that by placing Israel in comparative context and bringing the multivocal Palestinian experiences into discussion, we can move toward better attending to the politics of race, power, and the unfinished project of democracy in Israel/Palestine.

Political Science, Ethnic Studies, Race, and the Absence of Palestine

In the context of the success and growth of the Black Lives Matter movement beyond its base in the United States and of the murder of George Floyd at the hands of the Minneapolis police in May 2020, attention and awareness of race and racism have been heightened (Abu-Laban and Bakan 2021). However, to date, attention to race and racism in Israel/Palestine specifically has been scant.

Political science concerns itself with the study of states and power and is therefore an academic discipline arguably well suited to the study of race and racialization in Israel/Palestine. However, political science has not generally developed as a welcoming intellectual home for critical race analyses regardless of geographic region or country case study, which may be seen to hamper understanding, including of democracy. Specifically, "race" has been and remains only recently the subject of attention in political science (Nash 2011). This is highlighted in a report from 2011 that raises the question of whether the discipline itself can "broaden the understanding, and model the behavior necessary to build strong nation-states in a rapidly changing world where population shifts and related issues regarding race, ethnicity, immigration, and equal opportunity structure some of the most significant conflicts affecting politics and policy-making" (American Political Science Association 2011, 1). Indeed, to the extent that political science addresses race, it has traditionally subsumed race under or beside notions of "ethnicity" and has given processes of racialization in Israel/Palestine particularly limited attention. In the area of ethnic studies, race is addressed, but the case of Israel/Palestine has similarly received only marginal attention. As a discipline, political science has its origins in the developments of modern social science and was given renewed strength in the decades following World War II. Developments in the field in the United States since the mid–twentieth century have heavily shaped the discipline not only because some 75–80 percent of the world's political scientists were estimated to be located in the United States by the 1990s (R. Taylor 1999) but also because American narratives of the discipline are drawn upon both inside and outside of the US context (Abu-Laban 2017; Gunnell 2002).

This is not to suggest, however, that the subject of race has gone completely unnoticed in political science. In the case of comparative politics, one of the main subfields in the discipline, for much of the postwar period there was sporadic attention to issues of race and ethnicity, which further advanced in 1995 with the creation of a new section dealing with race/ethnicity in the American Political Science Association. The Canadian Political Science Association added a dedicated section on race, ethnicity, Indigenous peoples, and politics in 2009. However, analyses of racialization as a historically and socially constructed process remain marginal (R. Taylor 1999), as do analyses of the complex intersections of race, gender, and class, among other forms of inequality (Dawson and Cohen 2002, 503). According to Michael Hanchard and Erin Chung, "there has been little discussion of the conceptual and methodological implications of the comparative study of race and ethnicity on contemporary debates and discussion" in comparative politics in the United States (2004, 320), even though a more serious undertaking of these issues in cross-national perspective could greatly enhance the literature.

As Michael Dawson and Cathy Cohen noted in reviewing the study of race in the early 2000s,

> One central theme . . . is the need to understand the process of racialization and racial orderings throughout history and from the perspective of different racial and ethnic groups. More often than not political science seems oblivious to the different methods, times, and reasons groups become racialized subjects. Further, the dynamic trajectory of racial ordering and its consequences for not only policy areas such as immigration but also the evolution of state operations and orientations seems noticeably absent from our analyses. Exploring the historical and specific processes of racialization should provide greater insight into such staples of political science inquiry as electoral realignment, public opinion shifts, and interest group proliferation. (2002, 489)

In the subfield of political theory, the area within postwar American political science charged with considering normative questions (Gunnell 2006, 484–85), scholars of democratic theory have turned to the politics of multiculturalism and inclusion, which tend to frame racialization as a feature of illiberal attitudes and premodern practices. Notably, in the face of what has been termed the "behavioral revolution" and the concomitant privileging of certain kinds of research that could inform (American) policy makers, political theory continues to retain a surprising influence (Kettler 2006). In this regard, American political theorists, like their empiricist colleagues, have a strong concern for democratic theory (Berndston 1987). Over the 1970s and 1980s, democratic theory came to be characterized by the debate between liberals and communitarians. However, since 1989 and the attendant waning of the historic Cold War binary, political theory has more seriously taken up issues of national identity and multiculturalism. This turn is symbolized by the international influence of the Canadian political theorists Will Kymlicka (1989, 1995, 1998) and Charles Taylor (1994), which includes Kymlicka's joint edited work with Eva Pfôsti addressing issues of minority rights in the Middle East context (Kymlicka and Pfôsti 2014).

In short, dominant strands of political theory have gone multicultural (May, Modood, and Squires 2004, 3–8). The focus on cultural minorities—largely national minorities within liberal democratic nations—has tended in effect, however, to downplay and/or make less possible a focus on race and processes of racialization as well as on other forms of social differentiation and power relations by a privileging of "culture" (Arat-Koç 2014; Dhamoon 2006, 2010). Moreover, aside from some notable exceptions (e.g., Carens 2000), much of this work is theorized at a very abstract level, with limited attention to empirical realities in distinct contexts (May, Modood, and Squires 2004, 5–6) or historical specificities. Despite the impressive contributions by Canadian political scientists to studies of multicul-turalism, the absence of attention to racialization as both socially constructed and historically concrete has hampered the study of politics in Canada (Abu-Laban 2007). In her article "Is Race Political?" (2008), Debra Thompson addresses the awkward disconnect among the realities of race as a factor in power, social and political barriers, and representation as well as the near absence of attention to race in Canadian political science.

A legacy of "colonial amnesia" (Choudry 2010), characteristic of countries with settler histories, such as Canada and the United States, bears heavily on con-temporary political science. Other subfields in the discipline, notably in the field of international relations (IR), have similarly largely elided a focus on race and racialization. In the context of the Cold War as well as of American policy makers' interests and the dominance by American-based academics in state security in that period, much that was addressed took as its focus national security, nuclear deterrence, and military strength. As an area of study closely linking state policy to research, IR has been described variously as a field or subfield of political sci-ence or as a discipline in its own right. Regardless, it is clear that IR was shaped by the postwar development of political science as a discipline and has been closely associated with liberal democratic state military policy. As Bill McSweeney points out, "Measured in terms of growth since 1945, the study of security is probably the most prestigious sub-field of international relations" (1999, 25). Moreover, at least until the mid-1980s, many questions of international security were framed strictly within the boundaries of the discipline of political science and its objectivist tra-dition (McSweeney 1999, 33).

Even in the face of a narrow definition of security, however, there was con-siderable debate. As Ole Wæver notes, by the 1980s within the United States, where realism dominated, there was increased discussion of the "challenges" to this perspective's privileging of the state, power, and the military sphere; outside the United States, analysts highlighted an "interparadigm debate" among real-ism, liberalism, and Marxism (1997, 12–13). Of course, what is meant by "secu-rity" is complicated and contested (Kolodziej 2005, 1). However, it took the end of the Cold War—marked symbolically by the fall of the Berlin Wall in 1989—to challenge more decisively the manner in which IR tended to frame security in relation to the state and military power as well as to challenge the underlying epistemological and methodological tenets of positivism. The reframing of secu-rity has been evident, for example, in Thomas Homer-Dixon's (1991) discussion of the environment and the increased focus on human security. Epistemological and methodological challenges in the study of security are also increasingly influen-tial (Kolodziej 2005, 259–304).

Many writers contributed to these directions, including in post–Cold War discussions of "new security" and the constructed character of security within IR (Buzan and Wæver 2003; Buzan, Wæver, and Wilde 1998; Wæver et al. 1993). Nonetheless, in practical application, these authors tended to address the construction of global and regional security threats but paid scant attention to how processes of racialization define or affect definitions of security or its risks. Thus, as Geeta Chowdhry and Sheila Nair stated in the early twentieth century, "While conventional IR obscures the racialized, gendered and class bases of power, and in fact . . . normalizes these divisions, critical IR problematizes these sources and workings of power. However, the latter is less able or willing, with a few exceptions, to address the intersections of race, class and gender in the construction of power asymmetries" (2002, 2).

The case of Israel figures uneasily in approaches to global security and international relations because the claimed "Jewish" character of all the significant political parties in that state is normalized and accepted in international arenas. Moreover, Israel's exceptionality is widely taken as a given. As Reg Whitaker notes, this exceptionality has dramatically escalated in the post-9/11 context, not least associated specifically with airline security and antiterrorism (2011, 371). The inattention to the construction of racialization has enabled the Israeli state's claimed Jewish identity and representation to be accepted as a fact rather than as a feature of state hegemony and an ideological project. This framing has simultaneously effectively absented Palestinian experience, history, and identity claims. At its most problematic, this absenting is replaced with an assumed stereotype of the "Palestinian" as "terrorist" (Lentin 2008; Massad 2006). In this process, political science has been consistent with the social sciences generally, presuming Israel to be "a pioneering, settler-immigrant society that is democratic and has little in common with European-colonial ventures" (Zureik 2011, 5). Comparative studies that address Israeli politics tend to presume Israel to be on the same footing as Western liberal democracies (Haklai 2011; Migdal 2001). If history is brought to bear in the analysis, it is commonly according to the hegemonic narrative of a desert "land without a people" brought to bloom by Western settlement consistent with Zionist framings, which places European Jewish victims of antisemitism (anti-Jewish racism) as the innovative and industrious colonists. This frame absents Palestine and Palestinians and fails to view Zionism, as Edward Said ([1979] 1992) starkly poses the issue, from the standpoint of its victims.

In recent years, political science associations internationally have developed area studies focusing specifically on the politics of race and racism (Dawson and Cohen 2002; R. Taylor 1999), and political scientists have addressed the significance of race in state policies and practices domestically and internationally

(Abu-Laban 2000; Bakan 2014a; Chowdhry and Nair 2002; Saleé 2004; Stasiulis and Bakan 2005; D. Thompson 2008). However, they have largely continued not to address the specific nature of antiracism as a political project. If political science tends to absent or diminish the significance of race and racialization, ethnic studies should arguably serve as an alternative natural home. But here, too, the study of race and racialization regarding Israel/Palestine remains absent or marginal.

In the United States, ethnic studies "as a discipline, emerged in the post–Civil-Rights era" (Prashad 2006, 158). It developed in the context of struggles for academic legitimacy, where historic exclusions of "non-white intellectuals" and features of "faculty hesitancy" mitigated against the more rapid scholarly development demanded by the subject matter (Clarke 1977, 124). However, by the twenty-first century, ethnic studies had come of age as a recognized disciplinary focus. Combining a series of diverse studies of the minority "other" under a common rubric, the emergent discipline did not "disavow the importance of racialization and of racial oppression," even if perhaps it took the risk becoming "invested in the frozen tundra of identity" (Prashad 2006, 157). Critical challenges, however, have arisen concomitant to the mainstreaming of ethnic studies: "Every time the identity of the American people in this continent is celebrated today as a uniquely composite blend of European immigrants who settled the Atlantic colonies or passed through Ellis Island, a political decision and a historical judgment are being made. A decision is being made to represent the Others—American Indians, African Americans, Chicanos, Puerto Ricans, Asians, other peoples of colour—as missing, absent or supplemental" (San Juan 1991, 467).

Efforts to theorize differences and linkages among various types of racialized experiences generated distinct disciplinary foci and complex debates regarding the relationship between critical scholarship and social justice practices (Prashad 2006; San Juan 1991). Notably fraught in this context and relevant to the study of Israel/Palestine is the association of "Jewish studies" with both the historic exclusion of Jewish minorities comparable to the exclusion of other minority groups and the ascendance of Israel as a powerful militarized state that is closely associated with US imperialist interests in the Middle East. A series of debates regarding the ascribed "model minority" status of American Jews (Glazer 1964) and relationships between African Americans and Jewish Americans, with noted contributors including James Baldwin, have generally not found easy resolution (Prashad 2006, 166).

More recent developments in Jewish cultural studies (Boyarin and Boyarin 2002) hold more promise because they are premised explicitly on delinking Jewish diasporic cultural identity from a defense of or association with the Zionist ideology of the State of Israel, and emerging work in critical ethnic studies holds promise for exploring how understanding of race in America also shaped views toward Israel and Palestine (Feldman 2015). However, such perspectives are yet to be felt in much contemporary popular discussion, scholarship, and the political discourse of the complex geopolitics of the Middle East. Political science has an essential contribution to make in moving this discussion forward. To this end, the unequal power relations of states that are embedded in and in turn advance racialization demand attention.

Antisemitism has often been an ill-defined term, but we note it has been used to refer to three distinct forms of expression. The first is anti-Jewish racism, which involves prejudicial and contextually specific discriminatory practices toward Jewish populations defined as "less than white" and, at the violent extreme, the genocide that defined the Holocaust. The second is anti-Judaism, which is a prejudice based on a theological perspective or religious belief as opposed to race-based thinking. The third expression is sometimes referred to as the "new antisemitism" and conflates criticism of Israel's policies with antisemitism.[2] Without in any way minimizing the centuries-long legacy of anti-Judaism and anti-Jewish racism, particularly in European and North American politics, we argue that the colonial history and apartheid conditions of the Israeli state demand theoretical attention.

However, the disciplinary absence of a clear focus on race and racialization in Israel/Palestine cannot be simply redressed. This is not, as a common feminist critique of the absence of women as subjects in the social sciences used to note, a simple case of "add and stir." This point brings us to a discussion of the deeper epistemological challenges that have supported a sustained distortion of the idea of Israel and the concomitant absenting of Palestine.

The Idea of Israel

"Israel" is not only a state but also the concept or idea of a state. Although Ilan Pappé (2014) traces the relevance of the idea of Israel for many Israelis, we would stress that the idea of Israel is actually global. Established in 1948, the State of Israel marks the effective culmination, like a symbolic victory flag, of the Allies' success in defeating the Axis powers during World War II. The US, Canadian, and western European ideological frame was defined not only by the Cold War—claiming "democracy" in its liberal Western modernist form as the high point of humanity

2. The International Holocaust Remembrance Alliance's working definition of antisemitism, formulated in 2016, has been challenged precisely for, in its examples, conflating antisemitism with criticisms of Israel's policies toward Palestinians.

and "communism" in its Stalinist bureaucratic form as the low point—but also by the United Nations Declaration of Human Rights and the ascribed accomplishment of overcoming the global vision of Hitler's Nazis. Reclamation of Jewish victims of Nazi genocide became embedded in the normative assumptions of the day. US state power was also indicated in its ideological reach in Western countries. In this context there came a new assertion that the previously understood Christian Protestant mission of humanity and a sound work ethic dedicated to protecting "God's good earth" (Weber 1977; Connolly 2008), was now to be understood as "Judeo-Christian." The foundation of the State of Israel in 1948 coincided with increased acceptance of Jewish Americans—formerly subject to strict quotas in the university system (Soares 2007), among other barriers and expressions of anti-Jewish racism—in one of the most dramatic moments of upward class mobility known in liberal democracies (Brodkin 1998; Goldstein 2006).

The construction of this postwar democratic impulse, however, depended on a number of important absences. In Charles Mills's (1997) definition, these absences could also be seen as an indication of an "epistemology of ignorance." They included a failure to consider the racialized logic and legacy of the atomic bombing of Hiroshima and Nagasaki and the racist treatment of Asian Americans and Asian Canadians that was endemic to the security regime of World War II (Miki 2005). Also absented were the lived experiences of antisemitism of Jews in Europe, the United States, and Canada as well as the long traditions of progressive, antiracist organizing that united Jewish workers with other immigrant and minority populations in labor and socialist organizing (Bakan 2014b). Another absence was consideration of the concessions made to the Nazi genocide by the same states that claimed victory against it, not least a major international conference in Evian, France, in 1938 that refused asylum to Jewish refugees (Sacher 2005, 516). Further absented from consideration were the international corporate links that tied Western businesses to the German genocide machine (Black 2008).

The idea of Israel depends on a material foundation of Israel as a state, and the most enduring and significant absence in this context is the erasure of the Palestinian people. The moment of the establishment of Israel, projected and memorialized in the Zionist narrative as an achievement of "independence" from the British Mandate, is for Palestinians the Nakba, Arabic for "catastrophe." The establishment of the State of Israel was the result of the forced removal of tens of thousands of Indigenous Palestinian people from their homes and land in a violent moment of ethnic cleansing (Pappé 2007). This is not merely an historic event; it is also a current and continuing process of absenting, denial of the right of return, occupation of Palestinian territories, and denial of equal citizenship claims by Palestinians in Israel.

The enduring idea of Israel is framed alongside notions of "democracy" and "human rights." This framing was also sustained through the post–World War II ideological reach of the United States in the context of a bipolar world. Israel was imagined and understood as a progressive, humanistic state, consistent with liberal and even social democratic normative claims. The establishment of this frame was not a simple or linear process. An exhaustive documentation of this mythology goes beyond the scope of this chapter, but it is notable that it included a variety of formative moments on a number of levels, from media spectacles such as the Eichmann trial (Arendt [1963] 2006) to war and occupation, such as Israel's Six-Day War of 1967 (Gordon 2008), and an extensive international intellectual and political "branding" exercise on the part of Zionist advocates linking particular interpretations of the Holocaust to Israeli state practices (Finkelstein 2003, 2005).

Significantly, the constructed idea of Israel depends not only on a series of absences that render the claimed democratic and humanistic referents distortions of the actual practices of the Israeli state but also on a dismissal of the legitimacy of a counternarrative that could alter or correct such distortions. What we term the *mythologized exceptionalism* associated with the idea of Israel as a constructed uniqueness that challenges the possibility of comparison (and hence comparative politics as a method) is also grounded upon an array of widely accepted discursive objections to critiques of the mythology itself. Principal among these objections is the claim that any challenge to the hegemonic idea of Israel is tantamount to antisemitism. A specific variant of this claim takes on a particularly virulent affective form when its proponents are of Jewish faith, culture, or identity; the invective is applied not to the argument but to the person, who is charged with willfully suffering a distinct category of "self-hating," ascribing a particular psychological dimension to the conversation. Collectively, the idea of Israel therefore depends not only on an affirmative notion of positive characteristics that absent counternarratives but also on the silencing of critiques that could shift the focus to a comparative political or historical context. To advance this element of the epistemology of ignorance (Sullivan and Tuana 2007) associated with the idea of Israel, we briefly elaborate on each of the objections to these critiques.

The claim that critique of Israel is tantamount to antisemitism has taken on several distinct phases. The most recent iteration asserts that a "new" antisemitism has been advanced in the twenty-first century. This body of claims emerged notably, as Norman Finkelstein points out, "just as Palestinians renewed their resistance to occupation" (2005, 21) when the Second Intifada (Uprising) welcomed the new millennium. As the subsequent extreme repression by the Israeli state came under challenge, "a vast proliferation of books, articles, conferences, and the like alleg[ed] that—in the words of the Anti-Defamation League (ADL) national director Abraham Foxman—'we currently face as great a threat to the safety and security of the Jewish people as the one we faced in the 1930s—if not a greater one'" (Finkelstein 2005, 21).

The literature on the "new" antisemitism includes an array of authors finding a new common cause (Berenbaum 2008; Chesler 2003; Perry and Schweitzer 2008). From this perspective, international arenas for challenging racism and attending to the threats to the survival and rights of Palestinians under occupation have been identified as arenas of this new form of racism—for example, the World Conference against Racism, Racial Discrimination, Xenophobia, and Related Intolerance (WCAR) held in Durban, South Africa, in 2001; the Durban Review Conference in Geneva, Switzerland, in 2009; and the anniversary conference in New York in 2011. In all instances, major states, including the United States, Canada, and, not surprisingly, Israel, withdrew from the conferences on the grounds that these events were in fact not antiracist but antisemitic, thus abandoning the challenge to advance a common plan or even a common statement. A similar kind of response has attended debates surrounding the boycott, divestment, and sanctions movement against Israel, taken up by churches, unions, and student groups in Western countries (Bakan and Abu-Laban 2009; BDS National Committee 2021; Nadeau and Sears 2010).

As a consequence of how naming Israel's obviously racialized practices as equivalent to antisemitism, the atmosphere has not been one conducive to scholarly investigation. This might, for example, account for why the WCAR has earned scant attention in both scholarly and policy analysis (Jackson and Faupin 2008). However, conflating criticisms of Israel's policies toward Palestinians with charges of antisemitism not only trivializes the reality of actual antisemitism but is also counterproductive to fostering human rights and antiracism because it isolates movements and groups attempting to develop universalized responses to racism in its various forms, including antisemitism.

Another claim is directed specifically against Jewish critics of Israeli state policy. A discursive method that moves away from substance, regardless of agreement or disagreement, to one that discredits the person is not commonly accepted in protocols associated with professional and liberal democratic norms and practices in educational, legal, social, medical, or media institutions. However, a curious legitimacy is implied by the unchallenged acceptance of the charge when it is leveled by politically motivated defenders of the State of Israel who are Jewish against others who challenge Israel's policies and who are also Jewish. The specific genealogy of the charge of "self-hating Jew" against those Jews who adopt a critical view of Zionism and the policies and practices of the State of Israel is unclear. However, elements of it can be found in the way that the founder of modern Zionism,

Theodore Herzl, discursively presented the "new Jew" embracing colonial settlement as distinct from the "old Jews" of the eastern European ghetto (Bowman 2011). It was also expressed in critiques of the high-profile and public example of Hannah Arendt's journalistic analysis of the trial of Adolf Eichmann in 1962.

In her coverage, Arendt objected to the process of Eichman's kidnap, maintaining that this was "a clear violation of international law" ([1963] 2006, 263). Moreover, she described the event as less about justice and more about the construction of a show trial by the Ben Gurion government. She maintained that the effort to construct Eichmann as a central mastermind in the Holocaust was unfounded and that the evil manifest in him was less demonic than "banal," systemic in the Nazi political and industrial machine. In this system, she saw the members of the "Jewish councils" (Judenrate) that cooperated with the Nazis as both victims and victimizers. Moreover, she identified a cynical attempt by the Zionist state to use the trial to shape the memory of the Holocaust as a crime against the "Jews" rather than—what she saw as a more accurate account initiated by the Nuremburg trials—a crime against "humanity" (see also Bakan 2014). The reception of Arendt's analysis among leading Jewish Zionist writers was and in many ways remains vitriolic (Young-Bruehl 2004, 339). Arendt was referred to, notably, as a "self-hating Jew." In her very clear and dignified reply, Arendt noted the particular attention leveled toward her identification of the role of the Jewish councils. Among certain reviewers, the alleged charges were that she had, in her words, "claimed that the Jews had murdered themselves. And why had I told such a monstrously implausible lie? Out of 'self-hatred,' of course" (Arendt [1963] 2006, 284). This label continues to be attached to other intellectuals and scholars who are Jewish but who challenge Israel's policies (Nadeau and Sears 2010). The epistemology of ignorance associated with race and racialization in Israel/Palestine is thereby enhanced and perpetuated, enabling the hegemonic construction and further reproduction of the idea of Israel and the absenting of Palestine.

The Absence of Palestine

The profound absence of the Palestinians since 1948 is graphically illustrated by Prime Minister Golda Meir's insistence in the late 1960s, quoted in a leading British newspaper, that Palestinians did not "exist": "There was no such thing as a Palestinian. When was there an independent Palestinian people with a Palestinian state? . . . It was not as though there was a Palestinian people in Palestine considering itself as a Palestinian people and we came and threw them out and took their country away from them. They did not exist" (Giles 1969). Her statement in effect echoed the much earlier erasure of Palestine's Indigenous Arab (Christian and Muslim) population contained in the infamous early Zionist slogan calling for settlement of Palestine because it was a "land without a people." Even today, it is notable that considerable energy continues to be invested in attempts to sever the relevance of the Palestinian claims to the geographic space of mandatory Palestine. This is perhaps most commonly encountered in the long-enduring suggestion, still popular among some Israeli politicians, that Jordan should be the homeland of the Palestinian people (Peter and Prusher 2009). This proposal has been rejected by Jordan (Peter and Prusher 2009) and by Palestinians themselves (Ryan and Hallaj 1983). That during the US presidential Democratic primary debates in 2016 Bernie Sanders was said to have made "historic" comments for speaking not only about Israel's right to exist, as did rival Hilary Clinton, but distinctly also about Palestinians and their rights underscores the stunning absence of Palestine in the landscape of American political discourse (Lachman 2016).

To be clear, through their oral as well as written histories Palestinians have established both their presence in Israel/Palestine from antiquity and the ways in which the population identified as "Palestinian" existed there in the nineteenth and early twentieth centuries, including, therefore, the period long before 1948 (Farsoun and Aruri 2006; Khalidi [1997] 2010). In addition, a "post-Zionist" historiography has over the 2000s utilized archival documents made public in Israel to further document the militarized violence that produced and sustained the Nakba (Pappé 2007). In effect, this historiography challenges the official Israeli narrative of state founding, which, to paraphrase Golda Meir, holds that no one was "thrown out" but rather that the Palestinians voluntarily elected to depart. The work of Edward Said, widely read across the social sciences and humanities, has powerfully illuminated the peoples and societies of the Middle East and Palestine and provided a means for understanding their experiences in relation to human history and power differentials (Abu-Laban 2001). He made these corrections in his especially now classic discussion of the relevance of Orientalism to colonialism, including the Zionist settler-colonial project in Palestine (Said 1979) and in his work *The Question of Palestine* ([1979] 1992), which explicitly aimed to articulate for a Western/American audience "the Palestinian experience, which to all intents and purposes became a self-conscious experience when the first wave of Zionist colonialists reached the shores of Palestine in the early 1880s" (ix).

Said's ([1979] 1992) account is premised on the geopolitical constructed reality of Palestine's "nonexistence" after 1948; he simultaneously showed Palestine's relevance to the political imaginary and the experience of the Indigenous Arab population (who were and are, despite current assumptions of an Arab-equals-Muslim association, both Christian and Muslim). As Said put it with a clarity that continues to resonate, "The fact of the matter is that today Palestine does not exist, except as a memory or, more importantly as an idea, a political and human experience, and an act of sustained popular will" ([1979] 1992, 5). Moreover, Said recognized the difficulty of even finding ways to articulate Palestine as experience, memory, or idea, especially in the West. In his words, "the sheer impossibility of finding a space in which to speak for the Palestinians is enormous; indeed, every statement on behalf of Israel intensifies and concentrates pressure on the Palestinians to be silent, to accept repression" (39–40).

We attribute the difficulty in speaking as or in solidarity with what might be called the multivocal Palestinian narrative as well as the difficulty in hearing Palestinian voices at all to the epistemology of ignorance concerning sustained, systemic, hegemonic, and racialized processes of discrimination, repression, and exclusion. The cumulative effect of these racialized processes, combined with the challenges inherent in even naming these processes as racialized, sustains the absence of Palestine and the Palestinians.

The racialized processes that have led to the absenting of Palestine and Palestinians stem from several factors. First among them is the physical absence of Palestinians from mandatory Palestine. The Nakba itself served to all but obliterate Palestinian society when more than half the population in what became Israel was made refugees in lands outside of mandatory Palestine. Palestinians continue to be physically absent from the land of mandatory Palestine, and today they are one of the world's largest and oldest refugee groups.

Moreover, Palestinians are the targets of extreme repression. The historian Ilan Pappé (2007) has described in detail the process of "the ethnic cleansing of Palestine" preceding Israel's establishment as a state in 1948. Militarized repression then sustained the nonreturn of Palestinians, despite the fact that as early as 1948 United Nations Resolution 194 called for right of return of refugees. The small minority of Palestinian Arabs who remained in the new state were treated—and continue to be referred to—as a potential "fifth column." As such, they were the main objects of "emergency regulation" as well as a host of measures aimed at counting their presence and proportion in relation to the Jewish population and controlling their actions, movements, and ownership of land (see Zureik 2011). Indeed, Mahmoud Darwish, who was during his lifetime frequently referred to as Palestine's national poet, highlighted the militarized encounters that Arabs in Israel endured in his defiant poem "Identity Card" (1964). Its memorable opening stanza says:

> Record!
> I am an Arab
> And my identity card is fifty thousand
> I have eight children

And the ninth is coming after a summer
Will you be angry?
>   (Darwish [1964] 2011)

After the Six-Day War in 1967, the Israeli military occupation of the West
Bank, Gaza, and East Jerusalem furthered the ways and means by which Palestinians experienced disappearances, militarized repression, and control over their
land, resources, mobility, and daily activities—from education to services to travel
and employment (Gordon 2008). Because those under occupation lack Israeli citizenship, the racialized character of differential treatment is especially obvious.
The First Intifada (which may be dated from 1987 to 1993) brought to the world the
image of Palestinian youth resisting the Israeli military with nothing but stones.
It was in this context that Hanan Ashrawi wrote her poem "From the Diary of
an Almost-Four-Year-Old" (1988), based on the true story of a young child who
while standing on the balcony of her grandmother's house lost an eye when hit by
a rubber bullet fired by an Israeli soldier. As this incident was followed by other
infants losing eyes in similar ways, the poem's powerful last stanza focuses on the
almost-four-year-old narrator musing on an infant who lost an eye:

I'm old enough, almost four,
I've seen enough of life,
but she's just a baby
who didn't know any better.
>   (Ashrawi [1988] 1992, 341)

Since the Second Intifada (dating from 2000), the building of the separation
wall has further compounded the racialized experience of Palestinians living under
occupation. Although deemed in contravention of international law by the International Criminal Court, the wall—dubbed, significantly, the "apartheid wall"—
has further restricted the mobility of Palestinians and in many instances access to
their lands, while further segmenting their experience in relation to Israeli Jewish
settlers. As such, both Palestinians living under Israeli occupation and those who
hold Israeli citizenship experience discrimination as non-Jews by the Israeli state.
For Palestinians outside of mandatory Palestine, their "right" of return has been
continually denied.

Palestinians have faced unique challenges in being able to narrate their own
history and experiences. Although attention to "ethnic" history has been important to the evolution of "ethnic studies" in both the United States and Canada, the
history of the Palestinians faces obstacles not only because stateless people like

them have no national archive but also because Palestinians frequently lost their own private belongings—including photos, diaries, family heirlooms, and so on—in the forced removal from Palestine between 1947 and 1949 and in other wars in the region (Khalidi 2006, xxxv). Thus, while the Israeli state has helped to articulate a particular history—in the process fostering the idea of Israel's millennial ties to the "Holy Land"—Palestinians, lacking a state, also have lacked a parallel ability to articulate their history. Moreover, although there are many Palestinian writers, historians, and artists, such figures often face adverse conditions in presenting their works. For instance, in spurious attacks Edward Said was charged with being a "Professor of Terror" because he was Palestinian and simultaneously accused of lying about his claim to Palestinian identity because he had spent time in Egypt as a child (for a response to these attacks, see Shuraydi 2001). In short, the Palestinians have lacked the cultural capital to systematically break through these attempts at silencing and delegitimization. In addition, those taking up the cause of Palestine solidarity face a unique climate of repression, including in the academy (Nadeau and Sears 2010; J. Thompson 2011).

Another factor in the absenting process is quite literal, on the ground of Israel/Palestine, where the Palestinians' historic presence has been subject to erasure through Israel's state-sponsored process of "Judaization" in policies relating to settlement, land, planning, and development (Yiftachel 2006). At the same time, this Judaization has ironically not prevented what many Palestinians experience as an appropriation of elements of Palestinian culture. For example, North Americans and others outside the region associate such foods as falafel, hummus, and "Israeli couscous" with Israel or, more broadly, the Middle East rather than with Palestine. In this way, the cultural erasure of Palestinians may be seen to occur, with different degrees of intensity, both inside and outside Israel/Palestine.

A final factor contributing to the absenting of Palestine is that Palestinians have been compelled to endure and defend themselves against a recurrent pattern of dehumanizing and derogatory imagery. This stems from a very particular interpretation and usage of biblical imagery in which modern Israel is identified as a "biblical land" and in which a solely and singularly "Israelite" identity of this land is deemed beyond assail (Masalha 2007, 310–11). Such imagery is furthered through the discourse branding Palestinians to be the world's premier "terrorists" after the Six-Day War. David Theo Goldberg highlights this linking of biblical interpretation, history, and contemporary politics when he observes, "*Identified as the direct kin of biblical Philistines*, by the mid–twentieth century Palestinians as a people were often seen as Philistines as much in characterization as in scriptural name, conceived in the representational struggle as bloodthirsty and warmongering, constantly harassing modern-day Israelites, debauched and lacking altogether in liberal culture. *Terrorists, it seems, historically all the way down to the toenails of time. Goliath cut to size by David's perennial craftiness and military prowess*" (2009, 107–8, emphasis added).

In Goldberg's phrase "direct kin," what is left out is that even if the name "Philistine" appears to be an etymological predecessor of the name "Palestine," there is no clear ethnic or hereditary connection between modern Palestinians and the ancient Aegean "Sea People" known as the Philistines (Barkat 2009; Hare 2009; Masalha 2007, 99; *Seattle Times* 2002). Moreover, any precise identification of "ethnic" boundaries among such ancient cultures as the Canaanites, Israelites, Philistines, and so on has been argued to be "highly problematic and completely fictional in the critical period of 'Israelite origins' (Iron I Age)" (Masalha 2007, 255). Archaeological evidence, in fact, suggests that the original inhabitants of Israel/Palestine (i.e., Mizrahi Jews, Palestinian Christians, and Palestinian Muslims) are the products of the same shared Canaanite culture (Qumsieh 2004).

That "Palestinians" and "Philistines" are so easily connected is significant in relation to racialization, which is at the heart of Goldberg's argument. In particular, as Nur Masalha notes, the Philistines played the role of the archetypical enemy "other" in the story of the Israelites, most emphatically in the story of David and Goliath, which Goldberg suggests (2007, 99). Indeed, in subtle ways the story of David and Goliath is continually repeated in the imagery surrounding discussions of Israel/Palestine—for instance, in the oft-repeated phrasing of "little" Israel surrounded by "large" (and hostile) Arab states. More recently, Israel is claimed to be uniquely and unfairly "singled out" for human rights violations by ascribed "antisemitic" supporters of the boycott, divestment, and sanctions movement. According to Masalha, who in turn draws from the work of John McDonagh,

> In the Bible the Philistines became the archetypical Other, whose sole function in the text was to plot the destruction of civilization, and whose activities provided justification for the expansion of the Israelites. The Philistines—not unlike the modern Palestinians—had become the Other as a result of the challenge they posed to the bourgeoning collective Hebrew identity, within the parameters established by the biblical narrative. The "ignorant" and "demonic" Philistines, then, fulfilled a role in the construction of the great colonial edifice of Otherness that was later to be played by, among others, Arabs and Muslims, Africans, Indians, Aboriginals, [and] this role furthermore ironically played out to tragic effect by the Jews themselves over centuries of persecution in the West. (2007, 99–100)

We see here a construction of the direct linkage of Palestinians and Philistines (however historically debatable) grounded in the fear of the enemy Other, in this case in orientalized form. This fear fuels ideological justification for the repression of the Palestinians, who are perceived as entirely Muslim even if some 20 percent of them are Christian. It also fuels an ideological justification for Israel's continued colonial rule, occupation, and operations outside the rule of international law. This brings us to stress, once again, that the assertion of Israel's purported place as the sole "democracy" in the Middle East ignores the ways in which the politics of race and power shape the Israel/Palestine context and thus should necessarily give pause to scholars.

Conclusion: Toward Understanding the Unfinished Business of Race

In a moment when we are looking at the lessons of the Arab Spring and the possibilities of democratization as well as its constraints in Arab states, we should equally be addressing the possibilities of democratization and its constraints in Israel/Palestine. To do this, we need to attend more closely to race and power in the region. As this chapter has demonstrated, this attention in turn requires rethinking the dominant ways of knowing (and not knowing) that have conditioned scholarly work in disciplines such as political science and ethnic studies.

An absenting of the Palestinian experience and treatment of Israel as exceptional has affected discussions of democracy in the MENA region and has had cascading consequences for not only our understanding of democracy, the theme of this volume, but also specifically our understanding of the Middle East. It is only by placing Israel in comparative context and by listening to Palestinian voices that we can overcome a racialized epistemology of ignorance. As such, the Arab Spring should stand as a reminder of the incredible human impulse for fairness, inclusion, and equality as well as of the intellectual quest for better understanding and knowledge production.

References

Abu-Laban, Yasmeen. 2000. "Reconstructing an Inclusive Citizenship for a New Millennium." *International Politics* 37, no. 4 (Dec.): 509–26.

———. 2001. "Humanizing the Oriental: Edward Said and Western Scholarly Discourse." In *Revising Culture, Reinventing Peace: The Influence of Edward Said*, edited by Naseer Aruri and Muhammad A. Shuraydi, 74–85. New York: Interlink.

———. 2007. "Political Science, Race, Ethnicity, and Public Policy." In *Critical Public Policy Studies*, edited by Michael Orsini and Miriam Smith, 136–57. Vancouver: Univ. of British Columbia Press.

———. 2017. "Narrating Canadian Political Science: History Revisited. Presidential Address to the Canadian Political Science Association, Toronto, Ontario, May 30, 3017." *Canadian Journal of Political Science* 50, no. 4 (Dec.): 895–919.

Abu-Laban, Yasmeen, and Abigail B. Bakan. 2008. "The Racial Contract: Israel/Palestine and Canada." *Social Identities* 14, no. 5 (Sept.): 637–60.

———. 2021. "Anti-Palestinian Racism: Analyzing the Unnamed and Suppressed Reality." In "Racial Formations in Africa and the Middle East: A Transregional Approach," special issue of *POMEPS Studies* 44 (Sept.): 143–49. At https://pomeps.org /anti-palestinian-racism-analyzing-the-unnamed-and-suppressed-reality.

American Political Science Association. 2011. *Political Science in the 21st Century: Report of the Task Force on Political Science in the Twenty-First Century*. Washington, DC: American Political Science Association, Oct.

Arat-Koç, Sedef. 2014. "Rethinking Whiteness, 'Culturalism,' and Bourgeoisie in the Age of Neoliberalism." In *Theorizing Anti-racism: Linkages in Marxism and Critical Race Theories*, edited by Abigail B. Bakan and Enakshi Dua, 311–39. Toronto: Univ. of Toronto Press.

Arendt, Hannah. [1963] 2006. *Eichmann in Jerusalem: A Report on the Banality of Evil*. Introduction by Amos Elon. New York: Penguin.

Ashrawi, Mikha'il Hanan. [1988] 1992. "From the Diary of an Almost-Four-Year-Old." In *An Anthology of Modern Palestinian Literature*, edited by Salma Khadra Jayyusi, 340–41. New York: Columbia Univ. Press.

Bakan, Abigail B. 2014a. "Permanent Patriots and Temporary Predators? Post 9/11 Institutionalization of the Arab/Orientalized 'Other' in the United States and the Contributions of Arendt and Said." In *Liberating Temporariness? Migration, Work, and Citizenship in an Age of Insecurity*, edited by Leah F. Vosko, Valerie Preston, and Robert Latham, 60–75. Montreal: McGill-Queen's Univ. Press.

———. 2014b. "Race, Class, and Colonialism: Reconsidering the 'Jewish Question.'" In *Theorizing Anti-racism: Linkages in Marxism and Critical Race Theories*, edited by Abigail B. Bakan and Enakshi Dua, 252–79. Toronto: Univ. of Toronto Press.

Bakan, Abigail B., and Yasmeen Abu-Laban. 2009. "Palestinian Resistance and International Solidarity: The Israeli State, the BDS Campaign, and Hegemony." *Race and Class* 51, no. 1: 29–54.

Barkat, Amiran. 2009. "Dig Backs Biblical Account of Philistine City of Gat." *Haaretz*, Aug. 5. At http://www.haaretz.com/culture/arts-leisure/dig-backs-biblical-account-of -philistine-city-of-gat-1.166315.

BDS National Committee. 2021. "Updates from the Palestinian BDS National Committee (BNC)." At https://bdsmovement.net/.

Berenbaum, Michael, ed. 2008. *Not Your Father's Antisemitism: Hatred of the Jews in the 21st Century*. St. Paul, MN: Paragon House.

Berndston, Erkki. 1987. "The Rise and Fall of American Political Science: Personalities, Quotations, Speculations." *International Political Science Review* 8, no. 1: 85–100.

Bhandar, Brenna. 2018. *Colonial Lives of Property: Law, Land, and Racial Regimes of Ownership*. Durham, NC: Duke Univ. Press.

Black, Edwin. 2008. *IBM and the Holocaust: The Strategic Alliance between Nazi Germany and America's Most Powerful Corporation*. Washington, DC: Dialog Press.

Bowman, Glenn. 2011. "A Place for Palestinians in the *Altneuland*: Herzl, Antisemitism, and the Jewish State." In *Surveillance and Control in Israel/Palestine: Population, Territory, and Power*, edited by Elia Zureik, David Lyon, and Yasmeen Abu-Laban, 65–79. London: Routledge.

Boyarin, Jonathan, and Daniel Boyarin. 2002. *Powers of Diaspora: Two Essays on the Relevance of Jewish Culture*. Minneapolis: Univ. of Minnesota Press.

Brodkin, Karen. 1998. *How the Jews Became White Folks and What That Says about Race in America*. New Brunswick, NJ: Rutgers Univ. Press.

Buzan, Barry, and Ole Wæver. 2003. *Regions and Powers: The Structure of International Security*. Cambridge: Cambridge Univ. Press.

Buzan, Barry, Ole Wæver, and Jaap de Wilde. 1998. *Security: A New Framework for Analysis*. Boulder, CO: Lynne Rienner.

Carens, Joseph H. 2000. *Culture, Citizenship, and Community: A Contextual Exploration of Justice as Evenhandedness*. New York: Oxford Univ. Press.

Chesler, Phyllis. 2003. *The New Antisemitism: The Current Crisis and What We Must Do about It*. San Francisco: Jossey-Bass.

Choudry, Aziz. 2010. "What's Left? Canada's 'Global Justice' Movement and Colonial Amnesia." *Race and Class* 52, no. 1: 97–102.

Chowdhry, Geeta, and Sheila Nair. [2002] 2013. "Introduction." In *Power, Postcolonialism, and International Relations: Reading Race, Gender, and Class*, edited by Geeta Chowdhry and Sheila Nair, 1–32. New York: Routledge.

Clarke, Anthony. 1977. "Ethnic Studies: Reflection and Re-examination." *Journal of Negro Education* 46, no. 2 (Spring): 124–32.

Connolly, William E. 2008. *Capitalism and Christianity, American Style*. Durham, NC: Duke Univ. Press.

Darwish, Mahmoud. [1964] 2011. "Identity Card." At http://qumsiyeh.org/mahmoud darwish/.

Dawson, Michael C., and Cathy J. Cohen. 2002. "Problems in the Study of the Politics of Race." In *Political Science: State of the Discipline*, edited by Ira Katznelson and Helen V. Milner, 488–510. New York: Norton; Washington, DC: American Political Science Association.

Dhamoon, Rita. 2006. "Shifting from Culture to Cultural: Critical Theorizing of Identity/Difference Politics." *Constellations* 13, no. 3: 354–73.

———. 2010. *Identity/Difference Politics: How Difference Is Produced, and Why It Matters*. Vancouver: Univ. of British Columbia Press.

Diamond, Larry. 2015. "Facing Up to the Democratic Recession." *Journal of Democracy* 26, no. 1 (Jan.): 141–55.

Farsoun, Samih K., and Naseer H. Aruri. 2006. *Palestine and the Palestinians: A Social and Political History*. Boulder, CO: Westview Press.

Feldman, Keith. 2015. *A Shadow over Palestine: The Imperial Life of Race in America*. Minneapolis: Univ. of Minnesota Press.

Finkelstein, Norman. [2000] 2003. *The Holocaust Industry: Reflections on the Exploitation of Jewish Suffering*. London: Verso.

———. 2005. *Beyond Chutzpah: On the Misuse of Antisemitism and the Abuse of History*. Berkeley: Univ. of California Press.

Freedom House. 2021. "Tunisia." At https://freedomhouse.org/country/tunisia/freedom -world/2021.

Friends of Simon Weisenthal Center for Holocaust Studies. 2019. "Israel Only Free Country in the Middle East Says Freedom House." Sept. 19. At https://www.friends ofsimonwiesenthalcenter.com/news/israel-only-free-country-in-the-middle-east-says -freedom-house.

Giles, Frank. 1969. "Interview with Golda Meir." *Sunday Times* (London). June 15.

Glazer, Nathan. 1964. "Negroes and Jews: The New Challenge to Pluralism." *Commentary*, Dec., 6.

Goldberg, David Theo. 2009. *The Threat of Race: Reflections on Racial Neoliberalism*. Malden, MA: Wiley Blackwell.

Goldstein, Eric L. 2006. *The Price of Whiteness: Jews, Race, and American Identity*. Princeton, NJ: Princeton Univ. Press.

Gordon, Neve. 2008. *Israel's Occupation*. Berkeley: Univ. of California Press.

Gunnell, John G. 2002. "Handbooks and History: Is It Still the *American* Science of Politics?" *International Political Science Review* 23, no. 4: 339–54.

———. 2006. "The Founding of the American Political Science Association: Discipline, Profession, Political Theory, and Politics." *American Political Science Review* 100, no. 4: 479–86.

Haklai, Oded. 2011. *Palestinian Ethnonationalism in Israel*. Philadelphia: Univ. of Pennsylvania Press.

Hanchard, Michael, and Erin Aeran Chung. 2004. "From Race Relations to Comparative Racial Politics: A Survey of Cross-National Scholarship on Race in the Social Sciences." *Du Bois Review* 1, no. 2: 319–43.

Hare, John B. 2009. "Sacred Texts: *The Philistines* by R. A. S. Macalister." Internet Sacred Text Archive. At http://www.sacred-texts.com/ane/phc/index.htm.

Homer-Dixon, Thomas F. 1991. "On the Threshold: Environmental Changes as Causes of Acute Conflict." *International Security* 16, no. 2: 76–116.

Jackson, Peter, and Mathieu Faupin. 2008. "The United Nations Role in Fighting Racism and Racial Discrimination." *Ardent Review* 1 (Apr.): 1–8. At http://www.arts.ualberta .ca/~aadr/Journal.htm.

Kettler, David. 2006. "The Political Theory Question in Political Science." *American Political Science Review* 100, no. 4: 531–37.

Khalidi, Rashid. 2006. *The Iron Cage: The Story of the Palestinian Struggle for Statehood*. Boston: Beacon Press.

———. [1997] 2010. *Palestinian Identity: The Construction of Modern National Consciousness*. New York: Columbia Univ. Press.

Kolodziej, Edward A. 2005. *Security and International Relations*. Cambridge: Cambridge Univ. Press.

Kymlicka, Will. 1989. *Liberalism, Community, and Culture*. Oxford: Oxford Univ. Press.

———. 1995. *Multicultural Citizenship*. Oxford: Clarendon Press.

———. 1998. *Finding Our Way: Rethinking Ethnocultural Relations in Canada*. Don Mills, Canada: Oxford Univ. Press.

Kymlicka, Will, and Eva Pfôsti, eds. 2014. *Multiculturalism and Minority Rights in the Arab World*. Oxford: Oxford Univ. Press.

Lachman, Samanth. 2016. "Why Bernie Sanders' Comments on the Israeli–Palestinian Conflict Are Historic." *Huffington Post*, Apr. 15. At http://www.huffingtonpost.com/entry/bernie-sanders-hillary-clinton-israel_us_57114f60e4b0060ccda353ab?ir=Politics%3Fncid%3Dnewsltushpmg00000003.

Lentin, Ronit, ed. 2008. *Thinking Palestine*. London: Zed Books.

Lustick, Ian S. 2019. *Paradigm Lost: From Two State Solution to One State Reality*. Philadelphia: Univ. of Pennsylvania Press.

Masalha, Nur. 2007. *The Bible and Zionism: Invented Traditions, Archaeology, and Postcolonialism in Israel–Palestine*. London: Zed Books.

Massad, Joseph. 2006. *The Persistence of the Palestinian Question: Essays on Zionism and the Palestinians*. London: Routledge.

May, Stephen, Tariq Modood, and Judith Squires. 2004. "Ethnicity, Nationalism, and Minority Rights: Charting the Disciplinary Debates." In *Ethnicity, Nationalism, and Minority Rights*, edited by Stephen May, Tariq Modood, and Judith Squires, 1–24. Cambridge: Cambridge Univ. Press.

McSweeney, Bill. 1999. *Security, Identity, and Interests: A Sociology of International Relations*. Cambridge: Cambridge Univ. Press.

Migdal, Joel S. 2001. *Through the Lens of Israel: Explorations in State and Society*. Albany: State Univ. of New York Press.

Miki, Roy. 2005. *Redress: Inside the Japanese Canadian Call for Justice*. Vancouver: Raincoast Books.

Mills, Charles. 1997. *The Racial Contract*. Ithaca, NY: Cornell Univ. Press.

Nadeau, Mary-Jo, and Alan Sears. 2010. "The Palestine Test: Countering the Silencing Campaign." *Studies in Political Economy* 85 (Spring): 7–33.

Nash, Nisha. 2011. "Defining Narratives of Identity in Canadian Political Science: Accounting for the Absence of Race." *Canadian Journal of Political Science* 44, no. 1 (Mar.): 161–93.

Pappé, Ilan. 2007. *The Ethnic Cleansing of Palestine*. Oxford: Oneworld.

———. 2014. *The Idea of Israel: A History of Power and Knowledge*. London: Verso.

Perry, Marvin, and Frederick Schweitzer, eds. 2008. *Antisemitic Myths: A Historical and Contemporary Anthology*. Bloomington: Indiana Univ. Press.

Peter, Tom A., and Ilene R. Prusher. 2009. "Israeli Proposal: Make Jordan the Official Palestinian Homeland." *Christian Science Monitor*, June 1. At http://www.csmonitor.com/World/Middle-East/2009/0601/p06s01-wome.html.

Prashad, Vijay. 2006. "Ethnic Studies Inside Out." *Journal of Asian American Studies* 9, no. 2 (June): 157–76.

Qumsieh, Mazin B. 2004. *Sharing the Land of Canaan: Human Rights and the Israeli–Palestinian Struggle*. London: Pluto Press.

Ryan, Sheila, and Muhammad Hallaj. 1983. *Palestine Is, but Not in Jordan*. Belmont, MA: AAUG Press.

Sacher, Howard M. 2005. *A History of the Jews in the Modern World*. New York: Vintage.

Said, Edward. 1979. *Orientalism*. New York: Basic Books.

———. [1979] 1992. *The Question of Palestine*. With a new preface and epilogue. New York: Vintage.

San Juan, E. 1991. "Multiculturalism vs. Hegemony: Ethnic Studies, Asian Americans, and US Racial Politics." *Massachusetts Review* 32, no. 3 (Fall): 467–77.

Seattle Times. 2002. "Two Peoples, One Land: Understanding the Israeli–Palestinian Conflict." May 12. At http://seattletimes.nwsource.com/news/nation-world/mideast/roots/.

Shuraydi, Muhammad A. 2001. "Edward W. Said and His 'Beautiful Old House': A Response to Weiner." In *Revising Culture, Reinventing Peace: The Influence of Edward Said*, ed. Naseer Aruri and Muhammad A. Shuraydi, 170–78. New York: Interlink.

Slipowitz, Amy, and Amy Hawthorne. 2021. "An Unfree Region." *POMED/Project on Middle East Democracy*, Mar. 16. At https://pomed.org/an-unfree-region/.

Soares, Joseph A. 2007. *The Power of Privilege: Yale and America's Elite Colleges*. Stanford, CA: Stanford Univ. Press.

Stasiulis, Daiva, and Abigail B. Bakan. 2005. *Negotiating Citizenship: Migrant Women in Canada and the Global System*. Toronto: Univ. of Toronto Press, 2005.

Sullivan, Shannon, and Nancy Tuana, eds. 2007. *Race and Epistemologies of Ignorance*. New York: State Univ. of New York Press.

Taylor, Charles. 1994. "The Politics of Recognition." In *Multiculturalism: Examining the Politics of Recognition*, edited by Amy Gutmann, 25–74. Princeton, NJ: Princeton Univ. Press.

Taylor, Rupert. 1999. "Political Science Encounters 'Race' and 'Ethnicity.'" In *Ethnic and Racial Studies Today*, edited by Martin Bulmer and John Solomos, 115–23. London: Routledge.

Thompson, Debra. 2008. "Is Race Political?" *Canadian Journal of Political Science* 4, no. 3: 525–47.

Thompson, Jon. 2011. *No Debate: The Israel Lobby and Free Speech at Canadian Universities*. Toronto: Canadian Association of University Teachers.

Wæver, Ole. 1997. "Figures of International Thought; Introducing Persons Instead of Paradigms." In *The Future of International Relations: Masters in the Making*, edited by Iver B. Neumann and Ole Wæver, 7–37. London: Routledge.

Wæver, Ole, Barry Buzan, Morten Kelstrup, and Pierre Lemaitre. 1993. *Identity, Migration, and the New Security Agenda in Europe*. London: Pinter.

Weber, Max. 1977. *The Protestant Ethic and the Spirit of Capitalism*. Hoboken, NJ: Prentice Hall.

Whitaker, Reg. 2011. "Behavioural Profiling in Israeli Aviation Security as a Tool for Social Control." In *Surveillance and Control in Israel/Palestine: Population, Territory, and Power*, edited by Elia Zureik, David Lyon, and Yasmeen Abu-Laban, 371–85. London: Routledge.

Wolfe, Patrick. 2016. *Traces of History: Elementary Structures of Race*. London: Verso.

Yiftachel, Oren. 2006. *Ethnocracy: Land and Identity Politics in Israel/Palestine*. Philadelphia: Univ. of Pennsylvania Press.

Young-Bruehl, Elisabeth. 2004. *Hannah Arendt: For Love of the World*. New Haven, CT: Yale Univ. Press.

Zureik, Elia T. 2011. "Colonialism, Surveillance, and Population Control: Israel/Palestine." In *Surveillance and Control in Israel/Palestine: Population, Territory, and Power*, edited by Elia Zureik, David Lyon, and Yasmeen Abu-Laban, 3–46. London: Routledge.

3

How Applicable Are Leading Mainstream Social Movement Theories to the MENA Region?

Navid Pourmokhtari

This chapter argues that where contemporary Middle East and North African (MENA) societies are concerned, leading mainstream social movement theories ultimately fall short of explicating the mass mobilization of oppositional forces/ movements, chiefly because of the theories' provenance: all were developed in Western liberal democratic polities where collective action of an oppositional kind is not only tolerated by the state but also legitimized as a force for progress, both social and political. As such, they reflect, Steven Buechler reminds us, the "structural features of [those Western] societies" (1995, 447). This understanding of oppositional movements stands in stark contrast to the case in the MENA region, where they are viewed invariably as a dire threat by authoritarian states prepared to use whatever force necessary to preserve the status quo. In such settings, mass social movements tend to form, develop, emerge, and operate in circumstances where "repression [has] deeply left [its] mark," where "the collective dimension of protest is far from [a] given," and where "contention faces huge constraints" (Beinin and Vairel 2011, 19).

I begin my look at the applicability of social movement theories to the MENA region by interrogating the historical contexts, specifically American and European, that gave rise to theories of mass social movements, examining in the process their core principles and foundational assumptions. Only those leading mainstream theories that have been applied to or that reference the phenomenon

This chapter is based on my article "Protestation and Mobilization in the Middle East and North Africa: A Foucauldian Model," *Foucault Studies*, no. 22 (Jan. 2017): 177–207. I thank the *Foucault Studies* editorial board for granting me permission to use so much of the content of the original article in this chapter.

of social mobilization within MENA are surveyed here. Next, I show that leading mainstream theories, despite their dominance in social movement studies, a field that emerged during the 1960s, are prone to certain universalistic assumptions and West-centric orientations that render them incapable of accounting for the specificities and complexities of social movements within contemporary MENA societies—for example, the Iranian Revolution of 1979, the so-called Uprising of Dignity in Bahrain in 1994, the Iranian Green Movement of 2009, and the Arab Spring of 2011. For this reason, they fail to explicate adequately the precise conditions governing the emergence of oppositional movements in the region and the motives that impel their constituents to mobilize at certain historical junctures. An inquiry of this kind highlights the need for a fresh approach to thinking about how in the context of the authoritarian state broad social movements can effectively contest power.

Mainstream Social Movement Theories: Origins and Foundational Assumptions

In the United States, dominant social movement theories grew out of the civil rights, feminist, student liberation, and antiwar movements of the 1960s. Although each movement had a specific agenda—a legislated end to racial segregation, the emancipation of women, radical reform of the education system, withdrawal of US troops from South Vietnam, respectively—all were "self-consciously" politically oriented and looked exclusively to Washington for remedies (Davis 1999, 594). All, moreover, were perceived to be "forces for progress toward democracy" (Garner and Tenuto 1997, 5) based on two assumptions: "democracy materializes in the context of social movement activism" (Davis 1999, 599); and social movements emerge vis-à-vis "opportunities and constraints afforded by [the liberal democratic state]" (Garner and Tenuto 1997, 23).

American Social Movement Theories

Resource mobilization theory (RMT), one of "the dominant paradigm(s) for studying collective action in the United States," seeks to explain how in light of political opportunities—that is, conditions in the political system that either facilitate or inhibit collective action—actors come to recognize and seize opportunities to initiate action (Buechler 1995, 441). From this perspective, the resources available to oppositional groups prior to mobilizing and the ways in which these resources are pooled and employed play a critical role in determining how such groups make their presence felt and the level of effort they can bring to bear to effect social and political change (Jenkins 1983; McCarthy and Zald 1977). In this schema, structured leadership emerges as a pivotal aspect of social mobilization; indeed, for leading RMT theorists, such as John McCarthy and Mayer Zald, this factor plays a key role in identifying and defining grievances and in exploiting opportunities to initiate collective action. According to these luminaries, "Only after a well-defined leadership emerges do we find well-defined group action" (1973, 17).

RMT focuses primarily on economic factors—cost-reducing mechanisms, career benefits for cadres, the division of labor, management incentives—a focus that speaks to the centrality of aggregated resources, chiefly money and labor, to promoting collective action (McCarthy and Zald 1977; Oberschall 1973). Seen in this light, the emergence, endurance, and impact of a social movement organization (SMO) will hinge largely on the capacity to collectivize "what would otherwise remain individual grievances" (Wiktorowicz 2004a, 10)—a capacity predicated upon such factors as effective communications and the degree of professionalism among SMO staffs. Thus, a central tenet of RMT holds that "social change requires a high level of technical expertise" (Garner and Tenuto 1997, 23).

Other strands of social movement theory developed by American scholars shift the focus from the human and material resources available to SMOs to the political environment in which they operate (Kitschelt 1986; McAdam, McCarthy, and Zald 1996). The best known of these strands is political process theory (PPT). Shaped by social movement theorists of high stature, such as the late Charles Tilly, the late Mayer Zald, Doug McAdam, and Sidney Tarrow, PPT is "currently the hegemonic paradigm among social movement analysts," informing the field's "conceptual landscape, theoretical discourse, and research agenda" (Goodwin and Jasper 2004, 3–4). According to this model, it is the opening up of political opportunities or the structure of political opportunities that provides a window of opportunity for collective action. Doug McAdam (1996) identifies three "consensual" dimensions of political opportunity used to explicate the emergence of social movements: (1) access to a political system, which reflects the degree of its openness; (2) intraelite competition and/or elite allies who encourage or facilitate collective action; and (3) a state's declining capability to repress oppositional movements. These three broad structural factors have been joined recently by a fourth— any external factor, broadly understood as international/geopolitical pressure, that can provide "favorable conditions" or "open[] up . . . opportunit[ies]" for a movement to emerge (Markoff 2012, 53; see also McAdam 1996).

As suggested earlier, PPT constitutes a universal, causal theory of social movements predicated upon a set of structural factors—that is, "factors that are relatively stable . . . and . . . outside of the control of movement actors" (Goodwin and Jasper 2004, 4). For the most part, it is the state's susceptibility to popular political pressure, coinciding with the public's awareness of that susceptibility and willingness to exploit it, that triggers the mobilization of a mass movement. In this schema, the actors' wisdom and creativity, their conscious choices (i.e., their agency), and the outcome of those choices can be understood and evaluated by referencing "the rules of the games in which those choices are made"—that is, their structures (Meyer 2004, 128).

European Social Movement Theories

In Europe, the new social movement theories were directed at addressing what was deemed to be a deficiency in classical Marxism—namely, the failure to recognize the potential inherent in collective action for bringing about social change. For European social movement theorists, this failure stemmed from the economic and class reductionism to which classical Marxism was prone. According to the economic focus, all politically significant social action is to be grounded in the economic logic of capitalist production, "and . . . all other social logics [are] secondary at best in shaping such action" (Buechler 1995, 442). Such assumptions inevitably led Marxists to ground proletarian revolution in the sphere of production, thereby dismissing, or at least downgrading, other forms of social protest.

Against this background emerged new social movement theories rooted in traditions of continental European social theory and political philosophy, which could be used to reformulate the historical theory of emancipation (Cohen 1985; Klandermans 1991; Laraña, Johnston, and Gusfield 1994). With new social movements springing up in Europe in the 1960s—the student movements that erupted in 1968 as well as the environmental, feminist, ecological, and antinuclear movements, among others—social movement theorizing assumed a direction that was both "non-class and 'new' [in terms of] social and political logic" (Davis 1999, 594). Thus, theorists began to look to "other logics of action," in particular those based on politics, culture, and ideology, with a view to locating the mainspring of collective action, while also examining "other sources of identity such as ethnicity, gender and sexuality as the definers of collective identity" (Buechler 1995, 442). The term *new social movements* thus came to encompass a diverse array of movements that developed in large part "as a response to the inadequacies of classical Marxism for analyzing collective action" (Buechler 1995, 442).

One feature of the new social movements stands out. All were theoretically formulated in the context of a historically specific phase in the development of Western liberal societies, an attribute that speaks to, as Steven Buechler observes, "the most distinctive feature of new social movement theories" (1995, 443). Although different theories prescribe clearly differentiated models—postindustrial society

(Touraine 1988), postmaterialist society (Inglehart 1997), advanced capitalist society (Habermas 1975), information society (Melucci 1996), and so on—contingent upon the specific constituencies and issues under examination, they have one commonality: all are grounded in and work to reference a type of "societal totality" (Buechler 1995, 442) closely bound up with the new structural features emerging in western Europe that were giving rise to new patterns of social and political action as the old order was dissolving, in the process providing a context for collective action—a crucial point I revisit later when gauging the applicability of Alain Touraine's theory to MENA.

Social Movement Theories and Specificities
of MENA Oppositional Movements

As the previous discussion reveals, American social movement theorists view social movements as parcels of collective action that present, for the most part, an "organized, sustained, self-conscious challenge to existing authorities" (Tilly 1984, 304). In the "politically open and technologically advanced Western societies" (Bayat 2013, 20) in which such movements emerge, they operate more or less as formal business-like enterprises whose success is contingent upon resources, financial and otherwise, a centralized leadership, clearly defined division of labor, a high degree of professionalization, and strategic planning—factors having to do with technical expertise. It is, moreover, by acts of mobilization and protestation, chief among them petitioning and lobbying, that the actors engage and influence mainstream political institutions, such as parliaments, legislatures, and political parties, with a view to bringing about change (Bayat 2013).

But what of those political settings where mobilizing structures such as formal organizations, professional staffs, and centralized leaderships are nonexistent, rudimentary, and/or severely handicapped by authoritarian states; where acts of mobilization, such as petitioning and lobbying, are ineffectual in pressuring governments that are unaccountable to an electorate; and/or where the political channels for effecting meaningful change are controlled by factions having a monopoly over various levers of power?

Home to several states where mobilizing structures have been effectively ruled out, the MENA region can serve as an ideal laboratory for examining such questions. Indeed, although each state in the region possesses distinctive structural/societal features and modes of governance, one can discern among them common approaches to dealing with oppositional movements, all of which operate under severe handicaps. Of these states, Bahrain, Saudi Arabia, Syria, and Iran, each with its own distinctive brand of authoritarianism, represent outstanding cases of polities that have historically and to varying degrees proven most adept at denying opponents opportunities to build formal organizations with clearly defined command structures.

I say "each with its own distinctive brand of authoritarianism" and "to varying degrees" in order to differentiate these states in terms of the opportunities afforded to oppositional movements. Thus, for example, a republican, semidemocratic Iran under the reformist government of Mohammad Khatami (1997–2005) promoted the development of a civil society in which student, youth, and women's groups could operate with some degree of impunity; indeed, this was the case until Mahmoud Ahmadinejad's rise to power. Nothing of the kind has ever been possible in the far more authoritarian milieus of Bahrain, Syria, and Saudi Arabia, where oppositional groups have historically had little or no opportunity to engage in any kind of subversive action.

Those oppositional leaders who dared emerge from underground in such countries, including Iran, have variously been imprisoned for short periods, disappeared (Faeq al-Mir of Syria), detained and then arrested repeatedly (Louay Hussein of Syria), placed under house arrest (Mir Hossein Mousavi and Mehdi Karoubi of Iran), sentenced to long prison terms (Mohammed Saleh al-Bejadi of Saudi Arabia and Ibrahim Sharif of Bahrain), exiled (Sheikh Ali Salman of Bahrain), or in extreme cases executed (Sheikh Nimr Baqir al-Nimr of Saudi Arabia) (Alkarama 2016; al-Haj 2014; Saul 2015).

Even efforts on the part of civil society groups to advance reform agendas through official channels have often proven ineffectual. Such was the case even during the reform-minded Khatami administration, when the conservative establishment more often than not succeeded in obstructing or blocking the passage of reform measures through the Majlis, the Iranian Parliament. The establishment was enabled in this respect by the control it wielded over the judiciary and over the powerful supervisory bodies charged with approving legislation (Moslem 2002). This explains, for example, the Majlis's failure in the early 2000s to ratify the Convention on the Elimination of All Forms of Discrimination against Women (CEDAW), a United Nations initiative hailed by feminists as an international bill of rights for women.

If CEDAW had been adopted in Iran, it would have directly challenged a host of laws and practices that had long worked to marginalize and subordinate women. Following a press campaign by Iranian feminists aimed at pressuring the government to adopt CEDAW, in December 2001 the Khatami administration drafted the requisite legislation and submitted it for ratification to a Reformist-dominated Majlis. However, immediately before the final vote, the enabling bill was placed on hold because of, according to Speaker Mehdi Karoubi, concerns on the part of conservative clerics serving in the judiciary and elsewhere regarding its compatibility with shari'a (Pourmokhtari 2017; Tohidi 2006).

Under pressure from activists, Reformist deputies demanded over the course of the following two years an official inquiry, but to no avail. Finally, in August 2003 the Guardian Council, chief among the supervisory bodies, announced that CEDAW would not be ratified (*Feminist News* 2013). CEDAW's fate in Iran exemplifies how efforts to bring about social and political change even through official channels in such political settings are often frustrated by factions holding a monopoly over certain exercises of power.

When combined, all the factors listed earlier—closed political environments, government crackdowns on opposition cadres, the absence of formal leaderships, the inefficacy of acts of mobilization to pressure the state to adopt social and political reforms—work to imbue oppositional movements in the region with certain specificities. For example, far from posing an "organized [and] sustained . . . challenge to existing authorities" (Tilly 1984, 304), as is often the case with oppositional movements in the Western world, collective action in MENA more often than not takes the form of "open and fleeting struggles [waged] without [formal] leadership . . . or structured organization" (Bayat 2013, 46). Furthermore, owing to the absence of these features, it is predominately the power of ordinary people (Bayat 2013), not the efficacy of mobilization structures, that creates the potential to change the rules of the game and to bring about or at least push for social and political change and/or reform.

Relatedly, mobilizing actors may seek out alternative domains, most often of a public kind, in which to voice their demands and/or express discontent, thus transforming these domains into loci of resistance and defiance. Herein lies another specificity among those MENA states where social and political reform is likely to be blocked or at least hampered by factions with a monopoly over power, where open political channels are nonexistent, and/or where oppositional groups are denied political rights, particularly with respect to challenging government policy.

In the case of MENA, the urban streets lend themselves most readily to contesting the status quo. Ali Mirsepassi calls this spatial phenomenon the "tradition of democracy in the streets" (2010, ix). A primary venue for expressing discontent in the region, the street is a "consistent and powerful aspect of . . . protest movements" (Mirsepassi 2010, ix) across much of MENA, as evinced by the Iranian Revolution of 1979, the so-called Uprising of Dignity in Bahrain in 1994, the Iranian student movement of 1999, and the mass demonstrations in Yemen, Egypt, Tunisia, Bahrain, and elsewhere in the region during the Arab Spring.

Asef Bayat defines what he calls "street politics" as the participative use of streets for the purpose of "express[ing] grievances, forg[ing] identities[, and] enlarg[ing] solidarities." In this way, he asserts, "a small demonstration [can] grow into a massive exhibition of solidarity" aimed at contesting and negating the status quo (2013, 13). Thus, streets have become, in effect, the locus for a tug of war between the state and the masses. "[Owing to] this epidemic potential of street politics," not surprisingly, "almost every" major case of contention in MENA has ultimately "[found] expression in the urban streets" (Bayat 2013, 13). This means that it is not urban streets per se that are political, given the omnipresence of power, but rather the acts performed within them.

As a consequence, it might be more to the point to adopt what Nancy Fraser calls the "politics of everyday life" (1989, 18) as a point of departure for understanding and examining cases of collective action. The politics of everyday life serves as a domain wherein a people engage in everyday but cunning and contentious strategies, tactics, and acts aimed at subverting and challenging governmental rules. By examining the politics of everyday life, one can understand how rules, codes, norms, laws, and regulations come to be resisted and subverted at the point of application.

The phrase "politics of everyday life" refers to a strategy of defiance used by subjugated bodies, in this case protestors and demonstrators, to transform governmentalized zones into strongpoints from which to defy and contest power and by implication the very political order it reproduces. In this regard, what lends public spaces their significance is that although they have "increasingly becom[e] the domain of . . . state power" (Bayat 2013, 53)—which "regulates their use [and] mak[es] them 'orderly'" (Bayat 2013, 53) through laws and regulations—they have also become, simultaneously and contingently on the will of the masses, "[loci for] 'shaming' the authorities" (Mirsepassi, 2010, ix). In this way, such loci can be transformed into spaces of resistance or sites of political contestation and social negation of the status quo. Thus, it is hardly surprising that Tehran's Azadi Square (2009), Cairo's Tahrir Square (2011–12), and Istanbul's Taksim Square (2013) emerged as prominent signifiers of mass discontent during uprisings. In each case, immense crowds were able to showcase their counterpower by exploiting mainstream and social media to delegitimatize and de-authenticate governmental regimes. They succeeded by occupying these public spaces/governmentalized zones and in the process disrupting the normal flow of everyday life.

Indeed, as I have indicated elsewhere (Pourmokhtari 2017), a so-called politics of everyday life directed at winning social and political rights is no longer the monopoly of MENA oppositional movements. Its counterparts have sprung up in the liberal democracies of the West as well—the Occupy movement, Black Lives Matter, and Idle No More—and engage in an informal, spatial politics, replete with street demonstrations, such as sit-ins, as surrogate channels for a formal politics (Ancelovici, Dufour, and Nez 2016; Idle No More 2017). Thus, one can argue that even liberal institutions are not always responsive to grassroots demands. This point serves to transcend the false dichotomy of East versus West, in particular the view prevailing in the social and political sciences that the former comprises frozen, exceptional entities bereft of human rights, human dignity, equality, and freedom. Despite these commonalities, however, the fact remains there do exist significant differences in the social movements of the East and the West—for example, in their repertoires of contention, their actors' historical and context-dependent grievances, their modes and techniques of demonstrating and protesting, their leadership structures, and their specificities of power relations, reflecting the highly differentiated societies from which they have emerged (Ancelovici, Dufour, and Nez 2016; Idle No More 2017; Kaulingfreks 2015).

The politics of everyday life as played out in public spaces is by no means limited to expressing mass discontent. It also serves as a surrogate channel for demanding change and pursuing reforms where formal political institutions, such as parliaments and legislative assemblies, have failed. For example, in an effort to bring about political and socioeconomic reform, more than 1,500 Bahraini activists staged a sit-in in front of the headquarters of the Ministry of Labor in June 1994.[1] This single event sparked a series of uprisings (1994–99) that would undermine the al Khalifa monarchy and bring into question its very legitimacy. These manifestations of a profound discontent would also be among the first postideological cases of collective action within the region. The point to grasp here is that the demonstrators elected to engage in a politics of everyday life only upon discovering that the formal institutional channels for effecting change either were inadequate to the task or had been blocked entirely. In the years and months leading up to the Bahraini uprising, oppositional groups had sought repeatedly to reform/democratize the political process by petitioning the government. In each instance, their efforts had proved fruitless (Human Rights Watch 2006).

Unable to work through official channels, these groups were left with no option but to appropriate urban public spaces where they could express discontent and voice demands in ways the authorities might ignore only at their peril. By engaging in an everyday politics of resistance, they succeeded in "mut[ing] [politics as usual] within [spaces] . . . supposed to be its natural . . . habitat" (Walters 2012, 80), such as the Parliament, while transforming urban spaces and governmental zones into political loci of defiance whose very existence served to de-authenticate the status

---

1. The immediate cause of the demonstration was, according to a report published by Human Rights Watch (2006), soaring unemployment, at one point reaching 15 percent.

quo and delegitimize the political system as a whole. In this way, by putting into play this signal feature of defiance and principal strategy for conducting contention episodes, they worked to challenge and subvert the rules/norms of governmental rule.

Applying Political Process Theory to MENA Countries

Political process theory is informed by certain presuppositions that limit its efficacy for analyzing oppositional movements based in the MENA region. Owing to the emphasis on structural conditions, PPT theorists view mass mobilizations as a response to opportunities that reflect "the vulnerability of the state to popular political pressure" (Kurzman 1996, 153) or metaphorically as "'windows' that open and close" (John Kingdon, quoted in Goodwin and Jasper 2004, 12), which means "they are either there or not there" (Goodwin and Jasper 2004, 12). From this perspective, oppositional movements are assumed to comprise agents possessing an a priori and mechanistic essence, meaning "potential groups with preexisting desires . . . who only await the opportunity to pursue them" (Jasper 2012, 15). Not only does this assumption dispose PPT theorists to overextend "the concept of 'political opportunities'" by equating such opportunities with the "larger 'environment' in which social movements are embedded" (Goodwin and Jasper 2004, 27), but it also predisposes them to focus by and large on the "state or the polity as the only field of struggle that really matters" where mobilization and collective action are concerned (Jasper 2012, 15). However, as Jeff Goodwin and James Jasper argue, there exist "an extraordinarily large number of processes and events, political and otherwise, [that can] potentially influence movement mobilization, and they do so in historically complex combinations and sequences" (2004, 11).[2]

This fetishization of the state as an entity presenting social movements with opportunities to mobilize is highly problematic in places where such opportunities

---

2. In response to criticism from a number of social movement scholars—including Jeff Goodwin, James Jasper, and Charles Kurzman—Doug McAdam, Sidney Tarrow, and the late Charles Tilly did include in their collection *Dynamics of Contention* (2001) a revised PPT that articulates a more "relational" model of social movements, one far better suited to the study of oppositional movements in the MENA region. However, as Joel Beinin and Frédéric Vairel rightly opine, even this reformulated theory is overly complex in respect to the causal/empirical mechanics used to explicate oppositional movements, nor is it entirely free of structural bias in the sense that "[the authors] appear not to have completely changed their minds about the classical categories they helped to establish. They . . . reuse . . . or adjust them[, merely] modifying their meaning [or simply] reasserting them" (2011, 6).

are seldom, if ever, provided by polities determined to maintain the power status quo at whatever cost. For example, even during the reform-minded Khatami administration in Iran, oppositional groups functioned under the unrelenting scrutiny of a security apparatus directed by the conservative establishment, which included paramilitary groups prepared to use whatever means necessary to ensure the survival of the state as it was currently configured. Thus, in the Iranian context the so-called mobilizing structures—formal leaderships, organizational structures, professional staffs—that social movement theorists deem to be the foundational building blocks of social movements are at best rudimentary as well as severely handicapped by state repression.

Moreover, in Iran a Ministry of Intelligence dominated by hard-liners is able to exert a stranglehold on the media, whether state owned or private, resulting in the dissemination of misinformation and the framing of events in ways that advance a conservative agenda. This stranglehold is also applied to the state-sponsored social media. Thus, those dissidents courageous enough to transgress the narrow limits of public discourse imposed by the state risk arrest and show trials and are often sentenced to long jail terms, as was the case in the wake of the student movement of 1999 and the Green Movement of 2009 (Karami 2016). It is hardly credible that oppositional movements would have open opportunities to mobilize in political environments of this kind.

These realities compel us to seek out factors other than open opportunities to mobilize extant in the political environment if we are to plumb the root causes of the collective action that has occurred in the MENA region. Some recent cases of mobilization are instructive in this regard. For example, in the case of the Iranian Green Movement of 2009, oppositional forces—chiefly students and women's groups—took the lead in *creating* opportunities to mobilize (Pourmokhtari 2014). Both groups were motivated in part by discriminatory policies implemented by the Ahmadinejad administration during its first term in office (2005–9) and in part by the widespread perception of election fraud. At no time during this period or prior to it did the state provide anything that might be construed as an open opportunity to mobilize. Thus, opportunity was "what [the protestors made] of it" (Kurzman 2004, 117).

Two years later, a wave of protests would sweep through Tunisia, revealing the authoritative will of disparate peoples longing for the kind of fundamental change that alone might usher in a brighter future. Again, one might argue that those who filled the Arab streets created their own opportunities—opportunities that may be viewed as attributes of the actors themselves. Perhaps nothing better illustrates the latter point than the solitary act of defiance committed by a young Tunisian street vendor named Mohamed Bouazizi. In December 2010, Bouazizi set himself ablaze to protest the arbitrary confiscation of his wares and the harassment and humiliation he had suffered at the hands of a municipal official and her aides. This single incident triggered massive demonstrations throughout the country, precipitating what would come to be called the Arab Spring.

Thus, with respect to the Green Movement and this first flowering of the Arab Spring, one might argue that the demonstrators felt compelled to put their lives on the line, spurred on by moral outrage directed at governments that had violated their sense of justice beyond the point of endurance. No longer willing to be governed by those for whom human dignity, moral rights, and social justice were merely empty slogans, they took to the streets, determined to confront their tormentors. In such circumstances, a people may come to perceive themselves as agents of social change, as actors capable of advancing their interests and possessed of a sense of authority, legitimacy, and subjectivity that stems from a certainty that the status quo is fundamentally unjust—actors determined to leave their mark on history "under circumstances they have the power to change" (Kurzman 2004, 117).

New Social Movement Theories and Their Application to MENA Cases

The lived and context-based experience, trajectory, and history of those who filled the streets of Iranian and Tunisian cities demanding change are nowhere reflected in the new social movement theories—not surprisingly, given that such theories take as their datum the technologically advanced and politically open societies of the West. For this reason, these theories are prone to making grand and monolithic assumptions about social movements, which make their application highly problematic in the Middle East and North Africa. Alaine Touraine's highly influential postindustrial society theory, which rests upon the assumption that history unfolds in a succession of stages—commercial, industrial, and postindustrial—is a case in point. According to this luminary, postindustrial societies have attained an unparalleled level of historicity or historical development—the highest to be precise—wherein societal movements are no longer conceptualized as "dramatic events" but rather as "the work that society performs upon itself" (1981, 29). Henceforth in postindustrial societies, Touraine contends, "there can be no societal movement other than the collective actions that are aimed directly at the affirmation and defense of the rights of the subject—of his [*sic*] freedom and equality" (quoted in Adkin 2002, 290). For this reason, the new "societal movements have become moral movements," in contrast to their predecessors, which were of a religious, political, or economic character (quoted in Adkin 2002, 290).

Touraine uses the latter point to articulate the concept of levels of historicity from which he derives the corollary that only postindustrial societies can achieve the "highest level of historicity"—namely, that of self-production (1981, 105). In contrast, "traditional" societies still "lie within history," and for this reason their ability to produce the cultural models that govern how they function is more limited because the distance that historicity requires (from God, oneself, and the world as object) has not been achieved (Touraine 1981, 105). In terms of the opposition constructed here—that is, between postindustrial and traditional societies—MENA societies still lie within history because they are too close to God and therefore too preoccupied with religious concerns. Thus, they lack the kind of moral movements that are a hallmark of the postindustrial societies of the West—not to mention the postindustrial economies that represent the means for attaining the highest level of historicity along Touraine's evolutionary continuum.

The best that may be said about such overarching theorization is that it reflects a historically specific period of Western history; at its worst, Arturo Escobar opines, it conceives Third World societies and by implication their oppositional movements "as lacking historical agency or . . . as only having a diminished form of agency compared with the European case" (1992, 37).

What the preceding analyses reveal—and this is crucial to acknowledge—is that West-centric accounts such as Touraine's are unable to explain the recent rise of right-wing nationalist, populist, and racialist movements in western Europe and North America that are xenophobic and anti-LGBTQ+, among other things: for example, the Tea Party and the so-called Alt-Right in the United States (Skocpol and Williamson 2016). In contrast, more recent oppositional movements such as Black Lives Matter and Idle No More have articulated clear and specific demands for basic social justice and political rights that, one can only assume, are to be realized in a postindustrial society, at least according to the Tourainian view of an evolutionary continuum. Thus, it is readily apparent that such theories fail even to explain fully the complexity of Western liberal democracy itself. They are, as the example here clearly shows, neither universal nor representative of the particularities of the West.

Social Movement Studies and MENA Oppositional Movements

The previous discussion reveals that the new social movement theories as well as their Western forebears, which were formulated in light of European and North American experiences and trajectories, "coevolved with the relatively stable . . . democracies of the West" (Oliver, Cadena-Rao, and Strawn 2003, 215) and, by implication and despite all "claims to universality," are predicated on a set of "historically-specific developments occurring in the United States [and] Europe" (Davis 1999, 592). The latter context lends them much of their analytical power and empirical underpinning but at the same time, as Arthur Escobar points out, "greatly shapes and limits" their utility with respect to other contexts (1992, 30). All this has profound implications for conceptualizing MENA oppositional movements. Two of those implications in particular require elucidation.

MENA Societies, Social Movements, and Essentialism

The first problem has to do with the essentialist manner in which MENA oppositional movements—traditionally consigned to the margins of social movement studies—are construed as exceptionalist cases of mobilization, a view stemming from an understanding of them as rooted in a religious revivalism of a strictly fundamentalist nature and hence divorced from anything deemed to be even remotely utopian or progressive. Thus, both Alberto Melucci (1996, 104) and Alain Touraine (cited in Bayat 2005, 894) conceptualize MENA oppositional movements—for example, the Iranian Revolution of 1979—in terms of a "regressive utopianism" or as "anti-movement[s]," respectively, thereby reducing them to manifestations of Islamic fundamentalism—in effect dismissing them as reactionary, antidemocratic, and antimodern movements instigated by traditional peoples.

Other luminaries express similar views: Sidney Tarrow refers to the Middle East of the 1990s as a land of "ugly movements," "rooted in ethnic . . . claims [or] in religious fanaticism and racism" and dominated by "radical Islamic fundamentalists who slit the throats of folk singers and beat up women who dare to go unveiled" (1998, 194). These accounts work ultimately to relegate MENA movements to the margins of scholarly analysis, where they are dismissed as exceptionalist cases.

The positions taken by Melucci and Touraine can surely be questioned given that their modernist assumptions and West-centric orientation work to consign oppositional movements in MENA, along with the societies from which they spring and the conditions governing their emergence, to grand categories whose defining feature is an essentialism. One can discern in Touraine's (1988) thought, for example, how his normative concept of levels of historicity—according to which only social movements in the postindustrial societies of the West can achieve the highest level, a standing that lends them their progressive and modern character and that distinguishes them from all other societies, meaning those that still lie within history—leads inexorably to his dismissal of the Iranian Revolution as an antimovement.

Equally intriguing are the totalizing accounts of MENA societies presented by these theorists wherein a religiocentrism is assumed to be the defining feature of Islamist movements. These movements are understood almost exclusively as a kind of religious revivalism replete with primordial loyalties and signifying the peculiar and unique and are cast as the engine of as well as the dominant code for social mobilization (Bayat 2007). In other words, there exists a tendency to reify Islam as a static religion and Islamism as a monolithic social and political project and thus to overlook the variations of it that occur across time and space as well as among social strata and religious sects (Bayat 2007, 2013).

MENA social movements have therefore come to be perceived as Islamic movements: as monolithic entities with regressive and, indeed, backward-looking agendas, even as historically frozen entities prone to violence, all sense of their diversity and complexity lost. In characterizing a regressive utopianism, Melucci asserts that such movements, whose defining feature is a "totalizing monism," forge their "identit[ies] in terms of the past, drawing on a totalizing myth of rebirth" (1996, 104). These cases, he contends—the Iranian Revolution of 1979 stands as a prime example—represent nothing more than "a mythical quest for the Lost Paradise . . . [, which in turn] crystalizes into fanatic fundamentalism" (105).

Such accounts are like a "god trick," to borrow Donna Haraway's epithet for a vision that is "from everywhere [but in fact from] nowhere" (1988, 584). They show little interest in uncovering the complex forces propelling MENA movements forward. And yet the historical record is clear: the Iranian Revolution of 1979 was a convulsive reaction on the part of diverse societal groups, including but not limited to nationalists, social democrats, leftists, and other subvariants, among them Islamists and Muslim liberals and nationalists, all of whom took to the streets. It was, in fact, Ayatollah Khomeini's call for and pledge to promote pluralism in the postshah era—in particular the statements he issued during his brief period of exile in France—that rallied these diverse elements to his cause, a cause that received additional momentum by his repeated claims to have no interest in governing the country.[3]

At the outbreak of the Islamic Revolution, moreover, Iran possessed, contrary to popular belief, nothing remotely resembling a strong Islamist movement; rather,

---

3. While in exile, Ayatollah Khomeini declared repeatedly that he had no interest in governing the country. Thus, for example, in a *Le Monde* interview published on January 9, 1979, he vowed that "after the Shah's departure from Iran, I will not become a president nor accept any other leadership role. Just like before, I [shall] limit my activities only to guiding and directing the people." And in a *Le Journal* interview published on November 28, 1978, the future Supreme Leader opined that "it is the Iranian people who have to select their own capable and trustworthy individuals and give them . . . responsibilities. However, personally, I can't accept any special role or responsibility." In an earlier *United Press* interview on November 8, he emphasized, "I have repeatedly said that neither my desire nor my age nor my position allows me to govern." For an overview of Ayatollah Khomeini's remarks on any future role he might play in a post-Pahlavi Iran, see Matini 2003, where these quotations are given.

the latter was at an early stage of development when overtaken by the events of February 1979. Asef Bayat makes this point abundantly clear in his analysis of the social and political impact of Islamism upon Iran. In 1979, Islamists represented only one among many disaffected groups working to topple the monarchy; moreover, the subsequent seizure of the state apparatus was made possible only "by the popular mobilization of various sectors of the population" (2005, 897). Indeed, only well after the revolution had been consolidated and the Islamic Republic was established did Islamization proceed and state Islamization or Islamization from the top eventually prevail.

This is not to deny that the Middle East and North Africa are home to a number of extremist movements, including the Taliban and the Islamic State in Iraq and Syria; rather, it is to point out that during the 1990s there emerged in the region some remarkably progressive movements. Indeed, the first "post-Islamist" movements called for a "fus[ion of] religiosity and rights, faith and freedom, Islam and liberty" and advocated pluralism, the rule of law, and human rights and freedoms (Bayat 2013, 37)—a point lost amid the exceptionalist tendencies that inform much of what passes for scholarly analysis of MENA movements.

Social Movement Theories and Their Uncritical Application to MENA

The second problem to do with analyzing MENA social movements through the lens of leading mainstream social movement theories lies not with the theories themselves but rather with their uncritical application, as exemplified in Quintan Wiktorowicz's edited volume *Islamic Activism* (2004b), Mohammad Hafez's *Why Muslims Rebel* (2003), and Janine Clark's *Islam, Charity, and Activism* (2004). These works seek primarily to demonstrate that MENA social movements constitute normal cases of mobilization in that they confirm theoretical predictions, thus attesting to their universalistic assumptions regarding social mobilization and collective action.

To be sure, these scholarly efforts are encouraging in that they move the debate beyond the straightjacket of exceptionalist tendencies. Yet the manner in which the analysis is tailored to showcase the predictive power of mainstream theories has drawn criticism owing both to the failure to elucidate the full range, character, and dynamism of MENA movements and to the missed opportunities to contribute innovatively and critically to the broader social science scholarship on the region.

Undeniably, some of the more recent cases of mobilization to emerge in the Middle East and North Africa raise serious doubts as to the relevancy of dominant social movement theories in this context. For example, at the time Iran's

Green Movement was taking shape, there existed nothing that might be described as an open opportunity to mobilize. There existed no sign of dissension among ruling elites or of anything resembling a challenge to state institutions, most notably the Office of the Supreme Leader and the Guardian Council; no hint that the political system was willing to accept even the most modest of reform measures; no diminution in the state's capacity or willingness to crush resistance; and no indication of any geopolitical/international crisis looming on the horizon (Pourmokhtari 2014).

At the same time, owing to the authoritarian setting in which the Green Movement took shape and operated, it lacked the kind of mobilizing structures—most notably formal organizations, structured leadership, a clearly defined division of labor—thought by social movement theorists to be essential to organizing and sustaining collective action. Rather, as Paola Rivetti opines, "it is the interplay between formality and informality that offers a better explanation of how oppositional activism" such as the Green Movement will emerge (2017, 1179). Like most of its counterparts in the region, this movement would manifest itself primarily in spatial, mainly street, demonstrations. The latter's spontaneity, unpredictability, dynamism, and lack of centralized leadership speak to the Green Movement's informal organizational structure.

Nor was the Green Movement, as some social movement theorists may suggest, the product of religious sensibilities and tendencies; rather, characteristic of post-Islamist movements, it was grounded in demands for plurality, accountability, democratic rights, and freedoms as well as in a general wish to rein in the political role of state-sponsored religion (Bayat 2013; Pourmokhtari 2021).

From the preceding discussion, one might conclude, at least with reference to the cases delineated here, that recent mass movements in the MENA region are not necessarily theory confirming in that, however generally conceived, they do not conform to the chief presuppositions underpinning dominant social movement theories; nor are they, as was shown in the Tunisian case, exceptionalist, a position that works to dismiss nearly all MENA cases as regressive, fundamentalist, and antimodern, thus subjecting them to totalizing narratives.

Conclusion

This chapter has interrogated some of the leading mainstream theories informing social movement studies with a view to gauging their applicability to MENA. As has been shown, such theories fall short in elucidating the phenomenon of mass mobilization and political contestation in the region, for reasons pertaining to the theories' genesis and development in Western liberal democratic polities, which stand in stark contrast to MENA societies ruled by authoritarian states prepared to use whatever force necessary to preserve the status quo.

Further, as has been shown, leading mainstream theories are grounded in universalistic assumptions and West-centric orientations that render them incapable of addressing the specificities and complexities of MENA cases, which accounts for their failure to explicate the precise conditions that govern the emergence of mass social movements in the region, the forms and modes they assume, and the motives that impel their constituents to mobilize at certain historical junctures for the purpose of contesting power. I conclude by calling upon social movement theorists, in particular MENA specialists, to take context-sensitive theoretical approaches to explicating mass social movements.

References

Adkin, Laurie E. 2002. "The Rise and Fall of New Social Movement Theory?" In *Critical Political Studies: Debates and Dialogues from the Left*, edited by Abigail B. Bakan and Eleanor MacDonald, 281–318. Montreal: McGill-Queen's Univ. Press.

Alkarama. 2016. "Syria: Political Activist Faeq al Mir Disappeared for Three Years." Nov. 10. At http://www.alkarama.org/en/articles/syria-political-activist-faeq-al-mir-disappeared-three-years.

Ancelovici, Marcos, Pascale Dufour, and Héloïse Nez, eds. 2016. *Street Politics in the Age of Austerity: From the Indignados to Occupy*. Amsterdam: Amsterdam Univ. Press.

Bayat, Asef. 2005. "Islamism and Social Movement Theory." *Third World Quarterly* 26, no. 6: 891–908.

———. 2007. *Making Islam Democratic: Social Movements and the Post-Islamist Turn*. Stanford, CA: Stanford Univ. Press.

———. 2013. *Life as Politics: How Ordinary People Change the Middle East*. Stanford, CA: Stanford Univ. Press.

Beinin, Joel, and Frédéric Vairel. 2011. "Introduction: The Middle East and North Africa beyond Classical Social Movement Theory." In *Social Movements, Mobilization, and Contestation in the Middle East and North Africa*, edited by Joel Beinin and Frédéric Vairel, 1–32. Stanford, CA: Stanford Univ. Press.

Buechler, Steven. 1995. "New Social Movement Theories." *Sociological Quarterly* 3, no. 3: 441–64.

Clark, Janine A. 2004. *Islam, Charity, and Activism: Middle-Class Networks and Social Welfare in Egypt, Jordan, and Yemen*. Bloomington: Indiana Univ. Press.

Cohen, Jean. 1985. "Strategy or Identity? New Theoretical Paradigms and Contemporary Social Movements." *Social Research* 52, no. 4: 663–716.

Davis, Diane. 1999. "The Power of Distance: Re-theorizing Social Movements in Latin America." *Theory and Society* 28, no. 4: 585–638.

Escobar, Arturo. 1992. "Imagining a Post-development Era? Critical Thought, Development, and Social Movements." *Social Text* 31, no. 32: 20–56.

Feminist News. 2013. "CEDAW Rejected in Iran." Aug. 19. At http://www.feminist.org/news/newsbyte/uswirestory.asp?id=7996.

Fraser, Nancy. 1989. *Unruly Practices: Power, Discourse, and Gender in Contemporary Social Theory.* Minneapolis: Univ. of Minnesota Press.

Garner, Roberta, and John Tenuto. 1997. *Social Movement Theory and Research.* Lanham, MD: Scarecrow Press.

Goodwin, Jeff, and James M. Jasper. 2004. "Caught in a Winding, Snarling Vine: The Structural Bias of Political Process Theory." In *Rethinking Social Movements: Structure, Meaning, and Emotions,* edited by Jeff Goodwin and James M. Jasper, 3–30. New York: Littlefield.

Habermas, Jürgen. 1975. *Legitimation Crisis.* Boston: Beacon Press.

Hafez, Mohammed. 2003. *Why Muslims Rebel: Repression and Resistance in the Islamic World.* Boulder, CO: Lynne Reiner.

Al-Haj, Mustafa. 2014. "Syrian Authorities Arrest Opposition Leader." *Al-Monitor,* Nov. 13. At http://www.al-monitor.com/pulse/originals/2014/11/syria-regime-arrest-bss-leader.html.

Haraway, Donna. 1988. "Situated Knowledges: The Science Question in Feminism and the Privilege of Partial Perspective." *Feminist Studies* 14, no. 3: 575–97.

Human Rights Watch. 2006. *Routine Abuse, Routine Denial: Civil Rights and the Political Crisis in Bahrain.* New York: Human Rights Watch. At http://www.refworld.org/docid/45cafc9e2.html.

Idle No More. 2017. Idle No More Official Website. At http://www.idlenomore.ca/.

Inglehart, Ronald. 1997. *Modernization and Postmodernization: Cultural, Economic, and Political Change in 43 Societies.* Princeton, NJ: Princeton Univ. Press.

Jasper, James M. 2012. "Introduction: From Political Opportunity Structures to Strategic Interaction." In *Contention in Context: Political Opportunities and the Emergence of Protest,* edited by Jeff Goodwin and James M. Jasper, 1–34. Stanford, CA: Stanford Univ. Press.

Jenkins, J. Craig. 1983. "Resource Mobilization Theory and the Study of Social Movements." *Annual Review of Sociology* 9, no. 1: 527–53.

Karami, Arash. 2016. "Will House Arrests of Green Movement Leaders Come to an End?" *Al-Monitor,* Mar. 17. At http://www.al-monitor.com/pulse/originals/2016/03/rouhani-entezami-house-arrests-green-movement-leaders.html.

Kaulingfreks, Femke. 2015. *Uncivil Engagement and Unruly Politics: Disruptive Interventions of Urban Youth.* London: Palgrave MacMillan.

Kitschelt, Herbert. 1986. "Political Opportunity Structures and Political Protest: Antinuclear Movements in Four Democracies." *British Journal of Political Science* 16, no. 1: 57–85.

Klandermans, Bert. 1991. "New Social Movements and Resource Mobilization: The European and American Approaches Revisited." In *Research on Social Movements: The*

State of the Art in Western Europe and the USA, edited by Dieter Rucht, 17–46. Frankfurt am Main, Germany: Campus Verlag; Boulder, CO: Westview Press.

Kurzman, Charles. 1996. "Structural Opportunity and Perceived Opportunity in Social Movement Theory: The Iranian Revolution of 1979." *American Sociological Review* 61, no. 1: 153–70.

———. 2004. "The Poststructuralist Consensus in Social Movement Theory." In *Rethinking Social Movements: Structure, Meaning, and Emotion*, edited by Jeff Goodwin and James M. Jasper, 111–20. Lanham, MD: Rowman & Littlefield.

Laraña, Enrique, Hank Johnston, and Joseph R. Gusfield, eds. 1994. *New Social Movements: From Ideology to Identity*. Philadelphia: Temple Univ. Press.

Markoff, John. 2012. "Response to Jack Goldstone." In *Contention in Context: Political Opportunities and the Emergence of Protest*, edited by Jeff Goodwin and James M. Jasper, 52–58. Stanford, CA: Stanford Univ. Press.

Matini, Jalal. 2003. "Democracy? I Meant Theocracy: The Most Truthful Individual in Recent History." Translated by Farhad Mafie. *Iranian*, Aug. 5. At https://www.iranian.com/Opinion/2003/August/Khomeini/.

McAdam, Doug. 1996. "Conceptual Origins, Current Problems, Future Directions." In *Comparative Perspectives on Social Movements: Political Opportunities, Mobilizing Structures, and Cultural Framings*, edited by Doug McAdam, John McCarthy, and Mayer Zald, 23–40. Cambridge: Cambridge Univ. Press.

McAdam, Doug, John McCarthy, and Mayer Zald, eds. 1996. *Comparative Perspectives on Social Movements: Political Opportunities, Mobilizing Structures, and Cultural Framings*. Cambridge: Cambridge Univ. Press.

McAdam, Doug, Sidney Tarrow, and Charles Tilly. 2001. *Dynamics of Contention*. New York: Cambridge Univ. Press.

McCarthy, John, and Mayer Zald. 1973. *The Trends of Social Movements in America: Professionalization and Resource Mobilization*. Morristown, NJ: General Learning Corporation.

———. 1977. "Resource Mobilization and Social Movements: A Partial Theory." *American Journal of Sociology* 82, no. 2: 1212–40.

Melucci, Alberto. 1996. *Challenging Codes: Collective Action in the Information Age*. Cambridge: Cambridge Univ. Press.

Meyer, S. David. 2004. "Protest and Political Opportunities." *Annual Review of Sociology* 30, no. 1: 125–45.

Mirsepassi, Ali. 2010. *Democracy in Modern Iran*. New York: New York Univ. Press.

Moslem, Mehdi. 2002. *Factional Politics in Post-Khomeini Iran*. Syracuse, NY: Syracuse Univ. Press.

Oberschall, Anthony. 1973. *Social Conflict and Social Movements*. Englewood Cliffs, NJ: Prentice Hall.

Oliver, E. Pamela, Jorge Cadena-Rao, and D. Kelley Strawn. 2003. "Emerging Trends in the Study of Protest and Social Movements." *Research in Political Sociology* 12, no. 1: 213–44.

Pourmokhtari, Navid. 2014. "Understanding Iran's Green Movement as a 'Movement of Movements.'" *Sociology of Islam* 2, no. 3: 144–77.

———. 2017. "Protestation and Mobilization in the Middle East and North Africa: A Foucauldian Model." *Foucault Studies* 22:177–207.

———. 2021. *Iran's Green Movement: Everyday Resistance, Political Contestation, and Social Mobilization.* New York: Routledge.

Rivetti, Paola. 2017. "Political Activism in Iran: Strategies for Survival, Possibilities for Resistance, and Authoritarianism." *Democratization* 24, no. 6: 1178–94.

Saul, Heather. 2015. "French Journalist Confronts President Rouhani with Picture of an Iranian Woman without a Hijab." *Independent*, Nov. 12. At http://www.independent.co.uk/news/people/french-journalist-confronts-president-rouhani-with-picture-of-an-iranian-woman-without-a-hijab-from-a6732001.html.

Skocpol, Theda, and Vanessa Williamson. 2016. *The Tea Party and the Remaking of Republican Conservatism.* Oxford: Oxford Univ. Press.

Tarrow, Sidney. 1998. *Power in Movement: Social Movements and Contentious Politics.* Cambridge: Cambridge Univ. Press.

Tilly, Charles. 1984. "Social Movements and National Politics." In *State-Making and Social Movements: Essays in History and Theory,* edited by Charles Bright and Susan Friend Harding, 297–317. Ann Arbor: Univ. of Michigan Press.

Tohidi, Nayereh. 2006. "'Islamic Feminism': Negotiating Patriarchy and Modernity in Iran." In *The Blackwell Companion to Contemporary Islamic Thought,* edited by Ibrahim M. Abu-Rabi', 624–43. Oxford: Blackwell.

Touraine, Alain. 1981. *The Voice and the Eye: An Analysis of Social Movements.* Cambridge: Cambridge Univ. Press.

———. 1988. *The Return of the Actor: Social Theory in Postindustrial Society.* Minneapolis: Univ. of Minnesota Press.

Walters, William. 2012. *Governmentality Critical Encounters: Critical Issues in Global Politics.* Abingdon, UK: Routledge.

Wiktorowicz, Quintan. 2004a. "Introduction: Islamic Activism: A Social Movement Theory." In *Islamic Activism: A Social Movement Theory Approach,* edited by Quintan Wiktorowicz, 1–34. Bloomington: Indiana Univ. Press.

———, ed. 2004b. *Islamic Activism: A Social Movement Theory Approach.* Bloomington: Indiana Univ. Press.

4

China and Syria as an "Ideological Exception"?

Juan Cole

This chapter considers the motivations that underpinned Chinese policy toward Syria in 2011 and after, as the youth revolt turned to civil war, which then saw the rise of Muslim fundamentalist ministates in the hinterlands. Were economic considerations to the fore, especially after the inauguration of the New Silk Road policy by President Xi Jinping in 2013? How did Chinese governmental figures and the press feel about the Syrian opposition's initial demands for democracy? What part did rivalry with the United States and the North Atlantic Treaty Organization (NATO) play? How did suspicions of Western motives shape the Chinese reaction to these events?

The answers to these questions address some of the disputes among China observers concerning Beijing's foreign policy. The offensive realists have posited that as China grows in wealth and military strength, the country will seek more power, increasingly acting as a regional hegemon in East Asia, and attempting to displace the previous regional hegemon, the United States. This position implies increasing conflict between China and the United States. Defensive realists believe that Chinese foreign policy is changing but that it is seeking security rather than power for power's sake. They hold that the United States can avoid direct conflict by bandwagoning, allying with South Korea, Japan, and other regional powers to restrain Chinese ambitions. Liberal institutionalists hold that China's deep entanglement in international trade is potentially a brake on severe conflict with the United States, depending on how it is handled (Nye 2020). Constructivists envision an ongoing struggle in the Chinese foreign-policy apparatus among factions with varying goals and motivations, one of them being to restore China's standing in the world after the traumas of colonialism (Uemura 2018). All three schools are seeking to understand China's greater assertiveness in recent years, including its territorial disputes with the Philippines and Japan (see Feng and He 2017). Does China policy in Syria help address these questions?

China did not play a central role in Syria, but its position as a permanent, veto-wielding member of the United Nations Security Council (UNSC) did give it the opportunity to help determine events there (Dorsey 2019, 90–91). Interestingly, Beijing, despite its own suspicions of "color revolutions" and its view of demands for democracy as stalking horses for American and European neocolonialism, was careful both to cultivate the Syrian opposition and to foster negotiations with the al-Assad regime. China's long-standing opposition to foreign interference in the domestic affairs of other countries and its insistence that Syrians should reconcile and resolve their problems internally was challenged when Russia, with which it had generally good relations, intervened in Syria beginning in 2015.

Chinese foreign policy throughout this period for the most part demonstrated continuities, certainly in rhetoric if not always in concrete policy. China's leaders held to the Five Principles of Peaceful Coexistence: respect, nonaggression, equality, peaceful coexistence, and noninterference. They said they opposed the search for hegemony by any great power. Their strategy of harmonious development, of rising in the world through industry and commerce while avoiding foreign entanglements and quagmires, remained a touchstone. These policy highlights help explain China's Syria policy. They were, however, challenged in at least some ways by the rise of the so-called Islamic State group (the self-styled Islamic State of Iraq and the Levant, or ISIL, also known as the Islamic State of Iraq and Syria, ISIS), which made Beijing more willing to accept foreign interference, and by the new muscularity of Xi Jinping, who rose to the presidency in 2013 (Boon 2017). Xi Jinping de-emphasized Deng Xiaopeng's policy of "hiding strength and biding time" in favor of "striving for achievement" (Feng and He 2017, 19).

Syria as Ideological Exception

In the post-Soviet period, one Arab journalist who conducted discussions with Chinese experts in Beijing argued that China saw Syria as an "ideological exception" in the region (Zayd al-Marhun 2015). Presumably, the experts meant Syria's socialism, anti-imperialism, and secularism in a region rife with religious pro-American regimes, such as Saudi Arabia. The Ba'ath Party, characterizing itself as both Arab nationalist and socialist, had come to power in the 1960s, and in 1970 air force general Hafez al-Assad had made a coup and became president for life (see Hinnebusch 2001; Lesch 2012; Wedeen 1999; Wedeen and Stacher 2012). He was succeeded by his son Bashar al-Assad in 2000. Syria had been a Soviet client and in the early 2000s continued to maintain independence from the United States in part over the latter's stalwart support for Israel. Syrian intellectuals identified

Damascus as "the beating heart of Arabism," making the country a potential base for Chinese forays into the Arab world.

The George W. Bush administration's invasion of Iraq turned that country from a similar socialist, one-party, secularly ruled state into one dominated by religious Shi'ite parties, raising the alarm in China of being surrounded to the west by a capitalist, fundamentalist set of countries in Washington's Greater Middle East. The NATO intervention in Libya in 2011 provoked similar anxieties. In contrast, before 2011 Syria was seen in Beijing (incorrectly, as it transpired) as a stable country central to the Arab world and a "cohesive force" (Simpfendorfer 2011, chap. 4).

In 2010, China said it was encouraging the establishment of Chinese factories in Syria and expressed admiration for Syria's independent foreign policy (Xinhua News Agency 2010). China was also allegedly interested in Syria as part of a potential land bridge for Chinese exports to Europe through the Mediterranean Syrian port of Latakia. Syria would be one of the endpoints for the New Silk Road (as it had been in medieval times) and through the Barcelona agreement, which lowered Mediterranean tariffs, might provide a back door into Europe (Lin 2010). In 2010, on the eve of the outbreak of protests in Syria, China's annual trade with Syria came to a paltry US$2.5 billion, but with government encouragement Chinese firms were planning a big increase in investments. One manifestation of this interest in the Syrian economy was the Adra Free Zone industrial park east of Damascus, founded by Chinese investors from Zheijiang and aimed at being a place from which Chinese goods could be exported to the rest of the Middle East (Zayd al-Marhun 2015).

Youth Revolt

The outbreak of "Arab Spring" youth demonstrations throughout much of the Middle East, including in Syria, in March 2011 was unwelcome to China, especially because it coincided with the beginnings of NATO military intervention in Libya (Cole 2014). Shanghai's *Liberation Daily* wrote that the US intervention in Libya was intended as a "warning" to Syria, Iran, and Sudan in particular, adding, "It even has an intention to attempt to guide the regional turmoil towards these countries" (Baolai 2011). China was emerging as a major petroleum importer from the Middle East in those years. One concern raised by the Arab Spring revolts was the security of energy for China's growing economy, which in the wake of the US deep recession beginning in 2008 had become the engine of world growth. The Chinese Communist Youth League newspaper *China Youth Daily* worried in April 2011 that "PetroChina and Sinopec have projects in Sudan, Syria, Iran, Iraq, Venezuela and other countries, with bigger scale projects in Sudan, Venezuela and Iraq. So, it is necessary to guard against its impact on our country's oil supplies and to actively adjust the layout of overseas investments" (*Zhongguo qingnian bao* 2011).

As the unrest in Syria continued that spring, China supported Syrian government pledges of reform, which in the event proved worthless. The Chinese ambassador to the United Nations, Li Baodong, said in late April, "We hope that various parties in Syria will resolve their differences through political dialogue and cope with the current situation in an appropriate manner so as to maintain stability and normal order of the country" (Xinhua News Agency 2011). He commended Damascus for lifting the state of emergency and for vowing political reforms. Interestingly, Beijing did not come out at the beginning of the conflict with absolute backing for the al-Assad government's authoritarian practices, expressing approval of reform proposals and attempting to mollify the protesters.

As the demonstrations continued in the summer of 2011, Beijing clearly began planning measures that would make a UNSC-authorized Libya-style intervention in Syria impossible. A researcher at the Center for World Affairs Studies argued that Russia and China were "insurmountable obstacles" and would never agree to a UNSC resolution authorizing the use of force. Moreover, he thought, because the Libya intervention wasn't going well, the West might be less eager to rush into Syria, though the possibility could not be ruled out if the Libya intervention took a turn for the better and if the turbulence in Syria continued (Jizan 2011). This analysis proved prescient. Within about a year, China and Russia had vetoed three UNSC resolutions calling for action against or sanctions on the Syrian regime, which had from the fall of 2011 decided to use lethal force to put down the popular protests (*RT* 2012). Among the reasons for China's vetoes was a determination that the Libya precedent, where NATO used humanitarian intervention as a justification to force regime change and establish a new sphere of Western influence, not be repeated (Dorsey 2019, 90–91; Janik 2013).

Still, the fall of Qaddafi in August 2011, the continued Syrian protests, as well as the increasingly violent regime response (as at Hama in July) induced some caution in China. The *Global Times* (Beijing) warned in late August, "The situation in Syria continues to deteriorate, and the story of Libya could be repeated in Syria. This is clearly a test for China's diplomacy. China cannot join the Western camp to overthrow the current regime in Damascus, but if it stands in opposition to Western policy, this will be equally risky to China. . . . China may not be able to turn a blind eye to the Syrian opposition either and timely contact is not a bad option" (*Global Times* 2011).

That is, some Chinese observers worried that the al-Assad government might fall or be overthrown and that the new government would view any strong Chinese backing for the Ba'th Party in a poor light.

Civil War

Nevertheless, the Russo-Chinese bloc on the UNSC stood firm against resolutions that might take NATO into Syria. This determination may have been reinforced on November 15, 2012, when Xi Jinping was elected president by the Central Committee of the Chinese Communist Party. Xi championed a more vigorous Chinese foreign policy and had developed an economic vision that included the Middle East.

By the spring of 2013, the Support Front (Jabhat al-Nusra, then an al-Qaeda affiliate in Syria) and its allies were nearing an ability, through their dominance of Homs and Qusayr, to cut landlocked Damascus off from the key northwestern port of Latakia. China was getting pressure from France to soften its opposition to the overthrow of al-Assad but had determined to resist (*Shenzhen tequ bao* 2013). That spring, Iran asked Lebanon's Hezbollah to intervene in Qusayr and Homs, where it helped the Syrian Arab Army gradually retake these cities and restore secure routes between the capital and Latakia. The *Oriental Morning Post* of Shanghai expressed confidence that Iran retained substantial room for maneuver in Syria and was in no danger of falling victim to internal divisions (Zhongmin 2013).

At the same time, the United States announced it would begin providing "nonmilitary" aid to some rebel factions. The policy shift was met with a sharp rebuke by the Chinese press. Beijing's official mouthpiece, *China Daily*, wrote, "Helping the Syrian rebels is definitely not a move towards resolving the crisis peacefully and [is] contrary to the efforts of a majority of the international community. The mixed messages the US move has sent will embolden those keen on toppling the Syrian President Bashar al-Assad, which will result in more bloodshed in the country" (*China Daily* 2013b). Opposition to any foreign intervention in Syria characterized the Chinese stance until the fall of 2015.

Over time, the United States did rather more than offer "nonmilitary" aid. Washington initiated some covert operations to arm and train the rebels. One, a CIA project, involved providing antitank equipment to Saudi Arabia, which Riyadh then passed on to some thirty "vetted" groups, most of which probably had origins in the Muslim Brotherhood but who had gradually adopted a hardline Salafi religious stance (Bender 2015). Many US and Saudi munitions made their way to more radical groups, including the Support Front, al-Qaeda, and ISIL. As Beijing predicted, this US provision of medium weaponry intensified and prolonged the civil war, especially because it strengthened the most fundamentalist Sunni groups, who were completely unacceptable to a majority of Syrians, including Christians, Alawites, Druze, Twelver Shi'ites, leftist Kurds, and secular, urban Sunni Arabs.

In the summer of 2013, the rebels suffered a major setback in Qusayr, where Hezbollah was victorious. When the insurgents called for a cessation of hostilities during the holy fasting month, China strongly supported the idea. Indeed, Beijing asked for an immediate cease-fire (Xinhua News Agency 2013a). That fall, the Chinese press was still pushing for a cease-fire, pointing to the increasing problem of famine, which only a cessation of hostilities could ameliorate. The state-run *China Daily* blamed "the West" for speaking of democracy and freedom but turning a blind eye to mass starvation (*China Daily* 2013a).

In the summer of 2013, Xi Jinping, having just become president, announced a massive new economic program, the "New Silk Road." Some eight months later, the government released a map showing the extent of this planned set of trade networks. It would begin in central China and extend through the otherwise somewhat isolated Chinese cities of Urumqi and Khorgas in Xinjiang, China's traditionally Uighur Northwest, where Muslim separatism had been seen as a pressing problem in Beijing. The New Silk Road would then stretch through Kazakhstan and Uzbekistan into Iran and from there into Iraq, northern Syria, and Turkey. From Turkey, it would wind into Europe, up to Rotterdam, and then down to Venice. These trade routes would depend on new transportation infrastructure, including rail lines, but also on commercial depots and industrial parks. Important for our discussion here is China's aspiration of incorporating Iraq and Syria into the network, which would not have been necessary because a rail link already exists between Tehran and Istanbul, the last leg of the old Orient Express, and so the detour down to Baghdad and up to Aleppo could have been avoided in Chinese planning. It seems clear that Beijing was not interested in simple efficiency but rather in creating new trade possibilities. Ironically, in the early twentieth century a Tehran spike was suggested off the German-built Baghdad railway but was not implemented, in part because of Russian and British imperial rivalry (Cole 2017). There is a sense in which the New Silk Road has implications for Iran, Iraq, Syria, and Turkey like those of the Baghdad Railway project as it was initially envisaged by early twentieth-century entrepreneurs (Tiezzi 2014).

China was willing to take a long view regarding the incorporation of Syria into the New Silk Road, hoping the war would subside and leave enough of a stable government behind to start trade projects back up again. Even amid the fierce fighting in the summer of 2013, the Chinese ambassador in Damascus, Chang Shi Yon, discussed with the Syrian minister of electricity, Imad Khamis, a raft of power investments. Khamis sought memoranda of understanding with Chinese companies so as to import equipment for Syria's electricity sector. The ambassador said he welcomed this initiative, noting that the bulk of Sino-Syrian mutual cooperation at that point was in the electrical power sector (*SANA* 2013).

The Syrian government's use of chemical weapons in Ghouta near Damascus on August 21, 2013, provoked a crisis. President Barack Obama of the United States had designated chemical weapons use a "red line," and it seemed for a few weeks that he might be obliged to attack the al-Assad government, an action that might give a fillip to the rebels in the civil war. The crisis was resolved when Russia offered to oversee the destruction of Syrian government chemical weapons stockpiles. After this course was decided upon by Russia and the United States, on September 30 mortar shells landed near the Chinese embassy in Damascus. Hua Liming, a former Chinese ambassador to Iran, told the Chinese press that the shelling may not have been targeting the embassy. But he admitted the possibility that the rebels were frustrated that a diplomatic resolution of the poison gas crisis had been reached at the UNSC, which thus allowed the al-Assad government to escape threatened US bombing, and he observed that "the Syrian opposition's hopes that Western countries would attack the Syrian government have been dashed, so they may have unleashed anger at other countries." He added that the rebels were attempting to make Damascus unsafe and that "the opposition have long since planned to use mortar attacks on important targets, and the recent increase in them may be because they have had breakthroughs in technology" (Xinhua News Agency 2013b).

The autumn of 2013 saw several turbulent outcomes of the youth revolts of 2011. Fierce fighting continued in Syria. Libya was becoming increasingly unstable. Tunisian demonstrators took to the streets demanding new elections. In Egypt, General Abdel Fattah al-Sisi had begun consolidating his coup. The Chinese leadership took a dim view of all this turmoil and blamed it on a superficial Arab imitation of Western forms of governance—that is, bourgeois democracy. In a major, succinct statement of the problem, the Chinese Communist Party newspaper, the *People's Daily*, wrote,

> The occurrence of upheaval in the Arab world in 2011 is closely related to long-standing ideological confusion in Arab countries. Even after the upheaval in the Middle East, these countries in transition have accepted the "Arab Spring" theory without thinking, continued to copy Western theory and experience and simply see "democratization" as the road to get out of a predicament. . . . The end result of a lost direction is that their plight has become worse, and merely facilitated the transformation and control of the Middle East by Western countries. In contrast,

China's explored theory and path have more positive significance. The Chinese Communist Party believes in Marxism, but it advocates combining the basic principles of Marxism-Leninism with concrete practice in China and emphasizes taking the road of socialism with Chinese characteristics. (Wenlin 2013)

This analysis takes the Arabs to task for imitating Europe and North America rather than seeking their own system with regional characteristics. Moreover, the author appears to imply that the democratic system has facilitated European and American neoimperial dominance in the region.

It is not clear, however, that attributing the democratic aspirations in the region to Western influence could be substantiated with reference to actual developments. On the contrary, major Western figures such as Hillary Clinton lamented the overthrow of Egyptian dictator Hosni Mubarak, and the government of President Nicolas Sarkozy of France offered police training to Tunisian dictator Zine El Abidin Ben Ali. Democracy produced a Muslim Brotherhood government in Egypt, with which the West was visibly uncomfortable, whereas a subsequent military coup under al-Sisi in 2013 brought Egyptian policy closer, on the whole, to what the West would like to see.

By April 2014 in Syria, it was clear that Homs would fall to government forces, and in May those forces took control of the city. The strategy of al-Qaeda and its allies to use control of Homs and Qusayr to cut Damascus off from supply lines to Latakia was definitively defeated, in part because of the Hezbollah and Iranian intervention on the side of the Syrian Arab Army (Diyab 2014; R. Z. 2014). The Syrian political opposition was still relatively moderate (unlike the battlefield groups, which had come to be dominated by hard-liners and al-Qaeda affiliates) and was still engaging in diplomacy. China appears to have been one of the few diplomatic interlocutors acceptable both to the al-Assad government and to the opposition, and in mid-April 2014 Ahmad Jarba, president of the National Coalition of Syrian Revolutionary Forces, made a three-day visit to Beijing, where he met with Foreign Minister Wang Yi of China. Wang urged a cease-fire and called on all parties to allow the delivery of humanitarian aid to civilian populations. China Radio explained the visit, saying that the opposition had failed to make progress on the battlefield and had fallen off the radar of Western diplomacy. It cautioned, however, "It should be pointed out that China is only a coordinator supporting communication on the Syrian issue, and the key to resolving the issue lies with the Syrian government, the opposition and other external factors" (China Radio International 2014). Nevertheless, rather than only supporting Damascus, in the wake of Jarba's visit the Chinese Foreign Ministry called for the "start [of] an inclusive political transition as soon as possible," implying that the Ba'th Party could not hope to retain a one-party state and that the political opposition would have to be accommodated in some way (Xinhua News Agency 2014a). Beijing's willingness to mediate between the rebels and the al-Assad government showed the ways in which China, despite its best efforts, was being drawn into Syria. The Chinese ambassador to Washington, Cui Tiankai, predicted that his country's economic investments and entanglements would willy-nilly begin shaping China's foreign policy (Dorsey 2019, 76). China's thirst for Middle East petroleum was motivating a new engagement with the Middle East.

ISIL

In June 2014, the world was shocked when ISIL took over Mosul, the Iraqi army collapsed and fled, and then the al-Qaeda offshoot established itself in most of the Sunni Arab cities of northern and western Iraq (McCants 2015). Its Syrian base, the small eastern city of al-Raqqa in the province of the same name, became the capital of the world's newest country. ISIL leader Abu Bakr al-Baghdadi (the nom de guerre of the Iraqi Islamic studies academic Ibrahim al-Samarra'i) declared himself caliph, a lapsed Sunni Muslim institution akin to the papacy in Christianity.

These developments deeply alarmed Beijing, and not just because they might further inflame radicalism among the Muslim Uighur minority. The *People's Daily* warned, "It can be boldly said that the terrorism threat posed by the 'Islamic State' is the biggest development of international 'jihad' since the 'September 11 attack' and it marks a new phase of terrorism" (Xiaoqiang 2014). The party organ called for international cooperation in combating the new threat, invoking the image of the Great Wall of China, built to protect Beijing from Mongols and other Central Asian tribal threats: "Relevant countries must foster a consensus, strengthen their coordination in combatting terrorism, fully make use of mechanisms such as the United Nations Security Council and the Global Counterterrorism Forum and embark on preventive cooperation against terrorism in order to build a new wall guarding against the new round of threats posed by international terrorism" (Xiaoqiang 2014).

Other Chinese observers, however, critiqued the terrorism frame of US discourse about ISIL. Tian Wenlin wrote that ISIL must have some local credibility to have been able to spread so effectively in Syria and Iraq: "Scattered information suggests that the group has been providing water and electricity, paying salaries, controlling traffic, and operating institutions such as bakeries, banks, schools, courts and mosques and so on in the area that it controls. From this, it must be said that it is hard to conclude whether 'Islamic State' is indeed an evil terrorist group or a logical product of political evolutions in the Middle East" (Wenlin 2014).

In any case, Tian Wenlin said this outcome was the product of failed US policies in the region. The Chinese Communist Party, however, discounted the analysis of this Middle East expert, and Beijing even allegedly offered Baghdad practical military help against ISIL. Despite the specter of the ersatz caliphate, Beijing was not yet ready to abandon its principle of noninterference. James Dorsey observes that in a speech in London in mid-March 2015 senior Foreign Ministry adviser Wu Jianmen warned against any Chinese military alliances that would resurrect the Cold War and create enemies (Dorsey 2019, 76).

In mid-2015, President Xi Jinping called the rise of ISIL "both expected and unexpected." He appears to have meant not only that it was expected that US military intervention in Iraq should have produced pushback but also that the form this resistance took was a surprise. He urged an end to foreign intervention and instead pushed internal conciliation and unity, the typical Chinese Communist boilerplate. The official news agency reported, "Xi said China is concerned about the region, where conflicts between different ethnic groups, religions and religious sects have reemerged, and the Palestine–Israel, Syria and Iraq issues have intertwined and affected one another" (Xinhua News Agency 2014b).

Despite President Xi's apparent adherence to the long-standing Chinese doctrine of noninterference, it seems clear that unease about ISIL was provoking a reconsideration of the importance of counterterrorism and the need for partners in any such effort. In the fall of 2015, the state-run *China Daily* praised President Obama's condemnation of terrorism but implied that the United States continued to deploy terrorists for its own purposes. The paper said that denouncing a demon but then rejoicing when it attacked an enemy is inconsistent. "That such a policy is flawed can be surmised from the news that terrorists who attacked Chinese people aim to join the jihad in Syria. Therefore, China and US have no option but to combat the common enemy of terrorism together" (*China Daily* 2014). Reading between the lines, we can see here a reference to the alleged CIA support for Uighur separatists in Xinjiang Province. Beijing was appealing to the United States for closer security cooperation and an end to covert operations against China on the basis of the need to unite against ISIL, which threatened US interests in the Middle East and China's interests in its own Northwest.

The Iranian and Hezbollah intervention in Syria had its limits. US, Saudi, Gulf Cooperation Council, and Turkish support for the rebels over time allowed them to overrun some Syrian Arab Army positions. American provision of medium antitank weapons through the Saudis may have been particularly important in turning the tide through 2015. In the South, the rebels made advances in Deraa Province, and al-Qaeda had taken the Golan Heights. North of the capital, the Saudi-backed Salafi jihadi group the Army of Islam (Jaysh al-Islam) posed a constant danger to the regime. Al-Qaeda made a formal political and military alliance with some Salafi groups, including the Freemen of Syria (Ahrar al-Sham), and the new allies established positions northwest of Damascus near the Lebanese border and around Aleppo. In late March 2015, the al-Qaeda-led coalition called the Army of Conquest (Jaysh al-Fath) took Idlib City in the far Northwest.

Russian Intervention

By midsummer 2015, the al-Assad regime seemed in real trouble. There was a danger that the Army of Conquest, spear-headed by the Support Front, might sweep west from Idlib and south from the Turkish border into Latakia and take the port. That development would have the same effect of cutting Damascus off from resupply as the earlier failed plan to take and hold Homs would have had. At the same time, a range of rebel groups, which included Freemen of Syria, al-Qaeda, and ISIL, were increasingly likely to cut off supply routes north from Hama up to the regime-held enclave of West Aleppo, thus starving it out. The rebels had held East Aleppo since 2012. Aleppo is the largest city in Syria, and if it fell completely to the opposition, it was difficult so see how the al-Assad regime could survive in the medium to long term.

It is alleged that in the summer of 2015 Iran alerted the government of President Vladimir Putin of Russia to the danger that the Syrian regime would collapse, informing Moscow that Iran had done everything it could and had reached the limit of its ability to intervene. Hezbollah was a small guerrilla group with some five thousand to eight thousand fighters in Syria, and it could not spare more. Iran's Qods Brigade, a special forces unit of the Iranian Revolutionary Guards Corps, had put in around twenty-five hundred advisers, some of whom engaged in combat, but with resulting casualties that proved unpopular back home.

On September 30, 2015, at the request of the al-Assad regime, the Russian Federation came into the Syria conflict. It reinforced and expanded the naval facilities it was leasing from Syria at Tartus near Latakia in the northwest. It established a new airfield nearby, capable of receiving cargo airplanes that could bring in tanks and other heavy munitions to resupply the Syrian Arab Army. Russia deployed Sukhoi Su-24 attack aircraft as well as Tu-160 and Tu-95 heavy strategic bombers against rebel positions. The Russian strategy involved defending Latakia and Damascus, above all, and then relieving West Aleppo (which for two weeks in October was cut off from food and other supplies by rebel forces). Russia especially targeted the Support Front, the al-Qaeda affiliate, because it was the best opposition fighting force in the western part of the country and the one that most seriously threatened the regime. Russia and the regime were, however, interested in degrading rebel capabilities anywhere the rebels threatened regime-held cities, and so they attacked what the United States considered "moderate" (mainly Muslim Brotherhood) remnants of the Free Syrian Army—for instance, those north of Hama. ISIL positions tended to be in the eastern desert, and Russia viewed them as less of an immediate menace to al-Assad than the Free Syrian Army or al-Qaeda in the Northwest. Russia and the Damascus government gave the "caliphate" less attention—though Russia did run bombing raids against it and supported the Syrian Arab Army effort to take back Palmyra from it. The United States and its allies expressed anger that Russia seemed to be ignoring ISIL and hitting "moderates," but this narrative ignored the leading role of al-Qaeda in the western rebel coalition—a role that Vladimir Putin feared for what it might mean for the Russian Federation's Chechen Republic.

Beijing's *Global Times* defended Putin's strategy. In an editorial, it argued that three objectives had been discussed by the world community regarding Syria. Some wanted to see Bashar al-Assad's regime overthrown, others to see ISIL defeated, and yet others to see a democratic society built in Syria. As of 2015, the editors said, a fourth objective had been voiced: to prevent more refugees from being created in Syria. The paper insisted that all of these goals could not be attained simultaneously. The first, overthrowing al-Assad, the newspaper said, had proved "unrealistic." Even attempting this regime change had contributed to the rise of ISIL and to the stream of refugees fleeing the country. In contrast, Russia had intervened "brilliantly" to prop up the al-Assad regime and to push back ISIL. President Vladimir Putin, the editorial observed, had acted "in response to objective needs that the situation calls for." Even though many Western commentaries had focused only on aspects of the intervention with which they were uncomfortable, the editorial said, the Russian intervention carried benefits for the United States and for the countries opposed to ISIL (*Global Times* 2015). The late fall of 2015 saw a change in the previous Chinese stance against any outside interference in Syria when Chinese hostages were executed by ISIL, and the attacks by ISIL-linked militants in Paris in November made it difficult for Beijing to maintain that nothing should be done. Moreover, China generally tilted to Russia and Iran, both of which were committed to intervention (Shi 2015).

By late 2015, the right-wing paper the *Washington Times* in the United States was speculating that China itself might send troops to prevent the al-Assad government from falling (Gertz 2016). Professional China observers found this report fantastic (Bogdanov, Baltachyova, and Neroznikova 2016). Andrei Ostrovsky of the Russian Institute for Far Eastern Studies pointed out, "China has its own interests there, but China's main military doctrine is the so-called doctrine of defense sufficiency—not to interfere in foreign affairs." China's military would be reserved for use in defending Chinese borders, Ostrovsky said, not sent to distant Syria or Iraq, despite the existence of Uighur fighters in ISIL ranks. According to *Russia beyond the Headlines*, quoting from the Russian website Vzglyad, Ostrovsky added, "China is acting solely in terms of rationality, and its main concept in this context is that of the wise monkey Sun Wukong[1] that sits on a mountain, while tigers are fighting in the valley" (Ostrovsky quoted in Bogdanov, Baltachyova, and Neroznikova 2016). Still, China had not given up its economic ambitions for Syria, according to Alexei Maslov at Moscow's Higher School of Economics, also quoted in Vzglyad (Bogdanov, Baltachyova, and Neroznikova 2016). In late December 2015, Beijing pledged $6 million in humanitarian aid to Damascus (Xinhua News Agency 2015).

In February and March 2016, the Geneva process, of which China was a part, finally managed to implement a relatively successful cessation of hostilities in Syria. China had continued to act as a go-between for opposition elements willing to negotiate with the Damascus government, even though many in the opposition denounced Beijing for its four vetoes of UNSC resolutions that would have punished the al-Assad regime for war crimes (Kawa 'Isu 2016). Like Russia, China insisted that negotiations be without preconditions; that is, Beijing would not support the US demand that Bashar al-Assad step down before talks could begin (Xinhua Arabic 2016).

As Russian intervention and the continued support from Iran won the war for the Syrian regime, Damascus reestablished a fragile control over the country through the rest of the 2010s, except for the northwestern province of Idlib, where the remaining rebels took refuge along with 3 million residents and internal refugees. With the war all but over, the question of rebuilding came to the fore. China was still committed to its "One Belt, One Road" project of linking Eurasia with investments and infrastructure, its biggest commitment going to Pakistan and the Persian Gulf in the 2010s (Cole 2019). China did not make Syria a priority, but it did offer Damascus some aid in three tranches totaling $15–20 million between 2016 and 2019 (*SANA* 2019).

Washington seemed eager to prevent reconstruction by placing sanctions, in the form of the Caesar Act of 2020, on potential investors in Syria. Russia and China, in contrast, clearly wanted to restore the Syrian economy as a way of securing the al-Assad regime. For instance, in late 2020 there was talk of China putting an electric commuter-rail system into Damascus to connect the downtown with the suburbs that had swollen with internally displaced people (Mustafa 2020).

---

1. *Volume editor's note*: Sun Wukong is a figure from classical Chinese literature.

China continued to show interest in investing in Syria in a minor way, keeping a hand in. Syria would, after all, be the next-to-the-last stop before Europe on the New Silk Road route.

Syrians were clearly split on their views of China during the Civil War. Suriya al-Ikhbaria, a television network and YouTube channel connected to the Ministry of Information, carried interviews with what were characterized as people from "the Syrian Street" in September 2019 (Suriya al-Ikhbaria 2019). The anchor said that China had improved its popularity there. One casually but stylishly dressed man in a pretty Damascus city square said, "We thank China and its people generally because they are our friends and stood with us. They participated in economic activities." He concluded, "They are a country of construction and peace." A young shopkeeper selling children's clothes observed, "China is one of Syria's close friends. They did as Russia did, they exercised their [UN] veto more than once. They stood with us in an ideal way. They stood with us in lots of ways, including on the economy. They helped us a lot, China." A middle-aged man with a graying moustache, wearing a short-sleeved shirt, concurred: "Naturally, with regard to China, it is a great state in its economy and its political stances. It took a really beautiful position regarding the Syrian people." An older man in a plaid shirt standing outside a sidewalk fruit stand said of China, "We are grateful for its economic support, its moral support, its political support, even in international forums." A middle-aged woman enthused that she was grateful to China because "it stood by us in reconstruction." A young man, perhaps a college student, on a sidewalk in front of an Alpha Pharmacy in Damascus said he was grateful to China for its aid in fighting "the war on terrorism." The Syrian media are about as reliable as the North Korean media, though, and it is possible that at least some of these interviewees were trying to please the police state by expressing notions on television they knew would be palatable to it. Given, however, the extremely negative image of the fundamentalist rebels among middle-class urbanites in Damascus and West Aleppo, it is plausible that the statements accurately reflected the interviewees' views. Several mentioned Chinese economic aid, for which many Syrians would be grateful given Washington's policy of preventing economic reconstruction and thus punishing civilians for the Ba'th state's resilience. Syrian gratitude for Chinese help in facing the coronavirus pandemic in 2021 is plausible, given that China provided 150,000 doses of its vaccine to Damascus when only about one percent of Syrians had been inoculated. Wang Yi visited Damascus that summer, complaining that the United States was attempting to impede Syrian reconstruction and to harm the civilian economy even as Washington was talking pie in the sky about human rights (*South China Morning Post* 2021).

Conclusion

International relations' perspectives can offer insights for understanding Beijing's interest in Syria. China most powerfully pursued its foreign policy toward Syria in civil war through its string of vetoes of United Nations Security Council resolutions that would have placed sanctions on the regime (and some rebel groups) and might have opened the door to Western intervention and regime change. As a result of the Chinese and Russian vetoes, no "no-fly zone" was ever imposed over Syria, nor did NATO strike al-Assad regime targets. These vetoes are consistent with the constructivists' emphasis on the Chinese search for status; Beijing would have been demoted had NATO done to Syria what it did to Libya. Beijing felt badly used in 2011 and was determined not to be taken advantage of again. The most kinetic Western intervention was against ISIL in Syria's Northeast and to a lesser extent against al-Qaeda, which in the nature of the case helped the regime and was acceptable to China.

China's position for most of the period from 2011 to 2015 was that the opposition and the regime should engage in good-faith internal negotiations after reaching a cease-fire. It opposed the US, Turkish, and Gulf Cooperation Council's arming of the rebels but also implicitly criticized the al-Assad government's inflexibility. China's politicians and journalists critiqued the Syrian opposition's early discourse of democratization, seeing that process as a stalking horse for NATO influence or even dominance. Rather, China urged Syrians to develop their own political and economic pathway. Nevertheless, Beijing officials met repeatedly with the civilian leaders of the opposition in the Syrian National Council and perhaps passed messages back and forth. The Chinese press at some points expressed anxiety that freezing out the opposition would disadvantage Beijing were the government to fall. China was also a presence at the Geneva negotiations, which finally resulted in a brief cessation of hostilities in the first half of 2016.

In 2014–17, the rise of ISIL interposed a serious geopolitical obstacle to the New Silk Road plans inasmuch as the road would then have to run directly through the caliphate. Further, the enthusiasm for ISIL among a handful of Uighur militants gave Beijing pause. Thus, China uncharacteristically sought cooperation with the United States in intervening against ISIL as part of a global antiterrorism struggle, though its press continued to imply that the Obama administration was being hypocritical in covertly encouraging Uighur separatism.

When Russia decided to go into Syria in the fall of 2015, Beijing dropped its objection to foreign incursions and to striving for a unilateral victory in the conflict and instead praised Moscow's moves as "brilliant." China all along had an interest in seeing the Syrian conflict resolved, though it would have been unhappy if the resolution had involved a complete overthrow of the Syrian government, which it viewed through the lens of anti-imperial ideological exceptionalism. Beijing's turn to accepting Moscow's view that the al-Assad regime had to be propped up at all costs and its new willingness also to ally tacitly with the United States to crush ISIL marked a hardening of Xi Jinping's positions that contrasted with Beijing's earlier urging of a negotiated solution. This harder line, however, appears to have been reactive rather than, as in the case of playing hardball against Japan and Philippines over Pacific islands, driven by Xi Jinping's new emphasis on self-assertion. Moreover, this reactive line had status quo implications. China did not play a revisionist role as a challenger in Syria. This finding does not refute the realist position because realists expect China to seek regional hegemony only in East Asia, not elsewhere in the world.

We can conclude that China still does not make power plays in regions such as the Middle East and still acts there more as liberal institutionalists and constructivists would expect than as realists would. The liberal analysis of Chinese policy as centering on expansion of international trade rather than on mere power grabs or military entanglements also continues to be relevant to understanding China and Syria. Beijing has a long-standing interest in establishing Chinese factories and companies in Syria and using the country as an export base for the rest of the Arab world, which was frustrated during the 2010s. Syria is not a major oil producer, and China's Syria policy is not driven by its increased dependence on Persian Gulf oil. Still, the government of Xi Jinping hopes to incorporate Syria ultimately into the One Belt, One Road initiative, envisioning a rail link from Tehran to Baghdad that would proceed up to Aleppo and then on to Istanbul, connecting the northern Syria economy with both Europe and East Asia. In the meantime, as a marker on that future, Beijing provides minor amounts of aid and dangles the possibility of small infrastructural projects, continuing the tradition of the wise monkey Sun Wukong as Syria limps into a difficult postwar period.

References

Baolai, Liu. 2011. "Report." *Liberation Daily* (Shanghai), via BBC Monitoring, Apr. 1.

Bender, Jeremy. 2015. "There Are a Lot of CIA-Vetted Syrian Rebel Groups Taking It to Assad." *Business Insider*, Oct. 20. At http://www.businessinsider.com/cia-vetted-syrian -rebels-fighting-assad-2015-10.

Bogdanov, Yury, Marina Baltachyova, and Yekaterina Neroznikova. 2016. "China Will Not Fight in Syria." Translated in *Russia beyond the Headlines*, Jan. 15. At http://rbth .com/international/2016/01/15/china-will-not-fight-in-syria_559607.

Boon, Hoo Tiang. 2017. "Xi Jinping's Calibration of Chinese Foreign Policy." In *Chinese Foreign Policy*, edited by Hoo Tiang Boon, 3–16. London: Routledge.

China Daily (Beijing, via BBC Monitoring). 2013a. "Syria's Humanitarian Disaster." Nov. 4.

———. 2013b. "US Moves on Syria Risky." Mar. 4.

———. 2014. "Only a Sincere US Can Fight Terrorism." Nov. 14.

China Radio International (via BBC Monitoring). 2014. "What Is the Purpose of Syrian Opposition's China Visit?" Apr. 18.

Cole, Juan. 2014. *The New Arabs: How the Millennial Generation is Changing the Middle East.* New York: Simon and Schuster.

———. 2017. "Sanctioning Iran: A Nietzschean Theory of Negative Imperialism." *Farman-Farmaian Annual Lectures* 1:21–28.

———. 2019. *The China–Pakistan Economic Corridor and the Gulf Crisis.* Gulf Studies Center Series, no. 4. Doha: Qatar Univ., June. At https://www.qu.edu.qa/static_file/qu/research/Gulf%20Studies/documents/Monograph%20N%204%20Juan%20Cole.pdf.

Diyab, Muhammad. 2014. "Suqut Hums yutih li'l-nizam al-tawajjuh biquwwatihi ila rifiha al-shamali." *Al-Quds al-'Arabi*, May 7. At http://www.alquds.co.uk/?p=165415.

Dorsey, James M. 2019. *China and the Middle East.* London: Palgrave Macmillan.

Feng, Huiyun, and Kai He. 2017. "China under Xi Jinping." In *Chinese Foreign Policy under Xi*, edited by Hoo Tiang Boon, 19–35. London: Routledge.

Gertz, Bill. 2016. "China May Enter War against ISIS." *Washington Times*, Jan. 13. At http://www.washingtontimes.com/news/2016/jan/13/inside-ring-china-may-join-russia-war-against-isla/.

Global Times (Beijing, via BBC Monitoring). 2011. "Report." Aug. 31.

———. 2015. "Absurd for NATO to Have Military Confrontation against Russia in Syria." Oct. 8.

Hinnebusch, Raymond A. 2001. *Syria: Revolution from Above.* London: Routledge.

Janik, Ralph. 2013. "China, Russia, and the Failure of the Responsibility to Protect in Syria: Does the Fear of Regime Change Offer a Serviceable Explanation?" *Studia Europaea* 58, no. 1 (Mar.): 63–88.

Jizan, Tang. 2011. [No title.] *Liaowang xinwen zhoukan* (Outlook weekly, Beijing, via BBC Monitoring), June 21.

Kawa 'Isu. 2016. "Khujah: Al-Sin hawalat al-wuquf 'ala masafat mutasawiyah min al-nizam wal al-mu'aradah al-suriyyah." *AraNews*, Jan. 8. At http://aranews.org/2016/01/52637/.

Lesch, David W. 2012. *Syria: The Fall of the House of Assad.* New Haven, CT: Yale Univ. Press.

Lin, Christina. 2010. "Syria in China's New Silk Road Strategy." *China Brief* (Jamestown Foundation), Apr. 8. At http://www.jamestown.org/single/?tx_ttnews[tt_news]=36264&no_cache=1#.VuSGuKah7Ww.

McCants, William. 2015. *The ISIS Apocalypse: The History, Strategy, and Doomsday Vision of the Islamic State.* New York: St. Martin's Press.

Mustafa, Muhammad. 2020. "Al-Sin taftah nafidhah li al-isthmar fi al-Suriya." *Al-Mudun*, Nov. 27. At https://tinyurl.com/y34p5dnr.

Nye, Joseph S., Jr. 2020. "Power and Interdependence with China." *Washington Quarterly* 43, no. 1: 7–21.

RT. 2012. "Russia, China Veto Western-Backed Syria Resolution at UN Security Council." July 19. At https://www.rt.com/news/russia-china-unsc-veto-syria-584/.

R. Z. 2014. "The Fall of Homs." *Economist*, May 12. At http://www.economist.com/blogs /pomegranate/2014/05/syrias-war.

SANA (via BBC Monitoring). 2013. "Syria, China Discuss Energy Cooperation." July 13.

———. 2019. "China and Syria Sign Deal Worth $15m." Mar. 18.

Shenzhen tequ bao (via BBC Monitoring). 2013. "Report." Apr. 26.

Shi, Ting. 2015. "China Pulled Further into Syria Crisis amid Terrorism Threat." *Bloomberg Business*, Nov. 22. At http://www.bloomberg.com/news/articles/2015-11-22/china -pulled-further-into-syria-crisis-as-terrorism-threat-grows.

Simpfendorfer, Ben. 2011. *The New Silk Road: How a Rising Arab World Is Turning Away from the West and Rediscovering China.* New York: Palgrave Macmillan.

South China Morning Post. 2021. "China Says Syria Needs End to US Sanctions, Not a Colour Revolution." July 22. At https://www.scmp.com/news/china/diplomacy/article /3142089/china-says-syria-needs-end-us-sanctions-not-colour-revolution.

Suriya al-Ikhbaria. 2019. "Istitla' ra'y al-shari' al-suri." Sept. 29. At https://www.youtube .com/watch?v=8mDsYUQkW-A.

Tiezzi, Shannon. 2014. "China's 'New Silk Road' Vision Revealed." *Diplomat*, May 9. At http://thediplomat.com/2014/05/chinas-new-silk-road-vision-revealed/.

Uemura, Takeshi. 2018. "Constructivism and Chinese Studies," *Journal of Asia-Pacific Studies* (Waseda Univ.), no. 30: 49–63.

Wedeen, Lisa. 1999. *Ambiguities of Domination: Politics, Rhetoric, and Symbols in Contemporary Syria.* Chicago: Univ. of Chicago Press.

Wedeen, Lisa, and Joshua Stacher. 2012. *Adaptable Autocrats: Regime Power in Egypt and Syria.* Stanford, CA: Stanford Univ. Press.

Wenlin, Tian. 2013. "Arab-Style Confusion Merits Vigilance." *People's Daily* (Beijing, via BBC Monitoring), Oct. 1.

———. 2014. "US' Call to Fight ISIS Laden with Its Own Calculations." *Global Times* (via BBC Monitoring), Sept. 17.

Xiaoqiang, Fu. 2014. "Concerted Efforts Needed to Tackle New Threat of International Terrorism." *People's Daily* (via BBC Monitoring), Sept. 11.

Xinhua Arabic. 2016. "Al-Sin ta'mal fi sayr al-muhaddathat al-Suriyah dun shurut mus-baqah." Feb. 2. At http://arabic.cntv.cn/2016/02/02/ARTI6SzMWPRoPjJ5MlmIZRxY 160202.shtml.

Xinhua News Agency (via BBC Monitoring). 2010. "Chinese Top Political Adviser Vows to Boost Ties with Syria." Oct. 31.

———. 2011. "China Hopes Parties in Syria Will Resolve Differences through Political Dialogue." Apr. 28.

———. 2013a. "China Calls for Urgent Cease-Fire in Syria." July 11.

———. 2013b. "Chinese Embassy in Syria." Oct. 1.

———. 2014a. "China Calls for Inclusive Political Transition in Syria." Apr. 22.

———. 2014b. "President Says China to Back Iraqi Government in Stabilizing Situation." Aug. 16.

———. 2015. "China Announces over 6m Dollars Humanitarian Aid to Syria." Dec. 25.

Zayd al-Marhun, Abd al-Jalil. 2015. "Al-Sin wa al-Mas'ala al-Suriya." Al Jazeera, Jan. 20. At http://tinyurl.com/zah92ba.

Zhongmin, Liu. 2013. "Report." *Dongfang zaobao* (via BBC Monitoring), Mar. 4.

Zhongguo qingnian bao (via BBC Monitoring). 2011. "Report." Apr. 11.

5

The Rise of ISIS in Postinvasion Iraq

A Manifestation of (Neo)Colonial Violence

Mariam Georgis

Since October 2019, Iraqis across ages, religious sects, and genders have taken to the streets to demand a complete dismantling of a system they deem corrupt and illegitimate. These statewide protests have taken place against the backdrop of rampant violence, nonexistent security, and unaccountable governing elites who are far removed from those they govern both spatially and ideologically. This chapter focuses on one of the biggest issues plaguing postinvasion Iraq: containing violence from various militias who saw an opportunity to make political and economic gains in the security vacuum left in the wake of the removal of Saddam Hussein in 2003. The most prominent of these offshoots was the Islamic State of Iraq and Syria (ISIS), which took over Iraq's second-largest city, Mosul, in June 2014. By 2016, ISIS controlled a "wide swatch of territory in Iraq and Syria, as large as the United Kingdom, with a population estimated at roughly between six million and nine million people" (Gerges 2016, 1). In December 2017, Prime Minister Haider al Abadi declared victory over ISIS in Iraq, but ISIS continues to inspire and carry out attacks all over the world as its cells and ideology live on. The effects of ISIS in the region have been catastrophic, especially for Indigenous and minoritized communities who are unable to rely on the security apparatus of the Iraqi state for protection or their own sectarian militia. Sectarian militias are an increasing reality on the ground as they are one of the detrimental results of the 2003 invasion and occupation policies, which fragmented Iraqi politics and society. Following the fall of ISIS, the reality of sectarian militias has resulted in the dispute over "liberated" territories between major powers and their militias, to the exclusion of Indigenous and ethnoreligious minority groups' voices regarding political aspirations and local governance. This has further fragmented Iraqi politics and entrenched minoritized communities' feelings of vulnerability and mistrust toward political elites and their security apparatuses.

Although ISIS may have lost control in Iraq, there remains a great need to understand its origins and the factors that nurtured the growth and spread of its ideology. Recently, the Islamic State in Khorasan Province (ISIS-K) claimed responsibility for the Kabul airport attack on August 26, 2021. An affiliate of ISIS in Afghanistan, ISIS-K was formed in 2014 and has been responsible for some of the worst attacks in Afghanistan in recent years, reported Dareen Abughaida on al Jazeera's *Inside Story* on August 30, 2021. These events further substantiate my argument that if the roots of this violent ideology are not eradicated, it will continue to engulf the region, wreaking havoc on everyday people's lives. There has been much debate by Western media and political analysts regarding ISIS, the most problematic idea of which has been that ISIS represents a revolutionary or countercultural movement that has no foreseeable end or collapse (Kalyvas 2015; Vu and Van Orden 2020; Walt 2015). In contrast, drawing on anticolonial and decolonial theoretical approaches, this chapter begins with the position that ISIS does not represent a revolutionary movement but rather a regressive force symptomatic of the long-term colonial and neocolonial violent practices in the region. Specifically, I argue that its emergence and successes in occupying major cities did not happen overnight; a critical analysis of the US occupation and intervention in the region and of corrupt domestic policies and regional politics within a colonial global order is paramount to understanding the rise of extremist violent movements such as ISIS.

Specifically, I argue that certain political and strategic factors gave rise to ISIS, including the US invasion and occupation of Iraq; sectarian policies under occupation; corrupt and incompetent Iraqi political elites; the regional influence held by Iran, Saudi Arabia, and Syria; and the Syrian Civil War. Positing coloniality as a central feature of the international system, this chapter first contextualizes political violence. I argue that understanding this violence in terms of colonial power relations between "us" and "them" is important to understanding the way in which violence is instrumentalized in the international system—by both the Global North and the Global South—for political and economic ends. Then I investigate the factors that gave rise to ISIS—the invasion of Iraq, sectarian policies, the Syrian Civil War, and regional elements, including the ideologies of Wahhabism and Salafism. Drawing on the work of critical specialists of Southwest Asia[1] and

---

1. I use the name "Southwest Asia" to identify the region colonially and violently known as the "Middle East," the "Arab world," and the "Islamic world." The latter terms are used interchangeably by conventional and critical scholars alike without thought to the history of the region before colonial powers arbitrarily divided it to create the current states in the region. These names are used without recognition that Indigenous and non-Muslim and/or Arab groups are part and parcel of

interviews with Iraqis on the ground, I argue, first, that ISIS and sectarian violence do not accurately reflect Iraqis' desires. The ongoing mass protests during different periods since the invasion, up to and including the largest ones that began in 2019, illustrate this point. Second, I argue that to a large extent the initial appeal of movements such as al-Qaeda and ISIS in Iraq can be truly eradicated only when the conditions of social, economic, and political marginalization and oppression that act as "breeding grounds" for such movements are eliminated.

The Context of Political Violence: Understanding ISIS

This section argues that ISIS and other militant movements like it must be examined within a larger theoretical context of the use of political violence in the international system. One of the most useful tools that anticolonial and critical postcolonial theories[2] offer is their conceptualization of the reciprocal relationship between "us" and "them." The intention here is not to excuse the violent brutality of militant movements but rather to begin to understand them in their geohistorical context. Moreover, this approach provides a critique of the problematic historical amnesia that underpins the Orientalist discourse of the Iraq War in particular and of the war on terror in general.[3] In reference to ISIS, Ali al-Jaberi writes, "Mainstream western media continue to reduce the crisis to 'Arab-looking' men wielding beards and Kalashnikovs and spreading terror in a sectarian quagmire." Conveniently obscuring the undercurrents of the crisis, this Orientalist frame, argues al-Jaberi, renders "terror and sectarian violence a 'natural' phenomenon to the Arab world, entirely detached from western involvement." He concludes, "While Iraqis, who are massacred by the thousands, are portrayed as sectarian fanatics, western military superpowers can plead innocent once again" (2014). This is a familiar story; seemingly anti-Western sentiment among populations of the Global South is rarely contextualized, and anti-Western leaders in the Global

---

the fabric of Southwest Asia, to whom we do untold epistemic harm when we use such categories to exclude them.

2. I use "critical" as a marker here to indicate that while I draw on postcolonialism's conceptualization of a reciprocal relationship between "us" and "them," I recognize there is a theoretical debate regarding the "post" in postcolonialism, and I do not view Iraq as a postcolonial state despite its independence from the British Mandate, given Indigenous Assyrians' present colonial conditions and occupation of their land in the North.

3. I extend this argument to most instances of colonial violence between the world hegemon and the Global South. This argument is rooted in part in the American Empire's belief in itself as "benign," especially in relation to its imperial predecessors, and in part in the image of itself that the empire tries to propagate on the international stage.

South are also without context demonized as oppressive tyrants who hate American freedom. George W. Bush told the world in his State of the Union Address in 2001 that the terrorists hate America because of their sense of *lack*: "They hate what we see right here in this chamber, a democratically elected government. . . . They hate our freedoms—our freedom of religion, our freedom of speech, our freedom to vote and assemble and disagree with each other" (Bush 2001). Not only is Bush's statement nonsensical, but it is also dangerous. It fails to consider the decades of colonial and neocolonial violence via foreign intervention, the West's support for oppressive regimes it considered to be its allies, and collective punishment in the form of sanctions and other forms of violence inflicted on the region's people by colonial powers in their dealings with uncooperating regimes.

In "Muslims and Modernities: From Islamism to Post-Islamism?" (2013), Mojtaba Mahdavi provides a critique of both Western modernity and Islamism. He astutely writes, "The Western Orientalists' argument resonates [with] the Islamists' perception of a fundamental clash between Islam and modern notions of democracy, secularism and human rights" (58). For Mahdavi, both classical and contemporary Orientalists "argue that there is a fundamental irresolvable clash of values between Islam and modernity" (58). Drawing on the work of Ibrahim Abu-Rabi', Mahdavi argues that Islamism is a by-product of the "undemocratic imposition of a new world order" (60) and a response to the "economic and ecological violence of neo-liberalism, the fundamentalist orthodoxies of which fuel the growing divide between rich and poor" (60). It is possible to examine the historical and political context within which these types of movements arise and at the same time to critique them. Mahdavi writes, "[The] Islamist vision of politics and state therefore essentializes Muslim culture and traditions; it echoes the Orientalist stereotype of Islamic exceptionalism. Although different in power relations, both Orientalist and Islamist discourses advocate cultural essentialism. These particularist approaches undermine the possibility of a modern democratic Muslim society and polity" (2013, 62).

This comparative analysis of Orientalism and Islamism is useful not only to open the space for critique of both of these essentialist paradigms but also to open the space for decolonial alternatives to colonial modernity. One of the most significant aspects of decolonial alternatives is moving beyond a sole focus on Muslim conceptions of society in Southwest Asia and contending with Indigenous and ethnoreligious minoritized groups' demands for recognition, participation, and political aspirations, which for Indigenous nations includes sovereignty and self-governance. These groups are a fundamental part of the region, especially Indigenous nations whose lands these states are built on.

Gilbert Achcar also examines the mutually reinforcing mechanisms of the "West" and the "Islamic world." He writes, "Rather than a 'clash of civilizations,' the battle in progress is thus definitely a clash of the barbarisms that civilizations secrete in varying quantities in the course of the long historical and dialectical process of Civilization" (2002, 66). More troubling, Achcar continues, is the reality that "on both sides, 'absolute hostility' toward the 'absolute enemy,' to use Carl Schmitt's words, thus entails the deployment of extreme violence and a logic of extermination" (66). He is drawing on Guy Debord's work *The Society of the Spectacle* (1967, English translation 1994) to describe the dehumanization process that leads to such extermination. However, anticolonial scholars have long drawn our attention to the way in which the "Other," rooted in the specific context of coloniality, must be stripped of their humanity for "us" to conceive of and subsequently act out such violence (Fanon 2004) in our quest for the ever-elusive goal of "security." For instance, in thinking about the question "Why do they hate us?," which was continuously asked in the aftermath of the attacks on September 11, 2001, Derek Gregory writes that for Westerners the answer was "to be found among 'them' not among 'us': not in the foreign policy adventures of the USA, for example, but in what was portrayed as the chronic failure of Islamic societies to come to terms with the modern" (2004, 22). Indeed, Southwest Asia is home to some notable dictators, oppressive state policies, and civil rights violations. However, most of these regimes were set up and have been politically, financially, and militarily supported by colonial powers such as Great Britain, France, and the United States. Grappling with the many forms of terrorist violence in other spaces in Africa and Asia that are created by the configurations of colonial global and local forces, Veena Das importantly urges American citizens to ask themselves, "What kind of responsibility do they share when successive regimes elected by them have supported military regimes, brutal dictatorships, and warlords mired in corruption?" (2001, 109). To be clear, I am not condoning the violence of oppressive regimes in Southwest Asia or violent responses to the United States. I am, first, pointing to the reciprocal relationship between "our" and "their" actions; as Achcar states, "Without in any way 'excusing' mass terrorism, one can hold the government of the United States responsible for its own actions and the hatred that they call forth" (2002, 14). Second, I am purposefully defining American violence as *violence*. This definition stems from the observation that colonial state violence is rarely defined as such, or if it is, it is usually cloaked within a cloud of moral right or national interest and/or security.

Eve Tuck and K. Wayne Yang tell us that "settler colonialism fuels imperialism all around the globe. Oil is the motor and motive for war and so was salt, so will be water. Settler sovereignty over these very pieces of earth, air, and water is what makes possible these imperialisms" (2012, 31). This theoretical context for violence is essential to examine the way violence is used as a political and/or economic instrument by both state and nonstate actors in the international system. In "Understanding Iraq" (2009), Sabah Alnasseri argues,

> Ideas like Samuel Huntington's famous "clash of civilizations" are deployed to legitimate imperial control and rule over geo-strategically and economically important spaces in the South. The discursive construction of these spaces as dangerous, terrorist, and uncivilized areas is a necessary condition for ensuring and perpetuating such control and rule. To understand Iraq and situate the extreme violence and terror in their proper context, one must understand two specific moments: the *Guantanamo-isation* of Iraq, and the reactivation of *colonial* forms of rule and social forces under new circumstances. (78, emphasis in original)

In short, Alnasseri concludes that rather than characterizing the violence in Iraq as fanatical or extremist, one must examine the ways "the occupation has created a situation which provides a breeding-ground for all kinds of atrocities" (2009, 79). Many critical Iraqi scholars have shown how the ruling elites, especially the exiles who had no local support to draw from and relied heavily on sectarianism, use the rhetoric of "sectarianism" to meet their political and economic interests. I argue that the institutionalization of sectarianism is perhaps the most damaging legacy of the Anglo-American occupation; understanding the reasons for the conditions within which ISIS emerged are vital to working toward defeating its ideology, not just its geographical strongholds. This contention is a useful point of departure for an anticolonial analysis of the emergence of ISIS in Iraq and the region.

ISIS: A Manifestation of (Neo)Colonial Violence

Drawing on anticolonial and decolonial theoretical approaches, this section focuses on three dimensions of ISIS, which, taken together, offer a more valuable and generative analysis than the conventional understandings outlined in the previous section. First, it is important to note that looking at ISIS in strictly religious terms is Orientalist and serves to perpetuate the idea of a "clash between Islam and modernity." I argue that ISIS is a *modern* phenomenon and that its use of religious rhetoric should not place it in the colonial category of "traditional." I do not want to dismiss the religious rhetoric of ISIS's targeting of non-Muslim communities such as Yazidis, Assyrians and other Christians, and Shi'a Muslims or the impact of this violence on these groups. I mean that this religious basis can be more accurately understood as Islamism, and it is thus more fruitful to analyze the alliances between Islamist groups and American interests as well as US support for Islamist groups in the region when they are perceived to serve a strategic interest. Second, many critical scholars have attributed the rise of ISIS to the US invasion of Iraq and the occupation policies of neoliberalization, de-Ba'athification, sectarianism, and support for Nouri al-Maliki, whose corruption and sectarian politics further marginalized and incensed the Sunni population. Finally, the international and regional proxy war in Syria is another important aspect of the emergence of this group that must be taken into consideration. These three aspects are interconnected; each one alone cannot explain ISIS. I begin with the contention that ISIS is a modern phenomenon: although it has roots in al-Qaeda, it is a movement that has transformed into what it is within the context of the US invasion of Iraq and the Syrian Civil War.

Unlikely Allies: American Strategic Interests and Islamists

Religion should not be the main factor for studying ISIS, but the influential Wahhabi and Salafi movements in the region cannot be overlooked. There is an ongoing debate within Islamism between Wahhabism and Salafism (see Abu-Rabi' 2010); however, I leave this religious debate aside and instead focus on the political and economic ramifications of these movements. For the purposes of this chapter, I look at the correlation of interests between the elites in both the so-called Muslim world and the United States beginning in the Cold War era. Noam Chomsky and Gilbert Achcar argue, "Islamic fundamentalism—most of whose varieties allied under Wahhabite tutelage—subsequently became the main ideological tool of the anti-communist and antinationalist struggle in the Islamic world orchestrated by Washington in alliance with Riyadh" (2002, 36). In short, the "present strength of Islamic fundamentalism is a direct product of very direct U.S. policies" (2016, 28). Moreover, not only did the United States contribute directly to the spread of Islamic fundamentalism, but the combination of America's own "repression of progressive or secular ideologies and the subjective failure—the bankruptcy—of these ideologies, aggravated by the collapse of the Soviet Union, left the ground open to the only ideological channel of anti-Western protest available, which was Islamic fundamentalism" (Chomsky and Achcar 2016, 30). Accordingly, rather than reflecting an inherent radicalness in the region, Islamic fundamentalism became a viable default for anti-Western sentiments when other forms of opposition were eliminated.

Scholars such as Samir Amin (2007), Sabah Alnasseri (2007), and Omar Shahin (in Razazan 2015) emphasize the correlation of imperialist and Islamist interests. Amin writes, "In reality, the militants of political Islam are not truly interested in discussing the dogmas that form religion." Rather, he argues, "the exclusive emphasis on culture allows political Islam to eliminate from every sphere of life the real social confrontations between the popular classes and the globalized capitalist system that oppresses and exploits them. . . . They are not means of support for the struggles of the popular classes against the system responsible for their poverty." In short, in relation to real social issues, Amin suggests that "political Islam aligns itself with the camp of dependent capitalism and dominant imperialism. It defends the principle of the sacred character of property and legitimizes the inequality and all the requirements of capitalist reproduction" (2007). Similarly, Alnasseri contends that we cannot understand the conflict in Iraq and "sectarian" civil war without understanding the neoliberalization[4] of Iraq. Speaking specifically of the Iraqi case, Alnasseri also suggests that there was a correlation between the Bush administration's interests and the Iraqi ruling classes' interests; "both of them have their own agendas and the Iraqi government is not a puppet of the US, they have their own class project, but they rely heavily on the British and American occupation in Iraq to rebuild and cement their position within the state apparatus and outside" (2007). Similarly, in an interview in *Jaddaliyya*, Shahin, a Turkish political scientist, highlights the political and economic links between ISIS and Turkey. He says, "For a long time the Turkish government gave a free passage to those jihadists which were actually flowing into Syria from Europe and from the United States and Canada." According to Shahin, President Recep Tayyip Erdoğan of Turkey benefits from supporting ISIS militarily through providing arms to Support Front (Jabhat al-Nusra) and economically through the illegal oil trade and capital because of Turkey's political interests in weakening the Kurds. Specifically, "for several months, at least, the Turkish government[,] by turning a blind eye towards the oil trade, illegal oil trade, between ISIS and some Turkish authorities, provided ISIS with some capital, which was much needed" (in Razazin 2015). In other words, "the enemy of my enemy can be my friend for the time being" is a fitting characterization of the strategic alliances made between actors in the region.

The Anglo-American Invasion and Occupation

Despite the Bush administration's claims that the Saddam regime supported al-Qaeda, it is widely accepted now that "there was hardly any activity of al-Qaeda in Iraq at the time of the US invasion" (Achcar 2015). However, during the

---

4. The term *neoliberalization* is used here consciously to challenge the rhetoric of democratization used by the US administration as a pretext for the war on Iraq.

post-2003 period, the Anglo-American coalition as well as its Iraqi exile allies labeled all resistance to the occupation as "foreign in origin and anti-Iraqi" (Ismael and Ismael 2015, 217) to propagate a narrative of "fighting terror" to justify their use of violence. Alnasseri echoes this assertion: "This is the narrative now. If you opposed the invasion or cautioned that violence will ensue as opposed to democracy with the removal of Saddam, you were accused of being either a Ba'athist or a Sunni. There is no opposition to the government and no engaging with the government as a democratic subject" (2007). One of the policies that the application of the "Ba'athi" label supported was the detainment and confinement of Iraqis; most of those deemed "insurgents" were imprisoned by American forces during the occupation. This policy ironically not only provided these "inmates" with an opportunity to organize that they may have otherwise not had but also served to radicalize them. Although recognizing that the political system in Iraq was problematic, Zyad Saeed, an Iraqi international law expert, contends that the events of 2003 (the invasion and occupation of Iraq) "manufactured a system of violence" wherein thousands of mostly young men were randomly arrested and detained in prisons in Abu Ghraib, Bucca, Mosul, and northern Iraq for several months and then released.[5] These collective punishments on large areas were implemented due to Iraqis' resistance to American occupation, a resistance that, Saeed reminds me, is a right legislated/outlined in international law.

Similarly, Sa'ad Jawad, an Iraqi professor of political science who left Iraq in 2009, points to these occupation policies as a factor in the emergence of al-Qaeda and later of ISIS in postinvasion Iraq. He posits, "But more important was . . . the brutality of the Americans against the Sunnis and especially the army officers of the old army—Iraqi army—the humiliation they were subjected to. Any of them [could] find themselves in American Iraqi prisons. And these prisons or camps were really the schools where these people—where ISIS—were established. And some of them claimed that they were even trained by the Americans to fight al-Qaeda in Iraq."[6] The US military claimed that its detention operations were valid and necessary, but Saeed points out that collective torture (he is referring to the Abu Ghraib scandal) generates people who are spiteful, disgruntled, and unlawful toward the society, the system, and those perceived to be the causes of their malcontent.[7]

5. Zyad Saeed, legal adviser to the United Nations in Iraq, Skype interview by the author, Mar. 14, 2016.

6. Sa'ad Jawad, senior visiting fellow, Middle East Centre, London School of Economics, Skype interview by the author, Mar. 2, 2016.

7. Saeed, interview, Mar. 14, 2016.

Relatedly, unsecured borders in the aftermath of the invasion and occupation policies that left the state fragmented quickly turned Iraq into a breeding ground for groups such as al-Qaeda. Jawad describes the post-2003 situation as complete chaos; "this [American occupation] created the violence: no law, no order, no courts, no police force, [not] even a traffic ordinance—*shorta al muroor*—he [*sic*] couldn't do his duty." Furthermore, he recounts, the occupation "left the country open to organized crime, to revenge, to stealing—to the mobs, . . . and to the militias that came. And this is what created violence. Some of these people covered their crimes through 'sectarianism.' . . . And the government, the US, and their administration between 2003 and 2004 and 2005 did nothing."[8]

Echoing Jawad, Zaid al-Ali recalls, "Iraq was fertile soil for sectarian violence. . . . After 2003, the absence of the rule of law, the absence of security institutions, was a main contributor to violence."[9] This chaos was combined with a lack of state security, which further empowered various sectarian militias and contributed to the fragmentation of the state along sectarian lines. Within this context, criminal activity also became a source of financial gain; despite the sectarian rhetoric, many of my interviewees reported that financial gain in an atmosphere of lawlessness and severe unemployment (owing to the dissolution of the state) was a major contributing factor to this type of violence.

Under the occupation, the neoliberalization of the economy and the Iraqi state's failure to provide for its citizens also gave rise to conditions that led to a violent resistance to the occupation and allowed jihadist groups such as al-Qaeda and later ISIS to grow. The "Bremer Orders" created in 2004 by Paul Bremer under the Coalition Provisional Authority were essentially geared toward opening the Iraqi economy to foreign control; what is important to note here is that these orders entailed the remaking of Iraq in America's image while "virtually ignoring the pressing needs of the Iraqi people" (Juhasz 2004, 19). This lack of attention to the needs of ordinary Iraqis was a major advantage to al-Qaeda and later ISIS. The link between mass poverty and oppression, on the one side, and social upheaval and violence, on the other, is a well-established one. In grappling with the question of why we see the emergence of fanatical reactionary ideologies, Achcar argues, "In fact, these expressions of deep social frustrations cannot be separated from the dismantling of the welfare state, the rise of unemployment, and the increasing precariousness of life wrought by neoliberal policies." Furthermore, he states, we cannot defeat these currents through ideology; we "need above all to end the

8. Jawad, interview, Mar. 2, 2016.
9. Zaid al-Ali, legal adviser to the United Nations in Iraq, Skype interview by the author, Mar. 11, 2016.

conditions that constitute a breeding ground for their ideologies, and these are social, economic and political conditions" (2015). Indeed, these conditions were evident in Iraq because of the occupation policies; "the weight of the counterinsurgency operations from the Anglo-American occupation was followed by the neglect and military responses of the al-Maliki regime to any expression of local demands" (Ismael and Ismael 2015, 219).

These local demands included a perception that only the Shi'a were the beneficiaries of the newly created Iraqi state. I argue that rather than understanding sectarianism as a natural phenomenon in Iraq, we must acknowledge that institutionalized sectarianism in the post-2003 Iraqi political system under the occupation fueled much of this seeming "sectarian" violence. The al-Maliki government's lack of response to local Sunni demands further exacerbated the situation. Not only the government's neglect of the Sunni but also its violent response in Kirkuk escalated the tensions and strengthened the ISIS stronghold. It is important to highlight the marginal position of populations outside of the Kurdish- and Shi'a-controlled areas, especially following the withdrawal of the US military in 2011. Tarek Ismael and Jacqueline Ismael argue, "Without political representation, or basic security, this [withdrawal] left northern and western Iraq outside the writ of the KRG [Kurdistan Regional Government] particularly vulnerable. Composed of a majority of Sunni Arabs, as well as an enormously diverse array of ethnic and religious minorities, these regions had borne the brunt of heavy fighting in opposition to occupation and the new political order implanted by Anglo-American military power" (2015, 219). Two important things occurred following the US withdrawal from Iraq: one, there was a vast delinking of the Kurdish region and the "Iraqi federal project," and, two, al-Maliki's focus on Baghdad and the competition between the Shi'a groups in the South left "Anbar and the Nineveh provinces to wither" (Ismael and Ismael 2015, 220). These factors account for the lack of Iraqi state authority (or legitimacy) in these regions along with the regions' increasing dissatisfaction and opposition to the state.

Sectarianism was further institutionalized through another occupation policy under the leadership of Paul Bremer of the Coalition Provisional Authority: the "de-Ba'athification" of Iraq and the disbanding of the Iraqi army. Many widely held assumptions or narratives became dominant in the aftermath of 2003. One was that the Ba'ath regime was sectarian or Sunni in composition, as if "Sunni" is a homogenous category. Notwithstanding the fact that Saddam was a dictator who made no pretense to electoral legitimacy, the reality is that, aside from a narrow elite that benefited from the state, most Iraqis, regardless of sectarian identity, lived under a dictatorship with little to no civil and political rights and severe consequences for opposition to the regime. Sa'ad Jawad posits, "Saddam Hussein was brutal to Sunnis, Shi'is, Kurds, Christians, and . . . whoever challenged or opposed his policy. He did not concentrate on one section; he murdered, he assassinated or executed, people from his own town Tikrit in the same way that he executed people from Mosul or Baghdad or Najaf or Karbala or Basra. Or Kurds. Once he [felt] that there [was] a threat to his rule . . . he used to become very brutal and execute people."[10] More importantly, newly empowered Kurdish and Shi'a political parties,[11] in alliance with the United States, used this narrative of victimization or oppression by the previous regime strategically to gain legitimacy and political power "because it served them."[12] This is not to suggest that the Ba'ath regime did not marginalize certain groups religiously, politically, economically, or culturally; rather, I mean to complicate what have become simplified and homogenized sectarian categories, "Sunni" and "Shi'a." Moreover, dividing powers between Shi'a and Kurdish parties as a mechanism to "right the wrongs" of a regime but at the expense of every other group in Iraq is not just. Practically, de-Ba'athification and the disbanding of the army left a significant portion of the population not only without employment but also disenfranchised from the new state. This policy also had dangerous implications in that the increasingly disenfranchised population included a significant proportion of highly trained military personnel.

Regional Politics, the War in Syria

Other states' geostrategic concerns in the region are also important to take into consideration when analyzing seemingly regional support for ISIS. Saudi Arabia, a state that perceives itself as the keeper of the faith of the so-called Islamic world, has long rivaled Iran for hegemonic status in the region. Although the sectarian animosities between these two states can be real, as conventional analysis by Western political scientists suggests, the colonial and racist foundations that underpin leading international relations theories allow scholars to ignore such tenets in their examination of non-Western countries' foreign policies. That is, realist and neoliberal theories of international relations are used to analyze the foreign policies of states in the Global North, but the foreign policies of states in the Global South—in this case, Southwest Asia—are often characterized as dominated by irrational behaviors, tribal or sectarian affiliations, and fanaticism rather than by

---

10. Jawad, interview, Mar. 2, 2016.

11. It is important to emphasize political *parties* here because although these parties were empowered, the everyday lives of their constituents were not improved due to the party leaders' self-interest and corruption.

12. Jawad, interview, Mar. 2, 2016.

geostrategic or economic or political interests. This chapter is intended to serve as a critique and a challenge to this perception of Southwest Asia as "outside of the range" of international relations theory. As such, this subsection highlights regional politics and the war in Syria through the lens of geostrategy, economy, and politics.

The complete destruction of the Iraqi state had very real implications for the region. A longtime ally of the United States, King Abdullah of Jordan referred to the dangers of a "'Shia crescent' in December 2004, one stretching from Damascus to Tehran, passing through Baghdad" (Alaaldin 2015) because of the ambiguous nature of the newly "re-created" Iraq but also because of Iran's perceived heavy influence within the state. However, I suggest that what Ranj Alaaldin calls "sectarian polarisation of the region" (2015) is states behaving in accordance with realpolitik in the region, as the current colonial structure of the international system dictates.[13] That is, with a weakened Iraqi state as its neighbor, Iran seized the opportunity to utilize religious affiliations as a mechanism to build strategic alliances with parties in Iraq to ensure its own political interests in the region. Saudi Arabia's and other Persian Gulf states' subsequent support of ISIS initially can be seen as resulting from a perception of ISIS as serving to push back Iranian influence, a perception cloaked in a "Shi'a versus Sunni" discourse. I am not suggesting that the differences between these religious sects in Iraq are not real, especially considering that the differences have had a decade to coagulate; rather, I am arguing that the politicization of these identities gives them these specific meanings. Ironically, the politicization of these identities serves to *depoliticize* what is happening in Iraq and the region. Similarly, Turkey supports ISIS to elevate its position as Islamist in the Southwest Asia and North Africa region.[14] Osman Shahin argues, "Prime Minister Ahmet Davutoglu sees Turkey as a leader of the Islamic world. He sees and he thinks that Turkey has a potential to fulfill [that role] in

13. I recognize that I have critiqued conventional international relations theory throughout this chapter. I am not advocating the tenets of realpolitik; my intention here is to emphasize that conventional or predominant understandings of the international system are conventional because they are perpetuated by *all* actors in the system (in both the Global North and the Global South). I am pointing to the discrepancy between the labeling of behavior by states in the Global North as "rational" or based on "national interest" in accordance with conventional theory and the labeling of similar behavior by states in the Global South as "irrational" or "fanatical" according to a *different* standard. I am identifying this discrepancy as colonial and racist.

14. Like the category "Middle East," the designation "Middle East and North Africa" has colonial and problematic roots that do not reflect the rich, plural, and historical realities of this region. "Southwest Asia(n) and North Africa(n)," in contrast, is a decolonial name for the region and the states that compose it.

the Middle East." Committed to the revival of the Ottoman Empire, "[Davutoglu] says Turkey has to revive its potential and become the cultural, economic, and political leader of the region." Moreover, the "2011 uprisings from the perspective of Davutoglu gave the Turkish Republic the much-needed opportunity to seize the moment, so they wanted to actually create a Sunni belt. . . . Erdogan and Davutoglu think that Turkish Republic should be the leader of the Sunni world" (in Razazan 2015). Religious or sectarian rhetoric is used as a mechanism to compete with the Shi'ite Iranian state, a competition historically contextualized as a political and economic contest between the two empires turned nation-states.

The sectarianization of Iraqi politics was not a single phenomenon but had regional reverberations. Alnasseri calls this the "regional moment" wherein the "sectarianization and militarization of the conflict in Iraq and Syria and Libya, etc. are nothing but the mechanism through which the US and other, European imperialists, like the UK and France and their regional supporters[,] . . . push back against the Arab revolutions, . . . push back against people's demands, and . . . try to reproduce the status quo ante before the revolutions. So, it is a means through which the United States try [sic] to stabilize its regional allies against the demands of the people" (2014).

The invasion and occupation of Iraq gave Iran an opportunity to exert its influence in Iraq through certain Shi'a groups, such as the Supreme Council of the Islamic Revolution of Iraq and the Dawah Party. Achcar argues that "resentment against the US occupation was compounded by the fact that Iran was taking advantage of it in order to spread its influence. This prepared the ground for the growth of Al-Qaeda in Sunni Arab regions" (2015). These resentments incited domestic tensions among the various interest groups in Iraq. However, "regionally, the invasion of Iraq and the unfolding developments amplified sectarian tensions, with Jordanian King Abdullah warning of an incipient 'Shia crescent' threatening the region while Saudi King Abdullah—in a conversation with his American interlocutor—exhorted an attack on Iran to 'cut off the head of the (Shia) snake'" (Ismael and Ismael 2015, 40). At the same time, a moment of mass movements demanding civil and economic rights swept the region, giving way to optimism. This moment was quickly repressed when protests in Syria were met with violent government opposition, which turned into a civil war and sectarian conflict exacerbated by Iran, Saudi Arabia, and Qatar and drawing in Iraq, Lebanon, and Turkey (Ismael and Ismael 2015).

There were reports that Bashar al-Assad's government released jihadis from prison in 2011, thus militarizing the conflict within Syria to give credibility to his narrative that "his is a war against terrorism and not against a civil rebellion" (Prashad 2014). There is no evidence to suggest Assad created ISIS, though; "ISIS is a product of the U.S. war on Iraq, having been formed first as al-Qaeda in Iraq by the Jordanian militant Abu Musab al-Zarqawi" (Prashad 2014). However, Assad did play a role in strengthening ISIS and allowing it passage across Syria's borders, especially as it served his purposes in maintaining power. Achcar argues that Assad's motivation was to show that the only alternative to his regime was jihadism, which is why his government allowed al-Qaeda to enter Syria and released militants from jail in the fall of 2011 (Achcar 2015). Iraqi government officials emphasized this link, which was also fortified by the de-Ba'athification of Iraq. Speaking to the strategic alliance between the old Ba'athists and ISIS, Sa'ad Jawad asserts, "The golden opportunity came to ISIS when the Syrian situation exploded. They found a very good environment to develop, and, of course, the staff officers are mainly Iraqi old army officers, so they went in[to] Syria in the hope of establishing their main base there."[15] Cooperation between the former leaders of the Ba'ath Party and ISIS was strategic for both sides; the Ba'athis "thought they could use ISIS to occupy Mosul and advance to Tikrit and Anbar because there was no real army to get rid of them, and a lot of the members of the [new] Iraqi army were bribed by the members of ISIS and Ba'athists at that time, and [ISIS leaders] thought they could use [those members] to establish a base in Iraq."[16] Occupation policies, despite their persisting legacies, cannot at this juncture in Iraqi politics be the sole factor under consideration in understanding the violence in the region. American-selected and supported political elites' sectarian policies and corruption have also been damaging. More problematically, these elites are entrenched in the political sphere, even though they do not represent "the people" or reflect their will.

Conclusion: There Is Still a *Spark* in Iraq

To attempt to provide an exhaustive analysis of the emergence of violent and regressive movements such as ISIS in Iraq and Syria within the confines of a single chapter is an arduous task. Thus, my aim here is to provide a nuanced examination of ISIS rooted in the critical analyses by scholars from Southwest Asia. The successes of ISIS and its rapid or growing recruitment rate do not make it a revolutionary or countercultural movement; rather, a substantial critique grounded in the colonial global order reveals the underlying symptomatic causes of such regressive violence. In other words, it is important to understand the geopolitical, colonial, and imperial context that gives rise to Islamism in the wider Southwest Asia and North Africa region. Specifically, I contextualize the violence in post-2003 Iraq

15. Jawad, interview, Mar. 2, 2016.
16. Jawad, interview, Mar. 2, 2016.

within the Anglo-American invasion, occupation policies, the al-Maliki government, and regional politics, especially the war in Syria. I suggest that anticolonial
and decolonial theories offer a nuanced, historically contextualized, and *politicized* approach to studying ISIS. I am using a politicized analysis here as an alternative and a challenge to the depoliticized cultural analysis of sectarianism and
religion, which is based on Oriental and racist ideas about the region and its people. More importantly, I argue that we cannot understand this violence without
situating it within the dialectical relationship between the international and the
domestic—between "us" and "them." The colonial understanding that violence is
inherent to the "other" and that there will be an inevitable "clash between us and
them" is not only problematic but also dangerous; it is also ahistorical and results
in a perpetually reinforcing cycle of violence in the international system. This is
why although a military response can indeed "win the battle" against ISIS, it will
not eradicate the ideology on which ISIS draws and grows. Echoing many critical
scholars, I contend that a decolonial response to the social, economic, and political
grievances of historically and systemically marginalized groups is a more substantial solution to the crisis of colonial modernity that has characterized this era in
international relations.

It is especially important to avoid pointing to an ever-lasting conflict between
movements such as ISIS, which use the rhetoric of religion, and the West. This
is both a very simple and a problematic assertion. In contrast, I argue that ISIS
is a *symptom* of colonial modernity's failure to meet people's everyday needs.
It is also a *reaction* to violent colonial practices in the Global South, a reaction
that has been cultivated and nurtured by the alliances between Islamist groups,
regional powers such as Saudi Arabia, and American strategic interests. It is also
inaccurate to paint an entire country (and region) as inherently fundamentalist
or radical, a characterization rooted in colonial Orientalist understandings that
absolves foreign colonial powers of complicity in the violence that these movements inflict on everyday people and groups. Most of my interviewees pointed
to the large schism between the people and the American-installed or supported
political leaders in post-2003 Iraq. Yanar Mohammed, president of the Organization for Women's Freedom in Iraq, maintained that demonstrations in Baghdad's
Tahrir Square have been continuous and nonsectarian in nature, despite the Islamist parties' relentless attempts at taking over the demonstrations to *sectarianize*
them and render them meaningless.[17] In 2012 and 2013, there were protests against

---

17. Yanar Mohammed, president of the Organization for Women's Freedom in Iraq, Skype
interview by the author, Apr. 8, 2016.

corruption, sectarianism, and government incompetence; "there is a spark and there are people who really want to move beyond that, especially young people, especially women," states Nadje al-Ali.[18] Similarly, Mohammad recalls the mass protests in the summer of 2015 under the slogan "B'ism al-deen bagona al-harami-yah," meaning, "The thieves plundered us in the name of religion." She continues, "This happened in Baghdad, this happened in Basra, this happened in Nasiriyah," emphasizing that "these are major footholds or the castles of the Shi'a Islamist parties, who are the ones in power."[19] These sorts of protests were happening early in the occupation and continue today—even more intensely and on a wider scale since October 2019. Yet greater attention was and continues to be placed on those who took up arms (which were readily available in post-2003 Iraq).[20] To disregard the struggles of Iraqis—across sects and ethnicities—to make their voices heard against the occupation, American-selected or supported political elites, sectarianism, and the government's corruption and general incompetence—not only perpetuates Orientalist depictions of Iraqis as *fanatic*, *radical*, and *undemocratic* but also misses the critical grassroots mobilization that happens in Iraqi society.

References

Abughaida, Dareen. 2021. "Is ISIS-K a Challenge for the Taliban?" *Inside Story*, al Jazeera, Aug. 30. At https://www.aljazeera.com/program/inside-story/2021/8/30/is-isis-k-a-challenge-for-the-taliban.

Abu-Rabi', Ibrahim M., ed. 2010. *The Contemporary Arab Reader on Political Islam*. UK: Pluto Press.

Achcar, Gilbert. 2002. *The Clash of Barbarisms: September 11 and the Making of the New World Disorder*. New York: Monthly Review Press.

———. 2015. "Northing Mysterious about Islamic State." Interview by Farooq Sulehria. *News on Sunday*, Dec. 27. At http://tns.thenews.com.pk/nothing-mysterious-islamic-state-interview-gilbert-achcar/#.Vt3aVpMrKb8.

Alaaldin, Ranj. 2015. "Shia Crescent: Self-Fulfilling Prophecy." *Open Democracy*, Apr. 3. At https://www.opendemocracy.net/ranj-alaaldin/shia-crescent-selffulfilling-prophecy.

Alnasseri, Sabah. 2007. "Sectarianism and What's Going on in Iraq." Video episode of "Global Flashpoints: Reactions to Imperialism and Neoliberalism," *Socialist Register*, Nov. 16. At https://www.youtube.com/watch?v=O0vOOJVAuP0.

———. 2009. "Understanding Iraq." *Socialist Register* 44, no. 44: 76–100.

18. Nadje al-Ali, professor, School of African and Oriental Studies, Univ. of London, Skype interview by the author, Apr. 13, 2016.

19. Mohammed, interview, Apr. 8, 2016.

20. All of the interviewees made references to this phenomenon.

———. 2014. "ISIS Fills Power Vacuum in Iraq Fundamentally Created by U.S. Foreign Policy." Interview by Anton Woronczuk. *Real News*, June 12. At http://therealnews.com/t2/index.php?option=com_content&task=view&id=31&Itemid=74&jumival=11986.

Amin, Samir. 2007. "Political Islam in the Service of Imperialism." *Monthly Review* 59, no. 7. At http://monthlyreview.org/2007/12/01/political-islam-in-the-service-of-imperialism/.

Bush, George W. 2001. "State of the Union Address." *Washington Post*, Jan. 28. At https://www.washingtonpost.com/wp-srv/onpolitics/transcripts/bushtext_012803.html.

Chomsky, Noam, and Gilbert Achcar. 2016. *Perilous Power: The Middle East & U.S. Foreign Policy Dialogues on Terror, Democracy, War, and Justice.* Exp. ed. New York: Routledge.

Das, Veena. 2001. "Violence and Translation." *Anthropological Quarterly* 75, no. 1: 105–12.

Debord, Guy. 1994. *The Society of the Spectacle.* Translated by Donald Nicholson-Smith. Brooklyn, NY: Zone. Orig. pub. in French in 1967.

Fanon, Frantz. 2004. *The Wretched of the Earth.* Translated by Richard Philcox. With a foreword by Homi K. Bhabha and a preface by Jean-Paul Sartre. New York: Grove Press. Orig. pub. in French in 1961.

Gerges, Fawaz. 2016. *ISIS: A Short History.* Princeton, NJ: Princeton Univ. Press.

Gregory, Derek. 2004. *The Colonial Present: Afghanistan, Palestine, Iraq.* Oxford: Blackwell.

Ismael, Tarek Y., and Jacqueline S. Ismael. 2015. *Iraq in the Twenty-First Century: Regime Change and the Making of a Failed State.* New York: Routledge.

Al-Jaberi, Ali. 2014. "Iraq Crisis: Divide-and-Rule in Defence of a Neoliberal Political Economy." *Open Democracy*, July 1. At https://www.opendemocracy.net/arab-awakening/ali-aljaberi/iraq-crisis-divideandrule-in-defence-of-neoliberal-political-economy.

Juhasz, Antonio. 2004. "Capitalism Gone Wild." *Tikkun* 19, no. 1: 19–22.

Kalyvas, Stathis N. 2015. "Is ISIS a Revolutionary Group and If Yes, What Are the Implications?" *Perspective on Terrorism* 9, no. 4: 42–47.

Mahdavi, Mojtaba. 2013. "Muslims and Modernities: From Islamism to Post-Islamism?" *Religious Studies and Theology* 32, no. 1: 57–71.

Prashad, Vijay. 2014. "The Geopolitics of the Islamic State." *Hindu*, July 3. At http://www.thehindu.com/opinion/lead/the-geopolitics-of-the-islamic-state/article6170651.ece.

Razazan, Malihe. 2015. "A Shift in Turkey's Foreign Policy? An Interview with Osman Shahin." *Jadaliyya*, July 30. At http://www.jadaliyya.com/pages/index/22301/a-shift-in-turkeys-foreign-policy-an-interview-wit.

Tuck, Eve, and K. Wayne Yang. 2012. "Decolonization Is Not a Metaphor." *Decolonization: Indigeneity, Education, & Society* 1, no. 1: 1–40.

Vu, Tuong, and Patrick Van Orden. 2020. "Revolution and World Order: The Case of the Islamic State (ISIS)." *International Politics* 57, no. 1: 57–78.

Walt, Stephen M. 2015. "ISIS as Revolutionary State." *Foreign Affairs* 94 (Nov.–Dec.). At https://www.foreignaffairs.com//articles/middle-east/2015-11-01/isis-revolutionary-state.

6

Recolonizing the Arab World?

Tariq Ali

Fractious political scenes in Egypt and Tunisia, simmering strife in Yemen, armed anarchy in Libya, civil war in Syria, governmental crisis in Lebanon, crackdown in Bahrain, boosted regional weight for Saudi Arabia and Qatar—these are some of the salient outcomes that followed the uprisings of the Arab Spring (see Ali 2013a, 2013b).[1] Given these highly contested and contentious developments, how should we judge the outcomes of these uprisings that exploded across the Arab world in the spring of 2011? Are there any patterns to be discerned in the Arab present? In this chapter, I examine the development and the fate of the uprisings that swept the Arab region. I argue that to understand the Arab Spring and its mixed outcome, we need to situate it within the broader geopolitical politics of the region and its historical and modern struggles against Western colonialism and American imperialism.

In carrying out this analysis, the chapter adopts a fourfold approach. In the first two sections, I unpack the meaning and effect of European colonialism and American imperialism on the possibilities of democratic reforms in the region. The third section focuses on the spread of jihadist views in the Arab region; in it, I trace the rise of the Islamic State of Iraq and Syria (ISIS), also known as the Islamic State of Iraq and the Levant (ISIL), and highlight the role of the United States and its allies in the development of ISIS. In the final section, I elucidate the spread of Islamophobia in Europe and the United States and map the influence of Islamophobic policies on the politics of dissent and resistance in the region. The chapter concludes by emphasizing the effect of the social movements in the Arab world. I argue that although these social movements are experiencing a period of defeat, the new generation, which is now coming of political age, is different from

---

1. I detail the meaning and significance of these setbacks and their implications for democratic reform in the region in "Between Past and Future" (Ali 2013a).

preceding generations. Its members are forming and creating their own politics, and that is the greatest source of hope for the Middle East and North Africa.

Historicizing Arab Politics

I do not believe in "Arab exceptionalism," but in my view it is impossible to understand the Arab world without understanding the following three factors: European colonialism, American imperialism, and the creation of Israel.

European Colonialism and the Circumscribed States

Under Ottoman rule, people in the region were not divided into nation-states; they were part of the Ottoman Empire. The main travel routes were from city to city rather than from state to state: from Baghdad to Jerusalem, Jerusalem to Cairo, Baghdad to Amman, Amman to Damascus. People moved freely in the Ottoman Empire, not within circumscribed states. Such states were a "gift" from the British and French after they won World War I. It is always interesting to think of what might have happened had the Ottomans sided with the Western Allies and not with Germany in the war—how what became Yugoslavia and the Middle East would have differed. As a consequence of the war, these areas were given borders. For example, the region called "Syria" or "Greater Syria" was sliced, and the French created the coastal strip called "Lebanon" because they thought they needed to have a strip of land in case of emergency. A constitution imposed on "Lebanon" was problematic because it divided political positions along religious/ethnic lines.

All these states in the Arab world were created effectively after World War I and strengthened after World War II. For example, Saudi Arabia has been one of the biggest problems in the region since World War II, when the British Empire signed a compact with the House of Saud (al Sa'ud), the ruling royal family, which has been in power ever since. As the British Empire was collapsing, the Americans under the Franklin Roosevelt administration took over that empire's colonial interests and backed a monarchy based on a small religious sect, the Wahhabis, a sect that is also considered tiny within Sunni Islam globally. In the Arabian Peninsula, little tribal leaders were given tiny kingdoms, which became the imperial petrol stations that we now know as the Arab monarchies of the Persian Gulf states.

Outside the peninsula, Iraq had a monarchy; Jordan has a monarchy—cousins of the Wahhabis from a different family. The French, who were apportioned domination in Syria, refused to tolerate a monarchy for Syria because of their republican tradition, it was argued. "We are colonialist and imperialists, but our tradition is different: we are not going to impose a monarchy!"—something that apparently did not bother them in the case of Morocco. Hence, I am not inclined to treat this decision regarding Syria as demonstrating French republicanism.

It is worth noting that there was not even an ounce of democracy in the countries governed, if not directly ruled, by imperial powers, and yet the imperial powers proclaimed democracy to be one of their motivations for occupation and interference. They constantly talked about it but never allow it to be practiced in the colonies. Therefore, some of the early hostility to democracy in the former colonies arose from the fact that these states had been created and dominated by "democratic" British and French imperialists in the interval years.

The first wave of a break with the old European empires came in the 1950s and 1960s with military revolutions in Egypt, Syria, and Iraq, and for the first time there was discussion of a United Arab Nation with three concurrent capitals. This idea did not succeed, not because of the imperial powers but because of a problem within the newly independent entities. The weaknesses of the Arab revolutionary leaders made it impossible to create a meaningful alternative to the colonial rule. Moreover, because of their hostility to the West, the Arab revolutionary leaders preferred the Soviet one-party-dominated polity, which they genuinely thought a progressive alternative to the West. There has thus been no tradition of democratic rule in most of these countries. Democracy was not the priority of the European imperial powers, and democracy is not the priority of the American imperial power today.

Furthermore, we should not mystify the term *democracy*. It is known that the West and North America achieved democracy in the fullest sense of the word only after World War I, when women were given the right to vote. Prior to that, there was a truncated democracy based on gender and partially also based on property and race. So the idea that capitalism and democracy coexist is not true. Capitalism existed for six hundred years prior to the first signs of democracy. It is also worth recalling that democracy was obtained through struggle. The revolution in the United States, which did drive out the British, meant that the rebels had to write a constitution, but in that document they denied Blacks and women the right to vote. It was a democratic constitution within limits. Even in Britain, democracy came only through huge struggles over a period of two hundred years. We thus need to understand the quest for democracy on a global scale.

United States: Recolonizing the Arab World

To understand what has been happening in the Arab world since the early 1990s, one has to understand a huge event that took place in world history: the implosion of the Soviet Union and its satellite states in eastern Europe. This development resulted in the horrific reentry of capitalism into these countries, which punished the people, not the elite. In most cases, members of the former elite became oligarchs in the new regimes. A majority of Russian oligarchs continued to be members of the party apparatus in one way or another.

This event took the United States by surprise. It was not prepared for the upheaval despite the huge amount of money it expended on intelligence services and the buying of Soviet spies. The United States had made the mistake of exaggerating Soviet strength militarily and thus failed to see the internal dynamism; it could not believe that leaders from within would dismantle their state while not intending to do so. The collapse of this huge chunk of the world opened up the narrative of globalization but also the emergence of the United States as the world's only imperial power—something that has never before happened in the history of humanity.

From the period of the ancient world right until today, this is the first time that a single country has dominated the world, whose military strength equals that of all the major powers put together. Despite a lot of talk saying that the United States is collapsing or that it is near the end, which I do not believe, it remains a dominate player in the world: an empire from which arose the single most important development that more or less determines everything now—how we think, write, and communicate. The internet did not come from Japan, China, or Europe; it came from the United States. The United States is not finished; we have to deal with it and understand it for what it is.

Prior to the collapse of the Soviet Union, the US fight was against communism, which represented or was claimed to be an alternative socioeconomic system. The United States effectively and accurately claimed its superiority in that it had freedom or democratic rights, whose absence was a major failure in the Soviet system. However, in the post-Soviet era and long before September 11, 2001 (9/11), in the 1990s the George H. W. Bush administration was wondering how to function in a world where everyone has the same economic system as the United States. As a result, a process with the aim of articulating a new world order emerged: the United States was thinking about invading Iraq long before 9/11. When 9/11 happened, Secretary of State Condoleezza Rice said that the United States should now use it as an opportunity to change the world as the Americans saw fit (Ali 2015).

The recolonization of the Arab world is taking place because the world's only imperial power wants it to take place. The current model of recolonization favored by the United States differs from colonization practiced by other imperial powers. Historically speaking, the European empires, whether the British in India or the French in Africa, took large tracks of land, ran the countries, and set up countries on their own model.

The American model of empire has always been a bit different. In the old days, Americans didn't particularly like the model of directly occupying countries and keeping them with US troops there permanently. The way they governed the colonies of their empire, mainly in South America, was through local relays: local politicians, oligarchs, and crooks of one sort or the other. After the disastrous occupation of Iraq and its big political failure, Americans want to move back to an old way of governing the world, but they are not getting very far.

The Arab Spring took the United States by surprise. Despite all of its intelligence networks, it did not predict these rebellions. You can have all the surveillance you want, but you rarely predict such events because you are looking only for very obvious forms of revolt. When a revolt takes on a different form, it is virtually unpredictable to you, as was the Occupation of the Squares of the Tunisian movement in 2010. Moreover, the speed with which the Tunisian dictator, President Zin El Abidine Ben Ali, fled the country was another important aspect of that crisis. Victory was immediate. The French tried to persuade their loyal ally, Ben Ali, not to leave. The French defense minister communicated a special message to Ben Ali, asking him to hold on to power and promising that French troops would be on the way to protect the regime and save it from falling (Ali 2013b). Ben Ali, however, refused to wait. He knew more about himself and his wealth than the French did, in all likelihood. He thus got out with the money, and whether the money is in a Swiss bank or a Saudi Arabian bank we do not know, but probably in both.

The Creation of Israel

In addition to European colonialism and American imperialism, the third factor that entered the Arab world and partially explains the current crisis in the region is the creation of Israel in 1948 by the British Empire, which was later backed by the United States. The Arab population as a whole saw Israel as a huge wound in the Arab body politic. The more intelligent Israeli leaders knew what they were doing; it is clear in the writings of the early Zionists such as David Ben-Gurion and Moshe Dayan that they knew that the Arabs would fight back. "How could they not fight us," they argued, "when we are kicking them off the land and when we are stealing their property?" Some of the Zionist leaders were even determined to depopulate the new state of its non-Jewish residents; they wanted a home that matched the myth of a "land without a people" that they had fostered in Europe (Ali 2003). This idea was rejected, but the discussion certainly took place. The Israeli leaders knew what was going to come; they were not surprised.

It is an open question whether Israel would have been created had there not been a Judeocide in Europe, in which millions of Jewish people were wiped out with very little intervention by either the United States or Britain. The United States and Britain knew where the railway tracks were going; they received intelligence reports warning that Jews were being incinerated in the extermination camps. It is ironic that even though the United States and Britain did not bomb those railway lines, they continue to boast in some cases that they fought for Jews. Tony Blair, former prime minister of Great Britain, once claimed that Britain fought World War II to save the Jews. He is completely blind to history.

The West is complicit in the creation of Israel, which until now remains an unsolved problem. The Palestinian Arabs were not responsible for the genocide of the Jewish people in Europe, but they have become its indirect victims. They are treated as marginal people both by Israel and by its allies.

People are only beginning to take notice of the Palestinian struggle thanks to the boycott, divestment, and sanction movement (BDS), a grassroots movement that sprang up among young people on university campuses. BDS has scared Israel and its supporters much more than Hamas or other militant groups because BDS is much larger in scale and has both a moral and an economic effect.

It is troubling how the Israel–Palestine issue has become a forbidden subject. It is not a question of terrorism because many anti-Zionist Jews participate in the debates. I often ask North American journalists, "Could you not just plead with your editors to publish one article a week from the Israeli newspaper *Haaretz*? Just one. We are not asking for too much—articles by Amira Hass or Gideon Levy, people who write and tell the truth in Israel." I am not sure why this cannot be done in the West. What Israelis can read, it seems, Western citizens cannot read because the latter would get very upset and might actually begin to do something about the issue.

If discussion is sealed off, not just on this level but on other levels, too, then what is happening to democracy in the West indicates that we are in some ways close to the twilight years of democracy. What is permitted is decreed from above: you can talk about this, but you cannot talk about that (Ali 2015, 2016).

In my book *The Extreme Centre: A Warning* (2015), I warn against the decline of democracy in many Western societies. Scholars have been mapping what has been happening to democracy in the European Union and elsewhere (Mair 2013; Streeck 2014). Building upon their insights, I argue that the extreme center is the political expression of the neoliberal state. Economics and politics are so intertwined and interlinked that both mainstream politics and extreme-center politics are now little else but a version of concentrated economics. The implication of this entanglement is that any alternative—alternative capitalism, left Keynesianism, intervention by the state to help the poor, the rolling back of privatization—becomes a huge issue. The entire weight of the extreme center and its media is turned against any such alternative, a bullying that in reality now is beginning to harm democracy in the West. The ailing Western democratic model is thus not a very good example for the Arab world to emulate in its search for democratic reform.

What Went Wrong? Historicizing the Arab Spring

What went wrong with the Arab Spring? This mass movement was amazing. The spontaneity was fantastic, and the speed with which the movement spread from one country to the other was incredible. The demands, however, remained unclear. A week after the events in the Arab world, I wrote that what we were witnessing was perhaps an "Arab 1848" resembling events in Europe in 1848 (Ali 2011). But it was not quite like that. Some of the demands that the Europeans took up in 1848—freedom, justice, equality, and solidarity—were absent in the Arab Spring movement. A demand for freedom was present, but solidarity with the rest of the Arab world was not consciously sought on virtually any level, which marked a big move back from the movements of the 1950s and 1960s.

Everything that happens has a past; it has a history. By the time the Arab Spring happened, any remnant of progressive Arab politics had been virtually wiped out from the political landscape. Memories of the Arab Left, which used to be very strong, were absent. For example, the Iraqi Communist Party was one of the largest Communist parties in the Middle East, with Christians, Muslims, Sunnis, Shi'as, and women on its central committee. The former Iraqi president Saddam Hussein wiped the party out on the CIA's watch. Relations between Saddam Hussein and the West were once amiable; the West in fact used the former Iraqi president to fight Iran in the 1980s when revolutionary Iran became the big threat to Western powers. The fight involved an intolerable, appalling, and totally unnecessary eight-year war (1980–88) in which millions of Iraqis and Iranians suffered.

Moreover, the Six-Day War of 1967 was decisive in defeating Arab nationalism. It created a huge vacuum in which the traditional Islamist groups, such as the Jamaat Islami in Pakistan and the Muslim Brotherhood in Egypt and other parts of the region, rose. Many of the Islamists who worked with the United States in the Cold War era offered an alternative—an alternative that could be *loosely* termed progressive. They were simply opposed to the incumbent authoritarian and corrupt regimes. Given the lack of any other choice, they were thus successful in filling the gap created by the neoliberal policies being applied in all these countries. I remember interviewing a leader of the Muslim Brotherhood in Cairo several years ago, and I asked him very calmly, "How do you explain your popularity? I have seen it with my own eyes." He answered, "If you think that we go around forcing people to recite the Qur'an every time we talk to them, we would not get very far.

We do not do that." He then said, "Do you know what is the largest group that works with us in Egypt? It is the doctors. We control the Doctors' Union. We set up free clinics in many poor areas, not just in Cairo, and give people free medicine, free doctors, free consultation, and of course they know who we are." A Jamaat Islami leader once told me exactly the same thing in Pakistan.

Hence, the popularity of the Muslim Brotherhood in Egypt and of Jamaat Islami in Pakistan is not just owing to their ideology or religion; it stems more than that. It comes from taking over social services that the state no longer provides. It also comes from being the voice of a well-organized opposition, which no longer existed after the regimes completely wiped out the old leftist progressive oppositions.

The Arab Spring was therefore brought to an end very soon because there was no political alternative to authoritarian rule. It is true that the Muslim Brotherhood in Egypt won the first elections after the Mubarak regime was brought down. The Brotherhood, however, won because it was seen as the representative of the movement, and there was no other well-organized political party to compete against it. Algeria faced a similar challenge in the 1990s. The Algerian government, with heavy pressure from the French, stopped an election midway when it saw the Islamists were winning. This interference created a civil war in which both sides committed bloody crimes. The civil war destroyed the social fabric of Algeria, which is only now at long last beginning to recover from the grave repercussions of this conflict. In Egypt, the elections brought in Mohamed Morsi as the new president in June 2012. Luckily for the military, he lacked the necessary skills, cunningness, and intellect to rule the country. As in the rest of the world, the calibre of politics has declined in the Arab world. Some leaders of the Muslim Brotherhood were extremely intelligent, but they had left the party.

Morsi naively thought that he could simply take over the existing apparatus of the Egyptian state. He entered into deals with the Egyptian secret police, which had tortured many of the Muslim Brothers for years—saying to them, "Do for us what you did for Mubarak." But the Arab Spring in Egypt had been for democratization, for an end to the corrupt judiciary, and for the dismantling of various institutions of the state. Morsi and his party therefore rapidly became unpopular among the wider masses. The military then seized this opportunity and used the liberals as well as youths to organize a semifake election, while at the same time repressing the dissidents. Egypt ended up with a military dictator, General Abdel Fattah al-Sisi, who is worse than Mubarak. Morsi, the elected president, sat on death row in an Egyptian prison for six years; he died after collapsing at a court hearing where he was being tried for espionage; his death was blamed on the prison conditions.

The Middle East Now

It is hard to believe that any remotely progressive person would consider the occupation of Iraq in 2003 a victory given the amount of devastation and divisiveness that ensued from it. The question that arises thus is, Was Iraq better off under Saddam Hussein? Saddam certainly imprisoned many Iraqis. Nonetheless, when you talk to some Iraqi women who had suffered badly in his prisons but who campaigned against the American invasion of Iraq, they emphasize that there is no comparison between now and before under Saddam Hussein—life was better under Saddam. They further explain: Saddam Hussein was a dictator, but in terms of gender, education, and health, Iraq was among the more advanced countries in the world. Iraq employed more women in universities than any other Arab country (al-Ali 2005, 739; also see al-Ali, Pratt, and Enloe 2010). One Iraqi woman professor gave me a figure, which I later checked: she said Iraq in the 1980s had more women teaching at various levels in the universities in Baghdad than Princeton University has today.

The women describe how they lost this privileged status. The minute the Americans dismantled the entire sociopolitical structure of Iraq, darkness prevailed over the society. It is worth noting that after World War II the United States did not dismantle the entire sociopolitical structure in Japan, Germany, and Italy. Eighty percent of Mussolini's structure within the state, army, and judiciary was left in place, as was the case in Japan. In Germany, more people were charged with war crimes, but 60 percent of those who had worked for the Nazis were left in place because the new enemy was communism, and anyone who could help against communism was useful! This is why many of those who were on the side of the fascists were given refuge all over the Western world.

The Middle East is now divided up into tiny fragments. The unity of Iraq is gone. There is a Kurdish part of Iraq, which the Turks are not happy with. The Iranians are very dominant in southern Iraq, and the Saudis are intervening in Sunni Iraq. I am glad President Barack Obama at least had the decency to say that had the United States not gone into Iraq, ISIS would not exist (Saul 2015). This was the first attempt to accept some responsibility for the mess in Iraq.

Similar things are going on in Syria for which others bear different responsibilities; Syria has been broken. Much of the Arab Middle East is in a dire situation. I have not seen it in such a bad situation before.

Take the case of Libya. It is true that the initial uprising against Muammar Qaddafi was popular. The situation, however, changed when the British, French, and Qatari troops entered Libya, and North Atlantic Treaty Organization (NATO) forces started bombing the country; the tribes that initially opposed

Qaddafi changed their minds and decided to fight back against the foreigners. A seven-month NATO campaign ensued, and around twenty thousand to thirty thousand Libyans were killed in the conflict. Furthermore, after NATO deposed Qaddafi, three hard-core jihadi groups emerged and occupied Libya: al-Qaeda, ISIS, and a local group that was given pride of place in the NATO invasion. It is claimed that NATO gave the latter group carte blanche to destroy the old regime with the promise that its members would never be charged with war crimes or punished. They raped, butchered, and killed many people who were identified to be supporters—even in minor capacities—of the previous regime (Ali 2013a, 2013b).

A similar fight is now going on in Iraq, thanks to the Saudis and the Iranians. Many Iraqis would remind you that Iranian opposition to the Iraq War in 2003 would have made the United States think twice. The Iranian regime goes on the old motto of "the enemy of my enemy is my friend," and so because both Saddam Hussein in Iraq and the Taliban in Afghanistan were enemies of Iran, Iran did not oppose the US invasions of those two countries. Hence, the breakup of this region, with countries very narrowly defending their own interest, is partially responsible for conflicts and wars. All these conflicts in the region—starting with the invasion of Afghanistan in 2001—have gone on longer than World War I and World War II put together. We need to think of the effect of such long wars on the fabric of society and on the lives of ordinary people. No wonder ordinary people cannot bear this contentious environment anymore and seek refuge elsewhere—mostly in neighboring states.

However, European officials and citizens complain when they are asked to take a quarter of a million out of two million refugees. My answer to such complaints is very clear: "Do not go and fight wars when you will not accept refugees at this scale. You are responsible for them." This is the biggest wave of human movement the European states have seen since World War II, when they defeated Germany. The expulsion of ethnic Germans from Czech Slovakia and from parts of Russia and Poland instituted one of the largest masses to sweep across Europe. So the flight from the Arab Middle East to Europe is the second time such human flight has happened at this scale. It is unclear how this crisis is going to end; it is a Pandora's box: now that it has been opened, it is impossible to contain what emerged from it.

The Jihadists in Arab Politics

The influence of jihadists on Arab politics is an intriguing question. To explain it, we have to understand that ISIS did not come from a clear blue sky; it was not a thunderbolt. It was part of Saudi and Turkish policy to create a Sunni alliance against

Iran and the Shi'as, which is a huge tragedy for the world, but the policy succeeded. It succeeded because US policy gave power effectively to Shi'a clerical parties in Iraq and destroyed the political apparatus of the other side after 2003. Moreover, some of the Shi'a militias in Baghdad carried out large-scale ethnic cleansings, which cemented the divide (Weiss and Pregent 2015). This happened in a country where the Shi'as constituted more than 50 percent of the central committee of the Ba'ath Party when it was founded (Batatu 1978). *Sectarianism is not something deep inside people; it arises out of political events*, as it did in Iraq. The same applies to the Syrian war, which has wrecked the country. The idea that if President Bashar al-Assad were removed, we would have a pristine pure democracy in Syria is false (not that I support him), as the cases of Iraq and Libya demonstrate.

Another tragic war is taking place in Yemen, where the Saudis are completely wrecking large parts of the country in their intervention in the Yemen Civil War since 2015, and they have been ignored or supported. Despite that, Saudi Arabia was elected as the chairman of the United Nations Human Rights Commission that year (Brooks-Pollock 2015)—a new low for that organization, sending the wrong message to the Arab world.

Al-Qaeda was a product of the US jihad against the Russians in Afghanistan in the 1980s. ISIS is a product of the US occupation of Iraq. Such groups are now in competition with each other. Al-Qaeda targets Western interests and Western groups and accuses ISIS of targeting other Muslims and minorities, but both are wrong. What is interesting is that ISIS claims it is more modern. It has a very strong online presence. Its brochures are virtual carbon copies of NATO's. In NATO's brochures, you see a list of its military operations and equipment—planes, drones, and the wars it has been involved in. ISIS does the same, but because it is effectively a tiny group, it says: "You use drones, and we line up people and decapitate them with swords because we know it upsets you. We have knocked down all statues, and we do not care about cultural heritage." Here a serious question has to be raised, and it is a question of morality: Is killing fifteen totally innocent civilians with swords worse than killing fifty people with a drone attack in Somalia, Pakistan, and Afghanistan, where people die in this manner every day? How is one any better than the other? The West has become accustomed to a double standard: "What we do is automatically right, and what they do is automatically wrong." In most cases, both what they do and what we do are wrong.

Islamophobia

The wave of wars to remodel and reshape the energy-rich world has become part and parcel of a campaign that has created a powerful surge of Islamophobia in the

Western world. You will find that more books appeared on Islam and Muslims after 9/11 than in the centuries that preceded it. Although some are strong books, most are not; they attack Islam.

I have never been religious anytime in my life, but the situation for people like me is the same as the one for nonreligious Jews who when they saw crimes being committed were compelled to speak up. This does not mean that we defend the absurdities and atrocities carried out by Muslim fundamentalists against women, homosexuals, and minorities. This is a common problem with all religious fundamentalists—Muslims, Jews, Christians, and so on. The religious documents they read—the Old Testament in particular, which is the mother of all such documents in this regard—are filled with revenge, bloodshed, sodomy, killing, and war. So there is not just one fundamentalism that takes us up; fundamentalism in general is quite common, and it should not be defended. There is absolutely no reason for anyone attacking Islamophobia to justify Muslim fundamentalism.

Nonetheless, when we read what is being written about Muslims and Islam in France, Britain, the United States, and sometimes Germany and compare it with what was written about the Jews in the 1920s, 1930s, 1940s, and 1950s, it is not so different. "They are the *Other*," such texts say; "they are not part of us!" Even the language is the same. For example, a heading from the *Daily Mail*, one of the leading tabloid papers in Great Britain, stated in 1932, "Floods of Jewish Refugees Threaten Brit" (Brown 2016). Today the same paper, without any awareness of its own history, writes, "Floods of Syrian Refugees Pouring into Europe" (*Daily Mail Online* 2015)!

Conclusion: What Is to Be Done?

In today's world, where the situation is worse than I ever remember it being, what are we to do? The only thing we can do as citizens is to fight back, organize, protest, and fight for a better world. Change will come because history has taught us that huge mass movements can take us by surprise. Nobody thought that Hosni Mubarak, the former Egyptian president, would be defeated so easily. It is, however, important to note that Mubarak's speedy demise came about in part because of his decision to put his son in his place, which antagonized the army, so that the military did not defend him.

Although the social movements in the Arab world were defeated, and we still are living in a period of defeat, *this state of affairs is now beginning to change*. The new generation, which is now coming of political age, is different from preceding generations. Each generation is different from previous ones. These young people, alienated from traditional politics, are now realizing that they can form and create their own politics. And they do it the best way they can. Young people everywhere are saying, "Enough is enough; we have to do something." They choose the instrument nearest to them to bring change.

The speed at which the Occupy movements happened took everyone by surprise. The occupied squares as an *image* and an *idea* interestingly spread to the United States. The "occupy" idea came from the Arab world, and the squares moved from Cairo to New York, the Bay Area, Los Angeles, and other parts of the United States. The demands were almost the same. In the United States, the question did not go that far, but it came up again in that generation's incredibly enthusiastic campaign for Bernie Sanders. In Britain, the Movement of the Squares was not so huge, but it erupted again in the election of a leader of the Labour Party who could be arrested under the terrorism laws in place. Jeremy Corbyn, the former leader of the Labour Party, has been a solid supporter of the Palestinians for the past forty years and opposes nuclear weapons. He was the most left-wing leader in the history of that party from 1890 on. At the same time, he was caught in the most right-wing parliamentary Labour Party in Labour history as well. So you never get it all in the first round, but we must not lose hope. Not losing hope is difficult, though, especially in the Arab world at the present moment.

It is obvious that the hopes of those who sacrificed their lives in the heady days of the Arab Spring are far from being fulfilled. The coercive apparatuses remain intact, and the region's states do not offer any kind of social-democratic palliatives. However, the ability of the masses to topple long-running despotic regimes gave them an inner strength; the consciousness it produced has not evaporated in these countries, and it remains a real impediment to the governments' proceeding with neoliberal policies too far or too soon. There are two responses to this crisis. One is just total despair, which I understand, too. But *despair is a passive emotion*. It makes you very passive, whereas the other response, *hope, is an active emotion*. And on that activity rests the future of the Arab world and, of course, the planet.

References

Al-Ali, Nadje. 2005. "Reconstructing Gender: Iraqi Women between Dictatorship, War, Sanctions, and Occupation." *Third World Quarterly* 26, nos. 4–5: 739–58.

Al-Ali, Nadje, Nicola Pratt, and Cynthia Enloe. 2010. *What Kind of Liberation? Women and the Occupation of Iraq*. Berkeley: Univ. of California Press.

Ali, Tariq. 2003. *The Clash of Fundamentalisms: Crusades, Jihads, and Modernity*. London: Verso.

———. 2011. "This Is an Arab 1848. But US Hegemony Is Only Dented." *Guardian*, Feb. 22. At http://www.theguardian.com/commentisfree/2011/feb/22/arab-1848-us-hegemony -dented.

———. 2013a. "Between Past and Future." *New Left Review* 2, no. 80: 61–74.

———. 2013b. "On Libya, the Arab Spring and Syria." *Counterpunch*, Nov. 1. At http://www.counterpunch.org/2013/11/01/on-libya-the-arab-spring-and-syria/.

———. 2015. *The Extreme Centre: A Warning*. London: Verso.

———. 2016. "We Are Witnessing the Twilight of Democracy." At http://tariqali.org/archives/3007.

Batatu, Hanna. 1978. *The Old Social Classes and the Revolutionary Movement in Iraq*. Princeton, NJ: Princeton Univ. Press.

Brooks-Pollock, Tom. 2015. "Anger after Saudi Arabia 'Chosen to Head Key UN Human Rights Panel.'" *Independent*, Sept. 20. At http://www.independent.co.uk/news/world/anger-after-saudi-arabia-chosen-to-head-key-un-human-rights-panel-10509716.html.

Brown, Sophie. 2016. "This *Daily Mail* Headline from 1938 Is Eerily Similar to Today's Media Coverage." *Huffington Post UK*, July 31. At http://www.huffingtonpost.co.uk/2015/07/31/daily-mail-1938-jews_n_7909954.html.

Daily Mail Online. 2015. "Asylum Seekers Turn Holiday Island of Kos into 'Refugee Camp.'" May 27. At http://www.dailymail.co.uk/news/article-3099736/Holidaymakers-misery-boat-people-Syria-Afghanistan-seeking-asylum-set-migrant-camp-turn-popular-Greek-island-Kos-disgusting-hellhole.html.

Mair, Peter. 2013. *Ruling the Void: The Hollowing of Western Democracy*. London: Verso.

Saul, Heather. 2015. "President Obama Claims Rise of ISIS Is 'Unintended Consequence' of George W. Bush's Invasion in Iraq." *Independent*, Mar. 18. At http://www.independent.co.uk/news/world/middle-east/president-obama-claims-rise-of-isis-is-unintended-consequence-of-george-w-bush-s-invasion-in-iraq-10115243.html.

Streeck, Wolfgang. 2014. *Buying Time: The Delayed Crisis of Democratic Capitalism*. Translated by Patrick Camiller and David Fernbach. Brooklyn, NY: Verso.

Weiss, Michael, and Michael Pregent. 2015. "The U.S. Is Providing Air Cover for Ethnic Cleansing in Iraq." 2015. *Foreign Policy*, Mar. 28. At https://foreignpolicy.com/2015/03/28/the-united-states-is-providing-air-cover-for-ethnic-cleansing-in-iraq-shiite-militias-isis/.

Part Two

The Unfinished Project
of the Resilient Citizenship

7

Arab Youth Nonmovements

Resilient Citizenship in the Middle East

Bessma Momani and Melissa Finn

A story being told on the sidelines of dominant debates in Middle East studies, sociology, citizenship studies, and geography is about how enduring forms of social and political change manifest themselves in times of constraint, how ordinary people mobilize politics and citizenship through their daily practices, and how agency is enabled and constrained in authoritarian and democratic systems (Bayat 2013; Glenn 2011; Kasbari and Vinthagen 2020; Staeheli et al. 2012). Millions of daily acts of refusal by ordinary people pry open dysfunctional systems, show structures of domination where they are vulnerable, and provide guideposts that demarcate how society can be restructured when the system finally meets its demise or is reorganized beyond recognition.

It is a grand tale of people who are largely, if not entirely, invisible. They do not figure in international headlines; they are not necessarily followed by governments or secret service agencies; they do not necessarily demonstrate or manifest politically or ideologically oriented actions in the proverbial Arab street; and they are not necessarily part of the class of actors thought to make revolutions possible, such as the intellectuals, economic elites, armed forces, laborers, radicals, and moderates (Goldstone 1982), though they may be among them. Among these invisible citizens is the demographic of youth, who know how to survive and resist at the same time. Invisible though they may be, their ordinariness produces sites of citizenship contestation as well as of resolve and resilience, which help chisel away at power bulwarks and provide the groundwork and conditions for the building of new societies. Where they challenge conventions, they provide a way to map future innovations.

This chapter sheds further light on the nonmovements of ordinary Arab youth who by living authentically and even quietly are ensuring that the political status quo of authoritarian, detached, and unaccountable rule will one day reach its expiration date. We argue that the future of the Middle East and North Africa (MENA) can be charted in these nonmovements of youth and that they require more scholarly attention. Within the field of Middle East studies, the enormous energy devoted to debating the apparent incontrovertible nature of authoritarian resiliency, the entrenchment of military enclaves in the state's political economy, the pacification of political subjects by the lullabies of rentierism, the corroding forces of Islamism (or religion generally) on a body politic, and the democratic deficit inherent in Arab values, whose homogenous wholeness is itself the subject of further subdebates, drains research resources that might be otherwise focused on mapping contemporary undercurrents and future political configurations. The fear barrier that broke in 2011 when Arabs took to the street is still broken, and no matter how die-hard the old theories of MENA politics (often built on a misreading of history and deeply cynical views of the region), the trajectory in the years to come is going to be written by the new generation (Bishara 2016). As Khaled Diab notes, "The incremental and unprecedented use of force and coercion [in Egypt], not to mention efforts to frighten the population into submission, are signs of weakness, not of strength. It betrays just how desperate the regime has become after everything has failed to keep a rebellious population in check" (2016). As Jack Shenker comments further, "A profound gulf now exists between a ruling class intent on governing as if nothing has changed and large swaths of a democratic citizenry for whom something fundamental has altered" (quoted in Diab 2016). The purpose of this chapter is to survey some of the qualities of nonmovements among Arab youth years after the Arab Spring and to demonstrate that calls for change are persisting in often less revolutionary, more unassuming forms.

The Arab Spring and Nonmovements

As millions of Arabs poured into the streets and squares calling for the downfall of their autocratic regimes, those academics who study the region were baffled. Few political scientists specializing in the Middle East had predicted the Arab Spring. How could it be that area specialists, who often based their findings on empirical and field research in the region, could not have seen the coming wave of discontent? Of course, the question may be insulting to those social scientists who reject the idea that part of our craft involves having crystal balls that see into the future, but the oversight was nevertheless significant, particularly if one looks at the state of the conversation in Middle East studies. For at least a decade, political scientists' theoretical frame for understanding MENA politics was based on contrasting paradigms: "transition to democracy" and "authoritarian resilience" (Bellin 2012; Heydemann and Leenders 2011; Stepan 2012) or simply "change or continuity."

In support of the view of "change," scholars of the region suggested that the Arab Spring was a wakeup call to long-held perceptions of "Arab exceptionalism" reiterated through various connotations of a static, autocratic, and insular Middle East. Moreover, although many commentators noted that political unrest was not new to the region (see Alexander 2011; Gause 2011; Ottaway and Hamzawy 2011), the unprecedented nature of the mass protests, rallies, marches, demonstrations, use of social media, and the open and sustained opposition to the injustices of corrupt regimes violently suppressing unarmed citizens sparked analytical reevaluation.

With the benefit of time and modest retrospect, early proclamations of the Arab Spring as a "Facebook revolution"—a cataclysmic and monolithic event that swept the Arab world through mainly online media or through physical media mobilized by online modalities—have given way to more contextualized studies of regional transformation (Aliboni 2011). For many scholars, such as Marc Lynch (2012), the new Middle East was born after more than a decade of media diversification and liberalization, the spread of information communication technologies, and an aspirant and educated young population. To Lynch and others supporting the view that the region is experiencing change, the Arab Spring is one offspring of this structural transformation taking place in the region (see Momani 2015). More importantly, the tides moving the region forward cannot be turned back, and one should expect more MENA regimes to bow to popular unrest.

When explaining why the Middle East was resistant to democracy experienced in other parts of the developing world—or what has been coined Middle East "exceptionalism"—area scholars looked for markers of political liberalization in the form of active civil society organizations, nongovernmental organizations, political parties, and business associations, all of which were dormant or pacified in the region (see Bellin 2012, 139). Moreover, state centralization of the economy, high inequality, illiteracy, the prevalence of Islam, and no demonstration of having a successful Arab democracy were referenced to explain authoritarian resilience (Bellin 2012, 141). In analyzing the Middle East, Joel Beinin and Frédéric Vairel remind us about the importance of context in understanding contentious politics and that using only Western contexts to build theories of social movements, mobilization, and contestation is inadequate for understanding change in the Arab region because of how difficult it is to organize safely in many defensive, intolerant, and punitive autocratic regimes there. They note that the binary range of phenomena captured by the change and continuity literature is inadequate because Middle East politics often "takes place below the radar screen of the formal terrain that political science usually studies" (2013, 11). Moreover, as Carol Daniel Kasbari and Stellan Vinthagen elucidate, "A whole world of invisible politics is revealed through this research literature, where virtually everyone subordinated by some power is participating in politics through mundane or petty acts by circumventing, negotiating, manipulating, or undermining hegemonic power in their family, workplace, or neighborhood" (2020, 1).

While most academics studying the Middle East continued to focus on what was wrong with the region and the structural barriers preventing democratization and change, a minority of academics and Western policy makers saw and documented the everyday forms of protest through refusal in the region. They recognized that the "top-down" approach of looking at Arab governments instead of at Arab societies is why the Arab Spring was largely missed in academic and Western circles (Frangonikolopoulos and Chapsos 2012).

Asef Bayat argues that social nonmovements are the undercurrents of change in most of the Arab world but rarely get mentioned in academic tools and analysis:

> In the Middle East, the nonmovements have come to represent the mobilization of millions of the subaltern, chiefly the urban poor, Muslim women, and youth. The nonmovement of the urban dispossessed, which I have termed the "quiet encroachment of the ordinary," encapsulates the discreet and prolonged ways in which the poor struggle to survive and to better their lives by quietly impinging on the propertied and powerful, and on society at large. It embodies the protracted mobilization of millions of detached and dispersed individuals and families who strive to enhance their lives in a lifelong collective effort that bears few elements of pivotal leadership, ideology, or structured organization. (2013, 15)

In Bayat's formulation, the characteristics of nonmovements therefore include: (1) action-oriented rather than ideologically oriented behavior, behavior that is overwhelmingly quiet rather than audible and made by individuals rather than by united groups; (2) actors directly practicing what they claim in the face of government (or nongovernment) sanction as a politics of practice via direct and disparate actions; (3) ordinary practices of everyday life; and (4) actions occurring everywhere in public spaces, at the center and not at the margins of social life, by millions of people whose fragmented relationship to each other nevertheless builds significance through their collective instantiation. Nonmovements are passive networks, the collective actions of noncollective actors that build often unintentional resistance to power through an incremental encroachment on power and the subversion of conventions. The public enactments of any kind of refusal of dominant power provide the conditions for people to mutually identify with the resistance, to internalize how the revolt is manifesting itself, and to build with others an "imagined solidarity." Thus, the nonmovement builds critical momentum when millions of atomized individuals oriented toward action mutually recognize the interventions of others in public spaces when they see them (Bayat 2013).

Bayat's coverage of nonmovements has provided further groundwork to examine forms of protest under authoritarianism that are ordinary and yet can collectively be quite revolutionary in unexpected ways, as we saw with the Arab Spring protests in places where civil society social movements were essentially weak, thanks to authoritarianism (Bayat 2013).

Nonmovements are happenstance and yet powerful by virtue of their collective strength. Social movements and collective organization in the open are dangerous activities in Arab autocracies, and people are often jailed or tortured simply for associating with undesirable organizations. But noncollectives of Arabs are not necessarily passive or conformist in their ways just because they do not organize political parties or civil society associations to demand their rights. Rather, their ordinary and mundane acts of refusal collectively sustain protest, resilient citizenship, and the demand for justice and care in underground forms.

Research such as Bayat's on nonmovements in the Arab world attempts to theorize the agency of people, such as many Arab populations, who live under extremely socially and politically constraining conditions and to capture bottom-up political struggle that has too often been unaccounted for in political science (Aarts 2012). Nonmovements have taken many forms. For Arab women, a nonmovement can sometimes simply be going to work outside the home, going to school, taking part in sports, wearing a loose hijab, taking careers that challenge conventions, or even walking in areas where women are not usually seen (Bayat 2013; Harkness and Hongsermeier 2015; on Iran, see Hasani and Kazemi 2020). Nonmovements of the poor often position makeshift homes and carts of goods in places that encroach upon official state policy regarding the use of public space. For youth, defiance of conventions—for instance, playing rap or heavy metal in societies with conservative values to spread and make recognizable among others individual refusals or resilience against establishment violence—is a nonmovement. Various incarnations of the Syrian Mazaj (Mood) Band have made their presence known through music, especially through powerful songs such as "Down with the Homeland," that defies conventions while encroaching upon the state's centrifugal mechanisms of inducing silence (SyriaUntold 2015; Yassin-Kassab 2015). The point of nonmovements is that they involve noncollective actors who champion the art of presence and who encroach upon the free spaces that cannot be fully controlled by dysfunctional political systems.

Resilient Citizenship Claims Making by Youth in Nonmovements

The actions and practices of atomized and ordinary individuals in Arab youth nonmovements invoke resilient citizenship claims making that challenges Arab states to adhere to normative frameworks of justice and care (Staeheli et al. 2012). Lynn Staeheli and her colleagues (2012) argue that citizenship always involves presumptions of ordinariness (those with citizenship take it for granted), the demand for justice and care from the state, theories about how individuals themselves shift from subjects to citizens, mutual recognition of people in their encounters of others in daily life, and a command of "spaces" where citizenship is claimed, invoked, and granted. Citizenship is therefore a complex site of contestation that emerges not just from acts of insurrection (extraordinary acts) that rupture the status quo (Glenn 2011; Isin 2009) but also from ordinary acts, symbolically captured in the daily resistance of African Americans to streetcar segregation in the mid–twentieth century or in the bold refusals of the undocumented to be excluded from systems of justice and care. Citizenship is also enacted through the silent, unassuming actions of ordinary, largely invisible (or invisibilized) people—subalterns—who persist in presenting themselves authentically despite the panoptical regime that projects itself everywhere, or so it may claim, and that would have them be or act otherwise.

Over the past two decades, a productive turn has emerged in MENA studies that examines how contributions by nontraditional actors (e.g., nonelites) such as civil society organizations, the media, activists in political movements, political parties, and legal institutions have democratized local, state, and regional politics in the MENA region. These actors are attributed with having built, variously and disparately depending on the context, the necessary critical mass to a crescendo that challenged multiple Arab authoritarian systems in 2011. Much analysis focused on how these actors' apparently unprecedented revolts were going to provide the groundwork for a new blossoming in the Arab world (an "Arab spring"); the potential and need for a blossoming had, in fact, been residing for decades in the people's collective psyche and in the configurations of past revolts (al Jazeera English 2016).

What is particularly compelling about this progression toward and during the 2011 uprisings is how veteran activists and previously "ordinary" people mobilized others to take to the streets and fight the state via online media. Since 2011, social movements have been credited with having successfully removed authoritarian leaders from highly entrenched positions of power and control in Tunisia, Sudan, and Algeria. From our perspective, such activists' citizenship claims making through their public and private acts of resistance is undeniable. Acts that rupture the status quo and help to dispute, interrogate, and intervene in systems of oppression are forms of insurrectionary citizenship (Glenn 2011).

Dogged activist circles that continue to take to the streets, continue to put activists' lives on the line through political resistance, and continue to peacefully demand revolutionary political change claim the rights and duties of citizenship in its traditional liberal (rights-affording) and republican (duties-demanding) configurations. Such activism, when it builds solidarity, mutual aid, and *communitas* (Isin 2009), also constitutes nontraditional citizenship claims making that the state can deny only for so long. The speech acts of activists and ordinary people are a political *double sens* (entendre) against the state, demanding the rights and duties of citizenship that are untethered to the trappings of rights, duties, and community and state recognition and building the kind of momentum that will erode authoritarian entrenchment in very critical and historic ways. Such people who hold the authoritarian state accountable while simultaneously eroding it will one day be vindicated by their fight to survive and for their sacrifices in the struggle. We argue that given the fact that the largest demographic majority in the MENA region is Arab youth, profound political change in the Middle East is inevitable. We argue that this is the case, moreover, despite the immensity of the counter-revolutionary forces, including the large-scale centrifugal crackdowns by Bashar al-Assad on the Syrian people that continue to keep them subjected and hold them back; the rise of foreign-fighter movements and their proto-state territorial control in Syria, Libya, and Iraq; the reemergence (or reassertion) of military rule in Egypt; and the political paralysis in places such as Libya, Iraq, and Yemen. Provocatively, our argument here is that profound political change might not necessarily be locatable in the practices of activists but rather in the daily practices of ordinary citizens, including the youth.

To date, insufficient scholarly attention has been afforded to the role of non-movements—of ordinary people engaging in very unspectacular acts of refusal and acts of resilient citizenship that expand mutual aid, solidarity, and *communitas*, often armed only by their invisibility and their silence; of the millions of quiet daily acts of refusal that are profoundly transforming the MENA region and sustaining revolutionary momentum in the face of the supposedly resilient authoritarian system. Abdel Rahman Mansour, the cofounder of the "We Are All Khaled Said" Facebook page, which is credited with having provided decisive momentum to the revolutionary struggle in 2011, speaks about the invisible people whose quiet solidarity with the activist movements made the revolution possible: "They were the core of the protest movement, and we managed to embrace them and represent their interests. At the time, of course, we were not conscious of that fact, but in retrospect, what made the revolution a success and what made it work were those invisible citizens whose names we do not even know" (interviewed in al Jazeera English 2016). He argues further that the solution to the current Egyptian impasse may not be radical or revolutionary acts but rather the acts of ordinary citizens who will initiate meaningful change (al Jazeera English 2016).

Here, we are inquiring how analysis of Middle East politics shifts when the analytical tool kit includes the lived resistance by ordinary Arab youth (youth as a "level of analysis" in their own right), what they are saying, and how they are acting offline and online, away from the state apparatus's censors and the infamous freedom squares. Arab youth have not retreated in the face of the violence and oppression imposed by the counterrevolutionary sweep; on the contrary, their calls for change are still alive, active, often "under the radar," and at times unconsciously activist-like in their execution and impact.

Social scientists need to sharpen their tools of analysis to be able to see and understand this continuing cultural and social revolution from nontraditional levels of analysis if they are to better understand, first, the change that is coming to the Arab world when new generations take over state politics from aging technocrats and plutocrats, and, second, the citizenship claims making that emerges from people who invest a quiet, unassuming presence in the drive for mutual aid and solidarity (Bayat 2013). Nonmovements of individual Arab youth have collective power to fight for increased rights and to defy state authoritarianism through incredibly subversive means because of the invisibility of their political presence and the apparently mundane nature of their practices. Such youth use whatever invisibility can afford them to encroach upon political and social conventions that hold them back and erode their access to justice and care.

Arab Youth Nonmovements a Decade after the Arab Spring

We can observe Bayat's four characterizations of nonmovements throughout the decade after the Arab Spring. Indeed, they are individual, action oriented rather than ideologically oriented, quiet rather than audible, and disparate rather than collective. These nonmovements of millions occupy public spaces such as city centers and squares, do the ordinary practices of holding candles and signs, and are united by hashtags and slogans rather than by a single ideology or group formation. To begin, perhaps no Arab country resembles a complete regression of political liberalization and development than Egypt. The toppling of Hosni Mubarak during the Arab Spring of 2011 unleashed a wave of hope for democratization in the country and in the wider Arab region. Many looked to Egypt, the country with the highest number of Arabs, 100 million, with great hope for signs of political liberalization. But then in 2013, the coup d'état of the first democratically elected president to hold office in the Arab world was a blow to the hope that the region was about to begin a democratization domino effect. Although many have analyzed the counterrevolutionary forces that dominate Egypt, particularly in the security and military sectors, they have missed the budding youth revolutionary movement, which has not remained silent despite continued intimidation by the Egyptian government and its security apparatus.

Activist youth, supported by masses of nonactivists, continue to use online modalities, such as Facebook, to call for the return of the Egyptian people to the iconic Tahrir Square to demand change to the regime of General Abdel Fattah al-Sisi. One such group, Raga'oon, or "We Are Returning," continued to call for Egyptian youth to return to Tahrir Square on January 25, the anniversary of the Egyptian revolution (RAG3IN 2015). In years following the Arab revolts, graduate students went to Tahrir Square in the hundreds on Sunday afternoons to protest a lack of jobs. Government security forces arrested many protestors and fired tear gas on them, and yet they continued to return to downtown Cairo to protest for jobs and opportunities, including the mass demonstrations throughout September 2019. The protestors chant: "Oh officers, we are not terrorists, we are doctors" (*Mada Masr* 2015). The taking over of a public space by a mass of people who are united not by ideology but by everyday life experience is further support for labeling such action a nonmovement.

Just as protests at Tahrir Square were an important precursor to the Arab Spring, so were large workers' protests in the Mahala industrial sector. The Mahala protests for fair workers' rights and a decent wage were identified as a key precursor to the Tahrir protests and the April 6 Youth Movement. Again from 2015 to 2016, Egypt saw labor protests around the country that included industrial strikes and sit-ins to protest against mass layoffs as well as to call for increased wages. The protestors included employees in the hotels and resorts of Sharm el-Sheikh, the textile companies in Monufiya, and a fertilizer company in Assiut as well as Suez Canal workers. The most notable protest was in Alexandria, where twelve thousand workers of government-supported Petrotrade went on strike to demand a more equitable share of company profits (Charbel 2015). In another sector, doctors working at government-run hospitals protested for fairer wages, benefits, and better working conditions (Charbel 2015). Many of these struggles have emerged organically both from unionized and collectivized groups and from atomized individuals who are focused on change through concrete actions rather than change through ideological groundswells—a key characteristic of the nonmovement. Daily acts of refusal then complement and support more collectivized protests. Marie Duboc notes that although the relative power of trade unionism has been eroded by policies of liberalization in Egypt, this has not undermined the overt and hidden mobilization of workers, many of whom are youths. She points out that the political culture of protest in Egypt involves multiple forms that characterize traditional social movements and nonmovements of loosely affiliated people:

Egyptian factory workers are not only integrated into the formal labor market, sometimes as civil servants when employed by public companies, but they also engage in strikes and demonstrations, carry banners, write leaflets, and conduct interviews with the media to voice their grievances about wages and bonuses. The economic hardships they face involve the same daily struggles as shopkeepers, taxi drivers, and workers in the informal economy, and the same concerns about finding the resources to pay for medical expenses or private lessons for their children. For instance, factory workers, like state employees and the vast majority of the Egyptian population, are compelled to take on second jobs in addition to their work in the factory. Likewise, they may have bank accounts, but they do not take loans from banks, preferring to rely on a cooperative lending system organized with their neighbors to avoid paying interest. In other words, while they are part of the formal economy and engage in collective, public protests against their working conditions, they also devise informal tactics to improve their living conditions. (2015, 237–38)

Social media in MENA countries continues to provide a space for a politics of refusal through overt and covert rejection of what is deemed the ordinary or conventionally accepted. One example is the social media tumult in Egypt in 2015 against the pro-regime television host Riham Saed, who attempted to condone the sexual harassment of a woman that was caught on video. The uproar—driven mainly by Egyptian youth, who were repulsed by how Saed blamed the harassment on the young woman's clothing and lifestyle—led sponsors to pull their support for Saed's TV show. The TV station that aired the show announced it would cancel the show and investigate the matter (Youssef and Noman 2015). Here again, the action-oriented response of these quiet online nonmovements was direct and impactful. This nonmovement was nonideological in the sense of not using feminist or gender-norms discourse to protest against Saed. Rather, support for the victim and protests against the TV host were mobilized through collective uproar.

Perhaps one of the most interesting social media campaigns driven by Arab youth is the #YouStink movement in Lebanon. Starting in July 2015, Lebanese youth took the trash crisis to a new level by protesting throughout Beirut with proactive signs and slogans reminiscent of marches during the Arab Spring. The use of a hashtag to garner a nonmovement of fragmented individuals was effective because of its simplicity and ease on social media. The phrase "YouStink" was nonideological and nonpartisan and allowed the viral nature of social media to take action through disparate means. The #YouStink movement was an indictment of the corrupt politicians who had bankrupted the waste-management system and who were unable to find a resolution to the trash crisis because of government infighting across sectarian lines. The movement was youth led and cross-sectarian, and it garnered local and international attention. Organizers used online crowd-sourcing to raise money to buy protest material, hoping to get $2,000; they ended up receiving a total of $10,000 from more than 160 individuals (Annous 2015). The #YouStink movement protested every weekend for months and called for major reforms to combat government corruption, modernize social security, find an eco-friendly solution to the trash crisis, and—on top of all that—address the growing refugee crisis (Berthoud 2015). The cross-sectarian nature of the movement led some observers to argue that the youth were in essence calling for a change in the social contract to a post–Ta'if Agreement model where true democracy could be represented and the current sectarian model eschewed (Annous 2015). The #YouStink movement was reminiscent of the Arab Spring protests not only in its use of similar slogans, such as "Down with the regime," but also for its emphasis on the daily struggles of existence in an environment of corruption. The protestors highlighted the rise of prices and the government's inability to meet its citizens' basic needs.

As in the Lebanese #YouStink movement, young Iraqis also took to the streets in the summer of 2015 and again in 2019–20 to protest the lack of electricity and water in the soaring summer heat and the lack of jobs for university graduates. Thousands of young people went to the center of Baghdad (aptly named Tahrir Square), again occupying public spaces in the uncoordinated manner of nonmove-ments to demand government reform. The Iraqi government violently cleared out nearly five hundred protestors from the iconic square in October 2020. Like the Lebanese youth, the Iraqi youth blamed sectarian politics in their country for the poor provision of basic services and for corruption in government. Signs held in Tahrir Square blamed politicians, and protestors took the unusual step of lying bare-chested and in shorts to protest the soaring heat (Barnard 2015). Political parties did not take part in the protests, and protestors were nondenominational, as in the Lebanese antitrash movement. In both countries, the movements were also actively attended by and artistically appropriated by young artists, sometimes in graffiti and other street art forms (see Gilgamesh 2020).

Not since the Arab Spring had Morocco seen the sight of public protests. In the fall of 2015, however, protestors took to the streets of Tangier to demonstrate against high prices for water and electricity (El Yaakoubi 2015). Moroccan youth formed a Facebook campaign called "Revolt of Candles" to call for public demon-strations in Tangier's Place des nations (Maniani 2015). Protestors called on people to raise candles in protest against an expected rise in electricity prices that would come with the planned privatization of public utilities to a French firm (al Jazeera English 2011). It was estimated that sixty thousand people holding candles took part in the silent street marches across the northern city of Tangier (*Moroccan Times* 2015). The quiet use of candles to gather disparate individuals in an everyday protest is yet another example of Bayat's nonmovement protest. In 2016 and 2017, protests erupted after the death of a fishmonger when he was crushed by a garbage truck in his attempt to retrieve the fish he was selling after a police officer disposed of it as illegal merchandise. Thousands took to the streets in the Rif region of northern Morocco in what was called the "Rif movement."

There is perhaps no greater tragedy of the Arab Spring than the civil war in Syria. In response to a peaceful protest by young kids in the town of Der'aa, the Syrian regime repressed that town and every town and city thereafter that protested the regime's violence and repression. After years of civil war in Syria, the death toll exceeds 250,000, and the internally and externally displaced exceed 11 million. Yet even in the wake of full state repression of revolutionary movements and the rising tide of extremism, nonmovements continue to appear throughout Syria years after the Arab Spring.

One of the most interesting initiatives was Planet Syria, which described itself as "a wide network that includes over a hundred Syrian civil society groups, in order to make our voice heard again. We are determined to show the world that we can build solid institutions from scratch and reinstate order in liberated towns" (Planet Syria 2014). From the ashes of regime destruction, Planet Syria's network of volunteers and makeshift centers provided everyday necessities under extraordinary circumstances: "Centers concerned with women's well-being have opened their doors offering language courses to illiterate women and useful marketable skills to a young crowd. Subversive graffiti, revolutionary pamphlets, magazines and radio stations run by resistance groups, centers offering psychosocial support to children traumatized by the war, makeshift hospitals operating despite the lack of equipment, all those initiatives were made possible by Syria's vibrant and diverse civil society. People are experimenting with what could be possible from now on. Areas that the regime lost are filled to the brim with possibilities" (Planet Syria 2014).

This network of activists is not only desperately trying to fill a void that the Syrian regime has failed to fill but also doing so under constant attack by all sides of the Syrian conflict. Planet Syria activists constitute a classical nonmovement by protesting and existing every day in contested or liberated areas of the Syrian conflict.

One of the most interesting acts of everyday defiance spearheaded often by youth and propagandized by children was the use of political signs in the northwestern Syrian town of Kafranbel. Written in English, critical of the Assad regime, and embarrassing to Western powers, the Kafranbel signs often used dark humor and were reminders to the world that Syrian civilians were under the constant shelling of government forces (Mulder 2018; Noderer 2020). In December 2014, the residents of the town made a sign that read: "We stand in solidarity with the oppressed that cannot breathe. #BlackLivesMatter." Other signs read: "If we don't have oil, like Iraq or Libya, don't we deserve to live?" (2011); "Assad is the source of terrorism; no matter what efforts you make to humanize him, he has no future with us" (2015); and, ironically using a phrase from Assad's private emails revealed by Wikileaks (Morse 2012), "There is no egg in eggplant, no ham in hamburger, but let's face it, there is an ass in Assad" (2012). The daily defiance, refusal, and dogged presencing of ordinary people in the Kafranbel sign making legitimated these largely invisibilized actors' citizenship claims to be more than subjects and their demands on the state (and international community) to ensure that justice would endure and that their care (survival and freedom) would be assured.

Conclusion

In this chapter, we have argued that the mainly unassuming daily actions and practices of ordinary citizens have citizenship relevancy. Evelyn Nakano Glenn (2011) argues that citizenship is "omnirelevant," and we agree. Citizenship is invoked everywhere, not only in spaces and places where it is legitimated and formalized in the grandeur of stately assent but also in the backstreets by ordinary people who stake their claim no matter how battle hardened the regime-based institutions seeking relevance through control and oppression are. The story of these unassuming people conducting presumably unassuming acts is a story that is often missed in Middle East studies but that figures predominately on the sidelines of multiple fields of study under different names and concepts and that aptly characterizes social and political transformation in the Arab world that will have long-term traction and sustainability. Some of these actors are those traditionally regarded as revolutionary actors, such as workers and teachers, but many cannot be considered typical revolutionaries, such as housewives, the unemployed, and children. In this chapter, we have focused mainly on the contributions made by Arab youth. We invoke the hope that is imbued in theorizing how small actions have direct consequences for the development of citizenship as an idea, practice, space, and system of laws. The citizenship claims making of Arab youth in times of constraint is characterized by its resiliency in the face of a host of stoppages, barriers, assaults, and attempts at erasure. For those wishing to celebrate the gains of the Arab Spring and who desire to chart how the future will unfold, there is much explanatory power and predictive capacity in the youth nonmovements of the Middle East and their politics of presence(ing).

References

Aarts, Paul. 2012. *From Resilience to Revolt: Making Sense of the Arab Spring.* Amsterdam: Univ. of Amsterdam.

Alexander, Christopher. 2011. "Tunisia's Protest Wave: Where It Comes from and What It Means." *Foreign Policy*, Jan. 3. At http://foreignpolicy.com/2011/01/03/tunisias-protest-wave-where-it-comes-from-and-what-it-means/.

Aliboni, Roberto. 2011. "The International Dimension of the Arab Spring." *International Spectator* 46, no. 4: 5–9.

Annous, Samer. 2015. "Who Stinks? Social Protests and Political Change in Lebanon." Carnegie Middle East Center, Nov. 10. At http://carnegie-mec.org/2015/11/10/who-stinks-social-protests-and-political-change-in-lebanon.

Barnard, Anne. 2015. "120 Degrees and No Relief? ISIS Takes Back Seat for Iraqis." *New York Times*, Aug. 2. At http://www.nytimes.com/2015/08/02/world/middleeast/iraqis-protest-electricity-shortage-during-heat-wave.html?_r=0.

Bayat, Asef. 2013. *Life as Politics: How Ordinary People Change the Middle East.* Cairo: American Univ. in Cairo Press.

Beinin, Joel, and Frédéric Vairel. 2013. "Introduction: The Middle East and North Africa beyond Classical Social Movement Theory." In *Social Movements, Mobilization, and Contestation in the Middle East and North Africa*, 2nd ed., edited by Joel Beinin and Frédéric Vairel, 1–30. Stanford, CA: Stanford Univ. Press.

Bellin, Eva. 2012. "Reconsidering the Robustness of Authoritarianism in the Middle East: Lessons from the Arab Spring." *Comparative Politics* 44, no. 2: 127–49.

Berthoud, Oliver. 2015. "'There Is Hope': Lebanon's Protests and the Future of the Anti-corruption Movement." *Foreign Policy Journal*, Nov. 23. At http://www.foreignpolicyjournal.com/2015/11/23/there-is-hope-lebanons-protests-and-the-future-of-the-anti-corruption-movement/.

Bishara, Marwan. 2016. "Arabs in the Eye of History." Al Jazeera English, Jan. 19. At http://www.aljazeera.com/indepth/opinion/2016/01/arabs-eye-history-160119093305885.html.

Charbel, Jano. 2015. "Labor Unrest from North to South." *Mada Masr*, Dec. 19. At http://www.madamasr.com/sections/politics/labor-unrest-north-south.

Diab, Khaled. 2016. "Egypt's Revolutionary Conundrum." Al Jazeera English, Jan. 23. At http://www.aljazeera.com/indepth/opinion/2016/01/egypt-revolutionary-conundrum-160121052800363.html.

Duboc, Marie. 2015. "Challenging the Trade Union, Reclaiming the Nation." In *Beyond the Arab Spring: The Evolving Ruling Bargain in the Middle East*, edited by Mehran Kamrava, 223–48. Oxford: Oxford Univ. Press.

Frangonikolopoulos, Christos A., and Ioannis Chapsos. 2012. "Explaining the Role and the Impact of the Social Media in the Arab Spring." *GMJ: Mediterranean Edition* 8, no. 1: 10–20.

Gause, Gregory. 2011. "Why Middle East Studies Missed the Arab Spring." *Foreign Affairs*, June 20. At https://www.foreignaffairs.com/articles/north-africa/2011-07-01/why-middle-east-studies-missed-arab-spring.

Gilgamesh, Nabeel. 2020. "Protest Art Turns a Concrete Tunnel into a Vibrant Gallery." Al Fanar Media, Mar. 6. At https://www.al-fanarmedia.org/2020/03/protest-art-turns-a-concrete-tunnel-into-a-vibrant-gallery/.

Glenn, Evelyn Nakano. 2011. "Constructing Citizenship: Exclusion, Subordination, and Resistance." *American Sociological Review* 76, no. 1: 1–24.

Goldstone, Jack A. 1982. "The Comparative and Historical Study of Revolutions." *Annual Review of Sociology* 8:187–207.

Harkness, Geoff, and Natasha Hongsermeier. 2015. "Female Sports as Non-movement Resistance in the Middle East and North Africa." *Sociology Compass* 9, no. 12: 1082–93.

Hasani, Razieh, and Masoud Akhavan Kazemi. 2020. "Women's Non-movement in Iran and the Shift in Social Relations." *Sociological Cultural Studies* 11, no. 3: 61–88.

Heydemann, Steven, and Reinoud Leenders. 2011. "Authoritarian Learning and Authoritarian Resilience: Regime Responses to the 'Arab Awakening.'" *Globalizations* 8, no. 5: 647–53.

Isin, Engin F. 2009. "Citizenship in Flux: The Figure of the Activist Citizen." *Subjectivity* 29:367–88.

Al Jazeera English. 2011. "Moroccans Riot ahead of Protests." Feb. 19. At http://www.aljazeera.com/news/africa/2011/02/2011219163145111944.html.

———. 2016. "My Arab Spring: Egypt's Silent Protest." Jan. 25. At http://www.aljazeera.com/news/2016/01/arab-spring-egypt-silent-protest-160124101244868.html.

Kasbari, Carol Daniel, and Stellan Vinthagen. 2020. "The Visible Effects of 'Invisible Politics': 'Everyday Forms of Resistance' and Possible Outcomes." *Journal of Political Power* 13, no. 1: 1–21.

Lynch, Marc. 2012. *The Arab Uprising: The Unfinished Revolutions of the New Middle East.* New York: PublicAffairs.

Mada Masr. 2015. "Police Arrest Unemployed Postgraduates Protesting near Tahrir Square." Nov. 29. At http://www.madamasr.com/news/police-arrest-unemployed-postgraduates-protesting-near-tahrir-square.

Maniani, Jawad. 2015. "Tangier's 'Revolt of Candles' against Amendis Electricity Bills." *Morocco World News RSS*, Oct. 25. At http://www.moroccoworldnews.com/2015/10/171165/tangiers-revolt-of-candles-against-amendis-electricity-bills/.

Momani, Bessma. 2015. *Arab Dawn: Arab Youth and the Demographic Dividend They Will Bring.* Toronto: Univ. of Toronto Press.

Moroccan Times. 2015. "Tangier: Second Weekend of Huge Protests against Amendis." Oct. 25. At http://moroccantimes.com/2015/10/16969/tangier-second-weekend-huge-protests-amendis.

Morse, Felicity. 2012. "Syria Crisis: 'Occupied Kafranbel' Post Satirical Banners Attacking Bashar al-Assad." *Huffington Post*, July 17. At http://www.huffingtonpost.co.uk/2012/07/17/occupy-kafr-anbel-kafranbel-ass-in-assad-_n_1678857.html.

Mulder, Stephennie. 2018. "Beeshu's Laugh: The Arts of Satire in the Syrian Uprising." *Middle East Journal of Culture and Communication* 11, no. 2: 174–95.

Noderer, Sonja. 2020. "No Laughing Matter? The Potential of Political Humor as a Means of Nonviolent Resistance." *Zeitschrift für Friedens- und Konfliktforschung* 9, no. 2: 1–23.

Ottaway, Marina, and Amr Hamzawy. 2011. "The More Things Change . . . Political Reform in the Arab World." Carnegie Endowment for International Peace, Jan.–Feb. At http://carnegieendowment.org/files/OttawayHamzawy_Outlook_Jan11_Protest Movements.pdf.

Planet Syria. 2014. "The Evolution of Civil Resistance in Syria." Dec. 10. At http://on.planet syria.org/about/.

RaG3IN. 2015. "Egypt Youth Revolution." Facebook page. At https://www.facebook.com /events/1033151053385494/.

Staeheli, Lynn A., Patricia Ehrkamp, Helga Leitner, and Caroline R. Nagel. 2012. "Dreaming the Ordinary: Daily Life and the Complex Geographies of Citizenship." *Progress in Human Geography* 36, no. 5: 628–44.

Stepan, Alfred. 2012. "Tunisia's Transition and the Twin Tolerations." *Journal of Democracy* 23, no. 2: 89–103.

SyriaUntold. 2015. "Mazaj Band: Down with the Homeland." Dec. 8. At http://www.syria untold.com/en/creative/mazaj-band-homeland/.

El Yaakoubi, Aziz. 2015. "Thousands Protest Utility Prices in Morocco's Tangier." Reuters, Nov. 1. At http://www.reuters.com/article/us-morocco-protests-idUSKCN0SQ 1W720151101#dVBJT848T7W5zfeV.97.

Yassin-Kassab, Robin. 2015. "The Sound and the Fury: How Syria's Rappers, Rockers, and Writers Fought Back." *Guardian*, Nov. 25. At http://www.theguardian.com/music /2015/nov/26/how-hip-hop-and-heavy-metal-are-waging-war-in-syria.

Youssef, Naveen, and Mai Noman. 2015. "Alleged Assault Victim Asked: 'Do You Think You Were Dressed Appropriately?'" *BBC Trending*, Oct. 15. At http://www.bbc.com /news/blogs-trending-34668997.

8

What Happened to "Songs of the New Arab Revolutions"?

Michael Frishkopf, Guilnard Moufarrej, George Mürer, Carolyn Ramzy, Jonathan Shannon, Nermeen Youssef, and Iman Mersal

Introduction

Michael Frishkopf

What happens to revolutionary music after the revolution? Throughout the tumult of the Arab Spring, music demonstrated its power to galvanize sentiment and mobilize civil society. Such music included live performance, mediated live performance, and studio-based productions, the latter disseminated mainly through informal channels. Nearly all of this material wound up online, in whole or in part, spreading rapidly through social media.

As an ethnomusicologist focused on the Arab world, I felt it was important to chart this phenomenon. In June 2011, I founded a Facebook group, Songs of the New Arab Revolutions, in an attempt to harness the same social media for ethnomusicological documentation. Membership quickly grew to more than five hundred, posting and commenting on hundreds of links, offering a unique perspective on the complex sets of social dynamics, politics, and economic factors that culminated in the protests. The diversity of submissions from across the stylistic gamut, including folk, popular, and classical music, reflected the multifaceted roles of music in the Arab Spring and the heterogeneous interests of the group's members.

Later that year I issued a call to group members asking for volunteers to participate in a collaborative, web-based, filmmaking experiment. Each participant would draw materials from the stock of videos indexed by the Facebook group and edit and reassemble them to create critical, focused documentary shorts: personal

161

projections, linearizations, and interpretations of an enormous, tangled, and infinitely variegated collection.

Ten group members volunteered, representing a variety of backgrounds and perspectives. Working independently, each of us selected from the vast reservoir of online materials to fashion a five-minute film segment. As expected, a range of documentary foci and strategies emerged, from voiceovers and explicit narratives to more presentational and cinéma vérité approaches. I gathered these videos (in alphabetical sequence by the editors' names) into a fifty-five-minute documentary entitled *Songs of the New Arab Revolutions*, supplemented only by introductory titles for each segment and for the film as a whole (*Songs of the New Arab Revolutions* 2013).[1]

First screened at the meeting of the Society for Ethnomusicology in New Orleans in 2012 and viewed thousands of times since then, this composite film told stories of revolutions through music and stories of music through revolutions, celebrating music's power to express, to mobilize, to resist, to critique, and to change: music of and for grief, anger, and hope; music of and for empowerment; music of and for freedom and change. Some songs were newly inspired by current events; other songs repurposed or revived music of past times and places. Some songs were literal, others satirical; some crystal clear, others ambiguous. Some segments exhibited song's power to drive revolution, some showed revolution's power to drive song, whether for political or economic ends.

But subsequent events demand a reinterpretation of this material. What happened to "songs of the new Arab revolutions"—the songs themselves, the artists (composers, lyricists, performers) who produced them, the collective film, and the film collective that created it? What happened to the sentiments and the social movements they expressed and stirred? How have events of the past decade cast new light on the power of music—and of the arts generally—to effect social change? In retrospect, how do the filmmakers themselves interpret and experience this history? Ten years later, how do we feel about what we created? How do we assess the role of art in revolution today?

In this collectively crafted article, six of the ten original contributors plus one critical commentator (Iman Mersal) reflect on the "unfinished project of the Arab Spring" as expressed, propelled, and recollected through song, considering the possibilities of music's ability to be imbued with durable social meaning, revolutionary or otherwise, and the limits of its social power.

---

1. Before reading the remainder of this article, please view *Songs of the New Arab Revolutions* (2013) at http://bit.ly/snarvid or https://www.youtube.com/watch?v=9u4v7R9yF0o. If the video is unavailable, contact Michael Frishkopf at michaelf@ualberta.ca.

Music, Sport, and Political Protest

Michael Frishkopf

My film segment, "Music, Sport, and Political Protest," documents the evolution of a powerful synergy between song, carried by "singer of the revolution" Ramy Essam, and sport, the extreme soccer fandom of the Ultras Ahlawy (UA-07), supporting Egypt's al-Ahly club, in working toward sociopolitical action.

1. Stills from the documentary film *Songs of the New Arab Revolutions*. (1a). Ramy Essam performing his most famous song, "Irhal" (Leave), in Tahrir Square (February 2011), based on a political chant calling for President Hosni Mubarak to step down. (1b). A year later, Ramy performs "Ya majlis ya ibn al-haram" (Oh Council of Bastards), based on an Ultras Ahlawy chant protesting the role of the Supreme Council for Armed Forces (SCAF) in the Port Said stadium massacre of 2012.

In retrospect, much of the Egyptian revolution appears to have been powered by the fearless bravery of these young soccer fans, whose experience fighting police at matches was redirected toward political change. A synergy emerged between soccer chants, political chants, and song—not only those of Ramy Essam but also the many songs produced by the Ultras themselves.

Here was an alliance of music, sport, and political protest, undergirded by a powerful sense of authenticity. Ramy wasn't viewed as a refined Arab singer but as a sincere, fearless, and influential one. *Time Out* magazine hailed his "Irhal" as the "third-most world-changing song of all time" (NPR n.d.). Many admired the ragtag Ultras for their courageous dedication to the principles of freedom and brotherhood, God, and nation. Singers, protestors, and Ultras alike cleaved to the visceral power of their media—music, chant, and sport—to forge solidarity and precipitate action. The three gathered in a coalition of authenticity—rough-hewn, rowdy, but powerful and true. In an interview, Ramy expressed his admiration for the Ultras in these terms: they are *mukhlisin* (sincere), he told me. The Ultras returned the compliment.

In retrospect, however, it is difficult not to wax a bit cynical and wonder whether we all had overestimated the durable political power of music and sport. After the revolution, Ramy was unable to perform because he was constantly hounded by police. Finally, in late 2014 he left Egypt to take up an artistic residency in Sweden, initially for two years (Freemuse 2014). There he has remained, performing, recording, touring, and developing his art in a free environment. He releases new songs addressing Egyptians but cannot perform in his homeland. As he recently said, "My main audience is in countries where I can't go to" (Hiltunen 2021).

Ramy represents a broader pattern: the exodus of Arab activist artists to sanctuaries in the West, the contraction of their influence following exile from societies that nourished them, where their art has significant meaning and impact. If they remain in those societies, though, the only alternatives are silence, depoliticization, incarceration, or death.

The Ultras were also quickly disempowered by the new regime. After the Port Said massacre in 2012, soccer matches were halted for a time; then fans were prevented from attending. In 2015, the Ultras were officially declared to be terrorists. Some were imprisoned.

The symbolic power of the art/sport/politics synergy was neutralized as the military's material power emerged with its own musical soundtrack, as in "Tislam al-ayadi " (Bless the Hands), a song praising "the Great Egyptian Army" (Kamel 2013). Was the synergy ever a true engine of social change? Or was it simply an epiphenomenon of change driven by dominant material forces? Indeed, is art ever truly revolutionary? Or merely an expression? Or, worse, a veneer masking true social reality—an instrument of false consciousness?

One of the Egyptian revolution's problems was lack of clarity or unanimity about political objectives. It was clear who or what the protestors opposed but not who or what they supported. Sport and music prioritize emotion over perspicuity. Galvanizing an emotional response, they can unify and thus drive social movements for a spell. But they also obscure differences in a manner that may disempower once the revolution begins to succeed.

The Ultras represented diverse political positions, converging only in their struggle for the freedom to support their team. They were united in loyalty, bravery, a quest for justice and dignity—not in the establishment of a particular political order.

Music, too, has the strange power of making participants feel unified even when they're not. Leftists, Nasserists, and Islamists may sing or chant together without embracing a common agenda. Music can forge false consciousness by suppressing thought; as Maurice Bloch noted in an influential essay many years ago, one can't argue with a song (1974, 71).

What about the academy itself? The humanities are idealist and aesthetic; their media are words and art, not material forces, thus perhaps distorting humanists' understanding of how the world actually works. Perhaps we academicians underestimated the inertia of political structures undergirded by materiality; we overestimated the power of words and art to effect lasting change.

Do humanistic vocations blind us from seeing the reality of power, which is invariably material, anti-intellectual, anti-art . . . indeed, antihuman? The Islamic State of Iraq and Syria and the US military alike recklessly destroyed people and priceless heritage, whether in Palmyra or in the National Museum of Iraq.

To answer affirmatively is a cynical view that can lead to despair and inaction. But I prefer to believe that civil society collectivities, whether Ultras, revolutionary artists, or Facebook groups, do constitute a genuine source of social power by demonstrating what people, suitably motivated and allied, can achieve, by expressing collective fearlessness distilled into a durable social-aesthetic moment.

If such a distillation cannot transform political structures in the near term, it remains potent as an affirmation of human agency, the centrality of our fragile human lifeworld, poised against apparently invincible material forces of the global system. For, ultimately, that system draws all its strength from us.

Music, Social Media, and Bereaved Mothers in the New Arab Revolutions

GUILNARD MOUFARREJ

2. A frame from the video for the patriotic song "Ya bladi" (My Country) (Ezz 2011), composed by Baligh Hamdy, showing a martyr's mother singing it. The song is featured in the film *Al-ʿumr lahza*.

The Arab revolutions that began in 2010 have brought continuous distress and suffering to Arab women—from Tunisia, Egypt, and Libya to Iraq, Lebanon, Syria, and Yemen—who have borne the burdens of war. They have been displaced, arrested, assaulted, and raped, and, perhaps most importantly, they have endured the loss of beloved ones.

From the beginning of the uprisings, the notion of martyrdom dominated social media. Words such as *shahid* (martyr), *umm al-shahid* (martyr's mother), and *shahada* (martyrdom) appeared in countless speeches, slogans, and songs. Families took pride in their kinsmen's patriotic deaths, but mothers were especially praised as *umm al-shahid*. Many songs bearing the title "Ila umm al-shahid" (To the Martyr's Mother) encouraged mothers to be proud and not to grieve because their son was a *shahid* who died for his country. Although the lyrics aimed at helping mothers accept their loss, their use on social media altered their message: rather than alleviating mothers' pain, these songs often tended to promote ideologies and political agendas. Dozens of songs titled "Ila umm al-shahid" (To the Martyr's Mother) were posted on YouTube and shared on Facebook. Some songs were sung in the name of a son addressing his mother, comforting her, and asking her to forgive him for having caused her pain and suffering. The texts referred to the deceased's homeland as being his beloved worth his sacrifice.

An apt example, the video of the song "Ya bladi" (My Country), posted during the Egyptian uprisings in 2011, featured a martyr's mother leading a demonstration and singing while her fellow citizens surround her in support (Ezz 2011). The music and the attendant crowd empower her momentarily before she gives up and starts weeping, especially when she is told, in her son's name, to rejoice and accept that he preferred to die so his country could live. (See also Muhammad Fu'ad 2011; Muhammad Nur 2013.)

As I reflect back on these songs and videos, I wonder whether they really served as a tribute to the "martyrs" and a consolation to the afflicted mothers, as their title would suggest. I think that they instead helped spread and justify the culture of martyrdom: they reinforced political and social attitudes that encourage Arab women to raise their children to become martyrs and congratulate them for sacrificing their children for a noble cause. The Syrian historian Ibrahim Zaarour stated in a TV interview in 2005, "The mother in our Arab and Islamic history has always sacrificed her children and prepared them for martyrdom. This is rooted in our religion, our culture, in our values, and our upbringing. . . . As long as there are mothers who give birth, the processions of martyrs will march on" (*Arab Intellectuals Discuss* 2005). These discourses are emphasized through music and videos posted on social media, effectively spreading messages and capturing people's attention. Most of the videos featuring songs addressed to *umm al-shahid* show violent images of dead, disfigured bodies, the mothers wailing and screaming at their side. Such images, while gaining viewers' sympathy and fueling their anger, deepen the mothers' grief and suffering and prolong their healing process.

In this evolving culture of martyrdom, the mothers have been used as a means to gain sympathy and rally support without any consideration to their feelings. Although these metaphors may help the afflicted mother temporarily accept her son's death by submitting to God's will and to her son's desire, she will eventually have to face the reality of her loss. Discussing death in rural Greece, Loring Danforth describes this shift between denial and acceptance as "a shift between a subjective reality that denies the ultimate reality of death and an objective reality in which people adopt a common-sense perspective toward death and are able to accept it" (Danforth and Tsiaras 1982, 32).

As we contemplate the "unfinished project of the Arab Spring," we must acknowledge how many people were deceived: people who risked their lives hoping for a better country in which they could live with dignity and freedom, people who lost their lives believing that their death would make a difference and help resurrect their country from many years of stagnation and injustice. Those who died, the "martyrs," live today through their mothers, who face two losses: their beloved children and the cause they died for.

Tanbura: Port Said at Midan Tahrir

GEORGE MÜRER

Zakaria Ibrahim is an activist, researcher, and champion of local, community-based Egyptian musical practices, from Sudanese and Nubian Zar ceremonies to the exuberant popular songs of Port Said. His contributions to the empowerment of such spheres of musical and social activity include establishing the el-Mastaba Center in Cairo and nurturing the career of the Firqat at-Tanbura (*Tanbura* Ensemble) from Port Said. He himself is a native of Port Said, with roots in Upper Egypt, like many others whose families migrated to the port over the past century and a half. Long before the events known as the Arab Spring, Zakaria Ibrahim would generously introduce visitors (including me) to the community music forums. In the case of Port Said, he was quick to link public musical life to movements of popular resistance to imperialism and to confrontations for which the Suez Canal has served time and again as the front line (from the Suez Canal crisis to the Six-Day War of 1967, for example).

Since the five months I spent as a student in Cairo in 2000, I have retained an interest in Firqat at-Tanbura, whose riveting performances I was able to enjoy

3. Tanbura, Sudanese Zar ceremony, Cairo, 2000. Photograph by George Mürer.

in private in Port Said and in public in Cairo. In Philippe L. Dib's documentary *El Tanbura—Capturing a Vanishing Spirit* (2014), Zakaria Ibrahim points to two important facets of the ensemble's repertoire. The first is a popular genre known as *aghani al-damma*, often sung openly on the street as well as in cafés and at political demonstrations. In an interview in the film, he describes *aghani al-damma* as incorporating both the popular love song genre *al-suhbagiyya* and the type of ecstatic singing that animates local Sufi gatherings and festivals.

The second facet is the *simsimiyya*, a rhythmically strummed lyre, whose larger cousin gives the ensemble its name. The *simsimiyya* and closely related variations are part of local music not only in Port Said but also around the Red Sea in Sinai, Sudan, the Hijaz region, Ethiopia, and Yemen (especially Tihama but also among Hadramis from Mukalla and Shihr to Zanzibar). As an animating presence, the *simsimiyya* serves not only as an accompaniment but also as an emblem of local identity and history, while its baritone cousin the *tanbura*—the ensemble's namesake—is a powerful ritual object in many ceremonial contexts around the Red Sea, Persian Gulf, and Arabian Sea littorals.

When the Arab Spring gained in momentum, Tahrir Square was in many respects the epicenter of the protests and uprisings taking place from Tunis to Manama and Muharraq. Among the many singers, bands, activists, and rappers whose contributions to the demonstrations were captured and circulated, Firqat at-Tambura and Zakaria Ibrahim presided with an eloquent, historically cognizant, and impassioned combination of songs, chanted slogans, and oration, reminding the crowds of the sacrifices made by ordinary Egyptians in Port Said and Ismailia to safeguard Egypt from foreign intrusion and exploitation in the 1950s. In a clip posted on YouTube by Mamdouh el-Kady, one of Zakaria Ibrahim's close associates at el-Mastaba, we see the *simsimiyya* dramatically brandished aloft like a tour guide's umbrella as the ensemble makes its way through the crowd to the stage.

The songs chanted by the group throughout the clip echo the very themes that Zakaria Ibrahim posits to be at the heart of this strain of populist music making—themes of revolutionary patriotism, of the people as martyrs felled defending Egypt against foreign incursions, and slogans invoking Gamal Abdel Nasser, "patriotic Port Said," and January 25, 1952 (the date of a bloody confrontation between Egyptian police and the British army in Ismailia), and enjoining the youth (*shabab*) to rise up (*thuwar*).

In the aftermath of the Arab Spring, Egypt has continued to suffer social discord, popular discontent, severe political repression, and economic hardship, first under Mohamed Morsi and now under General Abdel Fattah al-Sisi. By resisting contextualization within either the ideological confines of concert or folkloric presentation or the push toward an aesthetic suited to the competitive global pop-music mediascape (as we find with the *mahraganat* scene), the musical sphere embodied by Firqat at-Tanbura offers both an open-ended inclusivity with respect to participation, sentiments, and ideas as well as an uncompromisingly critical position on Egypt's internal and external political, social, and economic relations.

In 2022, having weathered the pandemic, the ensemble continues to perform tirelessly, with weekly events in Port Said and frequent appearances elsewhere in Egypt. On social media, Zakaria Ibrahim continues to promote other ensembles and artists and to mourn the irreplaceable elder custodians of musical and cultural arts when they pass away. With support from this circle of dedicated performer-activists, a robust network of rising talents and archived memories is sustained.

"Bless My Country, O Lord": Coptic Christians
Negotiate Revolution through Song

CAROLYN RAMZY

In my contribution to *Songs of the New Arab Revolution* (2013), it is particularly poignant to watch Egypt's Muslims and Christians come together in Tahrir Square to sing Christian devotional songs, *taratil* (sing. *tartila*) a decade following the January 25 uprising in 2011. Although many from the Coptic Protestant community jubilantly embraced the revolution's possibilities and were among the first to rush to the square, Coptic Orthodox media outlets expressed the community's anxieties about the possible rise of Islamist parties to power following the uprising. In the making of my video segment, I hoped to highlight the seemingly dissonant juxtaposition of the narrative of "national" unity, sung by protestors in the square and touted by international media, and the anxiety expressed in *taratil* broadcast on official Coptic Orthodox outlets. As the spring ended, the election of a Muslim Brotherhood party and president (2012–13) as well as a rash of sectarian violence only justified these fears.

Although Egypt's new military president, General Abdel Fattah al-Sisi, has made considerable symbolic strides for the Coptic community, a sense of ambivalence continues to shape the community's satellite channels in and outside of Egypt. More specifically, *taratil* song videos that circulate on Coptic Television

4. Still from the music video for the *taratil* "Ya sahabat al-shuhud" (Cloud of Martyrs). Here, images of victims from recent sectarian-related incidents are pastiched side by side with pictures of Orthodox martyrs against a heavenly backdrop. Below the images, one of the lines from the song reads: "We are the sons of the martyrs." *Source*: From Coptic TV 2014.

(CTV; see, e.g., Coptic TV 2014), the church's official channel, as well as on other Christian satellite channels continue to emphasize martyr tropes and interpolate graphic images of victims from sectarian and military clashes with iconic images of saint hagiographies. In many of these videos, songs praise the dead as martyrs not for their Egyptian nation but rather for their Orthodox faith.

In my video, I begin with one particular moment. On February 6, 2011, *BBC Arabic News* along with countless other international new agencies broadcast what they thought was a Coptic mass in Tahrir Square, the heart of Egypt's ongoing revolution. Cameras panned on protesters as they yelled, "Christians, Muslims— one hand!" On an impromptu stage, the evangelical pastor Fawzy Khalil led a service accompanied by an instrumental ensemble and singers. They were singing the song "Barik biladi" (Bless My Country) by the popular and interdenominational ensemble Fari' Tasbih (literally Praise Team). In religiously generic terms, the song's text sounded a collective prayer to God to guide the ongoing revolution and to make Egypt "an Eden and to restore the rights of the abused." Just a few steps away from Tahrir Square, the liberal satellite news channel ON TV also broadcast a mixed congregation singing the song in Egypt's largest evangelical church, Kasr el-Dobara.

Back in Shubra, a middle-class neighborhood with the highest number of Coptic Christians in Cairo, many Orthodox viewers of this broadcast of a supposed Coptic mass in Tahrir Square were skeptical. First, much of the religious song's original text had been altered, removing all Christian markers. And, unlike what the BBC reported, this supposed mass was not a Sunday mass, at least not in the Orthodox sense. Instead, such misrepresentation only exacerbated existing interdenominational tensions between Orthodox and evangelical Christians and contributed to a growing sense of isolation among Orthodox Copts following the uprising. In turn, "Bless My Country" sounded very different on Orthodox TV and reflected the community's ambivalence about the current events. On the satellite channel Aghape TV, the song's music video highlighted its Christian references and placed a particular emphasis on Coptic martyrs and "the Holy Spirit, [who] gathers their bones from the valley." Drawing on Orthodox hagiographies, the song continued with a call to "raise the heavenly flag," played over images of ancient Egyptian monuments. Though this was the same song that demonstrators performed in Tahrir Square, on Orthodox TV "Bless my Country" reflected a very different understanding of Coptic *and* Orthodox Christian belonging during the uprising in Egypt.

Today, Abdel Fattah al-Sisi is the first Egyptian president to visit a Coptic cathedral during the celebration of the Orthodox liturgy (Ahram Online n.d.). His visits and pledge to rebuild churches torn down by religious extremists fuel the support for him among Orthodox Christians, and his warm relationship with the Orthodox pope, Tawadros II, inspires a cautious optimism among the community. Despite this shift, Orthodox media outlets have yet to change their tone. New *taratil*, such as "Cloud of Martyrs," continue to pastiche photographs of victims of sectarian-related violence, though special efforts are made to avoid articulating who the perpetrators are, in particular the military's role in the Maspero massacre in October 2011. The church's open and public support of the military continues, while satellite and digital media outlets privately continue to negotiate Coptic Orthodox ambivalence toward belonging to a postrevolutionary Egypt.

Humor in Syrian Revolutionary Music Videos: Songs by the Group Syrian Bear

JONATHAN SHANNON

The aim of my segment of *Songs of the New Arab Revolutions* was to reveal how humor and satire have played a large role in the musical responses to the crisis in Syria. At the time, I felt that most academic and mainstream media analysis of the conflict (initially called a rebellion, then a revolt or a conflict, and now a civil war) focused on global power plays but paid scant attention to the everyday lives of those most affected by the conflict. Even those reports that emphasized the human dimensions tended to focus on narratives of victimhood, and although such reports accurately captured the scale of suffering, in doing so they inadvertently perpetuated the trope that victims of violence have little or no agency. I wanted to show that amid their suffering—let us be clear, many Syrians have suffered on a scale not seen since World War II—Syrians drew on their vast and deep cultural resources of humor and wit in response to the violence.

Of course, satire and wit are often the best and even the only forms of political discourse feasible in dictatorial contexts, given the violence (implicit and explicit) of censorship. Syrians have also drawn on the rich repertoire of political protest song and chant, both local and global, in their response to their government's violent repression of dissent. The religious dimensions are also evident in the numerous Islamic chants (*anashid*) produced by actors as diverse as Islamic State supporters, al-Qaeda, and what Western media term "moderate" resistance fighters.

In my video segment, I wanted to show a different sort of response, one perhaps more nuanced and more powerful. The songs I selected, written by the anonymous group Syrian Bear, feature simple compositions with light, humorous, almost nursery-rhyme lyrics. The videos (from the simple to the more polished) that accompany them revealed in graphic imagery the Assad regime's savagery in its quest to quell the rebellion. At the same time, the songs marked a moment of optimism that the Syrian people would succeed, just as the Tunisians and Egyptians (at the time) had, in dislodging a feared and loathed dictator.

Alas, subsequent events in those countries and Libya reveal that the outcomes of the so-called Arab Spring uprisings were not what most protestors and commentators expected and hoped for. In Syria, after years of civil war, the situation is no better, and in fact it may be described as worse; witness the siege and mass starvation of the population of Madaya (a village not far from Damascus) by government and allied forces (mainly Lebanese Hezbollah). In the face of such brutality, the witty and satirical songs have largely dried up, and the Islamist *anashid* have proliferated. My video, then, captured a moment in time: a cautiously optimistic one in the midst of the grim realities of everyday violence. Today, barrel bombs, widespread starvation, massive flight to neighboring lands, and indescribable destruction have made such a response almost unthinkable.

Since the creation of the video project, the situation in Syria has worsened. The number of Syrians killed in the ongoing conflict exceeds 500,000, and more than 11 million have been displaced internally and externally, the majority ending up in neighboring countries and across Europe, where they have encountered receptions ranging from the lukewarm to the hostile. Now that the conflict has largely come to an end, the initial euphoria of a people mobilizing to overthrow a dictatorial regime has devolved into a state of desperation and despair. Syrians who remained within Syria waited for the regime to win or fall and for the international community to forge a solution. Now, with little hope for change, they attempt to rebuild lives in often desperate conditions. Protest-inspired musical practices within Syria have virtually come to an end, as have the number of Islamist *anashid*, and Syrian artists residing overseas either repeat the themes of 2011–13 or have fallen silent. A few voices still ring out (Samih Shoucair's is one, and those of younger artists in places such as Berlin are others), but the citizen journalism and guerrilla theater of 2011–13 have largely disappeared. Resistance to the violence of the state against its own people is now expressed as a collective silence. It's as if Syrian artists are holding their breath. The future remains uncertain.

From Potato Chips to Down with SCAF

Nermeen Youssef

Like many Egyptian expatriates, I watched the revolution unfold in Tahrir Square on January 25, 2011, by means of the internet. As previously observed during times of similar political turbulence, various changes on the social and cultural fronts occurred simultaneously. There was the melding of Egyptians from all walks of society in Tahrir Square—sharing food, spontaneously inventing teargas antidotes, and singing morale-boosting songs. In my segment of the video, I aimed to highlight five songs that were reappropriations of older well-known songs and commercials.

Mado, a singer and writer from the Cairo-based Taxi Band, repurposed music of three Egyptian television commercials and transformed them into humorous political songs. The products being advertised were True Chips, a new brand of potato chips; Dream Park, one of the biggest Egyptian theme parks; and Etisalat mobile phone plans.

The True Chips commercial, making fun of unskilled barbers who monopolize the conversation, hardly giving their customers a chance to talk, was an excellent analogy to how Mado viewed the Supreme Council of the Armed Forces (SCAF), which came to power after Hosni Mubarak stepped down in February 2011. The video shows Mado and Wael Amer on the street, addressing the military regime and telling it that despite its being in power for all these years, the country remained poor, prisoners were still being unjustly tried, and the people's demands were not being heeded—all to the tune of the True Chips commercial. Their cover ends with "Down with you, Mr. Tantawy," referring to Field Marshall Mohamed Tantawy, who headed SCAF at the time.

The contrast between the Dream Park commercial and the cover song by Taxi Band is striking and yielded a very amusing sing-along called "Sign Tora" (Tora Prison). Using the same uplifting and simple melody of a commercial, which invites children to spend an unforgettable day at the park, Mado invited Mubarak, his family, and his regime to Tora Prison, "where thieves belong," according to the song, to serve their sentences.

The commercial for Etisalat mobile communications revolves around how the company broke the mold with their new phone plans, even though everybody thought "they were crazy." Taxi Band created several versions of a song based on this commercial to address new events as they happened. The version included in my video shows Mado and Wael Amer at the time when the military was "transitionally" in power and new parties were being formed in preparation for Egypt's postrevolution Parliament. This cover highlights the confusion that the Egyptian youth were experiencing owing to the presence of too many political parties and the lack of trust in the military regime's propaganda. Yet the youth were hopeful that they could end the military rule, despite everybody thinking "they were crazy."

The Egyptian duo comprising composer and singer Sheikh Imam Eissa and poet Ahmed Fouad Negm created many political songs that were frequently banned and sent the duo to jail for their sharp criticism of the Nasser and Sadat regimes of the 1960s and 1970s. Their songs have been frequently used as symbols of resistance and revolution. My segment of the video shows them performing "Allah haii" (God Is Alive), an older song repurposed during the revolution using a more upbeat arrangement and a quicker tempo. The lyrics were also changed to praise Egypt's people, especially its youth. The happy melody symbolized hope and the youth's ability to change the stagnant political scene.

The song "Ya biladi ya biladi" ("My country, my country") was one of the musical icons of the revolution that emerged before Mubarak stepped down. The original melancholic melody, composed by Baligh Hamdy for the film *al-'Umr lahza* (Life Is but a Moment), was sung by a children's choir to accompany a scene where the heroine walks through the rubble of the Bahr al-Baqar primary school (near Port Said) after it is bombed by the Israeli air force in 1970, killing forty-six children. The chorus is a simple, repeated declaration of love to the country. Aziz El Shafei and Ramy Gamal used this same chorus and created new verses addressed to the mothers of the young martyrs who were killed during the revolution, comforting them that the martyrs were happy to give their lives for the sake of a better future for the country.

Although the production of political songs, reappropriated or original, has significantly declined in Egypt since 2011, the musical body of work produced in the first two years after the revolution remains the most memorable. At a time when Egyptians were united in a common goal, their sing-alongs would be carved in their collective memory, reminding them of times of hope, mourning, fear, and courage, a soundtrack to their revolution.

After the Revolution . . . What Happened to "Songs of the New Arab Revolutions"?

Iman Mersal

Illusion

Watching *Songs of the New Arab Revolutions* today generates a sense of illusion, like seeing a happy moment in a family photograph when you know that in reality this family is falling apart. Does this mean that what was revolutionary music—music inspiring action or celebrating change, music expressing hope—was a "false representation" or the representation of a failed hope? Has the film itself become a document of both the hope and its failing?

There are two moments here, carrying two emotions. There is a moment of hope: enthusiasm, unity, solidarity. The call for "*'aysh, hurriyya, 'adala ijtima'iyya*" (bread, freedom, and justice) resulted in the downfall of Zine El Abidine Ben Ali in Tunisia, Hosni Mubarak in Egypt, and Muammar Qaddafi in Libya. Then comes the moment of despair, hope transformed, as the army swept into control of Egypt, and the Islamic State gained territory in Syria and Iraq. The moment of despair is marked not only at the political, economic, and social levels (new military dictatorship, economic hardship, social disorder, sectarian violence, displacement, and refugee crises) but in the arts, including music, as well.

The singers and musicians of the Arab Spring are good examples of what individuals involved in such hope went through. The Syrian protest singer Ibrahim Kashoush was brutally murdered in Hama, Syria, in 2013, presumably by government thugs. In the same year, the Tunisian rapper Alaa Yacoubi, known as "Weld El 15," was sentenced to two years in prison for his famous song "Bulisiyya kilab" (The Police Are Dogs), criticizing the security services (Weld El 15 2013). In 2014, Egypt's "singer of the revolution," Ramy Essam, took up a two-year residency offered by the Malmö Municipality of Sweden because "in the past year I have not been able to perform freely in Egypt. Permission has not been granted to give concerts to large audiences. My songs are being censored by state media. I have been harassed by individual policemen and interrogated by National Security Police" (*Freemuse* 2014).

The public space that music of the Arab Spring once occupied no longer exists. In this chapter, Jonathan Shannon writes that "protest-inspired musical practices within Syria have virtually come to an end, as have the number of Islamist *anashid*, and Syrian artists residing overseas either repeat the themes of 2011–13 or have fallen silent." In Egypt, protest singers and musicians are lucky to be alive and free, but only because they are silent or in exile. Here, the contemporary musical scene is one that is instead preoccupied with songs praising the army: "mainstream sounding songs that ensure airtime by courting the state and listeners accustomed to monotonous pop" (El Sirgany n.d.). One of the most popular of these songs, "Tislam al-ayadi" (Bless the Hands), praises the Egyptian military and its leader, General Abdel-Fattah al-Sisi, for removing President Mohamed Morsi in July 2013 (Kamel 2013).

The music of the Arab Spring was characterized not only by its collective production and hopeful content but also by its success in occupying public space. Throughout thirty years of emergency law under Mubarak, Egyptians were never able to express their frustrations or hopes by inhabiting that space bodily; all one saw, scrawled on empty walls and under bridges, were slogans for the ruling National Democratic Party (which always received 99 percent of the vote), commercial products, and Islamic ideologies ("Islam is the solution," "the veil protects morality")—but never the people behind them.

One of the first chanted slogans to appear during the uprising was "al-Shariʻ lana" (The street is ours), taken from Majida El Roumi's famous song of the same title. This slogan, describing so many images and sounds during the eighteen days of revolution in Tahrir Square, presented a different sense of community and solidarity: there was public space for music. While some protestors charged their cell phones by hacking streetlights, others used their technical skills to power a sound system for a public concert. A group of young artists marked walls and floors with graffiti. A festival atmosphere prevailed, featuring music, art, comedy, even weddings. Music was an action that took part in what the American sociologist Charles Tilly (2008) calls "contentious performances." With each action, activists attempted to build upon and learn from the successes and failures of previous actions in a process of learning, revising, and improvising what Tilly calls a "repertoire of contention," stressing that this repertoire plays a role in standardizing and limiting the nature of contentious performance (see also Kriesi 2009, 341–49).

Reality

A few days after Mubarak stepped down in February 2011, I returned to my flat in Manial, a Cairo neighborhood located on an island in the Nile. There I found that a group of teenage boys and girls were constructing troughs in front of our building to hold flower beds, painting them in the bright colors of the Egyptian flag. Others were helping the teenagers in their work, buying them drinks, asking if they needed anything. Despite the neighborhood's middle-class pretensions, Manial's garbage is typically thrown into the streets, where it remains for two or three days before the garbagemen come along to sweep it up and cart it off, as elsewhere in the city. To my surprise, on this occasion there was no garbage: the streets were clean, decorated with flowers and the colors of the flag.

When I visited again in 2012, the flower beds were still there, but they were full of garbage. I couldn't help but imagine all the revolutionary musicians gathered again: they might not find squares or people; they might find the police awaiting them in numbers; but, more importantly, their gathering would be devoid of meaning except through the nostalgia for the past.

Questions

The public space that held this contentious performance is back in the hands of state authorities. The graffiti that appeared on the walls of Cairo and so many other Arab cities during the uprisings has been painted over by the police or by fellow citizens (see Naji 2011).

The valuable question that such a film about the music of the Arab Spring might be able to ask in a future moment is not "Has the Arab Spring failed?" or "What is the role of the arts in revolution?" but rather "What sorts of poems, songs, arts are required to support resistance, uprising, revolution? What is the artist's position at the moment of revolution? How and why are certain poems or songs recalled to play a specific function in every creation of national mythology? Finally, whether arts can transform revolution or not, can revolution also transform arts? If not, is this not also a sign of failure?

References

Ahram Online. N.d. "Egypt's Sisi Attends Coptic Christmas Mass for Second Straight Year." At http://english.ahram.org.eg/News/180296.aspx. Accessed Apr. 27, 2016.

Arab Intellectuals Discuss Martyrdom and Arab Women. 2005. Syrian TV, May. At http://www.youtube.com/watch?v=AO8eLID_pVw.

Bloch, Maurice. 1974. "Symbols, Song, Dance, and Features of Articulation: Is Religion an Extreme Form of Traditional Authority?" *European Journal of Sociology / Archives européennes de sociologie* 15, no. 1: 54–81.

Coptic TV. 2014. *Ya sahabat al-shuhud*. At https://www.youtube.com/watch?v=lQf4uz9_4NA.

Danforth, Loring M., and Alexander Tsiaras. 1982. *The Death Rituals of Rural Greece*. Princeton, NJ: Princeton Univ. Press.

Dib, Philippe L. 2014. *El Tanbura—Capturing a Vanishing Spirit*. At https://www.youtube.com/watch?v=ZSIpuVjfQec.

Ezz, Abdurrahman. 2011. *Umm al-shahid tughanni ya biladi ana bahibbak ya biladi*. Nov. At https://www.youtube.com/watch?v=dcy0BLmMeCk.

Freemuse. 2014. "Egyptian Singer Ramy Essam: 'Why I Moved to Sweden for Two Years.'" Oct. 24. At https://freemuse.org/news/egyptian-singer-ramy-essam-why-i-move-to-sweden-for-two-years/.

Hiltunen, Riikka. 2021. "Making Music for Justice in Exile—Musician Ramy Essam's Interview." *FMQ*, Mar. 29. At https://fmq.fi/articles/ramy-essam.

Kamel, Mustafa. 2013. "Tislam al-ayadi." At https://www.youtube.com/watch?v=_ETI-mMFAUU.

Kriesi, Hanspeter. 2009. "Charles Tilly: Contentious Performances, Campaigns, and Social Movements." *Swiss Political Science Review* 15, no. 2: 341–49.

Muhammad Fu'ad. 2011. "Ughniyat umm al-shahid." Mar. At https://www.youtube.com/watch?v=e8nMoH7v7UQ.

Muhammad Nur. 2013. "Ughniyat umm al-shahid." Aug. At https://www.youtube.com/watch?v=T3RUVtsDJLM.

Naji, Ahmed. 2011. "Al-Girafiti: Yahya al-fann al-za'il." *Akhbar al-adab*, June 11.

NPR. N.d. "Ramy Essam." *Live Sessions.* At https://livesessions.npr.org/artists/ramy-essam. Accessed Sept. 3, 2021.

El Sirgany, Sarah. N.d. "National Songs in Tune with the State." *Al Akhbar English.* At http://english.al-akhbar.com/blogs/labyrinth/national-songs-tune-state. Accessed Apr. 23, 2016.

Songs of the New Arab Revolutions. 2013. Documentary. At http://bit.ly/snarvid.

Tilly, Charles. 2008. *Contentious Performances.* Cambridge: Cambridge Univ. Press.

Weld El 15. 2013. *Weld EL 15—Boulicia Kleb (HD) (RAP TUNISIEN).* At https://www.youtube.com/watch?v=T_VYwkZmGIQ.

9

The Future of Nonviolence in the Middle East

Iran and Beyond

Ramin Jahanbegloo

The Middle East has entered a new era of sectarian tensions, civil conflicts, and regional wars. Syria unraveled into an ever more divisive and brutal conflict, jeopardizing the political and economic stability of Lebanon and Jordan. Egypt has returned to the strongman politics of the deep state. The geopolitics of the Persian Gulf region is affected by a proxy war between Iran and Saudi Arabia. One must also acknowledge that the Islamic State of Iraq and Syria (ISIS) surprised a large part of the Western community by taking advantage of a power vacuum in Syria, Iraq, and Libya within a short time to create its own safe havens in parts of Iraq, Syria, and Libya—all of them states that can be regarded as failed states with insufficient public control and authority.

It has become a cliché to talk of an inevitable and intractable sectarian divide between Sunni and Shi'a. But the reality is that the present rising tensions in the Middle East are far more complex than simple religious hatreds. They reflect a growing friction rooted in numerous struggles over power, rights, and identity initiated by both the US invasion of Iraq and the geopolitical reconfigurations of the Arab Spring.

More than ten years ago, waves of popular protest and revolutionary turmoil began to spread spontaneously and unexpectedly across the Middle East and North Africa (MENA). What was at the time ambiguously and romantically called the "Arab Spring" created great hope all around the region and the world about the establishment of long-awaited democracy in authoritarian Arab societies. This hope for a radical change in MENA was felt by activists, academics, and artists around the world. In this vein, the Iranian American scholar Hamid Dabashi wrote: "The Arab Spring is not a fulfillment but a delivery. This is what I mean by its being the end of post-colonialism: the Arab Spring is not the final fulfillment of a set of ideologies but the exhaustion of all ideologies, a final delivery from them all" (2012, 252). Though the Arab Spring did not put an end to the process of recolonization of the MENA region, it is certain that the fall of longtime dictators such as General Zine El Abidine Ben Ali, Hosni Mubarak, and Muammar Qaddafi as well as the rise of new civic actors and new social movements around the MENA region represented encouraging signs that a process of democratization was possible and that ideas of popular sovereignty and the rule of law could be taking hold.

Today, after a decade, the initial hope and wishful thinking about the Arab Spring have faded, while the political, social, and economic conditions that led to the uprisings of 2011 around the MENA region have for most part remained unchanged. The Middle East is in tatters, and the short period of hope and revolutionary ideals has been followed by new forms of authoritarianism and denial of civil liberties. It is clear that the result of the popular protests has been nothing but chaos in the form of either long-term wars (as in Syria) or sectarian conflicts (as in Yemen) or increased repression (as in Egypt). As for Libya, four years after the capture and execution of Muammer Qaddafi, the country resembles a failed state that has plunged into dangerous unrest.

Arguably, Tunisia is the only country where the Arab Spring appears to have succeeded principally through the establishment of a landmark pluralist constitution crafted through close dialogue and collaboration among the secularists and Islamists and without the interference of the West. Despite the experience of democratic transition in Tunisia, however, there appears little hope of democracy in the Middle East. Democracy needs certain conditions to flourish, notably the rule of law, civil liberties, and economic freedom, most of which are absent across the Arab world. We should add to this list a belief in social equality and ethnic diversity, which is now also missing in the political narrative and in actions, including those of the once "admired and landed" Justice and Development Party government in Turkey.

More importantly, since 2013 the Middle East has found itself facing the eruption of ISIS, a radical Sunni jihadist group that formally declared the establishment of a "caliphate." As one of the major consequences of the US invasion of Iraq in 2003, ISIS has become a central concern of governments across the world today. Based on a mixture of religious fanaticism and organizational hierarchy, the violence practiced by ISIS militants is neither Islamic nor sectarian but anticivilizational. The horrors perpetuated by members of this group—such as the massacre of civilians, the enslavement of women, destruction of entire religious communities, and annihilation of the monuments of old civilizations—represent a manifest rejection of the basic concepts of human heritage and shared values. Nevertheless, ISIS is a more complex phenomenon than we think because it links two important elements, the ideological and the geopolitical, that have been at work in the Middle East for a long time.

The Iranian Experience of Nonviolence

With respect to the Arab Spring, it would be certainly more correct to talk about "uprisings in the Middle East and North Africa" instead of using the phrase *intifadat al-Arabiya* (Arab uprisings), for the very good reason that there was also an *intifada al Iraniya* (Iranian uprising). In all and for all, we can say that the extraordinary uprisings in the Arab world that began in early 2011 had a Persian precursor in 2009, which more than any other civil uprising in this region of the world remains an unfinished project.

However, when interpreting something like the Iranian protests of 2009, people tend to project their own passions onto the screen. Young Iranian tweeters see a social media revolution; the Iranian Reformists see a reformist imperative in the Islamic Republic; and Iranian human rights groups see a backlash against routine abuses by the Iranian regime.

But, in fact, a full range of different "drivers of change" was involved in bringing about what is called the Green Movement of 2009, and it is because of this diversity of drivers of change that the movement not only remains a potential of democratization in Iranian society but also continues to suffer from some serious weaknesses. Considering the complexities of Iranian society and politics, it is important to highlight the fact that the Green Movement of 2009, specifically in regard to its democratic beliefs and liberal stance, did not suddenly materialize within Iranian consciousness in the aftermath of the fraudulent elections that year. Nader Hashemi and Danny Postel trace the roots of this historical event back to the rise of the Reform movement in Iran in the 1990s: "It was during this period, due primarily to the work of Iran's religious intellectuals, that Iranian political culture experienced a transformation in which the basic principles of liberal democracy and an indigenous understanding of 'Islamic secularism' emerged and sank deep roots into civil society" (2020, xx).

Iran's historical struggle to establish an accountable modern government can be traced back to the Constitutional Revolution of 1906, but without going back too far, we can say that in the past twenty-five years Iran has been on the course of a major political and societal evolution since the increasingly young population has become more educated, secular, and liberal. In those years, an explosive mix of high population growth leading to a "youth bulge," urbanization, growth in joblessness linked in part to structural adjustment, and the rapid expansion of university education has produced new sociological actors in Iran who are essentially young and educated (most of the them women) but have no political, economic, or social future. As a result, this generational gap has divided Iranian society between essentially money-making and powerful conservatives and young rebels without a cause. Iran has become a society divided between the Donald Trumps and the James Deans. Therefore, it is not strange that the Iranian youth has been at the forefront of support for the nuclear deal because they have suffered the most from unemployment and the Iranian currency devaluation owing to the international sanctions against Iran. Whether as internet users or spontaneous demonstrators, the young people of Iran, who represent today more than 60 percent of 81 million Iranians, are well educated and believe in gradual change of the Islamic Republic of Iran. Interestingly, more than half of Iranians between the ages of eighteen and twenty-five attend some form of higher-education institution, and more than 60 percent of the entries in the Iranian universities are women. Also, Iranian youngsters are by far the highest per capita users of the internet in the Middle East. The civic rebellion of 2009 was arguably the manifestation of such changing attitudes that have been slowly emerging among Iran's overall young population. These attitudes open up the options of nonviolent discontent among the Iranian youth. Back in 2009, this is how I described what I called "the Gandhian Moment" in Iran: "To many observers, the idea of the Gandhian moment in a despotic society like Iran is a fairy tale. However, one could respond to this objection with the words of Gandhi himself: 'The nonviolent technique does not depend for its success on the good will of the dictators. . . . Satyagraha is never vindictive. It believes not in destruction but in conversion.' It remains to be seen whether Iranian social movements could be committed wholly to the nonviolence of the brave, thereby realizing the Gandhian moment in Iran" (Jahanbegloo [2009] 2010, 19; also see Jahanbegloo 2013).

Though we do not have enough empirical evidence to conclude that all modes of resistance brought about through nonviolent action in Iran have been long-lasting, it seems that nonviolent attitudes regarding unveiling and garbage collecting are important social factors still present in Iranian society and undermine the legitimacy of the divine sovereignty of the Iranian government. Surprisingly, today the same nonviolent attitude shows itself across classes as supporting the nuclear deal with the United States. When the deal was announced on July 14, 2015, thousands of young Iranians took to the streets of Tehran to celebrate a new chapter in Iran's relations with the world. They held photos not of the country's supreme leader, Ali Khamenei, but of Foreign Minister Mohammad Javad Zarif. Some young participants also used the opportunity to hold up pictures of Mir Hossein Mousavi and

Mehdi Karoubi, two presidential candidates in 2009 who had been under house arrest since 2009 because of their opposition to the government.[1] Police dispersed those demonstrators, fearing they could spark wider protests.

Young Iranians have been at the forefront of support for the accords because they are among the hardest hit not only by the sanctions but also by the violent measures employed by the Ahmadinejad government after 2009. The same Baby Boomers came of age during the movement in 2009 when millions poured into the streets to protest fraudulent elections and call for major changes. This discontent boiled over when young Iranians voted for Hassan Rouhani even though he was not part of the Reformist camp. Many in the Iranian civil society argued that hard-liners used the West's hostility and the US-led sanctions as excuses for Iran's weak economic performance under Mahmoud Ahmadinejad and for the need for political repression. Although there are some skeptics, most civic actors in Iran predict that nonviolent resistance will continue in Iran even after economic sanctions are lifted. What counts most for Iranian civil society, however, is the effort to find a way out of economic difficulties in order to regain its forces to work toward a new Iran and enter an era of postideological politics. That is why for Iranian civil society the nuclear agreement marked a new era in Iranian politics. Yet we need to bear in mind that this new era is not only fragile but also affected by the limits of Iranian civil society, which is trying to empower itself by creating a competing and parallel political culture of its own. Though Iranian civil society does not romanticize the idea of revolution after forty-three years of revolutionary politics, the fact remains that most young Iranians have moved away from fundamentalist politics and utopian rationalities and have embraced value pluralism, dialogue with the West, and an understanding of both modern culture and Iranian heritage. The civic movement of 2009 is still carrying the heavy baggage of both suffering and unfulfilled promises. From a more critical perspective, to see the movement of 2009 in Iran as just a "civil rights" movement would be quite misleading.

1. As Laura Secor wrote in the *New Yorker* of October 12, 2010, "The Mehdi Karroubi who ran for president in 2009 barely resembled the Karroubi who ran in 2005. Now Karroubi emerged as the race's most outspoken proponent of human rights, women's rights, and political freedom. Some of the same young Iranians who scoffed at his campaign in 2005 told me with regret that they would vote for Mir-Hossein Mousavi—they saw him as the more electable candidate, with an appeal that extended from urban youth into Ahmadinejad's constituency—but that their hearts were with Karroubi. In a televised debate, Ahmadinejad displayed chart after chart to defend his claim that the Iranian economy was healthy; Karroubi all but called the President a liar. Although all the opposition candidates derided Ahmadinejad's Holocaust denial (if tepidly), it was Karroubi who indignantly told a rally, 'Denying the Holocaust is like defending Hitler. Have we come down so low that we need to defend Hitler's dignity?'" (Secor 2010, 409–10).

In reality, the movement of 2009 remains an unfinished project with a rebellious potential—not, as some people think, only a momentary show of rebellion that ultimately failed. "History will prove who the real participants of this movement are," wrote Ali Alizadeh (2010, 6). If there is still an element of nonviolence in Iranians' social attitude, it is about overcoming an ideology or, in better words, theological politics. However, two main elements are still missing in this potential of rebellion: leadership and a determined strategy. In 2009, the movement started strong but soon faced a violent crackdown by the regime and lost its momentum when the state incarcerated protestors and key figures. Another obstacle that the Green Movement failed to overcome was the fact that it was dealing with a "rentier state."

Rentier states receive much of their income from the sale of their natural resources, such as oil and natural gas, and do not rely on their citizens for income through taxation, thus making such states less obligated to satisfy the needs and wishes of their citizens. One reason why the Middle East has not changed much in its political development relates heavily to the fact that most of the governments in the region control the access to wealth and in turn are able to remain powerful and hinder any political reforms. As a matter of fact, the Green Movement of 2009 in Iran was unable to enlist the support of key segments of the Iranian economy, such as major industries, transportation and worker unions, government employees, bazaar merchants, and, most importantly, oil workers. Certainly, had the movement gained the support of such powerful economic groups, it would have financially weakened the state and possibly made the state more inclined to negotiate or engage in talks, as what happened in Poland with the Solidarity trade union.

Against this background, it is now possible to surmise the Green Movement's long-term effects. One of the movement's early achievements was that it mobilized millions of Iranians, far surpassing the numbers of protestors during the Revolution of 1979. The movement was made up of teachers, journalists, professors, clergymen, entrepreneurs, women, men, and the youth, and it attracted Iranians from all different socioeconomic backgrounds. Segments from the lower and middle classes came together, and many Iranians of different political views and affiliations set aside their differences and supported one another to oppose Mahmoud Ahmadinejad's government.

The Green Movement's ability to garner so many diverse supporters in such a short time can be attributed to several factors: years of built-up political, social, and economic dissatisfaction; the young population's political shift toward less ideology and more liberal and pluralistic values; the sociological evolution of Iranian women as main social and political actors in Iranian society; and, of course, the new communication technologies as civic tools of social organization. Not only did the Green Movement manage to gather widespread support, but it also channeled the dissatisfaction of its followers in a nonviolent way. The movement thus gained moral capital, which it still has not lost and which is certainly part of its unfinished project. Because of what happened in 2009, Iranian politics and Iranian political culture have for the foreseeable future been greatly affected by the idea of nonviolence. The movement of 2009 in Iran, as in the case of popular movements in Yemen, Bahrain, and Egypt, ended in violence, but in all these experiences the genie of nonviolence escaped the bottle.

Nonviolence in the Arab World and Beyond

The future of nonviolence in the MENA region lies in its creative use of social modes of resistance against illiberal regimes rather than in too much emphasis on the sainthood of its application, which would most likely keep millions of ordinary men and women from participating in it (see Jahanbegloo 2013, 2014, 2020, 2021a, 2021b). However, the Arab Spring showed us that the youth movement can play an important role in confronting the structural violence in Middle Eastern societies. As Jean-Pierre Filiu underlines in his book *The Arab Revolution* (2011), "This transnational youth movement bore some similarities to the multi-polarized uprising that took place on eight continents during the year 1968. Contexts and problematic [*sic*] were deeply heterogeneous, but the defiant generational stance, exemplified by the 'we won't get fooled again' motto, was widely shared from Czechoslovakia to Japan, and from the Latin Quarter to Berkeley" (41). When the East European dissidents of the 1980s were struggling against Communist authoritarian regimes, they returned to the concept of civil society. What East European intellectuals and civic actors understood by civil society included not just the eighteenth-century concept of the rule of law but also the notion of horizontal self-organized groups and institutions in the public sphere that could limit the power of the state by constructing a democratic space separate from the state and its ideological institutions. Democratic awakenings around the Middle East and North Africa in 2011 demonstrated once again that civil society can help to provide the independent space that is needed—to use Sir Isaiah Berlin's famous distinction—for "negative" rather than "positive" liberty. What united Tunisians and Egyptians—as well as Bahrainis, Yemenis, Libyans, Omanis, and Iranians—in their democratic uprisings was freedom from interference and a struggle against the concentration of arbitrary power. For those Egyptians who gathered for several weeks in Tahrir Square, freedom meant putting an end to the unjust accumulation of power by President Hosni Mubarak and his regime. In the effort to achieve this goal, they were constantly negotiating their desire for democratic governance based on secure civil society. Despite their heterogeneity, groups from Arab civil society throughout the MENA region that were leading the protests found a common enemy embodied in Arab authoritarian personalized regimes. The democratic protesters from Tunisia to Tehran demanded governments based on public accountability and popular sovereignty. Nonviolent modes of resistance played an important role in Tunisia, Egypt, and Iran. The fact that they succeeded in Tunisia but failed in Iran and Egypt had nothing to do with the philosophical and political nature of nonviolence but rather with how deeply it was internalized by civic actors in each of these societies. According to Jason Brownlee, Tarek Masoud, and Andrew Reynolds in their book *The Arab Spring: Pathways of Repression and Reform* (2015), "The Tunisian exception, if it continues to be one, only underscores the modest harvest of the Arab Spring—a bitter litany of failed uprisings, brutal crackdowns, flawed elections, and endemic violence" (228). But there is more to the Arab Spring and the Iranian Green Movement than just a momentary rupture in the art of politics in the Middle East.

If we take a closer look at the young people who launched the demands of the Green Movement, it is clear that they represent a "postideological generation." For this young generation of Arabs, the Iranian Revolution of 1979 and the great Islamist movements of the 1980s and 1990s are history. However, what their slogans expressed was mainly a demand for democracy and not necessarily for secularism. As such, the democratic revival in the Arab world occurred not necessarily through political ideologies in search of postindependence models of state building (for example, Kemalist or Arab nationalist) for these societies but through shared adherence to civic values that are fully compatible with the necessary pluralism of civil society. Interestingly, in such ethnically heterogeneous nations, a civil society allowing individuals to collaborate as individuals on nonethnic and democratic lines appears to be a real paradigm shift. Yet civil society structures in some Arab countries (as in the Persian Gulf region) might not be sufficiently robust to contain future ethnic and tribal conflicts. Civil society strategy, in other words, should assume that democratic passion is not enough to contain civil strife. Democratic passion cannot become real democracy until civil society becomes strong enough to control the state from the bottom up. It is in the institutions of civil society—a free press, trade unions, student and intellectual movements, private firms, publishing houses, and so on—that the future of a democratic society is written. Many analysts fail to imagine what models of social, political, and economic organization might come about in the near future from these mass mobilizations around the Middle East and the Maghreb. Pessimism about the prospects for a post-Islamist

Arab and Iranian world is centered on this issue. In western Europe, civil society took centuries to emerge from the bottom up, but Arab societies need democracy immediately. This said, without civil society, democracy is hobbled. But without democracy, civil society is blind. What does seem certain, however, is that within the political framework of each of these societies in ebullition, a new generation of civic actors will have a major part to play in writing the new rules of the game in the Arab world. Without a doubt, this process will entail ruptures of old systems and of illegitimate and corrupted regimes. The focus on constitutional changes accompanied by citizens' rights, political representation, and the accountability of governing bodies affirms the new political attitude that emanates from civil societies in the Arab world. This new political culture is the heart and soul of the change that Arab and Iranian citizens have initiated in their countries, noticeably without the use of violence or foreign intervention. It is still too early to speculate about the future effects of the Arab and Iranian revolts and whether unrest around the region will lead to the emergence of democratic regimes. There is also no reason to think that a similar wave of democratization will happen in countries such as Kuwait, Saudi Arabia, and Bahrain in the same way it has in Tunisia. Unlike Tunisia, countries such as Libya and Saudi Arabia do not possess civil society frameworks with the capacity to force out their leaders without engaging in a civil war. Also, in Tunisia the army saw itself as a mediator between the regime and civil society and in the end decided to take the side of civil society. In contrast, Libya, unlike its neighbor, lacks not only the mediating hand of a military institution but also trade unions, political parties, and nongovernmental agencies. Though free and democratic elections are not likely to be held soon in Iran or around the Persian Gulf region, the spread of freedom and democracy there is unquestionably a positive development for the future empowerment of civil societies in the Middle East and the Maghreb. We should not forget that in the case of eastern Europe, neither the Hungarian Revolution of 1956 nor the Prague Spring of 1968 nor Poland's Solidarity movement in 1981 succeeded in immediately creating a democracy. Yet each of these historic movements eroded forever the legitimacy of the communist ideology in these countries and challenged the states that represented it. In the same manner, we can say that the events of 2009 in Iran and of 2011 in Egypt at the very least have made authoritarianism increasingly unacceptable in Iranian and Egyptian societies, on the one hand, and nonviolent social, economic, and political change increasingly desired, on the other. "It is thus difficult to escape the conclusion that, when the definitive history of the Arab Spring of 2011–2013 is finally written, it will be remembered less as a momentous change in the region's political makeup than as a momentary break in a longer, more dismal story" (Brownlee, Masoud, and Reynolds 2015, 228).

Nonviolence as Complexity Management in the MENA Region

Whatever the outcome of the tumultuous events in Syria, Yemen, Iraq, and elsewhere in the Middle East in the past couple of decades, it is clear that the region is entering a new phase in its history. This era of change, twelve years after the uprisings known as the Arab Spring and a century after some Arabs started thinking of their independence from Ottoman and European rule, is also a defining moment of a new diplomacy of hope. It is in such historic moments that practitioners of politics and intellectual elites—Arab, Turkish, and Iranian—have an opportunity to prove whether they have acquired the necessary strength to help move their societies in a democratic direction.

The role of complexity management in any society is indeed one of the elements crucial to its peaceful development. Yet for many decades the Middle East has been held back by its political and intellectual elites, who seem to have surrendered their critical independence to the dogma of ideologies such as Marxism-Leninism and Islamism. As intellectuals in the Middle East constructed overarching narratives of modernization—whether framed in terms of liberalism, nationalism, fascism, or socialism—ahead of democracy, what could appear as "oppositional" intellectual practice was made to serve the quasi-theological dogmas of states and party or movement politics. These narratives did not succeed even in their own terms in part because they were anchored in Western ideologies and did not find any deep roots in Middle Eastern societies.

The unfolding of these narratives' monumental distortions and failures on the ground opened the way for Islamism as the only credible option. The result is that these elites have been less agents of hope and change than handmaidens of power who have merely reinterpreted local political realities in accord with their ideological purposes rather than putting ethical and critical issues at the heart of their civic and public activities. Although many elites in the MENA region became the icons of discontented, disillusioned, and frustrated generations, they also in turn allowed themselves to be used by political parties and Muslim clergy as instruments of organizational power and political control.

Instead of advancing a politics of nonviolence through a better understanding of the complex reality on the ground, elites chose to spread ideological messages: a choice that reflected their view of themselves as guardians of the "true" vocation of socialist, nationalist, or religious movements against those they saw as corrupt politicians willing to make unacceptable political compromises. The direct implication of this trend was that a culture of death and violence took over in the Middle East in the past hundred years. The more recent geopolitical developments in the Middle East pose a new challenge to public intellectuals regarding their role in the democratic evolution of their societies. Do they have anything more to offer than political opinions or a contract with power? Can they also respond to changing circumstances with an ethical engagement that allows them—via practical reason rather than politics—to struggle against all forms of tyranny? Indeed, the true struggle of public intellectuals in the Middle East today is a moral and nonviolent one against injustice and oppression and for democracy. This struggle requires courage and cannot be surrendered to any political elite, for it demands moving to a higher ground beyond particularistic interests to create and support new democratic spheres.

The question of nonviolence is indeed crucial. As the events in Tunis (2011), Tehran (2009), and Cairo's Tahrir Square (2011) demonstrated, violence needs to be tamed and transcended for societies to achieve democratic maturity. The East European dissidents of the 1980s, in their struggle against Communist authoritarian regimes, turned to the concept of nonviolence. What East European intellectuals and civic actors understood by nonviolence was not just the teleological concept of awaiting a better future, at best wishful thinking, but also the courage of giving meaning to change while changing themselves through self-organization and institution making in the public sphere. It was only through such a process that limits were placed on the state's power and a democratic space was constructed separate from the state and its ideological institutions. What united Tunisians and Egyptians in their democratic uprisings was an urge for freedom from interference and a struggle against the concentration of arbitrary power. They were thus constantly negotiating their desire for democratic governance with their desire for public accountability. The democratic revival in the Arab Spring did not happen necessarily through political ideologies in search of postindependence models of state building (for example, Kemalist or Arab nationalist) but more through a shared adherence to civic values that were fully compatible with the necessary pluralism of civil society. Yet civil society structures in some Arab countries (as in the Persian Gulf region and Libya) were not sufficiently robust to contain ethnic and ideological conflicts.

Conclusion

Many analysts have failed to imagine what models of social, political, and economic organization might evolve in the near future around the Middle East and the Maghreb. Pessimism about the prospects for the post-Islamist Arab world is centered on this issue. In western Europe, civil society took centuries to evolve from the bottom up, while Arab societies need democracy immediately. This said, without civil society, democracy would be hobbled. But without democracy, civil society will be blind. It is still too early to speculate about the future effects of the wars and conflicts around the Middle East in the past couple of decades and about whether intellectual and civic movements in the region will lead to the emergence of democratic regimes. Though free and democratic elections are not likely to be held any time soon, in many parts of the Arab world and in Iran the spread of nonviolent strategies will unquestionably be a positive development for the future empowerment of civil societies in the Middle East. However, if the question of nonviolence is placed once again on the agenda, intellectuals will have a vital role to play as part of the changes they seek—this time, free of the shackles of the past.

References

Alizadeh, Ali. 2010. "Why Are the Iranians Dreaming Again?" In *The People Reloaded: The Green Movement and the Struggle for Iran's Future*, edited by Nader Hashemi and Danny Postel, 3–6. New York: Melville House.

Brownlee, Jason, Tarek Masoud, and Andrew Reynolds. 2015. *The Arab Spring: Pathways of Repression and Reform*. Oxford: Oxford Univ. Press.

Dabashi, Hamid. 2012. *The Arab Spring: The End of Postcolonialism*. New York: Zed Books.

Filiu, Jean-Pierre. 2011. *The Arab Revolution: Ten Lessons from the Democratic Uprising*. London: Hurst.

Hashemi, Nader, and Danny Postel. 2010. Introduction to *The People Reloaded: The Green Movement and the Struggle for Iran's Future*, edited by Nader Hashemi and Danny Postel, xi–xxi. New York: Melville House.

Jahanbegloo, Ramin. [2009] 2010. "The Gandhian Moment." In *The People Reloaded: The Green Movement and The Struggle for Iran's Future*, edited by Nader Hashemi and Danny Postel, 18–21. New York: Melville House.

———. 2013. *The Gandhian Moment*. Foreword by the Dalai Lama. Cambridge, MA: Harvard Univ. Press.

———. 2014. *Introduction to Nonviolence*. New York: Palgrave.

———. 2020. *The Passion of Politics: Conversations with Contemporary American Political Philosophers: Gene Sharp, Andrew Arato, and Michael Walzer*. New Delhi, India: Har-Anand.

———. 2021a. *Mahatma Gandhi: A Nonviolent Perspective on Peace*. London: Routledge.

———. 2021b. *Nonviolent Resistance as a Philosophy of Life*. London: Bloomsbury.

Secor, Laura. 2010. "Iran's Green Movement: An Interview with Mehdi Karoubi." *New Yorker*, Oct. 12. Reprinted in *The People Reloaded: The Green Movement and the Struggle for Iran's Future*, edited by Nader Hashemi and Danny Postel, 408–14. New York: Melville House.

10

The Rise and Fall
of the Student Movements
in Postrevolutionary Iran

Roozbeh Safshekan

The cycles of student activism since the inception of the higher-education system in Iran in 1933 demonstrate that public universities have been a mirror of society, absorbing and reflecting its mood with stunning clarity. Before long, universities became a battlefield where sociopolitical forces and ideas confronted each other and the state. After the coup d'état of August 19, 1953, against Prime Minister Mohammad Mosaddeq, the military government violently suppressed University of Tehran (UT) students on December 7, a date that has become emblazoned in the historical memory of Iranians as 16 Azar, or University Students' Day. During the 1960s, when the guerrilla movement against the shah took the political stage by storm, university students and graduates made up the majority of the guerrilla bands and their supporters, making the universities one of the main strongholds for the revolutionary forces that ultimately brought down the shah's regime in 1979. When the Islamists under the leadership of Ayatollah Ruhollah Khomeini initiated their plan to purge Iranian society of "un-Islamic" influences immediately after the revolution, public universities dominated by opposition students and faculty were one of the purge's main targets in the Cultural Revolution (1980–83). Soon after Iraq invaded Iran in September 1980, university students answered the call of duty when just months earlier few of them probably imagined themselves in combat fatigues holding assault rifles in filthy trenches. In the rise of the Reformist movement in the late 1990s, university students played a crucial

An earlier version of some sections of this chapter first appeared in my master's thesis, Columbia University, 2011. I thank my thesis advisers, Hamid Dabashi and Lawrence Potter, for their guidance and insightful feedback. I am also thankful for the constructive comments and suggestions on this chapter provided by Mojtaba Mahdavi and the reviewers of this volume.

role in Mohammad Khatami's victory as voters, campaign activists, and a reference group that shaped public opinion in favor of Reformists, a trend repeated in support of Reformist candidates in the presidential election of 2009. This history demonstrates that student activism has been at the center of almost all significant phases of modern Iran's political trajectory.

By placing Iranian student activism in a historical perspective, this chapter attempts to capture and analyze its cyclical rise and fall in postrevolutionary Iran. It further contributes to the literature on Iranian student activism mainly by highlighting that the level and type of student political activism in each cycle has depended on (*a*) the level of freedom and extent of the political space opened up or closed down by different administrations and (*b*) characteristics of political and social forces in society. During periods of relative freedom, the student movement has expressed itself as a complete social movement. In periods of repression, it has gradually ceased to exist but has remanifested itself in alliance with social forces as society starts to resist repression. In each cycle, student activism has been closely dependent on and linked to political and social forces in society and has followed the latter's national political demands.

This chapter is divided into four parts, presenting how the aforementioned factors have affected the student movement's cyclical rise and fall. The first part shows that the Cultural Revolution and the Iran–Iraq War (1980–88) created a repressive atmosphere for the student movement that snuffed it out. The second part highlights how the economic liberalization of the Reconstruction era (1989–97), followed by social and political liberalization during the Reform era (1997–2005), created a small but sufficient political space for a new student movement to be born in the late 1990s. The third part shows how the authoritarianism of Mahmoud Ahmadinejad's presidency (2005–13) reversed the trend of social and political liberalization and suppressed the student movement once more. The last part briefly discusses how Hassan Rouhani's presidency (2013–21) initially could have created a new opening for the student movement and how this trend reversed during his second term in office owing to the interplay of different domestic and foreign factors. The chapter concludes by proposing a set of insights and critical reflections on the cycles of student activism in postrevolutionary Iran.

From Bastion of Freedom to War Trench

After decades of stifling repression under the Pahlavi regime, Iranian students used the freedom and open political space afforded by the Revolution of 1979 to engage in activism on two distinct levels. At the level of the university administration, this meant running universities democratically by creating an elected council composed of student representatives, faculty, and other university employees. The main university coordination council based at UT realized that there was a distinct absence of a law for governing universities and so commissioned Nasser Katouzian, head of UT's Faculty of Law, to study university governance laws from around the world and come up with one for Iran. This project was ready by July 1979 and promptly sent to the Ministry of Science, but there was never a reply.

At the political level, the situation was more favorable for activism, with a plethora of active student groups and organizations disseminating their visions about the future of the nascent revolution and organizing strong social bases on campus to advance their agendas. In this period, student organizations on university campuses were not centered around university issues but around political parties. The five leading student organizations at this time were (1) the Muslim Students Association, affiliated with the People's Mojahedin Organization of Iran; (2) the Pishgam Organization, affiliated with the Organization of Iranian People's Fadein Guerillas; (3) the Militant Students Organization, affiliated with the Marxist *Peykar* Organization; (4) the Democrat Students' Organization of Iran, affiliated with the Tudeh Party of Iran; and (5) the Office for Consolidating Unity (OCU), affiliated with the Islamists under the leadership of Ayatollah Khomeini.[1] Of these organizations, the OCU was the least successful in gaining significant traction among students.

On November 4, 1979, however, a group of Khomeinist students called the Muslim Student Followers of the Imam's Line or Students of the Line of the Imam (SLI) executed what was supposed to be a short takeover of the US embassy in Tehran to establish their revolutionary and anti-imperialist credentials. In what became a 444-day saga known as the Iran Hostage Crisis, the Khomeinist students went from a marginal to a major force in universities by affirming "the clerics' anti-imperialist posture" and stealing "the limelight from the radical left" (Azimi 2008, 361). The moment was now ripe for confronting the opposition and for a purge of universities, which were a bastion of freedom for opposition forces. In this context, Ayatollah Khomeini in his address on Nowruz (New Year's Day) in 1980 declared that the revolution must reach universities to "purge the professors associated with the West and the East and make the university a decent place for teaching superior Islamic sciences" (Khomeini 1980b).

A pretext for the purge of universities was found on April 15, 1980, when students heckled Ali-Akbar Hashemi-Rafsanjani, a member of the ruling Council of

---

1. The OCU's full name is "Etehaadiyeh-ye Anjoman-haye Eslaami-e Daneshjooyan-e Daneshgaah-ha va Maraakez-e Amoozesh-e Ali-e Keshvar" (Union of Student Islamic Associations of Universities and Higher Educational Centers of the Country).

the Islamic Revolution, while he was giving a lecture at the University of Tabriz. On April 19, 1980, the new president, Abol-Hassan Banisadr, issued an ultimatum to the opposition political parties and groups that had set up operation bases in universities, demanding they withdraw from the schools within three days from the date of order. This order, of course, did not apply to the OCU, which was affiliated with Khomeini. The Muslim Students Association, the Pishgam Organization, and the Democrat Students' Organization agreed to comply with Banisadr's order, but the Militant Students Organization decided to resist. The Khomeinists and their student supporters used this refusal as a justification to attack the opposition student groups even before the deadline had expired, resulting in the deaths of at least thirty-seven students and the injury and arrest of hundreds of others (Mashayekhi 2001, 292). Commenting on the tragic events taking place on campuses across the country, Ayatollah Khomeini once again emphasized the need for Islamizing universities: "Our universities are foreign dependent. Our universities are of the colonial type. . . . Now that we want to set up an independent university and make fundamental changes, so that it would not be dependent on the West and Communism, dependent on Marxism, they confront us. This, in itself, shows that our universities are not Islamic and we do not have, and never have had, universities that would educate our youth. This, in itself, is a proof that our youth has not received proper education. . . . The university must become Islamic" (quoted in Behdad 1995, 194).

On July 13, 1980, Ayatollah Khomeini issued an order to create the Council of the Cultural Revolution (CCR), officially launching the Cultural Revolution (Khomeini 1980a). The CCR, in close collaboration with the Center for Cooperation of Seminaries and Universities, was in charge of Islamizing the curriculum. According to Sohrab Behdad, the cooperation between these two bodies was encouraged by Ayatollah Khomeini and other *hawzeh* (seminary) scholars, who claimed almost exclusive expertise in the field of humanities. According to Ayatollah Khomeini, "Islam has dealt more deeply than anyone else or any school of thought with humanities and human development. You need specialists? You must ask the hawzeh. . . . Open the universities, but for humanities they must gradually ask the scholars of the hawzehs in Iran, especially in Qum" (quoted in Behdad 1995, 194). At the same time, the purging committees enforced a strict Islamic code on campuses and expelled opposition students and faculty (Razavi 2009).

As a consequence of the Cultural Revolution, universities were closed for three years, 57,069 students were expelled, many high school students were not allowed to enter university, and, as CCR member Abdul-Karim Soroush has asserted, at least seven hundred university professors and lecturers were also purged (Maleki 2000; Soroush 1999). Besides the purges, the government put in place "a highly selective and ideological screening mechanism" to impede the admission of "non-religious students" to higher education institutions (Mashayekhi 2001, 292). The Cultural Revolution not only undermined the student movement but also lowered academic standards at Iranian universities and decreased the quality of the student body. Nikki R. Keddie describes how "the Cultural Revolution was a major blow to Iran's cultural and intellectual life and achievement, interrupting the education and professional livelihood of many and encouraging further emigration by students, teachers, and other professionals" (2003, 250).

While the new ruling elite was dealing a blow to the opposition throughout Iran and to the universities in particular, Saddam Hussein's invasion of Iran in 1980 and the commencement of the eight-year Iran–Iraq War further worsened the conditions of student activism. To begin with, independent student activism effectively ceased to exist, and all energy was canalized toward the war effort through the state and affiliated bodies such as the OCU. Students who just a year earlier may not have viewed themselves as revolutionaries, let alone soldiers, found themselves in a life-and-death struggle against a well-armed Iraqi adversary. A shining example of such students was Seyed Hossein Alamol-Hoda, the twenty-two-year-old commander of the Howeizeh and SLI units of the Revolutionary Guards. On January 6, 1981, Alamol-Hoda and his fellow students took part in the Battle of Howeizeh in preparation for the operation Liberation of Khorramshahr and were killed en masse because of the absence of necessary logistics and operational coordination among the Iranian units (Yazdaanfaam 2004).

Student life was also transformed in other ways. In 1987, the War Logistics Office called for a draft of university students, and soon after that a law was passed instituting mandatory six-month military service for all male students (Rayatnazari and Safshekan 2002). Study conditions were completely transformed by the war, not only in terms of shortages but also in terms of the toll taken by having to deal with air-raid drills and bombings on a daily basis. During the war, university organizations backed by the government and its affiliates—such as the OCU and the Academic Center for Education, Culture, and Research—had a near complete monopoly on political activities and life on campus. Except for sports, which were allowed under supervision, extracurricular activities were banned. State authoritarianism during the Cultural Revolution and war, which undermined all national opposition groups that had guided student politics on campuses, decreased the overall level of student activism and directed the remainder through myriad officially sponsored entities. By the end of the war in 1988 and the death of Ayatollah Khomeini in 1989, the last tinge of color had disappeared from universities, and student activism was a shadow of its former self. But change was in the air.

The Dawn and Dusk of Reform

By the early 1990s, the Islamic Republic's leadership realized that the end of the revolutionary era, the Iran–Iraq War, and the Cold War would bring new challenges and that the country thus would need to take a new direction. The most pressing of these challenges was the stagnant war economy, which had served well during the war but was completely unfit for an era of economic globalization. To answer this challenge, then newly elected president Ali-Akbar Hashemi-Rafsanjani commenced the Reconstruction era, which attempted to repair the damage done by the war and to introduce economic liberalization. The strong emphasis on neoliberal policies led to the emergence of greater socioeconomic divergence and an increasing stratification of society based on class as well as decreasing socioeconomic diversity in public universities to the benefit of affluent students. At the political level, restrictions continued, albeit on a smaller scale than in the first decade of the Islamic Republic, leaving limited opportunities for student activism. Asef Bayat has aptly highlighted the confluence of these two factors and their impact on student activism under Rafsanjani: "The student body was a potential social force, but one whose desire for better material life and political participation had been dashed by the sluggish economy and the clergy's tight control over political institutions and everyday life. The poor economy turned their expectations into outrage, while moral surveillance and political suppression stifled the expression of their youthful dispositions and made them even more frustrated" (2007, 69).

In the Reconstruction era, the OCU, with its deep roots in the social-justice-driven agenda of the Islamic Left, maintained a near monopoly over student activism and became a vocal critic of Rafsanjani's neoliberal policies. The Islamic Right, which had come to dominate the Iranian political structure after the death of Ayatollah Khomeini, realized that as long as universities remained under the monopoly of the left-leaning OCU, they could become centers of dissent and resistance to the implementation of the Right's agenda. To break the OCU's monopoly, the Islamic Right enhanced the Student Basij (Mobilization) and supported the formation of a new student organization, the Islamic Union of Student Associations of Universities and Higher Educational Centers in 1992. Despite the challenge by these Islamic Right–backed student organizations, however, the OCU was successful in maintaining its dominance over student activism and retaining universities as strongholds of the Islamic Left, whose power had declined after the loss of its main backer, Ayatollah Khomeini.

The OCU's continued domination was in part underpinned by drawing on the works of religious intellectuals outside politically repressed university campuses to revitalize student activism. These religious intellectuals included, ironically, the likes of Abdol-Karim Soroush, who had been a member of the CCR. Beginning with a series of articles in the monthly *Kayhan Farhangi* in the early 1990s and culminating in his book *Qabz va bast teorik shari'a* (The Theoretical Contraction and Expansion of Shari'a), published in 1991, Soroush criticized the state's jurisprudential and conservative reading of Islam and suggested an alternative conception of Islam more compatible with modern social sciences and democratic ideals. The religious intellectual figures eagerly utilized the on-campus lectures and debates held by the OCU as a public platform to popularize and spread their ideas throughout society.

Exile from power and the influence of religious intellectuals forced the Islamic Left to reexamine its record and contemporary social circumstances and to embark on a new path to reclaim power. Forsaking their former politics, which had emphasized anti-imperialism, economic redistribution, and strict adherence to the restrictive interpretation of Islamic social and political values, the new Islamic Left took on a more liberal orientation and introduced the discourse of reforming the political structure and enhancing civil society. This change trickled down to their student followers in the OCU, which now began advocating greater freedom and democracy (Rivetti and Cavatorta 2013).

As noted earlier, in the presidential election of 1997, the OCU and university students played a crucial role in the Reformist Mohammad Khatami's landslide victory (Mashayekhi 2001, 297). The Reformists in turn became actively involved in universities and helped to bring about a new student movement in Iran bound to the Reformist political current.

By 1999, the Islamic Right began to recover from the shock of Khatami's victory and started reorganizing, rebranding itself as the Principlists. Distrusting the OCU, the Principlist-dominated Parliament passed the Law for the Formation, Enhancement, and Development of the Student Basij on university campuses in 1998, which allowed the Student Basij to assume the mantle of a pressure group that the OCU had once worn. The OCU, for its part, was no longer a rigid ideological instrument for the state but rather a broad-based student group with a fairly politically diverse membership.

The Principlist reaction to the rise of the Reform movement and the ensuing struggle that drew in the student movement set in motion a chain of events that resulted in the 18 Tir (July 9) student uprising in 1999. The first salvo in this struggle was the Chain Murders, an assassination campaign whose most famous murder victims were the Iran Nation Party leader Dariush Forouhar and his wife, Parvaneh Eskandari, as well as the leftist writers and intellectuals Mohammad Jafar Puyandeh and Mohammad Mokhtari. Although the Ministry of Intelligence and Security official Saeed Emami took the fall for the murders as a "rogue agent" and died in prison under mysterious circumstances, no one was ultimately tried for the murders. Events came to a head in 1999 when the Principlists' Press Law Reform bill in the Majlis sought to put greater restrictions on the media. In a counterattack, the pro-Khatami newspaper *Salaam* published an article claiming that the Press Law Reform bill had been suggested by none other than Saeed Emami, citing and publishing his secret letter to the minister of intelligence. On July 6, 1999, the Judiciary ordered *Salaam* closed for publishing a classified document.

The OCU quickly mobilized in reaction to the closing of *Salaam*. UT students staged a sit-in at the University Hill dormitory, and the protest spilled over onto the streets. On 18 Tir, police antiriot units descended on the University Hill dormitory and forcefully removed students with the aid of the Basij paramilitary force. In the anarchy that ensued, one student, Ezatollah Ebrahimnejad, was killed; several were severely injured; and many were arrested. The attack on the dormitory polarized and politicized students across the country overnight, and the OCU called for a day of mourning. It was clear that in the battle to come, the reform project itself was at stake, and students rose up in universities and later took to the streets in its defense, with thousands of ordinary people from all walks of life joining them, especially in Tehran.

As the crisis escalated, society slid toward conflict, and the protest movement gained momentum and became increasingly popular, with students at its forefront. Besides the hundreds of injuries from fighting on the streets, dozens of students were arrested. At later trials, the police and security forces who attacked the student dormitory were acquitted, but the students were sentenced to imprisonment for organizing and participating in the unrest.

Student discontent once again boiled over into an uprising at UT in July 2003 over the impending privatization of Iranian public universities. UT's president, Reza Faraji-Dana, managed to prevent an attack on student dormitories by security forces through his on-the-scene presence. The protest ended only after the student leaders were arrested, but the students' concerns over privatization remained unaddressed. This further eroded Khatami's popularity among the students, and his minister of science, research, and technology, Mostafa Moin, one of the last remaining Reformist leaders with credibility among the student movement, resigned over the mistreatment of arrested students.

The events of 18 Tir and the July 2003 uprising, among myriad other episodes, demonstrated that the Reformist leadership was more concerned with their factional interests than with meeting the demands of their social base, including students. Although the student movement had been decisive in helping the Reform movement achieve electoral victory and advance its agenda, students found themselves abandoned by the Reformist leadership during their moment of greatest need. The divide between the Reformist leadership and student base was clearly reflected in Reformist fortunes after the tragic events of 18 Tir and July 2003: a long retreat that resulted in the decline of the Reform movement for several years.

Between 2003 and 2005, the Reformists lost power at every level as a result of their shrinking popular support and the rolling back of reforms by the Principlists. In 2003, the Reformists lost the city and village council elections to a new generation of Principlists, led by Mahmoud Ahmadinejad, who became mayor of Tehran that year. In 2004, they lost the Majlis and in 2005 the presidency, completing their plummet from power. At the university level, the Reformist base fractured into several groups. Although the OCU continued to exist and retained a not inconsiderable hold on universities, it was a shadow of its former self, ultimately splitting into two branches: the majority Allameh branch, which was more radical and advocated for the student movement to be independent of Reformists and all other state political factions, and the minority Shiraz branch, which was conservative and joined the camp of Khatami's opponents. As Paola Rivetti and Francesco Cavatorta (2014) have aptly shown in their work, the OCU example demonstrates that student movements, like many other civil society actors in authoritarian contexts, do not always enhance democratization and often can be co-opted by and strengthen the authoritarian rule.

As reformism declined, space for novel oppositional discourses opened up, most prominently that of the New Left. The latter gradually developed a platform that gained traction on campuses across the country. Its platform included but was not limited to the following three pillars. First, although the New Left accepted the ideals of social and political liberalization, they made socioeconomic justice the core pillar of their platform, something that had been relatively unheard of since the Cultural Revolution. Second, unlike the Reformist student movement, the New Left rejected cooperation with the state's political factions altogether. Instead, they advocated an alliance of social movements, including primarily the labor movement and the women's movement. Third, the New Left rejected any foreign intervention, including military intervention or economic sanctions, to resolve Iran's domestic problems. This rejection was, in part, a response to the rise of some New Right student activists after September 11, 2001, and the beginning of the war on terror. Unlike the New Left's vision of political change based on domestic social movements, the New Right tacitly advocated foreign intervention, whether wars or sanctions, as a means of resolving the political impasse in the country. They took the examples of the US invasion of Afghanistan in 2001 and Iraq in 2003 as models that could be replicated in Iran. Although this group viewed itself as "liberal" in the context of Iran's domestic politics, it bore a strong resemblance to American neoconservatism.

Cultural Revolution Redux

Reformism was in retreat long before the election of Mahmoud Ahmadinejad in 2005, but the Principlist seizure of the presidency confirmed reformism's downward trajectory. The new Ahmadinejad administration quickly set about closing the social and political space that had been expanded to some extent under the Reformists. It initiated what can be viewed as a second major attempt after the Cultural Revolution to purge dissident students and to Islamize the curriculum. The social sciences, once again viewed as a threatening foreign discipline, were placed under sustained attack, with the expulsion of professors and the temporary closing of facilities to rewrite curricula in cooperation with the religious seminaries. Moreover, the administration introduced the Star System to classify political students and impede their academic advancement. One star on a student's record meant that the student was issued a warning about being politically active and had to sign a statement forswearing that activity before resuming studies. After receiving two stars, a student underwent interrogation at the Central Selection Committee of the Ministry of Science, Research, and Technology and was given a warning about involvement in student political activism. Finally, a student with three stars was banned from further studies. The number of stars increased with the level and nature of a student's political activities. Besides measures such as the Star System, the Ahmadinejad administration increased gender segregation, going as far as to prescribe separate study materials and even subjects for men and women in some disciplines. It is believed that in just the first year of this process, some seventy students were suspended, nearly thirty students were given warnings, and upward of one hundred professors were forced into early retirement (Fathi 2006).

The closure of the social and political space, akin to what happened after the Cultural Revolution, inevitably meant the decline of the legal opposition and, critically for our analysis, of the student movement that had grown alongside it. The OCU had increasingly become impotent before 2005 but found it even more difficult to operate under these new conditions. The New Right, too, however, declined when faced with the failure of the American neoconservatives to establish viable and prosperous democratic regimes in Afghanistan and Iraq by around 2006. The New Left, although successful in occupying increasingly greater amounts of the university space, also found it hard to operate in this hostile new environment. They were vanquished as an active force following a crackdown on a major demonstration at UT on December 4, 2007, which swept up much of the leadership. The student movement, which had flourished during the Reform era, would largely lie dormant until the presidential elections of June 12, 2009, and the rise of the Green Movement.

In the lead-up to the Iranian presidential elections of 2009, there was major dissatisfaction among broad swaths of the population about the policies of the Ahmadinejad administration. As the Islamic Republic was oft inclined to do during elections, it allowed greater social and political freedoms to increase electoral participation. In this freer space, expectations rose, and the campaign of the Reformist Mir Hossein Mousavi, a former prime minister (1980–89), gained considerable traction. Students played a major role in his campaign by participating in street rallies and holding debates and demonstrations at universities, expressing their frustration with the political situation in the country under Ahmadinejad.

With heightened expectations about the prospect of change through the election, the reelection of Ahmadinejad came as shock to many voters and, combined with allegations of electoral fraud, mobilized millions under the banner of the Green Movement and the slogan "Where is my vote?" to overturn the election result. Before long, universities became battlefields between students who sought to demonstrate their discontent with the election results and security forces who sought to suppress the protests. Students rose up at universities in cities across the country, including Tehran, Shiraz, Isfahan, Tabriz, and Hamedan, and as with 18 Tir and July 2003, university campuses and student dormitories became a focus of attacks by security forces. One particularly severe attack, captured on video and seared into students' memory, was the brutal assault on UT dormitories on June 14, 2009, which is thought to have killed five students, injured dozens more through violent and merciless beatings, and wrought enormous physical destruction to the facilities (Tait and Kamali Dehghan 2009).

Students' Day, or 16 Azar (December 7), became another major flashpoint in the Green Movement, with hundreds descending onto the streets but once again being confronted with batons and arrests by security forces. At the Amir Kabir University event commemorating 16 Azar, one of the leading student figures, Majid Tavakkoli, became a symbol of the Green Movement when security forces sought to humiliate him by claiming he had tried to escape arrest by donning the veil and pretending to be a woman. Rather than discrediting him, this fabrication turned Tavakkoli into a social media phenomenon, with hundreds of men uploading photos of themselves in the veil to demonstrate their solidarity with him and raise objections to the practice of forced veiling of women in Iran.

The events of 16 Azar became a link in a long chain of events in the demonstrations in 2009 that showed the integral role students were playing in the

Green Movement; the movement's leader, Mir Hossein Mousavi, declared that the "three million informed students of the country are the biggest asset of the Green Movement" (Mousavi 2012, 171). With the gradual decline of the Green Movement, however, students found themselves unable to engage in activism.

Reform Redux?

The relatively open political space around the presidential elections of 2013 and the rise of Hassan Rouhani once again gave life to student activism, and the pulse of the movement could once again be detected. In the election campaign, one of the main pillars of Rouhani's platform was the state of social and political freedoms in Iran and in particular the hypersecuritized atmosphere of universities in the country, a message behind which students consolidated. Students thus paved the way to victory for Rouhani, much as they had for Mohammad Khatami and had attempted to for Mir Hossein Mousavi. Student activism therefore once again reestablished the symbiotic, albeit subservient, relationship it historically had with major national political forces.

Given the importance of student activism to his election campaign, Rouhani, for his part, was mindful of trying to fulfill his promises to students within the limits of his power. One of the most meaningful actions he took was to appoint a minister of science, research, and technology who would be acceptable to students. Jafar Tofighi and Jafar Meili-Monfared, both Reformist figures with significant experience in the higher-education field, were candidates for this position but failed to become permanent officeholders when members of Parliament rejected them because of their support of the Green Movement and criticism of the election results in 2009. Reza Faraji-Dana, the respected and popular Reformist former head of UT who had personally helped prevent a violent assault by security forces on student dormitories through his physical presence on the scene of the July 2003 student uprising, was finally appointed to this position. However, he was ultimately impeached by Parliament after only ten months because of his efforts to fulfill Rouhani's campaign promises, such as ending the Star System in universities, reinstating professors who had been removed under Ahmadinejad, and opening up the social and political space in universities. Despite Faraji-Dana's impeachment, these efforts continued, albeit to a lesser extent.

During Rouhani's first term in office, many aspects of Ahmadinejad's restrictive policies toward the higher-education system and student activism were dismantled, the university space was revitalized to some extent, and student activism was on the rise (Honari 2018). However, this trend somewhat reversed during

Rouhani's second term in office. The US "maximum-pressure" campaign under President Donald Trump put tremendous strain on the Iranian economy and curtailed the major foreign-policy objectives that Rouhani had managed to achieve during his first term in office. Chief among these objectives was to reach a nuclear deal called the Joint Comprehensive Plan of Action (JCPOA) in July 2015. The Trump administration's withdrawal from the JCPOA and reimposition of sanctions in May 2018 as well as domestic economic mismanagement created a bitter economic situation in the country and major dissatisfactions among the public. Moreover, the rise of tensions between Iran and the United States as well as major regional players, such as Saudi Arabia and Israel, led to further securitization of public space. The combination of these factors diminished the former open political space, and the student movement once again found it quite hard to be active in this new restrictive environment. Student activism has been in a state of limbo ever since as these deteriorating conditions have continued.

Conclusion

This chapter has analyzed the cyclical rise and fall of student activism in post-revolutionary Iran and showed how the level and type of activism in each cycle depended on the level of political freedom and the characteristics of political and social forces in society. In falling into this cyclical pattern, whereby student activists follow the agenda of national political forces when there is relatively open political space, the student movement risks having two important blind spots that may weaken it during potential future periods of repression. On one level, it may ignore other important social forces, especially the women's and labor movements. The student movement has historically reached out to other social forces during periods of repression only when it has been unable to align with a larger national political force. By establishing ties to and solidarity with women, workers, and other social strata during times of relative political openness, the student movement would be better able to utilize the opportunities of political openness and better prepared for periods of potential future repression. This also applies to the relationship between students and the wider public. Because students have historically been part of the elite crème de la crème of the country, and given the securitized atmosphere of university spaces, to which nonstudents have physically limited access, students have at times been isolated from the broader society. By utilizing new communication technologies, student activists can disseminate their message to a broader audience and involve the public in university events such as lectures, debates, and rallies. This trend is already underway, but its full potential remains unrealized.

On another level, the student movement also needs to focus on the demands of students within universities. The student movement's activist core has typically focused on social and political issues to the detriment of issues such as the cost of education, quality of instruction and teaching materials, and the condition of university facilities, which are critical to the broader and more politically apathetic student body. The relatively nonpolitical nature of this type of activism may enable the student movement to better institutionalize itself within Iranian higher education. By paying more attention to the larger student body and the conditions of higher education in the country, the student movement would be able to broaden its social base, take on a grander mission that would enhance its importance, and better institutionalize itself to survive in times of repression. Ultimately, the student movement appears destined to remain a key feature of Iranian political life, and greater attention to the student body within universities and ties with society beyond the campus are only likely to enhance the movement's durability and importance in future struggles.

References

Azimi, Fakhreddin. 2008. *The Quest for Democracy in Iran: A Century of Struggle against Authoritarian Rule*. Cambridge, MA: Harvard Univ. Press.

Bayat, Asef. 2007. *Making Islam Democratic: Social Movements and the Post-Islamist Turn*. Stanford, CA: Stanford Univ. Press.

Behdad, Sohrab. 1995. "Islamization of Economics in Iranian Universities." *International Journal of Middle East Studies* 27, no. 2: 193–217.

Fathi, Nazila. 2006. "Iran President Facing Revival of Students' Ire." *New York Times*, Dec. 20.

Honari, Ali. 2018. "Struggles for Revival: The Iranian Student Movement under the 'Moderate' Government, 2013–2017." In *Human Rights and Agents of Change in Iran: Towards a Theory of Change*, edited by Rebecca Barlow and Shahram Akbarzadeh, 127–41. Singapore: Palgrave Macmillan.

Keddie, Nikki R. 2003. *Modern Iran: Roots and Results of Revolution*. New Haven, CT: Yale Univ. Press.

Khomeini, Ruhollah. 1980a. "Tashkil-e Setad-e Enghelab- Farhangi" (Formation of the Council of the Cultural Revolution) (July 13, 1980). In *Imam Khomeini*. Tehran: Institute for Compilation and Publication of Imam Khomeini's Works. At http://www.imam-khomeini.ir/fa/C207_43139/.

———. 1980b. "Tosieh-haye sizdahganeh be Mosalmanan" (Thirteen pieces of advice to Muslims) (Mar. 21, 1980). In *Imam Khomeini*. Tehran: Institute for Compilation and Publication of Imam Khomeini's Works. At http://www.imam-khomeini.ir/fa/c17_14879/.

Maleki, Mohammad. 2000. "Goftogu-ye Mehrak Kamali ba Mohammad Maleki: Kasi az ma nazar nakhast" (Mehrak Kamali's interview with Mohammad Maleki: No one asked for our opinion). *Lowh* 7:25–40.

Mashayekhi, Mehrdad. 2001. "The Revival of the Student Movement in Post-revolutionary Iran." *International Journal of Politics, Culture, and Society* 15, no. 2: 283–313.

Mousavi, Mir Hossein. 2012. *Nurturing the Seed of Hope, a Green Strategy for Liberation: Statements of Mir Hossein Mousavi*. Translated by Daryoush Mohammad Poor. London: H & S Media.

Rayatnazari, Amir, and Roozbeh Safshekan. 2002. "Daneshkadeh-ye Fanni-ye Daneshgah-e Tehran" (The Faculty of Engineering at the University of Tehran)." *Lowh* 14:30–52.

Razavi, Reza. 2009. "The Cultural Revolution in Iran, with Close Regard to the Universities, and Its Impact on the Student Movement." *Middle Eastern Studies* 45, no. 1: 1–17.

Rivetti, Paola, and Francesco Cavatorta. 2013. "'The Importance of Being Civil Society': Student Politics and the Reformist Movement in Khatami's Iran." *Middle Eastern Studies* 49, no. 4: 645–60.

———. 2014. "Iranian Student Activism between Authoritarianism and Democratization: Patterns of Conflict and Cooperation between the Office for the Strengthening of Unity and the Regime." *Democratization* 21, no. 2: 289–310.

Soroush, Abdul-Karim. 1999. "'Goftogu-ye Mehrak Kamali ba Abdul-Karim Soroush': Akharash ham nadanestand manzalgah-e maqsud kojast" (Mehrak Kamali's interview with Mohammad Maleki: Right to the end they could not find where they were meant to be going). *Lowh* 6:34–44.

Tait, Robert, and Saeed Kamali Dehghan. 2009. "Iran: 12 Students Reported Killed in Crackdown after Violent Clashes." *Guardian*, June 15.

Yazdaanfaam, Mahmood. 2004. "Hamaseh-ye Howeizeh va tasir aan bar ravand-e jang" (Epic of Howeizeh and its impact on the war process). *Negin-e Iran* 1, no. 3: 85–95.

11

Finished or Unfinished? The Uncertain Future of Christians in the Middle East

Paul S. Rowe

Over the past decade, Christian populations in the Middle East have undergone severe trials, leading to the dramatic acceleration of their displacement and exile. Ancient Christian communities in Syria and Iraq have fled to safe havens within and outside their home countries. In Lebanon, Jordan, and Egypt as well as among the Palestinians, Christians also face numerous pressures. The departure of Christians from the Middle East undermines pluralism in a region transformed by demands for change. If the health of pluralism is measured by the Christian exodus, is there hope for the future of reform?

Despite the ambivalence shown by established church hierarchies and elites, many Christians participated in the Egyptian and Syrian Arab Spring protests. In the period of transition that ensued, Copts pursued pluralist strategies to represent their interests. Similar efforts in Syria and Jordan quickly came to a halt with the collapse of Syria into civil war and the overthrow of Mohamed Morsi in Egypt in the summer of 2013. The crisis brought about by the takeover of northern Syria and Iraq by the Islamic State of Iraq and Syria (ISIS) in the summer of 2014 forced Christians into organizing merely to survive in small sanctuaries or in exile.

Arab Christians seeking to represent their interests are left with few options. The Arab Spring highlighted the possibility of a new pluralist form of representation, only to be dashed by destabilization. Most Arab regimes continue to seek neo-millet elite bargains with Christian leaders, which gain support among Christians fearful of a return to chaotic democratic transition. The neomillet system serves as a continuation of the Ottoman-era practice of granting Christian communities autonomous control over their own internal affairs. It presumes the corporatist organization of Christian society under the aegis of traditional churches, the authorities of which represent Christian interests to the state. Even so, a struggling

Christian civil society seeks the modernization of entrenched sectarian relation-ships. For Christians, the unfinished project of the Arab Spring is the expansion of their opportunity to organize and celebrate their differences through civil activ-ism and community engagement.

Christians and Authoritarianism in the Middle East

Popular and scholarly treatments of religion and politics in the Middle East often emphasize the dominant if multiple Islamic cultures that permeate the region. Until recently, the reality of cultural and religious pluralism has been only occasionally acknowledged. However, the destabilization of Egypt and the Levant and the rise of extreme violent radicalism in the movements linked to al-Qaeda in Iraq and Syria and to ISIS have shone a light on the reality of social pluralism in those contexts.

Among the various religious and ethnic minority communities in the Middle East are several Christian communities, numbering up to 14.5 million in pop-ulation.[1] In most cases, these communities boast a historic presence that dates back to the earliest history of Christianity. As a result, many Christians describe themselves as truly indigenous, tracing their ancestry back to communities that predated the Islamic conquest. Christian controversies had divided many of these groups before the rise of Islam, though, so there is relatively little ecumenical unity among the Christians of the region, rendering them vulnerable to strategies that would isolate each Christian community in its national context.

National churches predominate throughout the Middle East (see Bailey and Bailey 2010). The largest group by absolute numbers is the Coptic Orthodox Church of Egypt. Somewhere close to 95 percent of Egypt's population of up to 9 million Christians are Coptic Orthodox, and all Egyptian Christians are popularly known as "Copts," a word referring to the historic Byzantine name of Egypt.[2] Propor-tionately, Christians have been the largest sectarian group in Lebanon, where they

---

1. In 2017, the Catholic Near East Welfare Association provided detailed estimates for the Christian population of the Middle East. It found there to be a little more than 14.5 million Chris-tians in the region. This may be an overestimate given the difficulty of calculating the figures for those countries undergoing civil conflict. See Catholic Near East Welfare Association 2017.

2. According to S. S. Hasan, "The scholar has the choice of picking a figure in between [the official and the church-based estimates of], say, 8–12 percent, or of consoling himself [sic] with the thought that even if one accepts the low government estimate of 6 percent there is still the fact that the Christian population of Egypt is as large as the Jewish population of the entire state of Israel" (2003, 18).

remain somewhere in the neighborhood of 30 percent of the population (Harris 1996, 68–72). Lebanese Christians are divided by sect, but the historic importance of the Maronite Church in Lebanon provides it with a uniquely significant position as an influence on politics, in particular given the fact that the National Pact (Mithaq al-Watani) consigns the presidency to a Maronite. Lebanese Catholics of the Greek Catholic rite are also prominent, as are Greek Orthodox and Armenians.

Similar divisions apply among the native Syrian Christian population of approximately 2 million (*BBC News* 2015). Although the historic Christian community of Iraq is rooted in the ancient Church of the East, whose adherents refer to themselves as Assyrians, rooted in an ancient northern Iraqi civilization, the majority of Iraqi Christians are divided among the Syriac Orthodox and Chaldaean Churches. Among Palestinians and Jordanians, there are likely around 400,000 Christians, divided among various Latin and Eastern Rite Catholics and the Eastern Orthodox (see *BBC News* 2011; Sabella 2006).

Almost all of the relative numbers of Christians in the Middle East are based on both official numbers and the independent assessments of scholars and Christians themselves, for, as Andrea Zaki Stephanous points out, "the calculation of the numbers of Christians in the Arab World was, and still is, a political issue rather than a demographic fact" (2010, 119).

History has divided the Arab Christian population, but contemporary challenges to the faith have forced these Christians to rethink their age-old divides. The modern ecumenical movement among the churches may be dated back to the foundation of the Middle East Council of Churches in 1974. But the churches' preoccupation with local issues has limited cooperation even within the ecumenical movement. Added to this are the normal tensions that have arisen between the denominations over Protestant and Catholic evangelism among the historic churches, and there has been little desire to provide a united voice across the region to speak for Christian concerns.

More recently, the growth of media initiatives and the attendant spread of television ministries and personalities have given new impetus to a feeling of regional solidarity among Christians. For example, Sat-7, a satellite channel founded in 1996, provides religious programming by and for all the denominations of Christians in the Middle East. Over recent years, there has been an increase in the number of regional councils and events that gather the leaders of various churches and Christian organizations in the region. In October 2010, the Roman Catholic Church summoned a synod to discuss the plight of Christians in the Middle East, focusing on the decline in the Christian population (Special Assembly 2010). In September 2013, the king of Jordan hosted an international research conference on the status of Christians amid the Arab Spring (Josua 2014, 128–29). The inauguration of a new movement "in defense of Christians" convened in Washington, DC, in September 2014 that included a wide array of church leaders, lay activists, and interested politicians. Though it deliberately aimed at an ecumenical and nonpartisan effort, the conference demonstrated some of the inherent difficulties of uniting efforts on behalf of the Christians of the region when it gained headlines for the politicized pro-Israel speech delivered by Senator Ted Cruz (R-Tex.), which was cut short by an unwelcoming crowd (Markoe 2014).

Despite such efforts to present a united front in response to challenges shared among the Christian communities, national churches predominate in the Middle East, and these churches tend to form peak organizations of Christians that shape Christian life from state to state. Although regional efforts have been made to expand the influence of civil society, the dominant form of interest representation among Christians is the neomillet model, in which church hierarchies forge direct relationships with the regime (Rowe 2007). In 2007, Fiona McCallum observed that where religious identity is politicized, it "has become more pronounced as a consequence of the difficulties faced by the nation state. This identity helps to maintain the cohesiveness of the community. Thus, it is natural that the leader of the institution would be given the opportunity to act as both the spiritual and civil leader of the group" (2007, 937). Church hierarchies jealously guard this prerogative to preserve their own status within the community as well as to preserve the survival of their flocks.

The partnerships that national churches have built with the state in the Arab world in turn shape the political options available. In particular, this pattern has limited the extension of full citizenship to Christians. As states responded to the wave of political Islam that arose in the 1970s, they embraced reforms that more deeply entrenched shariʿa in the legal tradition. Most notably, the Egyptian Constitution was amended in 1980 to introduce the Islamic shariʿa as "the" source of Egyptian law rather than "a" source. In a context of political crisis, Egyptian Christians responded to this change with protests and marches (Farah 1986).

Nevertheless, the wording was retained through two redraftings of the Constitution in 2012 and 2014, but with the acquiescence of most Egyptian Christians. Elsewhere in the Middle East, the practice of enshrining shariʿa as a basis of secular legal systems has become normal. Christians have accepted these provisions, at least in part because they have been granted exceptions provided under traditional Islamic practice for religious minority communities (Nabo 2020, 36). Most importantly, civil status for Christians is adjudicated separately on the basis of Christian tradition and in most cases by Christian lay courts. Concerns over the construction of churches, the status of holy places, and legal cases that involve communal disputes are typically taken up by the church hierarchies.

This neomillet system has undermined the full participation of Christians as citizens by relegating their issues to the status of communal concerns. In auto-cratic societies, corporatist forms of interest mediation are a time-tested strategy by which the regime co-opts support from organized interests. This system per-petuates the authoritarian regime's power while handing a minimal level of auton-omy to groups based on vocation or class or identity. Christians in Middle Eastern states acquiesce to corporatism as a means of maintaining their position rather than embracing the far more dangerous option of full democratization, in which their particular concerns will be thrown in among the multiple demands from civil society (Belge and Karacoç 2015).

Indeed, full democratization in most postauthoritarian societies of the Arab Spring period from 2011 to 2013 involved the rapid rise of Islamist political parties. Better organized, playing on sympathies for their past suppression, and benefiting by the structures of the electoral contests in Egypt and Tunisia in particular, these Islamist groups became the chief beneficiaries of the democratic project (Brynen et al. 2012, 166–67). Christians would only ever play second fiddle in parties that are coalitions of liberal or conservative Muslims and like-minded Christians.

Nevertheless, the unfortunate truth is that the neomillet partnership creates a self-perpetuating trap for Christian populations. Their communal support for the regime attaches them to its survival. Any desire for changes to the regime in the form of a pluralist accommodation of civil interests would require the dismantling of the informal elite consensus and the attendant reduction of corporatist influence. Thus, authentic desire for change among Christians meets up against entrenched privilege and the fear of undermining the minimal autonomy and freedom that Christians enjoy under the authoritarian regime. For these reasons, McCallum writes, Arab Christians have typically favored authoritarian regimes: "As long as the state is perceived as promoting tolerant policies towards the Christian com-munities, recognising their contribution to society and not condoning rhetorical or physical attacks against their presence, the churches are willing to accept lim-itation on societal freedom" (2012, 122). As a result, authoritarian regimes have maintained liberal attitudes toward Christian civil initiatives attached to the his-toric churches as a means of maintaining their authority (Rowe 2009) and engag-ing in what Steven Heydemann (2007) calls "authoritarian upgrading." When regimes are no longer able to guarantee the security of Christian communities, or when communal consensus about the model breaks down, the model erodes and presents a crisis for the community.

Christians and the Arab Spring

Such a crisis arose during the Arab Spring protests of 2011. Internal communal identity and general consensus about the authority of patriarchs and church hierarchs declined amid the demand for democratic freedoms, as did the certainty that aging regimes could maintain a lid on societal protest. Christians took part in these protests with a view to creating a new consensus that would obviate the neomillet partnership: a cosmopolitan form of citizenship that would promote Christians and Christian civil organizations as partners in new republics based on liberal-democratic values. However, transition to such a system was fraught with many dangers. Mariz Tadros notes that "countries that have undergone transitions without an escalation of sectarian tensions . . . shared one common political strategy despite their very different contexts, and that is that they did not focus only on introducing democratic procedures, such as elections, and building institutions for reorganizing state–society relations, but also paid special attention to building *inclusive democracies*" (2013, 5, emphasis in original). As the Arab Spring spread, it became clear that majoritarianism was a stronger force than inclusion. The downfall of the ancien régime in Egypt led to a failed democratic experiment in which Christians became one of the chief targets of Islamist anger. The breakdown of Ba'ath Party authority in Syria provided opportunities for the expansion of extremism that also targeted Christians for persecution and genocide. The only remaining option for Christians in the absence of such a cosmopolitan form of governance was either a return to a corporatist arrangement with newly restored authoritarian regimes or exit via emigration or flight.

These stark choices have characterized the Christian dilemma for the past ten years. By and large, they have contributed to the serious erosion of the Arab Christian population. Though Christians continue to be a vibrant part of the social and political life of many Middle Eastern states, "the reality is that the Christian population in the Middle East is shrinking at a faster rate than ever before, through emigration and wholesale killings, as well as a lower birthrate than its Muslim counterpart's" (Flamini 2013, 71). Some argue that although Western governments and the international media have recognized the significance of the crisis, their efforts to solve it are "woefully lacking" (Khashan 2014, 9). Initial Christian support for democratization under the Arab Spring led to a significant malaise when the protests led to instability and civil strife rather than to liberal-democratic reform. Christians' general response has been either to support retrenchment under authoritarian regimes that will engage in corporatist protection of religious minorities or to depart the region.

Christians fled ISIS in far larger numbers than their proportion of the population. The majority fled to Western countries, unlikely to return. Many others fled to semiauthoritarian states where Christian minorities remain protected by friendly regimes, such as Turkey, Jordan, Lebanon, and the Kurdistan Regional Government of northern Iraq. Though coverage of the refugee crisis throughout the Middle East emphasized the expansion of refugee camps across border regions abutting the affected areas of Iraq and Syria since the outbreak of civil war in 2011, most Christians tended to find shelter among local churches. In Turkey, Syrian Christian refugees largely eschewed camps set up by multilateral aid agencies for fear of being targeted by compatriots who might associate them with the regime of Bashar al-Assad, which is widely perceived to enjoy the support of religious minorities (Martone 2013). In Jordan, local churches provided shelter to many Christians fleeing displacement from the Nineveh Plains of northern Iraq, including at least a thousand in the churches of Amman alone (Lynn 2015). Closer to home, many of the displaced Christians found their way to In Ankawa, a suburb of Erbil in the Kurdish region of northern Iraq, where they settled in large numbers in refugee camps on the property of churches and an unfinished shopping center. In many of these situations, there are few prospects for naturalized citizenship or open advocacy of domestic guarantees of essential freedoms.

Elsewhere, the participation of Christians in the popular revolutions in Egypt and Syria gave way to a return to former patterns of interest representation. The restoration of authoritarian rule in Egypt in 2014 provided a new opportunity for corporatist neomillet partnership with the regime in that country. The Syrian regime's resistance to democratization led Syrian Christians to find shelter in local communities or in church-based refugee camps in Lebanon and Jordan. These and other trends set the stage for the unfinished resolution of Christian participation in the transitional period after the 2011 revolutions. Here I consider the two states with Christian populations most affected by the unfinished project of the Arab Spring.

Case 1: The Disillusioned—Egypt's Copts

The unique interest of Christian Egyptians, largely known as Copts, in the Arab Spring protests of 2011 is occasionally emphasized in accounts of the January 25 revolution. The ongoing malaise of governance by the National Democratic Party, disgust with Hosni Mubarak's unacknowledged plan to appoint his son Gamal as his successor, the return to gross fraud and intimidation in the elections of 2010, and, of course, the impetus provided by the protests that drove President Zine El Abidine Ben Ali of Tunisia out of office—all had an effect on the average Egyptian.

However, among Christians a gradual erosion of confidence in the regime dated back to early 2010, if not earlier. Amid the politicization of Egyptian society common during an election campaign, Christians felt targeted by both the regime and the opposition. Elizabeth Iskander relates how in late November 2010 Copts persisted in a church-construction project in defiance of the Giza governor's refusal to authorize a building permit, leading to a government clampdown on their efforts. In response, the Coptic patriarch, Pope Shenouda III, took the unusual step of vocally condemning the security services for their partisan stance against Christian religious freedom. Iskander notes that the various Christian denominations in Egypt endorsed the US State Department's report on international religious freedom in Egypt for the first time that same month (2012, 158).

In this context, the bombing of the Two Saints Church in Alexandria on January 1, 2011, in which twenty-three were killed and dozens injured, had particular resonance for the Christian community (Tadros 2013, 125). The Mubarak government laid official blame at the door of a shadowy Islamist movement; later press reports, however, implicated the regime. In either case, Copts no longer felt that regime protection was sufficient to prevent vigilante attacks against the community.

From the initial gatherings at Tahrir Square on January 25, Christians were participating equally in the organization and execution of the mass protests. One of the common slogans in Tahrir Square was the chant that boasted, "Muslims and Christians, one hand." Christian participation flouted the injunctions announced by the Coptic patriarch, Pope Shenouda III, who sought to deter the laity from joining the protests in the square (Tadros 2013, 128). Despite the church's efforts, lay Copts were active both as organizers of the revolutionary movement and as protestors in the square. The nearby Qasr al Doubara Evangelical Church served as a makeshift hospital during the prolonged sit-in.

The outcome of regime change was initially ambiguous for the Christian minority. The scent of freedom led many to believe that new church building would be one benefit of the overthrow of the Mubarak regime. In fact, Christian defiance of government strictures on building was one of the major actions that had defined Christian resistance to the regime in the months prior to the revolution. There was hope that a democratic state might open up doors for a new form of citizenship and for a redrafting of the Constitution in a way that would enshrine human rights and the rule of law in Egypt. However, the growth of Islamist and Salafist power over the months that followed the revolution created a strong sense of anxiety among Egyptian Christians.

The collapse of the old order appeared to many Christians to be an opportunity to assume a new stance toward the government on the basis of shared citizenship.

Individual Copts had been involved in opposition movements in the past. For example, George Ishaq, a Coptic intellectual and layman, was one of the founding members of the *kifaya* movement that challenged the Mubarak government in 2005. The postrevolutionary opening for new political parties created opportunities for many individual Copts to participate in organizing and running new political movements. Prominent Coptic billionaire Naguib Sawiris came out as a public supporter of the Free Egyptians Party, a newly formed liberal party that contested legislative elections in 2011–12. Other Copts participated as candidates, and eight in total were elected to the People's Assembly that year. Several were appointed to the Constituent Assembly appointed to draft a new Egyptian constitution.

Amid the new landscape of Egyptian politics, new lay movements arose to demand individual rights for Copts. The demands focused on the age-old concern of church construction, but it was clear that other issues motivated Coptic activism, such as the relaxation of regulations surrounding religious identification on official identity cards and the creation of a uniform civil code that would subvert church rules against divorce. In response to vigilante attacks on churches in Upper Egypt throughout the summer of 2011, a new protest movement developed among the Copts.

Though dozens of new Coptic movements arose during the early postrevolutionary period, the most notable was the Maspero Youth Union (MYU). This group included two controversial priests in its ranks, but the leadership insisted upon its lay credentials as a movement aimed at speaking for Coptic interests outside the church hierarchy. Over the course of 2011, the group's organizational strength was recognized by the media, which increasingly sought out its leadership to understand where Copts stood on public issues. For the MYU, a top concern was the publicization of government management of church-construction activities in Upper Egypt. In September 2011, a controversy over the construction of a church in Marinab, Aswan, led to calls for public protests to demand equal rights for Coptic citizens within the city of Cairo. Several allied groups of activists began what was called an "open-ended strike" at the National Radio and Television Headquarters in Maspero, after which the youth movement was named (Leila 2011). The protests persisted over the next two weeks and began to test the nerves of the government, which was now led by the Supreme Council of the Armed Forces (SCAF).

When the MYU launched a large street protest outside Egyptian television headquarters in Maspero on October 9, 2011, it was met with lethal force. That night, twenty-seven people were killed in the melee that ensued. Average Copts viewed the Egyptian military's actions as a betrayal that ultimately contributed to growing disaffection with the SCAF regime. The "Maspero Massacre" had the effect of intimidating the Coptic lay movement at a time when the church was also unable to tap into formerly regular channels of influence with the regime. Its impact on Copts' trust in the military was severe. However, future events demonstrated that a renewal of personal relations between the church hierarchy and the military was still within the realm of possibility. When civil order broke down under a civilian regime, the Coptic Church would resume its support for a military-backed secularist order.

Copts were disappointed by the SCAF military regime, and they met the election of Islamist and Salafist parties to lead the National Assembly and the election of Mohamed Morsi to the presidency in June 2012 with even greater skepticism. Morsi's early attempts to demonstrate a commitment to a multisectarian presidency by appointing a Copt to the cabinet were immediately undermined by developments in the autumn of 2012. His decision to rule by decree, announced in November 2012, was followed by the mass resignation of his Coptic advisers and members of the Constituent Assembly drafting the Constitution and ruined his reputation among Christians long before his regime began to crumble. Those who resigned from the Constituent Assembly were quickly replaced by Muslim Brotherhood loyalists.

The new Constitution enshrined a special role for the ulama of al-Azhar University in interpreting the way in which the Islamic shari'a would be applied, deepening Christians' concerns that the Muslim Brotherhood was seeking to move toward a theocratic agenda at odds with the revolution's democratic aims. At the same time, the appointment of a new Coptic pope to replace Shenouda III, who had passed away in March 2012, ushered in a new era in church–state relations. The newly enthroned patriarch, Tawadros III, rose to the papacy by deliberately minimizing his political involvement. Nevertheless, the events of late 2012 and the expansion of the Tamarod movement to drive Morsi from the presidency ultimately engulfed the church as well. Tawadros's decision to embrace a political role in restoring the former relationship between the church and the state appears to have developed over the early months of 2013. In early February 2013, Tawadros publicly criticized the administration's efforts to engage in a dialogue following the rejection of popular sectors for the Constituent Assembly, arguing that the "dialogue ends before its starts and none of its results are implemented" (*Ahram Online* 2013). The pope voiced the popular view of most Christians that the newly restrictive environment ushered in by the Islamist-dominated Constitutional Assembly was something less than the liberal democracy they had hoped for after the fall of Mubarak.

The Christian public's support of the Coptic patriarch was on full display when General Abdel Fatah al-Sisi announced the overthrow of the Morsi regime on July 3, 2013, and the pope was easily recognizable standing beside the general during

Sisi's televised announcement. The message taken by the Muslim Brotherhood was clear: Christians supported the military government. Throughout the summer of 2013, the Islamist movement attacked churches as soft targets of the regime, and several Christians were killed in targeted attacks. By the end of July 2013, there had been "at least six" separate attacks on Copts, in which seven had died and large-scale damage had been done to Christians' properties. As the Sisi regime consolidated its hold on the Egyptian government and engaged in the forced dispersal of Islamist protestors from the camp at Rabaa al-Adawiya in August 2013, Copts registered their hope that despite the difficulties they faced at the hands of the previous government's supporters, the future would be brighter for religious minorities. The words of one Coptic graduate student interviewed at the time, "we're still better off," reflected a common Coptic response to the overthrow of the Muslim Brotherhood government (Kholaif 2013).

The patriarch's support for the July coup and the price paid in lives and institutions were an investment in a renewal of official church support for the authoritarian government of General Sisi, who was elected president the following year. Egyptian Copts had passed through the revolutionary period as proponents of regime change but ultimately benefited by the resumption of politics as normal. On January 6, 2015, President Sisi visited the Coptic Cathedral in Abbasiyya, the seat of the Coptic patriarch, for Coptic Christmas celebrations—the first time an Egyptian president had chosen to do so. Coming on the heels of Tawadros's public comments that Copts should not hold the military responsible for the Maspero massacre of October 2011, the visit was a demonstration of the extremely close relationship that had developed between the pope and the new president (Kirkpatrick and Thomas 2015). Nor was the pope's forgiving attitude toward the regime unique, given the level of applause that the president enjoyed upon his entrance to the cathedral.

Although the Coptic laity had demonstrated a clear preference for the implementation of a more liberal-democratic state with pluralist forms of interest representation, the erosion of citizenship rights under the SCAF regime and the resort to majoritarian policies represented by the Morsi interregnum seemed to Copts proof of the futility of pursuing a postsectarian Egypt. The transitional period introduced by the revolution of 2011 had instead provided only a limited opportunity for the parallel democratization of state and church. The challenge posed by political Islam more than justified a return to the status quo for most Copts, who were concerned about the rising threat of extremism. As civil conflict deepened in neighboring Libya and in Syria, dramatic stories of Christian martyrdom only seemed to justify further Christian support for a regime that aimed its full force at counterterrorist actions. This support persisted despite increasingly draconian approaches undertaken by the Egyptian state in the years following the summer of 2013.

Case 2: The Refugees—Iraqi Christians

The US invasion of Iraq in 2003 set in motion momentous changes that continue to reverberate today. Among various effects, it led to the violent targeting of churches and hierarchs in central and northern Iraq and the mass exodus of a large proportion of the prewar Christian population. The introduction of a democratic form of government handed power to the Arab Shiʻi majority, while disenfranchising earlier elites among the Arab Sunni population. Ultimately, this shift has empowered Shiʻi Arab majoritarianism and led to the marginalization of most of the minority populations, except in the case of the autonomous Kurdistan Regional Government of northern Iraq.

In 2003, Iraq had a small population of 800,000 to one million Christians, divided among the Chaldaean Catholic, Assyrian, and Syriac Churches. Their subdivision arose out of a long history of ethnic and cultural marginalization of the Indigenous Christian Assyrian population. Rivalry between the three indigenous churches has made it difficult for them to form a common front for the articulation of the Christian community's interests. These Christian groups have maintained unique cultural practices in addition to their religious distinction from the Iraqi Arab majority: for example, to this day, most Iraqi Christians speak a form of Syriac or Aramaic either in common parlance or in the liturgy. Under the Hashemite monarchy from the 1920s to the 1950s and into the early republican period, Iraqi Christians were increasingly broadly categorized as Arab Christians, a process of "acculturation" that Sargon Donabed describes as a gradual campaign aimed at the "social death" of the community (2015, 244).

This long history of assimilation had both marginalized the community and provided it with a singular survival strategy as Christians came to be associated with the larger Arab society. It also sowed the seeds for the destruction of their communities when Iraq descended into sectarianism in the 2000s. Iraqi Christians had enjoyed relative quiet under the regime of Saddam Hussein. Though some had benefited under Baʻath Party dominance (most famously under Tariq Aziz, the former foreign minister and deputy prime minister), more generally the Christian population had remained apolitical. The Baʻath regime had seen little purpose in solidifying a formal relationship with the indigenous churches, and the new regime founded by the American occupation deepened the inherent political divisions in Iraq, magnifying the sectarian divides that served to polarize the country.

Sectarianism and the Iraqi multiple-member proportional list system based on governorates does not generally benefit Christians running for Parliament. Even if the state were to adopt a proportional system that includes the entire population, a party representing Christian interests would remain tiny and marginal. Mokhtar Lamani observes that "the contemporary Iraqi political system that has divided Iraqi people into three ethnic groups has actually emphasized minorities' vulnerabilities to the dangers that have persisted since 2003" (2010, 97). Iraq's Constitution provides for the appointment of five Christian members to Parliament, and Christian members have been elected in partnership with the majoritarian alliances among Arab Sunnis and Kurds. However, the ongoing polarization of Iraqi politics between the governing faction led by Shiʻi coalitions and the extra-parliamentary Sunni opposition set the stage for the invasion by ISIS in June 2014.

Since 2003, the tensions that beset the area of northern Iraq have led Iraqi Christians to seek a longer-term solution to enhancing the security of the embattled minority. In the face of the ISIS advance on Mosul that June, the vast majority of Christians fled the city. Those who remained were quickly identified by the militants, who famously labeled Christian residences and property with the Arabic letter *nuun* for "Nasiri," a name eschewed by Christians themselves. By August 2014, the nearby town of Qaraqosh, the center of Christian settlement in the Nineveh Plains on the borders of the Kurdish regional administration, was also abandoned by both its native Assyrian population and the Kurdish *pesh merga*, military forces, who had briefly defended the area.

The Christian population of Mosul and the Nineveh Plains demonstrated immense resilience in the face of adversity. Though ISIS forces engaged in rape, enslavement, and slaughter of many in the minority communities, a large proportion of the Christian population was able to flee before the takeover of Mosul and the Nineveh Plains. They found their way either to refugee camps in Erbil and other parts of Iraqi Kurdistan or to sanctuaries farther afield. In Erbil, several Christian organizations and the traditional churches set up educational and relief services for the displaced population. The civil initiatives established by internal exiles spearheaded a movement for a safe haven to be established in the area of the Nineveh Plains, an idea floated ever since the US invasion. Small numbers formed five separate defense militias, some of which joined with Kurdish *pesh merga* in the fight against ISIS (Griswold 2015). Although Kurdish forces provided a safe haven for many Christians, the Kurds' desire for a state separate from Iraq with influence over areas of the Nineveh Plains raised suspicion among most Christians in northern Iraq. Their concern was that Kurdish interest in expanding influence over the territory of the Nineveh Plains had little to do with creating a pluralist Kurdish state and more to do with the resource wealth of the border regions of Iraqi Kurdistan (Griswold 2015). Assyrians have spent the better part of ten decades resisting Arabist assimilation and fear that it will merely be replaced by a new and stronger Kurdish variant in which Assyrians are subsumed into the Kurdish ethnicity.

In the years since the defeat of ISIS in Mosul in 2017, small numbers of Christians have returned to their homes in the Nineveh Plains, particularly in towns such as Teleskof and Qaraqosh. Nevertheless, these communities are vastly diminished following the trauma of the ISIS invasion. In the case of Qaraqosh, the largest of the Christian settlements, the population is estimated to be only a little more than half what it was in 2015 (Rasche 2018, 136). The rise of *hashd al-shaabi* (popular militias) among various groups empowered to fight ISIS after the collapse of the Iraqi armed forces in northern Iraq in 2015 has presented a singular challenge both for the government of Iraq and for minority communities. Although on the one hand it opened up the possibility of creating a Christian militia in the Nineveh Plains, it also on the other hand empowered various other groups that had intimidated Christians in their former homes. Many Christians are likely to remain in exile in the Kurdish region or abroad.

Case 3: The Reticent—Syria's Christians

Amid the civil war that emerged out of the US invasion of Iraq, many Arab Sunni leaders fled to safe haven in Syria. These elements joined forces with Syrian Sunni dissidents to create their own sphere of influence in northeastern Syria after 2011, eventually declaring the restoration of the caliphate as the "Islamic State," based in Raqqa. ISIS eventually occupied most of eastern Syria and various parts of the central portions of the country. Other Islamist militias of varying stripes took up the conflict against the Syrian government in the North and South. Along the northern border with Turkey, the Kurdish movement embodied by the Democratic Union Party and its irregular forces, known as the People's Defense Units (Yekîneyên Parastina Gel, YPG), formed the "most organized and visible opposition movement in Syria" (Allsopp 2017, 291). From mid-2012, the YPG staked out control over a territory referred to by its Kurdish name, "Rojava," until Turkish forces pushed them out of the border region in 2018. ISIS, the various Islamist militias, the YPG, and other groups, such as Turkish-sponsored rebel movements, engaged in periodic clashes with the Syrian government and one another over the years from 2011 to 2019.

Based in Damascus, the regime of Syrian president Bashar al-Assad oversees a secular corporatist state that has discouraged the active civil engagement of religious organizations in public life. Although the state's decades-long repression of civil society has left church hierarchies in place, it, in tandem with the repression by Islamist organizations, has minimized the social role undertaken by the churches. Coupled with the natural division of the churches among Eastern and Oriental Orthodox as well as Catholic churches, Syrian Christian civil society has remained limited, despite the fact that Christians make up somewhere close to 10 percent of the population. Although Christians have no central role in the top ranks of the Ba'athist hierarchy in Syria, they have filled minor cabinet positions under the Assad administration. What is more, the church hierarchies have enjoyed a relatively harmonious relationship with the regime. One scholar of Syrian Christian descent laments that "the highest ranks of their spiritual and clerical prelates have colluded with the al-Assad (senior and junior) tyrannical regime in a multi-faceted relational network of allegiance, subordination, opportunism, mutual interest and self-seeking" (Awad 2017, 71). Indeed, in December 2011 the Syrian patriarchs united in a statement rejecting foreign intervention. Nevertheless, Mark Farha and Salma Moussa argue, based in part on qualitative analysis of social media posts, that this elite consensus reflects the perspective of most Syrian Christians. Although some Christians backed protests against the regime in March and April 2011, as the civil war dragged on, "the regime . . . invested much of its energies in intertwining the fate of Christians with its own to scare them into submission" (2015, 186).

The descent into civil war therefore led most of the Christian population to flee or to seek refuge in government-controlled areas. Their status in Syria came to be closely linked to the state's overall security situation. One Damascene Christian interviewed in 2013 put it bluntly: "Either everything will be O.K. in one year, or there will be no Christians here" (quoted in Barnard 2013). The assertion may have been an overstatement, but it demonstrated the way in which the breakdown of order disproportionately hit the Christian minority. The limited scope of civil society also rendered the Christian minority dependent on the vicissitudes of either government or rebel tolerance of pluralism.

During the war, Syrian Christians were generally clustered in three areas: the northern city of Aleppo, the northeastern fringe of the country surrounding the city of Qamishli, and the land surrounding the capital, Damascus. The Christian population of Aleppo fled in large numbers over the border to Turkey and abroad into exile in Western states. In Rojava, Syrian Christians were able to remain in place or to seek refuge. The larger population of Christians in the capital Damascus and surrounding regions either fled or remained in areas under government control.

Conclusion

To be or not to be? The past couple of decades have placed in stark relief the precarious survival of Christian communities throughout the Middle East. The Arab Spring protests opened up a delicate expansion of civil society activity that both quickly flowered and rapidly withered under the pressure of entrenched interests, radicalism, and desperation. Traditionally, civil society had been marginalized by Middle Eastern authoritarian regimes, which viewed social movements and independently organized groups as direct threats to their rule. Christian organizations had some immunity from restrictions on their activity given that they were unlikely to pose a threat to the government of any Muslim-majority state. Christian civil society survived and in some isolated cases even thrived in authoritarian environments such as Egypt, where limited liberalization had been introduced as a form of authoritarian upgrading.

As a result, Arab Christian civil society was already established as an important force before the Arab Spring, even if it was generally tethered to the recognized indigenous churches. Statist authoritarianism had sought to cultivate support among Christians through corporatist means that reinforced regime stability. In the words of Andrea Zaki Stephanous, "Societal institutions [other than the state]—such as the Church and the Mosque—that represent the plurality of the civil society simply imitate the state or try to control it" (2010, 173). Christians had no chance of implementing control over the state, but through partnerships with the regime they had enjoyed some shelter.

But the revolutions in 2011 opened up the possibility that Christian organizations, including both churches and parachurch organizations, might emerge from the shadow of state corporatism. Seeking pluralism, Christian civil society met up against majoritarianism—even if it did not represent the majority's views and desires. The assertion of Islamist majoritarianism did not enshrine a newly democratic impulse, which Christians had demanded amid the Arab Spring protests. The democratic project remained unfinished. Christians wanted an equilibrium in which their free pursuit of civil participation would be allowed under a nascent democratic system. They required a nation that would include them while also affirming the right of all citizens, both Muslim and Christian, to the free pursuit of their interests—what Stephanous calls "dynamic citizenship" under a system of "inclusive pluralism" (2010, 211). But as majoritarianism turned toward an uncompromising Islamism, Christians fled back toward the shelter of authoritarian corporatism. In short, the dream of democratic pluralism remained, but the permissive environment limited Christians' options.

Hopeful Christians participated in Arab Spring protests from Egypt to Syria and beyond. Their goals for the revolutionary movement were the establishment of more liberal politics, including nonsectarian and pluralist systems that might afford them better access to the rights of citizenship and the normalization of civil status for both Muslims and Christians. The Arab Spring encouraged Christians to pursue greater autonomous civil activism outside the realm of the traditional neo-millet corporatist partnership that yoked the national and historic churches to the authoritarian state. Nevertheless, the descent of the Arab Spring into majoritarian politics benefited the sometimes politicized and sometimes radicalized wings of the Islamist movement and only served to deepen Arab Christians' anxieties about a future that was already uncertain. They were faced with a stark choice between supporting renewed authoritarianism and emigrating. Their favored choice, plu-ralist participation in a newly emergent civil society, became an impossibility as majoritarian social movements worked to overturn the liberal establishment in Egypt or to overthrow sectarian administrations in Iraq and Syria. Delicate and vulnerable civil societies in Lebanon and Jordan, each of which received Christian immigrants, were able to provide shelter to Christian groups under semiauthori-tarian auspices.

The short-term solution for most Christian populations has been to seek shelter under the traditional neomillet corporatist partnership with authoritar-ian regimes. This strategy, however, does not achieve most Christians' long-term desire for social change under a pluralist regime and seems likely to damage Christian–Muslim relations into the future, possibly irreparably. The short-lived dream of pluralist social engagement under a democratizing regime remains the Christians' long-term hope. The unfinished project of the Christian Arab Spring is the establishment of just such an enduring inclusive pluralism.

References

Ahram Online. 2013. "Coptic Pope Tawadros II Criticises Egypt's Islamist Leadership, New Constitution." Feb. 5. At https://english.ahram.org.eg/NewsContent/1/64/64135 /Egypt/Politics-/Coptic-Pope-Tawadros-II-criticises-Egypts-Islamist.aspx.

Allsopp, Harriet. 2017. "Kurdish Political Parties and the Syrian Uprising." In *The Kurdish Question Revisited*, edited by Gareth Stansfield and Mohammed Shareef, 289–304. Oxford: Oxford Univ. Press.

Awad, Najib George. 2017. "Social Harmony in the Middle East: The Christian Contri-butions." In *Christian Citizenship in the Middle East: Divided Allegiance or Dual Be-longing?*, edited by Mohammed Girma and Cristian Romocea, 63–82. London: Jessica Kingsley.

Bailey, Betty Jane, and J. Martin Bailey. 2010. *Who Are the Christians in the Middle East?* 2nd ed. Grand Rapids, MI: Eerdmans.

Barnard, Anne. 2013. "A Wary Easter Weekend for Christians in Syria." *New York Times*, Mar. 30.

BBC News. 2011. "Guide: Christians in the Middle East." Oct. 11. At http://www.bbc.com/news/world-middle-east-15239529.

———. 2015. "Syria's Beleaguered Christians." Feb. 25. At http://www.bbc.com/news/world-middle-east-22270455.

Belge, Ceren, and Ekrem Karacoç. 2015. "Minorities in the Middle East: Ethnicity, Religion, and Support for Authoritarianism." *Political Research Quarterly* 68, no. 2: 280–92.

Brynen, Rex, Pete W. Moore, Bassel Salloukh, and Marie-Joelle Zahar. 2012. *Beyond the Arab Spring: Authoritarianism and Democratization in the Arab World.* Boulder, CO: Lynne Rienner.

Catholic Near East Welfare Association. 2017. "Middle East Populations, 2017." At https://www.cnewa.org/pdf/popul_data.pdf.

Donabed, Sargon. 2015. *Reforging a Forgotten History: Iraq and the Assyrians in the Twentieth Century.* Edinburgh: Edinburgh Univ. Press.

Farah, Nadia Ramses. 1986. *Religious Strife in Egypt.* New York: Gordon and Breach.

Farha, Mark, and Salma Moussa. 2015. "Secular Autocracy vs. Sectarian Democracy? Weighing Reasons for Christian Support for Regime Transition in Syria and Egypt." *Mediterranean Politics* 20, no. 2: 178–97.

Flamini, Roland. 2013. "Forced Exodus: Christians in the Middle East." *World Affairs* 176, no. 4: 65–71.

Griswold, Eliza. 2015. "Is This the End of Christianity in the Middle East?" *New York Times Magazine*, July 26. At http://www.nytimes.com/2015/07/26/magazine/is-this-the-end-of-christianity-in-the-middle-east.html?_r=0.

Harris, William. 1996. *Faces of Lebanon: Sects, Wars, and Global Extensions.* Princeton, NJ: Markus Wiener.

Hasan, S. S. 2003. *Christians versus Muslims in Modern Egypt: The Century-Long Struggle for Coptic Equality.* Oxford: Oxford Univ. Press.

Heydemann, Stephen. 2007. *Upgrading Authoritarianism in the Arab World.* Washington, DC: Brookings Institution Press.

Iskander, Elizabeth. 2012. *Sectarian Conflict in Egypt: Coptic Media, Identity, and Representation.* London: Routledge.

Josua, Hanna Nouri. 2014. "The Middle East: A Future Region without Christians." *International Journal for Religious Freedom* 7, nos. 1–2: 127–56.

Khashan, Hilal. 2014. "*Dateline*: Arab Uprisings May Doom Middle East Christians." *Middle East Quarterly* 21, no. 4: 1–9.

Kholaif, Dahlia. 2013. "Egypt's Sectarian Tensions Become Politicised." Al Jazeera Online, July 26. At https://www.aljazeera.com/features/2013/7/26/egypts-sectarian-tensions-become-politicised.

Kirkpatrick, David D., and Merna Thomas. 2015. "Egyptian Leader Visits Coptic Christmas Eve Service." *New York Times*, Jan. 6.

Lamani, Mokhtar. 2010. "The Extinction of Iraqi Minorities: Challenge or Catastrophe?" In *From Desolation to Reconstruction: Iraq's Troubled Journey*, edited by Mokhtar Lamani and Bessma Momani, 95–116. Waterloo, Canada: Wilfrid Laurier Univ. Press.

Leila, Reem. 2011. "Church Fire Fires Up Copts." *Al Ahram Weekly*, Oct. 6–12.

Lynn, Kelly. 2015. "Life on Hold for Iraqi Christian Refugees in Jordan." Al Jazeera Online, Sept. 18. At http://www.aljazeera.com/indepth/inpictures/2015/09/life-hold-iraqi-christian-refugees-jordan-150914112759635.html.

Markoe, Lauren. 2014. "Ted Cruz Booed Offstage at Defense of Christians Gathering for Israel Comments." *Huffington Post*, Sept. 11. At http://www.huffingtonpost.com/2014/09/11/ted-cruz-booed-offstage_n_5805332.html.

Martone, James. 2013. "Syrian Christians Turn to Turkish Churches, Not Refugee Camps, for Help." *Catholic News Service*, Mar. 20. At http://www.catholicnews.com/services/englishnews/2013/syrian-christians-turn-to-turkish-churches-not-refugee-camps-for-help.cfm.

McCallum, Fiona. 2007. "The Political Role of the Patriarch in the Contemporary Middle East." *Middle Eastern Studies* 43, no. 6: 923–40.

———. 2012. "Religious Institutions and Authoritarian States: Church–State Relations in the Middle East." *Third World Quarterly* 33, no. 1: 109–24.

Nabo, Mitra Moussa. 2020. "Eastern Subjectivities and Islam's Hegemony in the Arab World." In *Middle East Christianity: Local Practices, World Societal Engagements*, edited by Stephan Stetter and Mitra Moussa Nabo, 25–47. London: Palgrave Macmillan.

Rasche, Stephen. 2018. *The Disappearing People: The Tragic Fate of Christians in the Middle East*. New York: Bombardier.

Rowe, Paul S. 2007. "Neo-millet Systems and Transnational Religious Movements: The Humayun Decrees and Church Construction in Egypt." *Journal of Church and State* 49, no. 2: 329–50.

———. 2009. "Building Coptic Civil Society: Christian Groups and the State in Mubarak's Egypt." *Middle Eastern Studies* 45, no. 1: 111–26.

Sabella, Bernard. 2006. *The Sabeel Survey on Palestinian Christians in the West Bank and Israel*. Jerusalem: Sabeel.

Special Assembly for the Middle East of the Synod of Bishops. 2010. Oct. 10–12. At http://www.vatican.va/news_services/press/sinodo/documents/bollettino_24_speciale-medio-oriente-2010/bollettino_24_speciale-medio-oriente-2010_index_en.html.

Stephanous, Andrea Zaki. 2010. *Political Islam, Citizenship, and Minorities: The Future of Arab Christians in the Islamic Middle East*. Lanham, MD: Univ. Press of America.

Tadros, Mariz. 2013. *Copts at the Crossroads*. Cairo: American Univ. of Cairo Press.

Part Three

Gendering the MENA Movements

12

Toward a Democratization of Authority in Islamic Thought

*Gender as a Category of Thought
in Light of the Arab Spring*

amina wadud

As the Arab Spring began to unfold, it brought global attention to the need and desire for change in Muslim-majority contexts. It became symbolic of the aspirations for both minority and majority Muslim communities. Ironically, the rise and spread of its philosophical and political opposite in the form of Da'ish, or the so-called Islamic State, also becomes symbolic of ways to resist the impact of that unfolding. Among the foundational ideas distinguishing these two movements are diametrically opposed notions of authority in Islam. The Islamic State operates under a hegemonic-based notion of authority, and the Arab Spring heralded a more democratic notion of authority.

The habit of hegemonic- and charismatic-based notions of authority in Islam has developed, changed, and been resisted since the Islamic Classical period. This chapter explores the construction of more democratic authority in an effort to dismantle the tendency of deference to earlier notions of authority. I contend that the Arab Spring constitutes the most profound message that Muslims as a whole are waking up to their own need for more collective determination of their governance and ways of being.

The tendency to defer unquestionably to certain types of authority can lead to problematic abuses, as all can see with the Da'ish movement. As Muslims claim political agency, whether that be in the Arab Spring or at any other moment, they must also construct more inclusive forms of authority. To move toward more democratic political systems in civil society, we need a paradigm shift toward greater collective competence. Like much of my work, this chapter uses a gender-inclusive analysis to indicate how it has shaped my perspective. However, this gender-inclusive analysis is not about women.

The Islamic intellectual tradition accepts God as the Ultimate Authority. God communicated to humankind through revelation to the Prophet Muhammad (S). Sunni Islam "lack[s] a formal institutional and hierarchical structure of authority" because "there is no authoritative center other than God and the Prophet" (Abou El Fadl 2001, 11). This makes any idea of religious authority dubious. After the death of the Prophet—and thus for almost the entirety of Islamic history—both God and the Prophet were represented in texts. Interpretation of these texts stood as authority but was completely open, diverse, contested, and even contradictory. In the aftermath of direct revelation to the Prophet, Muslim thinkers established the idea of authority in the Qur'an, sunna, and hadith as primary sources, but also to varying degrees in shari'a—or really *fiqh*.

In this sense, the question of authority is about whose interpretations are valid and applicable or who has the authority to provide interpretations that will be enacted. Certainly, those with the power—be it the state or another entity—have forcibly implemented their interpretations. However, they could face contestation of the authority of their interpretations by other interpretations with unshakeable evidence that establishes different reasoning and legitimacy. At the very least, new interpretations could disprove the logic used by those in power. This is the place of revolution, as in the Arab Spring. This is also the place of Islamic feminism as one of the modern reformist projects.

The Qur'an remains the primary basis for all human claims to authority in Islamic thought. Yet meaning must be derived from that source and then implemented. Most Muslims know very little about the mechanisms for finding meaning and the ways such meanings are implemented, so they defer to experts, scholars, and leaders—who become authorities.

For Khaled Abou El Fadl, "only God has the power to define and identify" the meanings of some passages. He questions the extent to which "a reader [can] decide a meaning for the text." He proposes that the legal process is "a dialectical engagement with God. God, in one form or another speaks to human beings and human beings engage God's speech through interpretation and praxis" (2001, 3–7). When Muslims are unaware of the nature of, consequences of, and influences upon interpretations, they depend on others—as authorities—to provide interpretations that dictate the full spectrum of right and wrong, thus defining what it means to be human and Muslim. Certain static notions about the nature of reality have sometimes been given authority, while other interpretations are closed off from legitimacy. Are there limits to legitimacy? Who decides? Why are "limits" even a question if God is the Ultimate Sovereign? "Wal aa yuhituna bi-shayin min ilmihi illa bi maa sha" (And you will not encompass ought of His knowledge except as He wills).

The first crisis in the early Muslim *ummah* (community) was over the question of legitimate political authority. After the conflict that initiated the longest-standing dispute between Sunni and Shi'ah, political leadership for Sunnis would largely remain separate from interpretive authority, which fell to the jurists. The jurists could determine what was legitimate within the community and even who could lead the community. The jurists were seen as repositories of a certain amount of knowledge about the primary sources, which they used to answer questions regarding right praxis. Although there were continued and extensive historical transformations in all aspects of interpretations, even Abou El Fadl does not consider the extent to which interpretive methodologies were steeped in the existing patriarchal and hegemonic social order. Patriarchy left its mark on all aspects of interpretation, including the approved methodologies and the major canonical principles. Although Classical thinkers were neither irresponsible nor amoral, they were located in their time and place. This brings us to the question of how they may or may not be qualified to speak for us now.

In particular, I am concerned with the question of gender as a category of thought. Despite endless assertions about the role and "nature" of men and women, no coherent interrogation of the social construction of gender existed until the end of the twentieth century. However, patriarchal privilege and gender locations left their mark on categories of authority and questions of legitimacy as well as on methods used to assert both. Even with detailed criteria about knowledge acquisition concerning who can claim authority, that role comes into question if the one who fulfills those criteria is a woman.

In more than fifty years of scholarship and activism, I have observed rhetorical assertions of power and authority and even been subjected to them. Can such rhetoric stand in place of criteria, or are the established criteria dubious? All criteria were constructed during the Classical period with certain contextual conditions in which they were thought to do service. Yet those contexts were steeped in patriarchal privilege, leaving the mark of time and place on the criteria themselves. Yet no context of human civilization and organization is permanent, fixed, or divine. It is time to rethink the matter of authority in order to serve a growing community that has developed in ways perhaps not foreseen in the Classical period.

For example, during the Classical period, the operative understanding of what it means to be a human being was selectively based on the free male Muslim human being. The definition of that base needed exceptions, additions, or deletions to apply to non-Muslims and to slaves. This was also the case for female Muslim human beings, who likewise would appear deficient, deviant, or subhuman against this male standard. For example, when Attar of Nishapur (c. 1145–c. 1220) included Rabi'ah al-'Adawiyyah in his famous Sufi hagiographies, he was forced to explain her presence by inadvertently making her "other-than" female. He said, "When an aspirant reaches the level of spiritual acumen that Rabi'ah has, she ceases to be a woman. She is amongst the men" (Shaikh 2012, 52–53). Thus, high spiritual attainment was conditioned upon maleness. When a woman reaches that height, she would/could no longer be (just?) a woman. Do all human beings who achieve spiritual heights cease to be their gendered self—men no longer men and women no longer women? To offer such gender transcendence only to females privileges in one direction but reinforces male hegemony in the other. Not only are there ethical questions about this literary "othering," but also the whole project of what constitutes authority is suspect.

Thus, Classical constructions of legitimacy and authority were based on a patriarchal framework that cannot meet the challenge of a rapidly moving and increasingly diverse world. The divine mission of guidance to all humankind must encompass more than the standard male patriarch that comes to us from the first few centuries after revelation. Throughout the development of an Islamic intellectual and ethical worldview, even constructing what the term *Islam* means or discussing what we understand to be Allah—the Ultimate Reality and Supreme Divinity—has been subject to human discourse. No wonder, then, that for much of this discourse, Allah, the Ultimate Reality, is viewed as an all-powerful male being. Is that model sufficient to every aspect of a faith mission? What happens to Allah's intimate nurturing capacity under such a remote notion?

To be sure, there is a distinction between being *an authority* and being *in authority*. Being *in authority* is coercive, with the ability to direct the conduct of another person through the use of inducements benefits, threats, or punishments, so that reasonable people would conclude that for all practical purposes they have no choice but to comply. Being *in authority* means one can obtain compliance with one's commands or directives. There is no surrender of private judgment because that judgment is made irrelevant. You may disagree, but you have to comply.

Obeying one who is *an authority* involves a surrender of private judgment or opinion in deference to "the perceived special knowledge" the authority possesses. Here, the authority must show their knowledge or expertise. Deference to an authority involves transference of reason to another person's will even if within a common belief system. Being an authority is persuasive, involving the ability to direct the belief or conduct of a person through trust (Abou El Fadl 2001, 18).

According to Abou El Fadl, the authoritative structure can be one in which a person agrees but does not lose their ability to develop their own opinions because the Islamic system is egalitarian and diverse, unless the person loses that ability against the pressure of an authoritative structure. Thus, it is only in the event of disagreement that the question of coercion comes in. When I encounter rhetorical assertions of male hegemony as authority, such persons claim privilege simply because they are male—even when they lack comparable knowledge or expertise. This is one reason why I have found tracing questions of authority so compelling.[1]

Although Abou El Fadl asserts that knowledge authority in this Islamic system is egalitarian and diverse, I contend that it has become hegemonic and coercive. Being an authority also involves assertion of power and privilege, which we need to dismantle. That is the motivation behind this chapter.

Ethics, Knowledge, and Authority

Where does the sense of authority—the privilege to become an authority and the designation of who gets to assert a judgment over another—come from in Muslim discourses? In the Classical period of Islamic intellectual history, we witness the signs of broad and even encyclopedic knowledge acquisition. Yet although the Classical scholars' knowledge was broad and deep—and we still consider their words integral to our intellectual traditions—they were never presumptuous about their knowledge. They accepted with humility the challenge or potential for error. After intense research, deep reflections, and the conclusion of their treatises, they wrote, "Wa-Allahu A'lam"—indeed, (only) Allah knows best.

This surrender I consider an indication that they had not given up the aspiration to go further with their knowledge, to the place where only Allah could take them. Even with the knowledge acquired, they returned to a place of humble surrender. Today we find those who want the power of asserting authority without the responsibility of acquiring knowledge with humility. For there is tremendous power in knowing, but knowledge also means responsibility to others. Power always serves. Power without service to others is self-serving.

In a conference in Exeter in 2015, "a male, in the audience asked why Dr. Amina Wadud . . . led the gender-mixed prayer *knowing* very well that it'd further diminish her chances at a position of authority in the Muslim community" (*Freedom from Forbidden* 2015).

How does one person lose authority they never knew they had? How does another person read that person's intention to covet any sort of authority (let alone

---

1. How can a twenty-something male make assertions not only over my opinion or judgment but also over my person and my faith with so little to show except the force of patriarchal privilege? Similar assertions are made by certain Arabic speakers, presuming they know more than I just because of an accident of birth. It is possible to acquire Arabic for specialization in Islamic disciplines. Even after fifty years of scholarship, somehow I can never know as much as a twenty-year-old because he was born to Arabic-speaking parents?!

the patriarchal hegemonic charismatic type, which I am critiquing) without asking the person first? How is the one who makes such an assertion demonstrating their claim to authority and flexing their power to limit access to authority for another? Are there obvious criteria of authority used here? Statements such as the one made at the conference attempt to remove the authority that has been heaped upon me since I began to lead mixed-gender prayer in 2005. They are rhetorical assertions of power that limit the possibilities of developing more democratic norms of authority.

Another definition of authority is the "ability to assert an opinion or perspective and by its assertion to thus become a marker for the community conversation and even transformation" (Abou El Fadl 2001, 19). No discussion of Muslim women leaders today can occur without considering this demonstration of authority as a female imam—even if only to dispute it. Such a demonstration has become the marker for Muslim communities globally.

As for rhetorical assertions of power, how do Muslims promote their claims to authority over me and over my capacity to have authority? Authority must be accessible to every human being, or its criteria are flawed. Authority must be fluid in principle. It must be attainable by coherent methods within an integral system that concludes with an Islamic worldview. Such a system cannot simply be one of only male persons—regardless of their competence and integrity.

Furthermore, must there be hierarchy in human relationship? How do certain assertions of authority indict the one who asserts them by closing off the transformative potential? Such assertions do not form a full circle; they are circumstantial and arbitrary. When the circumstances change, these assertions can equally be used against the ones previously claiming authority. All assertions of power are conditional and fragile. Their fragility is even more evident when they lead to violence.

Therefore, the question of authority is an ethical one, related to our notion of the divine will and of Allah Herself. If one person has an idea about God/Allah, how can they assert their notion over that of another person and still consider their idea to be valid? Everyone must be completely free to establish their own notion of the divine, or it is *shirk*. Yet such an establishment presumes knowledge and access to knowledge construction.

My work with the Musawah movement, a knowledge-building project done primarily by women, helped me to see the potential for a democratization of authority as part of reformist Islam. Although Musawah's contributions are authentically garnished from our experiences as women living in Muslim communities, it is also a movement toward women's full and equal rights. In the formulation of traditional jurisprudence, women were the subject of the discourse, not its agents. This meant that men took license to presume the conclusion of all principal discourses, including definitions and application of claims to authority. In this millennium, we are exercising the right to construct new understandings and applications of Islamic thought and practice. There are two main features to this proposal for more democratic authority: ethics and knowledge production.

Islamic ethics is more than do's and don'ts or simply rules and postulates. The divine will extends beyond the historical constructions of human communities and affects the entire universe. Key to the order of the universe is *tawhid*. The universe is unified, orderly, and harmonious. By this Qur'anic construction, the human being is a moral agent of *tawhid*. Thus, it is the moral responsibility of all humans to support and maintain the universal harmony, and this means maintaining equality and reciprocity between self and other.

Throughout my years of study in Islamic ethics and spirituality, I noticed the way the dominant discourse constructed human relations in a vertical line. Allah, the highest metaphysical essence, was at the top. Man, or the male person, was in the middle; this position was not only in a direct line below Allah but also above woman or the female person, who was on the bottom. Although my consideration of a tawhidic paradigm began with concerns over unequal gender relationships as encoded in Islamic jurisprudence and practiced in patriarchal cultures worldwide—including among Muslims—the implications of *tawhid* were more widespread. I unraveled an Islamic equivalent of the Buber ethics of reciprocity.

Whenever one human being makes another human being into a utility lacking full and independent moral agency, that second person becomes an "it" to the "I" of the first person. That is exploitation, corruption, and inequality (Buber 1958). Not only was this an important personal discovery for me when I applied it to re-reading Islamic ethics, but it also shed light on the basic paradigmatic flaw that undergirds so much of jurisprudence, patriarchal ethics, and philosophy within the Islamic intellectual legacy. It was then necessary to consider how a tawhidic paradigm of equality and justice could be applied to social contracts, including marriage. Although I found traces of this discourse about *tawhid* as an applied term for shaping social justice, those traces were limited to relationships between male persons—ruler and ruled, teacher and student—and lacked application to gender relations (Lakhani 2006, 42–52).

Clearly, it was necessary to understand how gender relations affect the way we think and are thus worthy of examination as a category of thought. Do our constructs and postulates privilege one human being over another on the basis of gender (or race, religion, class, sexual orientation, etc.)? Although human systems might prefer one group over another, such a construct cannot be assigned divine sanction because doing so removes us from the full responsibility and consequence of our actions and reduces the divine to a projection of our whims.

Every human being, male or female, was created to be a *khalifah* (successor) before Allah, according to the Qur'an. Each is responsible not only in a patriarchal system but beyond patriarchy and in an egalitarian system. Any construct of the divine human relation that reduces another person to a subcategory is not sustainable. When we apply this understanding to gender, we see that no matter how long patriarchy has been the bulwark of human communities, it is untenable and thus un-Islamic. Muslim Personal Status Laws are up against the error of unequal relations. It is futile to ignore the realities of diverse family constructs by continually resorting back to a system that is no longer tenable today. Women are full agents in Islam as human beings and as members of the family and society. We have the capacity and responsibility to fulfill roles according to our diverse circumstances and ecological arrangements—public, private, and spiritual. We need a way to think about agency and authority as constructs.

From the time of the Prophet, ideas about authority in Islam have changed and been challenged. In part, this is due to the divine nature of *risalah*, or prophethood, which is how he became an authority. From his divinely assigned authority, we get a glimpse of all the characteristics and types of authority that would follow. All subsequent authorities lack that divine assignment, yet, as Abou El Fadl has elaborated, many still claim to be "speaking in the name of God." Beyond the divinely sanctioned authority of the Prophet, what other features of authority in one person should concern us now? From the moment of the Prophet's death, challenges to the meaning of authority—who qualifies to have it and how they qualify—have been a part of the development of Islamic intellectual, spiritual, and political history. It is no less so today with the question of the authority of women and who has authority to speak for women. Authority must not only be established in someone but must be confirmed by a community for it to be complete in all its dimensions.

The question of authority today includes important dimensions of gender. As mentioned earlier, in those instances when authority is built upon tangible qualifications, these qualifications have been brought into question when they adhere to a woman. Whoever has the power to confirm and implement practices in a community is an authority over that community. Why do we tend to think of "whoever" as referring to singular persons rather than to the community as a whole in consultation or even in contestation?

To discuss authority as knowledge of Truth or as expertise, we must also discuss knowledge. How is it acquired? How does it operate? And what does it mean?

The Prophet's experience of knowledge was unique, bestowed directly by God in the form of revelation. His knowledge also grew. Within the first generation after his death, leadership and knowledge were split among those who followed him such that religious authorities would be the ones with knowledge but without power. Nevertheless, new knowledge flourished within the first few centuries of Islam even after the question of authoritative leadership was separated from it. In this, we see that the question of "new" knowledge, epistemologically, did not arise. Imagine what that must have been like. All fields of human knowledge flourished, blossomed, were challenged and rethought. New paradigms came in and went out in all fields, from religious knowledge, strictly speaking, to the sciences, philosophy, mathematics, medicine, and so on.

The one proposing new knowledge had only to demonstrate the legitimacy of their arguments and postulates, which were open to contestation, further development, or abandonment in the face of evidence more compelling or relevant. This is a healthy part of the development of the Islamic intellectual legacy, heralding Islam's golden age, while the rest of the world yet slept. An authority is a knowledge expert who must substantiate their claims by producing results. Otherwise, people would lose their trust altogether. At the very least, the practice of consulting with more than one authority indicates how significant it is to have evidence to confirm the authority.

Sometimes authority in one person rests upon that person's charisma. Sometimes they are afforded trust in areas without evidence to support the legitimacy of this claim to authority. This is like asking a podiatrist about a problem with your eyes or asking an ophthalmologist about a problem with your feet. When Muslims defer to the authority of certain experts regarding a subject beyond the experts' expertise, they indicate the placement of authority is in the person not in the person's demonstrated area of competence or specific knowledge. Why would I, as a Qur'anic scholar, be asked questions on *fiqh*?

Mastery of these sources in sometimes quantitative amounts but also in qualitative amounts with the assignment if *ijazah*, or certifications, has long been the norm within the Islamic intellectual traditions. The question for us today is how to sustain this legitimacy based on knowledge of sources without having authority adhere to some place over there or to some time back then. We have the agency to create new knowledge and to establish authority in that knowledge from our here and our now. This agency is especially important with respect to the question of gender and more particularly with respect to the matter of women's authority. It relates fundamentally to the idea that Islam is what we live and that it must be continuously lived by the people, who then become equal contributors to what is Islam and to creating authority in each living circumstance. How can Islam be alive if the life of the ones who live it here and now is not reflected in what is taken as authoritative?

As for knowledge production and ideas about authority, how do we know what we know? The Islamic community emphasizes knowledge received from or confirmed by a transcendent source. How does the one who knows respond to the truth unveiled in that system? Four positions in knowledge development can be taken from empirical research based on women's ways of knowing (Field Belenky et al. 1986). Prior to this research, however, the main architects of knowledge and morality acquisition excluded women from their research samples. This research also fills in gaps about the context of Islam as a received-knowledge tradition. Thus, it is not exclusive to women, although it is among women that my point will find significance.

The first position is that of received knowledge, when knowledge is always out there—adhering to an authority or an expert, if not altogether unattainable because transcendent. In the context of Islam, a received-knowledge tradition, somewhere out there in the realm of the Ultimate, real knowledge of absolute Truth exists. It was passed through revelation directly to the Prophet, who made it accessible to all by both word and praxis. For the received knower, knowledge is always secondhand. We can never really know for ourselves, so we must learn through the voices of others who have authority. There is no way to tell the truth except from an authority, who is all powerful and all-knowing and who requires our obedience to survive. If one wishes to demonstrate one's capacity with knowledge, one does so by parroting the authority, who gives only a single answer to each problem. By parroting the authority, the received knower can speak the truth. This position is affirmed by living in gender stereotypical roles. Everything is black or white, either–or, *halal* (permissible) or *haram* (forbidden), and literal. The value and imperative of this received knowledge are almost cosmic, as in eternal salvation. The affirmation that one is doing right—or is right—means one will be rewarded with paradise, a compelling impetus to accept the knowledge received without question or debate, much less personal affirmation.

At some point in the lives of many women, no matter how well or for how long they fulfill gender roles established in patriarchal cultures, a rupture occurs between what is received and the inner experience. This is the second position. To affirm that inner experience sometimes becomes a matter of life and death—say, in the case of domestic violence but also in the case of alienation and unhappiness within those stereotypical roles. Are we meant to be so unhappy? Is life in Islam so complex that it does not recognize our struggles within it or within our families and communities? Soon that inner voice is so loud it cannot be silenced without difficulty and must be responded to.

Here is an important initiative of women's agency because it is so intimate to the self—what Carole Christ (1980) calls "diving deep and surfacing." This surfacing of the self becomes evidence enough. "I know in my gut" is all that is required to affirm one's individual location on certain matters. This leads to a trust in oneself, with the inward affirmation necessary to confirm any truth to which one will adhere.

Among some Muslim women, it is not uncommon that the patriarchal experience of Islam is so incongruent with their inner being that they reject all of Islam as the rubric for understanding and praxis. This is evident in the articulations of staunchly secular, anti-Islam, post-Muslim women. However, even for many believing Muslim women, there might be inward displacement and outward silence. For one thing, although the community no longer speaks to the reality of this inward experience, this affirmation of the self does not require community approval. Meanwhile, the community's force and its authority may seem too strong to contend with. There is great ambivalence about the community's relationship to this new kind of awareness, which in and of itself is so authentic that it is confirmed, no matter the feeling or experience of alienation from the community at large. However, a stubborn commitment to one's internal views can also lead to unwillingness to expose one's self to the views of others because subjective knowledge is often characterized by few tools to express or persuade others.

The next position is the third, or procedural knowledge, which respects the complexity of things, wherein some truths are truer than others. Some things are open to more than one interpretation, and some interpretations are better than others. Besides, the intuition can deceive, and the gut can be wrong. It is better to develop a systematic way to confirm truth and affirm knowledge. At this position, knowledge is the result of a procedure that involves conscious, systematic analysis. Ideas must measure up to an objective standard and methodology. Experts are only as good as their argument on behalf of what they claim to know. In fact, a general kind of suspicion challenges the assertions of all who claim authority. This suspicion includes what Toni Morrison (1993) calls the calcification of the academy. Within academia, Muslim women endeavor to develop their competence in this *methodolatry* and to distance themselves from too personal an analysis.[2]

2. It is interesting to note how often the analysis itself is overly preoccupied with the experiences of Muslim women subjects, with rendering these experiences comprehensible by the methods, procedures, and standards of the objective academy. For example, Saba Mahmoud's book *The Politics of Piety* (2011) renders experience into a coherent philosophy or a procedural formula, which means we really "understand" it now, we really know.

At the final position, or fourth, is constructive knowledge. These positions in knowledge development are by no means comprehensive. A person manages them with leaps and bounds or remains stuck in one or another position. In this fourth position, all knowledge is constructed, and the knower is an intimate part of what is known. Constructive knowledge integrates the voice of the subjective knower with the procedure and process of the procedural knower. Our consciousness is part of the world, which we create as we think about it. In this position, there is a place for reason and intuition in balance with the expertise of others. The knower accepts responsibility for evaluating and reevaluating the assumptions about knowledge. There is an appreciation for the challenge of disagreement. Truth is mutable, combining personal history, timing, and circumstances. Moral responsibility guides the intellect and the collective commitments to both self and others. Constructive knowledge leads to tolerance of ambiguities and contradictions as well as to acceptance of diversity of opinion and identity.

In this final position, a knower remains self-aware and becomes aware of the workings of the mind in such a way as to stretch the boundaries of consciousness. Constructive knowledge is more than just procedure; the self is an instrument of understanding. It is more than subjectivity or objectivity because passion and intellect are woven into a whole, giving one the empathy or capacity to attend to others despite differences.

In 1994, I gave the Friday *khutbah* at the Claremont Main Road Mosque in Cape Town, South Africa. The text of the sermon used the female particular reality of giving birth as public discourse to construct a normative articulation of what it means to be "Muslim" and human. Before that, Islamic public discourse most often focused on the male experience and rendered that experience the only appropriate one not only for men in public spaces but also for women. Yet when the voice of a woman offers something about herself particularly as a woman, this, too, must be incorporated into what it means to be human in Islam. I am *not* more human if I am like a man. I am woman, I am human, and my humanity is female.

To the morally responsible role of knowledge construction, I bring back the question of authority as the "ability to assert an opinion or perspective and by its assertion to thus become a marker for the community conversation and even transformation" (Abou El Fadl 2001, 19). This is very simple: women's lived realities are a measure of the success or failure of Islam in all its dimensions. If the goal of Islam is not achieved in the lives of women living as Muslim, then Islam itself fails. Women do not have to do anything to achieve this result. They don't have to be wives, mothers, obedient or even good. They just have to be. Their subjectivity becomes an evaluative instrument to determine if the goals of Islam have been fulfilled.

This view is built upon a principle encoded in Islamic jurisprudence (which I demonstrate here using advanced medical technologies). Whenever an Islamic opinion (or fatwa) is needed about a matter of medical advancement (stem cell research or technologically assisted reproduction), religious scholars must confer with the experts in medicine to fully understand what the advancement entails. The mufti is a received knower, a repository of Islamic *usul al-fiqh*, who must now receive information about the medical advancement.

To make informed decisions about women's lives, a reference to experts is also required. Experts in women's lives are, of course, women themselves but also those who work in the community to negotiate women's lives: social workers, psychologists, therapists, counselors, activists, and so on. This is where the subjective part comes in. These experts are then addressed by analysis: the procedural part. The analysis includes interpretive works done by women scholars in our time. What results is a woman-friendly Islam that also completes what Abu-Qayyim Ibn al-Jawziyyah has determined is the *maqasid* (intended purpose) of shari'a: justice. Can Islam be just if women do not experience that justice?

Bringing this question to the international human rights arena, I learned from the work of Madhavi Sunder (2003) that we face an epistemological difficulty involving the historical postulates about an inherent conflict between women's rights and religion. This is a problem of traditional legal construction that is premised on Enlightenment theory that justified reason in the public sphere by allowing deference to religious despotism in the private sphere. "Human rights law," states Sunder, "continues to define religion . . . as a sovereign, extralegal jurisdiction in which inequality is not only accepted, but expected." In international law, religion is viewed as "natural, irrational, incontestable, and imposed—in contrast to the public sphere, the only viable space for freedom and reason." Religion is the "other" of international law. Observing Muslim women pro-faith activists and Islamic feminists, Sunder demonstrates that "despite law's formal refusal to acknowledge claims of internal dissent, women are claiming their rights to challenge religious and cultural authorities and to imagine religious community on more egalitarian and democratic terms" (1402–3).

Because of the way international law operates, an individual has only two choices: to remain in a discriminatory culture or religion—on the terms set by established authority—or to exit it. There is no understanding of the right for those who dissent to stay in their communities and to contest or reform them. There is no right to a religion or culture on one's own terms—that is, to plurality and choice *within* culture. In effect, the law requires women to choose between religion and rights. Secular feminists accept this framework, arguing that when weighing religious freedom against equality, women's rights should trump religion. Here, religion is held as unjust, with unchanging beliefs. However, contemporary theo-rists argue that religion is much more internally contested and subject to reasoned argument and change than earlier theorists acknowledged. The human aspects of religion and culture are subject to tests of rationality and legitimacy. Humans define and interpret the divine will. They should show why they interpret their religion in one way rather than another.

Faith "involves judgment, choice and decision, and hence reason and personal responsibility" (Sunder 2003, 1424). Muslim women's human rights activism sig-nifies a world in transition because they embrace the universal concepts of justice, equality, and democracy and seek to apply them within explicitly religious and cultural contexts. Islamic feminists argue that the same democratic principles that guide the public sphere should apply within the family, culture, and religion—despite the way family, culture, and religion were traditionally defined by Muslim Personal Status Law, by notions of authority, or by international human rights law, which rendered them private and virtually unregulated. This is a radical shift from traditional human rights law, which posits freedom only in secular terms.

Current international law allocates to religious and cultural authorities the right to define the community. Now Muslim women are asserting that individual members of a community ought to be able to participate in defining the religion in terms that are not oppressive to any group of people. This is also part of the man-date of the Arab Spring: for people to help define the future of their autonomy and public participation, let alone governance. Islamic feminism takes the agency of authority to interpret both the notions of human rights and the notions of Islam. In our dependency on leaders to be authorities over us and to determine our ways of knowing, we have abandoned the capacity to act as full agents of Allah on earth. To regain the equanimity of responsibility, we all must take part in determining what will constitute the living reality of Islam.

Furthermore, any public policy that is put over the lives of citizens in the cur-rent reality of the nation-state has been made by human beings, who thus in turn retain the power to change the policies—including policies that are claimed in abstraction as if "in the name of Islam." All laws in today's nation-state were for-mulated by people. Although the Arab Spring is not exclusive to Muslims, the mandates for autonomy are now being put to the challenge of reified definitions of Islam and how to adjudicate it in the context of a new nation-state. Should we simply defer to a select few, or do we all have responsibility to be a part of the process? Now we are putting forward a mandate for total recognition of "we" the people. Therefore, "we" the people must take back the authority over policies that govern our lives. We must construct sustainable systems that allow us to grapple with whose truth holds sway over how our lives are governed. This is the mandate expressed during the Arab Spring, where the people moved to the streets and to accept more responsibility as citizens and to demand more accountability of those who previously had laid claim to leadership.

This reminds me of a discussion on Twitter during the Black Lives Matter movement. Someone asked, Who are our leaders? Another responded that we no longer defer to that old-time position of waiting for a leader to come take us to the promised land. That model of leadership is over. We *all* are leaders. We make this road by walking it. We construct Islam by living it. We acknowledge the contributions we all make by giving authority to our collective effort to represent Islam, and we no longer defer to neoconservative male elites as the only authority. We all have authority.

References

Abou El Fadl, Khaled. 2001. *Speaking in God's Name: Islamic Law, Authority, and Women.* London: Oneworld.

Buber, Martin. 1958. *I and Thou.* Translated by Ronald Gregor Smith. New York: MacMillan.

Christ, Carole. 1980. *Diving Deep and Surfacing: Women Writers on Spiritual Quest.* Boston: Beacon Press.

Field Belenky, Mary, Blythe McVicker Clinchy, Nancy Rule Goldberger, and Jill Mattuck Tarule. 1986. *Women's Ways of Knowing: The Development of Self, Voice, and Mind.* New York: Basic.

Freedom from Forbidden. 2015. "The Islamic Reform Symposium in Exeter: Authority, Muslim Feminists, and Woman-Led Prayers." Aug. 17. At https://orbala.net/2015/08/17/the-islamic-reform-symposium-in-exeter-authority-muslim-feminists-and-women-led-prayers/.

Lakhani, M. Ali. 2006. "The Metaphysics of Human Governance: Imam ʿAli, Truth, and Justice." In *The Sacred Foundations of Justice in Islam: The Teachings of ʿAli Ibn Abi-Talib,* edited by M. Ali Lakhani, 3–60. North Vancouver, Canada: Sacred Web.

Mahmoud, Saba. 2011. *The Politics of Piety: The Islamic Revival and the Feminist Subject.* Princeton, NJ: Princeton Univ. Press.

Morrison, Toni. 1993. "Toni Morrison Banquet Speech." Nobel Prize. At https://www.nobelprize.org/prizes/literature/1993/morrison/speech/.

Shaikh, Saʿdiyya. 2012. *Sufi Narratives of Intimacy: Ibn ʿArabi, Gender, and Sexuality.* Chapel Hill: Univ. of North Carolina Press.

Sunder, Madhavi. 2003. "Piercing the Veil." *Yale Law Journal* 112, no. 6: 1399–472. At http://www.yalelawjournal.org/article/piercing-the-veil.

13

Remembering Istanbul

*Women and Anarchistic-Queer Openings
in a Belated Modernity*

Poyraz Kolluoglu

When the momentum unleashed by the Istanbul protests of 2013 began to pre-occupy Turkish academic circles and experts on the Middle East, many framed it as yet another iteration of the Arab Spring wave and accordingly labeled it the "Turkish Summer" (J. Butler 2014; Özkırımlı 2014, 2) in parallel to frame it within mainstream political and sociological explanations. In subsequent years, how-ever, it has become ethnographically difficult to decide on the conditions of the similarity between the Arab Spring and the "Turkish Summer." Yet when looked at in terms of the forms of protests implemented on the ground, many scholars, who draw their inspiration from autonomist Marxist theory and anarchist school of thought, such as Michael Hardt, Antonio Negri, and David Graeber, actually observe a continuation among the first forms of direct-action-oriented collective actions that surfaced in the late 1990s, the so-called Arab Spring, and the Occupy movements (see Gibson 2013; Hammond 2015; Hardt and Negri 2011). Aside from a stress on the modular forms of protests, what unites these radical tradition-based approaches is their common emphasis on the shortcomings of liberal democracy and socialist visions, which do not resonate across the lifeworld of the millennial generation, I would suggest. Departing from this heuristic deduction, in this chap-ter I intend to present activist-based ethnographic findings that verify the offerings of the radical school of thought. In doing so, I am also hoping to demonstrate the

This research would not have been possible without Richard Day. He taught me how to criti-cally study and analyze complex social movements such as Gezi with a deep critical introspection. Thanks to him, I have both academically and personally matured and broken off the shackles of the social cosmos in which I live. He has been always there to help me out, just an email away, even after I graduated, which led to the biggest struggle of my life.

extent to which the new millennials of the Middle East are capable of having a critical stance to mobilize, organize, desire, and imagine a sociopolitical establishment whose preliminary configurations transcend the decaying structures of the twentieth-century nation-state and its gender regimes. In this way, I draw scholarly attention to the ways in which post-2010 dissident initiatives emerged as collective actions in constant state of becoming, which I associate with the basic principles of anarchist school of thought.

By celebrating the "energy" left behind the antiglobalization movements of the 2000s, Richard Day, one of the leading scholars in radical thought, observes an intriguing slide toward "anarchistic" openings in contemporary forms of activism, starting with the Seattle protests in 1999 (2005, 1–13). He has further argued that the "newest" struggles of the twenty-first century have rendered both post-Marxist and neoliberal paradigms of social movements inadequate in their theoretical explanations and ethical judgments about which motivational factors draw protestors to sites of action (2005, 95–97). Acknowledging that the possibility of organized mobilization processes that would lead to social revolutions or reforms/betterment dwindled on the ground, Day suggests we are now looking at a new paradigm shift from "hegemony of hegemony"—that is, an ideological-theoretical position that involves a blend of socialist-liberal visions—to a point he characterizes as "affinity for affinity" (2005, 46–54)—that is, new forms of alliances that are not contaminated by the already-existing ideologies provided by nation-state politics until now. In a nutshell, he suggests that affinity groups that spontaneously surface in the course of collective action allow protesters to form new political and social relations that serve as alternatives to the ontological normalcy of the neoliberal system for a while. And this experimental mindset, he argues, has now replaced the old revolutionary hopes and reformist desires of a bygone century.

The resonances that the Arab Spring created across the whole Middle East and North Africa (MENA) region as well as the subsequent rise of Occupy movements in the Global North seem to validate Day's heuristic observations. Especially since 2011, we have been witnessing the spread of direct-action-oriented and horizontally organized encampments at large and small scales in public spaces of metropolitan areas all across the globe. Millennials have taken this improvisational state of being together, which I characterize as the "commune repertoire" (Kolluoglu 2020), to the world protest stage regardless of their ideological backgrounds or of the social or political gains they would achieve. The so-called Occupy repertoire has now become a modular protest form in almost all types of regime space, although with slight modifications and changes, as seen in Ukraine's Euromaidan protests of 2014 and the Hong Kong protests of 2019. This protest scenery raises a couple of questions that need to be answered regarding the future of social protest forms to come. Do occupiers or dissidents—whom we might also consider "communards" according to a better normative terminology—have genuine anarchistic visions and desires? Have they really given up hope of transforming their movements into political and social gains through sustained party politics, organizational formations, and revolutionary attempts, as Day suggests? How do they organize the mobilization processes leading up to the commune encampments? Are liberal democracy and the softened versions of socialist desires and aspirations that help to sustain the capitalist system—that is, demands for democratic citizenship—nearing their end in the twenty-first century? If so, more importantly, do all these changes in social protest mindset reflect themselves over heteronormative values and principles? I am hoping to open up this set of questions to discussion by providing an ethnographic glimpse into the Istanbul Commune of 2013, the grassroots politics it set in motion in the following years, as well as its gender ingredients that not only equipped the protesters with the necessary mobilization ingredients but also enabled them to reconsider in a queer mindset the gender roles we know.

Women of the Insurrection

Like the other commune repertoires seen in other parks and squares of the globe, the encampment at Gezi Park in Istanbul had a multilayered participant profile, spanning the political spectrum and cultural life in Turkey's fragmented and polarized social milieu. Aside from the counterhegemonic identities and groups such as the Kurdish and Alevi minorities, LGBTQI+ people, anarchist youths, environmentalists, and Marxist groups, the young generations of conservative segments—such as the nationalist republican youth organizations, ultranationalists, and even some of the young supporters of the neoliberal Islamic government—took to the streets to protect the last green space left in the heart of a neoliberal metropolis. In this regard, I would suggest that the Gezi Park protests initially emerged as an urban struggle that took shape around green sensitivities and public commons (Harmanşah 2014). Therefore, it was the urban space that gathered all these contrasting and differentiating identities and groups in the same protest mise-en-scéne, I would suggest (Kolluoglu 2020, 455–58).

It all started on May 29, 2013, after four days of picketing staged by a small environmentalist group, which was backed by the local "not in my backyard yard" civil society organization Taksim Solidarity (Taksim Dayanışması, TD). Environmentalists and a few TD members gathered in the park, which is located in the cultural heart of Istanbul, in response to the current government's decades of neo-liberal urban policies—the so-called urban-renewal projects that have been aggressively commodifying and symbolically Islamizing the urban commons since 1994, the year when the current president, Recep Tayyip Erdoğan, became the mayor of the city. Turning the whole city into a colossal construction project, this undesirable urban vortex increased in intensity after Erdoğan won the national elections in 2002. When the party he rules, the Justice and Development Party (Adalet ve Kalkınma Partisi, AKP), announced the construction of yet another privatization project for the park under the guise of the restoration of Ottoman barracks, a small group of architects, graduate students, urban planners, Kurdish parliamentarians, and local dwellers began occupying the site to halt the unlawful construction process. Some demonstrators who lived in the vicinity pitched tents to keep watch and continue the occupation during the night. Inevitably, tensions rose when the police executed a forceful eviction. Thereafter, Gezi reenacted the dramatic scenes we usually see in other ecological protest events and the Arab Spring protests.

The images of a female protester being brutally attacked by the police during the clashes particularly captured public attention and went viral on social media. Just as what happened following Mohamed Bouazizi's self-immolation in Tunisia, this social media reverberation galvanized all other Istanbulites, who were weary of the government's arbitrary urban policies and furious at the injustice done to this female protester. One photograph of her displaying perhaps one of the most dramatic moments in all the Gezi events emerged before us as a watershed moment for the whole cause. Also known as "The Red Woman," this iconic image (Seel 2013), I would argue, can be viewed as the representational expression of all the intersecting and diverging reasons for mobilization defining the groups and identities who participated in the Istanbul experience. Each collective-action process or political incident interrupting the flow of daily routine has just such an affective threshold moment (Bertelson and Murphie 2010; Della Porta 2011, 2018), and I would argue that the attack directed on the red woman's body precisely corresponds to that moment in the Gezi mobilization. As happened so many times before in other acts of civil disobedience we saw in the Arab Spring, this moment of rupture marked the beginning of a total, spontaneous mobilization process going beyond all the ideology and organizational formations structuring the country's regime space. I would suggest that the image of the red woman was metaphorically the harbinger of systemic eruptions to come in the relatively calm universe of the new Turkish middle classes, just like a red giant right before the supernova.

A majority of the interviewees (twelve out of seventeen) whom I carefully chose for my ethnographic research to reflect the overall cultural and political profile of the commune[1] underlined that the courage showed by the red woman as well as by other sexual minorities, such as trans and gay individuals in similar ways, was the main factor that pulled them into the gravitational force of the first night of mobilization. This common response came upon me quite unexpectedly as a researcher who did not take into account the fact that all social movements have gendered dimensions even though they are not entirely and necessarily gender oriented (V. Taylor 1999).[2] For me, the discovery was bewildering in the sense

1. In order not to pollute or taint the claim to objectivity and to channel all the voices involved in the commune, I conducted semistructured interviews with seventeen participants (approximately two members from each group and subjectivity), whom I recruited according to the ethical research principles set out in activist ethnography (Graeber 2009). In this mindset, by positioning myself as "critical insider," I began my research by reaching out ideologically and culturally to the most distant groups and identities in parallel to my own subjectivity within the movement. Among the first groups I got in touch were members of the Union of Turkish Youth (TGB)—that is, the ultranationalists— then government supporters and the anticapitalist Muslims. To test the notion of solidarity within the so-called movement, I asked my first conservative comrades to hook me up with other prospective participants outside of their social and organizational circles. In this way, I questioned if the solidarity maintained back at the park was still continuing. That request led me to speak to socialists, communists, and republican communards outside of my own political and social entourage. Finally, I also used my own activist circles in Turkey's various LGBTQI+ and environmentalist movements to extend the scope of the participant profile I tried to structure throughout this ethnographic journey. All interviews were conducted in Turkish, and I translated quotations from them for this chapter.

2. I filtered the ethnographic data I obtained through epistemological matrices derived from memory studies (Bornat 2013; Brown and Reavey 2013; Fivush 2013; Kansteiner 2002; Keightley 2010; Radstone 2016; Roediger and Wertsch 2008; D. Taylor 2003) and critical approaches to narrative analysis techniques, which basically encourage researchers to use their emotions as investigative tools during both transcription and data-collection processes (Arditti et al. 2010; Hubbard, Backett-Milburn, and Kemmer 2001; Kleinman and Copp 1993). As a result of this methodological combination, I focused on consciously and/or unconsciously included and/or excluded metaphorical expressions as well as on common or diverging accounts that surfaced during the dialogical exchanges of the interviews (Keightley 2010, 57–58, 64). I then made use of the statements, assessments, metaphorical expressions that compelled me to see the incident in a different light from the perspective of my own lifeworld positioned in the panorama of Gezi. In layman's terms, I would suggest in this regard that it never crossed my mind to characterize Gezi as a commune, let alone to frame gay and trans individuals and women as the main reasons for mobilization. Based on my own theoretical projections and literature analysis, I assumed that protest participants would bring up political freedoms, economic-class matters, and the Occupy movements or the Arab Spring in general to frame Gezi. My entire analysis is not structured upon third-person narratives, however. In this chapter, I am opening up space for the researcher's own insights and accounts as much as possible to bring a narrative and analytical harmony to my analysis. Because my own positionality within the picture of Gezi and the research process also changed and evolved, I tried to reflect this subjectivity change in this text as much as possible to present an ethnographic analysis.

that I assumed my interviewees would address political or social injustices related to their own ideological backgrounds. Rather than such macrostructural motivational incentives, the struggles of women and sexually dissident protesters were foregrounded in their commentaries as if they were turning Turkey's heteronormative culture upside down.

When I asked one of those interviewees, a young, educated pan-Turkist,[3] what his main reason was for participating in the uprising, he told me, "I was impressed by ordinary people's bravery during the insurrection night, especially that of women. They did not seem to possess extraordinary talents and skills, like the heroic characters we see in the films; . . . the courage they showed just impressed me. That is how I found myself amidst the crowds trying to reach the park."[4] Another participant, a Kurdish laborer who was affiliated with various anarchist organizations, recounted that he first saw the shot of the red woman on his smartphone while he was working on the "twenty-fifth floor of [a] construction [site]." He added, "After that, I made up my mind to go Taksim as soon as I finish[ed] off the work." After I asked him what made this image special for him, he replied: "I felt the whole country was under invasion. It was as if the public emerged as enemy. . . . 'How could they do that to this girl?,' I kept mumbling to myself." This anarchist Kurd's answer to the probing questions I directed at him sounded quite creative and intriguing to me: I would never have expected him to comment on the safety of the nation because as an outlaw Kurd he tends to take a position against it.

Another intriguing anecdote the anarchist Kurd shared was about a transgender individual. When I asked him "what sorts of things differentiate" Gezi from his previous encounters with the police as an outlaw and "experienced protester," he told me: "That night I almost passed out in the gas fume[s]. One trans individual pulled me out of that gas cloud and dragged my motionless body into her place. She gave me the usual stuff to ease the side effects; you know milk, lemon. It was my first time in my life, you know, being saved by a trans person. I would have never thought of anything like that before Gezi, if you are asking that."

Women of the insurrection, the ever-expanding red giant of Istanbul's neo-liberal-Islamic urban space, brought not only two diametrically opposed identities, one anarchist Kurd and one Turkish ultranationalist, together in the same mobilization process but also attracted others like me, who participated in the

3. Pan-Turkism, which is involved in the three main political ideologies in Turkish political culture, aside from laic-republicanism and political Islam, advocates the unification of Turkic countries in Central Asia, with racialized and ethnic references.

4. In quotations from my interviews, ellipses indicate omissions of statements rather than pauses.

events in a way independent of any political ideology or organization. Soon after the police maced the red woman—in other words, right before the protests went supernova—I found myself hopelessly drifting on a large boulevard leading to one of Istanbul's busiest commercial districts. Small groups walking toward the action site and disrupting the flow of traffic caught my eye on my way to this busy commercial area known for its bumper-to-bumper traffic lasting all day long. It appeared to me that they were mostly white-collar workers dressed in business suits. In groups of three to five, workers in "smokeless industries," perhaps having never tasted the privilege of unionization, were walking hastily on the boulevard and slowing down the traffic. In the blink of an eye, it was as if a large nest of ants had suddenly been disturbed; the crowd was filling the boulevard and the small lanes connecting to it.

In the late evening hours, the first shock waves of this chaotic momentum hit. Not even a single vehicle was left on the boulevard. It was an extraordinary and eerie feeling to see the area that way. The daily routine of the never-stopping city had now been interrupted. The picketing transmuted truly into a supernova, a cosmic cocktail spreading its remnants. Protesters were hurling stones to mitigate the anger that had grown inside them, in other words. The ambiguous borders of the nebula that the supernova explosion created were stretching as far as Gezi Park. Neither a centralized political body nor an organizational formation nor a leadership cult could have orchestrated such a spontaneous cosmic event. From the red woman, the red giant had grown over the past three decades into an insurrection without organization and ideology overnight. Istanbul was caught in the allure of anarchism. None of the mainstream political ideologies of Turkish regime space had managed to bring about such an urban uprising or a demonstration at this scale in the neoliberal era.

Yet a few relatively organized ideological groups attempting to solidify in the anarchistic nebula were capturing attention as well. They seemed to me like youngsters from a republican-nationalist background. I heard some shouting in a militarist fashion, "We are the soldiers of Mustafa Kemal." Rather than the counterhegemonic remnants of the supernova, they seemed like the light beams traveling from an already dead pulsar within this mise-en-scène. One protestor standing next to me teased them by shouting back, "We are the soldiers of Zeki Müren," referring to a famous Turkish queer icon. By reminding the others there of this figure who has received publicity since the late 1940s, this protestor cursed the toxic masculinity and militarist, patriarchal national ideology that has been feeding not only conservative segments but also the Turkish laic middle classes, who are inclined to display a not much different stance when it comes to matters of morality and national interests. This symbolic challenge directed toward the founding ideology was as if the last children of Atatürk, the establishing father figure of the secular Turkish nation-state, were slowly drowning in the poisonous, anarchistic gasses of the nebula yet were also destined to be resurrected in the form of a new subjectivity in the commune to arise in the next few hours.

Another interviewee, a young member coming from the nationalist-Ataturkist Union of Turkish Youth (Türkiye Gençlik Birliği, TGB) recounted to me how the chaotic and spontaneous insurrection caught him as well as his organization unprepared, as if verifying my own ethnographic observations narrated earlier. He said he usually participates in "demonstrations" with his "brothers" in an organized manner and with a specific agenda and explained to me how that approach changed during "the Gezi uprising." After following the news on social media, he told me they agreed on a rendezvous point so that they could share out the placards and banners they usually brought from their headquarters.

> Yet this was not possible anymore. I could not meet my comrades in the midst of that chaos. I felt like I was a fish out of water. Not knowing what to do and lingering around, I came across a middle-aged woman in a work suit and high heels. She was building barricades along with two young boys who were wearing the aprons of a famous chain food company. Seeing them in that way, doing something together, just stunned me. I kept watching them for a while. I think the guys were Kurdish because they were speaking Kurdish among themselves. [Seeing] two Kurds and one office woman in the same picture was almost surreal for me. As my eyes were fixed on them, the woman in black scolded me for standing there and doing nothing, after giving me an angry look. It was a wake-up call for me. My body thereupon just began to follow and mimicked what they were doing.

Other accounts given by interviewees who witnessed the insurrection or actively participated firsthand more or less echo and verify one another. The women and LGBTQI+ people there as well as the anarchistic, disorganized mobilization dynamics, which I associated earlier with a nebula, stand out almost in all the anecdotes given, regardless of the participants' ideological and political profiles. Therefore, I would argue that Gezi was truly an anarchistic, urban uprising whose inspiration came from the sexual minorities and women struggling at the front lines.

As matter of fact, the history of revolution could verify that such an inference is not surprising at all. Almost 150 years earlier, iconography featuring women had animated and given inspiration to another rebellion that took shape around the notion of the right to the city (Bertelson and Murphie 2010). The erotic representation of a half-naked female body, which corresponds to the imagination of motherland calling for sacrifice, and oil paintings depicting brave women rising over the barricades often appeared in the brochures and pamphlets during the French Revolution, which eventually culminated in the Commune of 1871 (Harvey 2004, 4, 280–85). Serendipitously, when I asked the interviewees selected for my activist ethnography what the day following the night of the Gezi insurrection reminded them of, aside from situationist-like expressions such as "utopia," "utopian space," "liberated zone," "dream," "space of hope," "commune," they also mentioned historically distant but analogous events such as "the Spanish Civil War," "the Paris Commune," and "the French Revolution." Based on my own theoretical projections, and considering the power of new media and computing technologies, which enable protesters to record every millisecond of a demonstration and picketing event and instantly share those moments with others in different parts of the world, I was expecting the Gezi people to mention more contemporary cases, such as the Occupy movements in the Global North or at the very least the Arab Spring as a culturally and politically less distant geopolitical event. One of those nostalgic yearnings very surprisingly came from a right-wing, nationalist actor. The Pan-Turkist communard, whom I dubbed "Sheriff" because of his studies in law faculty, recounted his observations over the late hours of the rebellion: "Unlike other demonstrations organized by the Left—you know, where you usually see people lifting up left fists—this was without organization, without ideology. 'This is a historic moment,' I kept telling myself as I followed what other protesters were doing. Taksim was engulfed in flames."

When I asked him to describe what those scenes reminded him of, immediately in a way that left no room for doubt he said, "The French Revolution—you know, like 'the Paris Commune.'" And he was not the only communard to frame Gezi around the nostalgic representation of the Commune of 1871, which widened the ideological cleavages between the Marxist tradition and Prodhounian approaches by compelling Marx to dismiss any protest attempt other than workers' takeover of the state (Marx and Engels 1981, 396; Ross 2015, 31–32, 111–12, 175–76).

Petit Anarchists of the Commune

The Istanbul police forces were left with no choice but to withdraw from Taksim Square in the early morning hours of the following day. The security forces, government, and local municipal authorities, in other words, failed to create a response to a spontaneously performed protest repertoire at this scale, which was unprecedented in the country's history. In a sense, they took a wait-and-see attitude to monitor and give meaning to what was happening. After the hegemonic center took its hand off the square, the insurrectionists restored the occupation, yet this time with the support of culturally, socially, and politically much more diverse crowds. Like other occupations we have witnessed in Lower Manhattan and Tahrir Square, they pitched the tents once again and set up platforms and podiums to organize social relations and direct-democracy initiatives. A democratic culture beyond ballots was sprouting. Thereafter, countercultural activities, workshops, discussion forums, public lectures, postmodern art performances blossomed in every corner of the park in a carnivalesque fashion despite the ongoing clashes in near vicinities. With its infirmary, free food court, botanic garden, radio broadcasts, library, daily newspaper, and communards who set out for work from the place they now called "home," life at the park literally emerged as a commune where Emma Goldman could dance in the first week of June 2013. Perhaps for the first time, unions, Marxist groups, and socialist parties, which are excessively romanticized by Turkish socialists, who sometimes even justify Joseph Stalin's atrocities from time to time, did not dominate this rendezvous in a belated "festival" of 1968 (Evren 2013). Another member of the TGB described this festival scene after first setting foot in the park as follows: "There were overwhelmingly too many colors. There were too many organizations. Yet I felt something new there at the same time. I could have never imagined the Left resisting with humor and art before. Yet at the same time there was a self-organized network. I think all the previous organizations and movements without ideologies came together that day. I was really impressed then."

As this nationalist communard indicates, one of the most visible characteristics of the Istanbul commune was its "self-organizing" nature, which allowed the most contemporary forms of collective action to implement an experimental political and social understanding, as I suggested earlier. Such an improvisational movement mindset, which is not anchored in a concrete ideology or any democratic principles we know from mainstream politics, also contributes to the maintenance of social relations in politically and culturally heterogeneous protest sites like Gezi by veiling over the necessity of organizational structure. As a matter of fact, such a social fusion and the imagination of an alternative societal order would otherwise not be possible. This anarchistic tendency, the inclination to "create the future . . . in new social relations," as Marina Sitrin puts it (2006, 6), or the process of being created in a Deleuzean sense nonetheless has received a fair amount of criticism from liberal and Marxist-based scholars for not having political and social implications to any degree. Such critiques have also underlined that the search for new societal forms in similar liberated cultural zones does nothing except limit the potential of progressive politics to closed sites such as parks and squares, thereby preventing the spread of democratic visions and social justice values among other segments of society. The lack of organizational reflexes and of motivational political agendas has always been marked as the main reason behind the gaps and failures of the so-called newest social movements (Bamyeh and Hanafi 2015; Calhoun 2013; Day 2011; Gitlin 2013; Kamrava 2014; Leveille 2017; Lustiger-Thaler 2014; Roberts 2012; Shihade, Flesher Fominaya, and Cox 2012; Velut 2015), a criticism that can also be applied to the waves of the Arab Spring and the democratic initiatives taken afterward.

Taking into account such critiques, which arguably arise from the "hegemony" of liberal and Marxist paradigms in social sciences (Day 2005, 46–65), I asked the communards to put their "opinions" and "feelings" into words regarding Gezi's seemingly chaotic and aimless operational mechanism. In other words, I questioned them regarding what they think of the conundrum of social movements without ideology and party politics in the new millennium. A public figure who is known for founding a New Left oriented party after Gezi said to me, "The movement was shaping us, not the [other] way around," when asked if he would rather have seen "more organization" in retrospect. Another communard who introduced herself as a "socialist-bisexual feminist" suggested "there was no need to organize anything. Gezi was a yearning for a commune." One gay communard emphasized that the commune had a "common sense in its own way" when asked if he encountered any conflict between groups resulting from the commune's seemingly chaotic atmosphere. Overall, these responses suggest that the general opinion regarding the incident's chaotic organizational structure was affirmatory.

My own experiences throughout the first week of the commune seem to verify the accounts given by the communards. Because so many different groups and identities were involved in this collective action, it was without question impossible to get organized and act like a hive under any sort of ideology. The dynamism of just being there and encountering people you would not normally come across in fast-paced metropolitan life was in itself an organizational force of sorts. Gezi was something new to Turkish protest culture and political understanding, so people there were just experiencing this new protest repertoire in the making. I would argue that it was exactly this sense of newness, this sense of exploration, this creative chaos that was alluring to the conservative communards who are generally overlooked by Turkish studies. One government sympathizer, who introduced himself as an "Erdoğan" supporter and an "entrepreneur" in the proliferating construction business, told me he came to understand "what a commune life would look like" in response to my question regarding what he thought was the most memorable moment of the Gezi uprising. He mentioned the communards carrying water packs in chains of participants and recounted how that "solidarity spirit" mesmerized him. He added: "When people lined up to carry plastic bottles to the park in rows, I actually came to understand that [the] Turkish Left was not just about lifting up left fists in times of demonstrations. A sense of thrilling excitement filled us as we [he and his wife] kept on watching them. Actually, I realized there was a petit anarchist [*anarşik*] lying inside me at that moment."

Yet the commune's irresistible, charming affective facade was interrupted a bit toward the end of the first week after government and state officials made statements criticizing Erdoğan's harsh response to the events, which had caused more than seven deaths and wounded thousands. His insulting comments to the "future generations," calling them the thugs and looters of the country, was the last straw for his government partners and other power figures in his party. Gezi reshuffled the cards inside Erdoğan's party, in other words. When the differences of opinion and cracks opened up by the commune's seismic activities in regime space were coupled with Erdoğan's unplanned diplomatic visit abroad, communards began discussing the possibility of "overthrowing" the government and making "revolution." In other words, at that point the encampment's overall discourse, I would suggest, slid from "just being there" to the fantasy of socialist revolution. When Erdoğan went on his trip, government officials who seemed to be going against him, such as the president at that time (Abdullah Gül), invited the communards to the negotiation table to discuss the terms of withdrawal by guaranteeing the end of all construction projects for the park. A state of confusion of sorts pervaded the commune thereafter. The logic of just being there, the self-organizing nature of the commune, was traded off for socialist daydreams and fantasies as well as realist discussions of the terms of withdrawal.

I also exchanged views with my socialist friends regarding the withdrawal option and the demands to be made of the state as we hung around one of the tents after we heard the news. They vehemently opposed the idea of emptying the park by pointing to people who had sacrificed their lives for this "cause." The withdrawal option nonetheless seemed to be more appealing and practical to me. Things were different on my side, in other words. I knew if the government really wanted us out of the park, we had no chance against the firepower of security officers. I explained to my friends how it would look like "victory" for us if we quit while ahead. One of the socialists criticized me for not seeing the bigger picture. "Look here, this is a great opportunity to unify the fragmented Turkish Left under one red flag. This reminds me of the May 1 demonstration in 1977," she told me, as if she really had been present at that mythic gathering on May 1 that was sabotaged by the right-wing contra-guerrilla actors supported by the North Atlantic Treaty Organization and the Turkish military. Also known as "Bloody May 1," this dramatic incident occurred at the square right next to the park (Baykan and Hatuka 2010). Retrospectively, I would suggest that it was as if the communal affects were now calling for a worker demonstration rather than for the genesis of commune repertoire.

Another communard, the socialist bisexual who told me Gezi was yearning for a commune, shared an interesting anecdote about her second-week experiences when I asked her if she also had observed any changes after "Erdoğan's flight." "I went to the Odak periodical tent several times. Because there was good food there. They are old-school socialists who were constantly bringing food to the commune. They were like parents feeding their children. Once, I heard they were talking about getting organized. Yet this happened in the second week of the commune—you know, when Erdoğan left the country. They wanted the park to get more organized. They wanted more people to participate and criticized unions for not mobilizing enough people."

"You think they were right? Perhaps we could have made political and social gains in that way with more organization or under a common ideology," I interrupted, once again playing the role of critical insider. "To me," responded the socialist bisexual communard, "we did not need to get organized. There was already a state of being organized in itself. That multitude would not have come together if we had tried to organize it, I think."

I also directed a couple of questions to the pan-Turkist participant regarding whether he observed changes in the communards' attitudes and perceptions after the prime minister "fled" the country. I was curious about his input because even though he appeared to be very critical of socialist ideology, I also expected him, as a Turkish nationalist, to defend the idea of a well-planned revolution. Yet his comments about the dilemma over the political/social gains and losses from leaving the commune and about the changes in the communards' attitudes were not very much different from my own observations or from those of the socialist bisexual. Confirming that he had observed "a change of air" among his own "socialist" friends, he answered: "The story is always predictable for socialists. They dreamed of establishing a new state coming out of Gezi. But this [Gezi] was more of a social experiment. You cannot produce political implications out of try-outs. It would not be very smart!"

A Glimpse into the Post-Gezi Alliance Politics

Besides the interviews I conducted between the winters of 2014 and 2015, I also paid visits to the organizational meetings and quorums of the groups constituting the commune in order to make ethnographic observations of the post-Gezi activism and alliance initiatives. Such a participant-observant-based methodological approach was in fact not on my agenda back then. I meant to focus on one-on-one individual interviews to realize the ethical principles of intersectionality in the context of social movements. Yet I could not decline the invitations made by the group leaders, who were quite eager to recruit new members to their organizations in the afterglow of Gezi. On second thought, I decided that attending meetings could be a great opportunity to make observations on the increasing mobilization activity and extend the temporal scope of my research, so I made short visits to organizations and groups that ranged from newly founded environmentalist movements, such as the Northern Forest Solidarity, to already-established groups, such as the TGB, in this period. Among all the movements that welcomed me, the June Unity Movement (JUM, Birleşik Haziran Hareketi), a sort of socialist-communist umbrella organization, gave me a great deal of intriguing material to write on regarding the trajectory of political ideologies and democracy in the country's future.

JUM was founded in the fall of 2013 following the momentum set in motion by the commune. As socialist communards desperately hoped, the movement brought together the scattered flanks of the Turkish Left, which have never bound together because of disagreements over the nuances of Marxist ideology. This platform acted as a crossroads for Marxists, Leninists, Maoists, and their national-leftist-oriented organizations, party factions, and small unionist groups to meet regularly on weekends to discuss and find out the things to do after the fall of Gezi. In a sense, Gezi was an unfinished business back then. One of my interviewees, who was the representative of the Turkish Communist Party in this platform, took me to one of those meetings, which were held in the Taksim area in proximity to the park. This activist woman, whom I dubbed "Iron Rose," was a very proud socialist and was never sympathetic to my anarchistic openings and the critical comments I made during our interview. When I asked whether she felt "regrets" because Gezi did not lead to any "political change" or "revolution of sorts," she threw me a terrible look as if sensing my cynicism. Remaining quiet, Iron Rose, once a mayoral candidate for Taksim as Turkey's first transexual political figure, took me to the JUM quorum instead of scolding for me for not being a loyal socialist. I was never loyal enough for her, anyway.

Our visit to the JUM quorum occurred at the same time that the coalition of the radical Left popularly known as SYRIZA in Greece swept all the voting districts across the Aegean Sea. At that time, Turkey, too, was en route to the first election after Gezi, so the JUM representatives were talking up a storm about their movement's position in this upcoming democracy showdown when we entered the quorum hall. The delegates were exchanging views as to whether the "movement" should enter the election race as a block or publicly give support to the pro-Kurdish People's Democratic Party (Halkların Demokratik Partisi, HDP), which was founded with the promise of radical democracy for the country after Gezi. Amid the heated debates and speeches, it seemed to me in general that the young generations of the Turkish Left were caught up in the allure of SYRIZA's victory.

Contrary to overall approaches that had surfaced during the two-week occupation, the Turkish New Left now seemed to be closer to traditional party politics than to the experimental, anarchistic try-outs in the streets. In contrast, old-school leftists present at the quorum, who had pressed for organized mobilization back in the commune days, were displaying inclinations toward grassroots politics. A former member of the Revolutionary Path Organization, a hard-core militant-Marxist movement of the 1970s, made a statement: "Socialism has failed us. You cannot expect a revolution from this society. We, as the Turkish Left, are not patient; we have to learn to be patient and perform politics in that sense." This gray-haired apologetic Marxist was not the only one to support the idea of politics in a different sense—that is, the understanding of politics in the streets. Another JUM member made similar comments: "Elections have been regularly held in these lands since the 1870s [when the Ottoman Parliament had gathered representatives from all across the Balkans and the Middle East]," cried this elder, experienced socialist amid a general sound of disapproval. Those making the noise probably disliked the idea of associating the first Ottoman Parliament with democracy. "We must definitely not scalarize the elections," the wise socialist added with a determined tone in his voice. In the same spirit, a relatively young speaker underlined the fact that "the struggle must be from the bottom" to defeat capitalism not just in elections but in every aspect of life. "This is why there shall be a second Gezi," he roared at the crowd after throwing his head back despite his shaky voice. But not all of the delegates in the quorum agreed. Murmuring sounds filled up the quorum hall. Younger Turkish socialists and communists, probably encouraged by SYRIZA's landslide victory in Europe, which was at that point being ripped apart by right-wing populist leaders throughout the Poland–Hungry corridor, gave speeches like political leaders and defended the notion of elections. They underlined that JUM should act as an umbrella party on behalf of the whole Left by using the impetus that Gezi had created. One of those delegates, who also acted as the chair, ended the meeting with a highly cynical explanation: "What happened after the Spanish Civil War, what would happen after another Gezi. One [can of] tear gas, and then we would all scatter like flies again. We should be an actor in the elections!"

Despite all other similar views, JUM did not enter the general election of June 2015; nonetheless, the block members publicly announced their support for the new pro-Kurdish, left-oriented party, the HDP, right before the race began. By getting the support of new middle classes at urban centers in addition to the Kurdish votes, the HDP won seats for eighty members of Parliament by the end of this election. This surprising vertical leap in the country's regime space led to a hung Parliament for the first time since 2001, thereby preventing Erdoğan from forming a majority government. Nonetheless, the representatives of the Nationalist

Movement Party (Milliyetçi Hareket Partisi) and cautious republican nationalists were not very willing to form a coalition with the HDP, and so came a political deadlock, which completely reshuffled all the cards in the political game. At the end of six months of uncertainty, the pan-Turkist party and Erdoğan, who was looking for alternatives to replace the Kurdish votes he lost to the HDP, found themselves aligned more or less along similar Islamist-nationalist lines and against the party they now stigmatized as the "terrorists."

These massive shifts in the country's alliance politics, I would argue, can be attributed to the Gezi commune itself, which revealed the first signs of a power conflict between Erdoğan and his party's so-called civil society extension—that is, the Gülen movement. The Sufi-inspired Gülen movement's arcane support for the "innocent kid" in the commune and disagreements over the share of economic and social resources (Tugal 2014) had already forced the hand of neoliberal political Islam, the AKP, to look for other alliances to maintain its hegemony. When the pan-Turkists called for a snap election in November 2015 following the political deadlock, they were already in the same boat with Erdoğan. Thereafter, Turkey bore witness to the agglomeration of neoliberal Islamism and ultranationalism at the same ideological point.

This political development at the national level may seem like an insignificant, singular event; nonetheless, I would argue that increasing nationalist rhetoric and the intensifying conflict between the Gülen movement and the Turkish state have implications not only for Turkey's regime space but also for the whole Middle East region by undermining the autonomous position of the Turkish army after an alleged coup attempt, thereby dragging it into the bloody civil war unfolding in Syria. A country in political chaos and international conflicts gave Erdoğan all he needed to consolidate his new totalitarian regime, which is now slowly positioned against the Western world as well. Arbitrary arrests and indictments, media censorship, restriction of civil liberties through executive decrees issued by Erdoğan himself, persecution of academics on a regular basis, and public hate speeches by top-ranked state figures against the LGBTQI+ community became the realities of the new Turkey, once known as a role model for the Middle East with its broken but functioning democracy and relatively better economic welfare.

For the past couple of years, Turkey's new ideological fusion seems to have redrawn the overall public discourses along two main fault lines: democracy and authoritarianism. In other words, the political turbulences and chaotic social environment that came with Gezi's anarchistic openings, I would argue, laid the foundations of a popular front of sorts against the dance of Turkish nationalism and neoliberal Islamism. Perhaps in a way more than ever, republican nationalists of the country's founding party nowadays display inclinations to position themselves in the same camp with the Kurds and with all other political and cultural minorities, such as the LGBTQI+ individuals who pose a threat to the solidarist-nationalist spirit that the republicans embrace. This new popular front has also caused a spilt in the pan-Turkish party, thereby carrying a new nationalist party whose female leader was heard openly advocating LGBTQI+ rights against Erdoğan. This new, multilegged cosmopolitan democratic alliance even managed to take down the two biggest urban centers, Istanbul and Ankara, in the local elections of 2019.

Thus, when looked at through the prism of ideological history, Gezi seems to set an example that proves wrong all the unfair comments and assessments made about the Occupy and Arab Spring movements. As I suggested earlier, the Occupy movements overall received a fair amount of criticism for not creating the desired political and social resonances in their retreat processes. It has been repetitively argued that the new political understandings of Occupy's posterity, whose life-world takes shape around middle-class values and views, tend to remain stuck in these occupied spaces, thereby not resonating with lower segments of society, who are inclined to vote for populist leaders such as Erdoğan, Vladimir Putin, and Donald Trump. In a similar fashion, the alliances that blossomed in the Arab Spring were criticized for not preparing for the subsequent electoral races and not internalizing core democratic values.

At first look, Gezi also seems to have given Erdoğan the necessary tool to justify his policies and seems inadvertently to have caused an agglomeration in the Islamic–nationalist axis. But at the same time, it also provided the Turkish Left and other democratic actors with a temporal-distortion field of sorts to make a thirty-year time jump. In other words, Gezi matured the notion of collective civil society consciousness, which should have emerged in the Middle East in the 1970s, as it did in the Western world. Such a democratic civil society formation was delayed because of the strong state tradition and a corporatist view of society, which has also been embraced by Turkish republicans from head to foot since the war of independence. But what could be a more transformative force than placing the founding ideology of the country in the same anarchistic trench dug against the corporatist state that ideology established a hundred years ago? Perhaps gays infiltrating into nationalist and heterosexual domains.

In Lieu of Conclusion: The Allure of Anarchism and Queerness

Because a cosmopolitan civil society understanding was delayed and therefore new social movements could not find enough space for themselves to display their cultural vitrines in the heyday of post-1960 mobilization scenery in Turkey, the matter of queerness and sexual minorities' rights never acquired the publicity it did in Western societies. For sure, Islamic cultural values and the reconfiguration of the whole society as the sacred family nation in the 1930s (White 2003) could be counted among other factors that restrained the rise of gay rights as well. Nonetheless, the LGBTQI+ movement made a great deal of effort to be visible and get its message across throughout the 1980s and early 1990s. Decades before the Gezi commune, one of the very first protest events came from the nonbinary dissidents in Gezi Park, which was closed to all public demonstrations during the coup administration. Throughout the early 1980s, Taksim Square was marked as no man's land by the junta regime, which was determined to suppress all the protest activity in the country and had embarked on a ruthless journey to neoliberalism. Yet the LGBTQI+ movement and trans sex workers, who were exposed to various discrimination and harassment practices by the army administration and its security forces, managed to breach the ban by enacting a successful collective hunger strike at the park on an open-air protest stage, an action seen for the first time in the country's history (Güneş 2016).

I would suggest that this is exactly why the space itself holds symbolic significance for queer communards. It was the first site where the notion of gay resistance blossomed, as happened at New York's Stonewall. Moreover, the park had served—and actually is still serving—as cruising ground for working-class gay men deprived of access to the glamourous night clubs of Istiklal Street, which put on the biggest gay pride events ever held in a predominantly Muslim country in the early 2000s. By weaving the earlier queer repertoires to itself, the park provided a venue even for heterosexual communards to reconsider and remold the known heteronormative values and notions during the commune days, I would argue.

I am making such an argument once again by relying on the open-ended questions I posed in my fieldwork. When I asked my interviewees to put their opinions into words regarding the "most celebrated groups of the commune," they enthusiastically listed the anarchist football fans, also known as the Çarşı group (Turan and Özçetin 2017), and members of the LGBTQI+ movement first, and then they recounted their serendipitous encounters with the latter group and how the commune was changing the image of being gay in the eyes of the new middle classes and in their own perception. "People came to understand we are not just about sex, thanks to Gezi," one prominent public gay figure told me, as if verifying the other side of the picture. "We have been politicized well before Gezi, but nobody was paying attention to that. Our flag was nailed to the trees before June," he added with a proud expression on his face. Other accounts given by both heterosexual and nonbinary communards seemed to echo the statements made by this famous public figure who got into trouble because of comments he made about the president.

One of the members of the TGB, who also confirmed that the LGBTQI+ movement was the most popular group in the commune, explained to me how he observed an "attitude change toward gays" in his own organization, which is set up according to a male-dominant, militarist cultural understanding, as I noted earlier. When I asked him what he meant by the "attitude change," he said, "After Gezi, we began discussing to what extend gays would be compatible with our cause." Not only the nationalist youths but also more militant left anarchistic organizations began to consider gays as potential recruits after Gezi. The Kurdish anarchist who recounted a similar anecdote told me his comrades began to think of gays as a "major political force" to make an alliance against the state after the emotional reverberations the commune created. "Çarşı fans and many other out-lawed organizations I am part of, we even participated in the first pride [parade] after Gezi. Maybe you won't believe, but it is true! Gezi has caused a change in perceptions," he recounted after marking "gays" as the most celebrated group.

Without a doubt, another iconic image burned into the communards' memo-ries was the one that depicted the rapprochement between the gay community and anarchist football fans, the most celebrated groups of the commune. In this shot, they paraded shoulder to shoulder through the streets and avenues surrounding the park on the first day of victory. In a belated modern milieu, the political ideologies of the past centuries were again, against all odds, left behind; it was as if they could not catch up to the speed and the allure of anarchism and queerness. The queerness was so alluring that a couple of my interviewees told me they saw alpha-male-type, republican, nationalist communards as well as independent protesters publicly coming out in the deepest hours of the commune nights. "At my workplace, every-one stopped hiding that they were gay during Gezi," one white-collar communard told me in response to my question about "his most memorable moment of Gezi." In answering the same question, a feminist conjured up the image of the "bear flag draped over the TGB tent." "I am not sure if they knew the meaning of that flag; even if not, it was very compatible with their ideology on the outlook," she added with a cynical smile.

Of course, further ethnographic research is required to decipher the codes of these changing gender perceptions in the political ideologies that have held ground in Turkey for the past century. I hope that the ethnographic findings as well as the critical approach I have taken to the matter of ideology in this chapter will provide the necessary launching point for new researchers who would be willing to look at changing modular patterns of mainstream political and gender ideologies not only in Turkey but in other experiences as well.

References

Arditti, Joyce, Karen Joest, Jennifer Lamber-Shute, and Latanya Walker. 2010. "The Role of Emotions in Fieldwork: A Self-Study of Family Research in a Corrections Setting." *Qualitative Report* 15, no. 6: 1387–414.

Bamyeh, Mohammed, and Sari Hanafi. 2015. "Introduction to the Special Issue on Arab Uprisings." *International Sociology* 30, no. 4: 343–47.

Baykan, Aysegul, and Tali Hatuka. 2010. "Politics and Culture in the Making of Public Space: Taksim Square, 1 May 1977, Istanbul." *Planning Perspectives* 25, no. 1: 49–68.

Bertelson, Lone, and Andrew Murphie. 2010. "An Ethics of Everyday Infinities and Powers: Félix Guattari on Affect and the Refrain." In *The Affect Theory Reader*, edited by Melissa Gregg and Gregory J. Seigworth, 138–57. Durham, NC: Duke Univ. Press.

Bornat, Joanna. 2013. "Oral History and Remembering." In *Research Methods for Memory Studies*, edited by Emily Keightley and Michael Pickering, 29–42. Edinburgh: Edinburgh Univ. Press.

Brown, Steven D., and Paula Reavey. 2013. "Experience and Memory." In *Research Methods for Memory Studies*, edited by Emily Keightley and Michael Pickering, 45–59. Edinburgh: Edinburgh Univ. Press.

Butler, Judith. 2014. Foreword to *The Making of a Protest Movement in Turkey: #occupygezi*, edited by Umut Özkırımlı, vii–xvi. New York: Palgrave Macmillan.

Calhoun, Craig. 2013. "Occupy Wall Street in Perspective." *British Journal of Sociology* 64, no. 1: 26–38.

Day, Richard J. F. 2005. *Gramsci Is Dead: Anarchist Currents in the Newest Social Movements*. London: Pluto Press.

———. 2011. "Hegemony, Affinity, and the Newest Social Movements: At the End of the 00s." In *Post-anarchism: A Reader*, edited by Duane Rousselle and Süreyya Evren, 95–116. London: Pluto Press.

Della Porta, Donatella. 2011. "Eventful Protest, Global Conflicts: Social Mechanisms in the Reproduction of Protest." In *Contention in Context: Political Opportunities and the Emergence of Protest*, edited by Jeff Goodwin and James M. Jasper, 256–76. Stanford, CA: Stanford Univ. Press.

———. 2018. "Protests as Critical Junctures: Some Reflections towards a Momentous Approach to Social Movements." *Social Movement Studies* 19, no. 1: 1–20.

Evren, Süreyya. 2013. "Gezi Resistance in Istanbul: Something in between Tahrir, Occupy, and a Turkish 1968." *Anarchist Studies* 21, no. 2: 7–10.

Fivush, Robyn. 2013. "Autobiographical Memory." In *Research Methods for Memory Studies*, edited by Emily Keightley and Michael Pickering, 13–28. Edinburgh: Edinburgh Univ. Press.

Gibson, Morgan Rodgers. 2013. "The Anarchism of the Occupy Movement." *Australian Journal of Political Science* 48, no. 3: 335–48.

Gitlin, Todd. 2013. "Occupy's Predicament: The Moment and the Prospects for the Movement." *British Journal of Sociology* 64, no. 1: 3–25.

Graeber, David. 2009. *Direct Action: An Ethnography*. Edinburgh: AK Press UK.

Güneş, Ahmet. 2016. *Göğe Kuşan Lazım*. Istanbul: Sel Yayincilik.

Hammond, John L. 2015. "The Anarchism of Occupy Wall Street." *Science & Society* 79, no. 2: 288–313.

Hardt, Michael, and Antonio Negri. 2011. "The Fight for 'Real Democracy' at the Heart of Occupy Wall Street." *Foreign Affairs*, Oct. 11. At https://www.foreignaffairs.com/articles/north-america/2011-10-11/fight-real-democracy-heart-occupy-wall-street.

Harmanşah, Ömür. 2014. "Urban Utopias and How They Fell Apart: The Political Ecology of Gezi Park." In *The Making of a Protest Movement in Turkey: #occupygezi*, edited by Umut Özkırımlı, 121–33. New York: Palgrave Macmillan.

Harvey, David. 2004. *Paris, Capital of Modernity*. London: Routledge.

Hubbard, Gill, Kathryn Backett-Milburn, and Debbie Kemmer. 2001. "Working with Emotion: Issues for the Researcher in Fieldwork and Teamwork." *International Journal of Social Research Methodology* 4, no. 2: 119–37.

Kamrava, Mehran. 2014. *Beyond the Arab Spring: The Evolving Ruling Bargain in the Middle East*. New York: Oxford Univ. Press.

Kansteiner, Wulf. 2002. "Finding Meaning in Memory: A Methodological Critique of Collective Memory Studies." *History and Theory* 41, no. 2: 179–97.

Keightley, Emily. 2010. "Remembering Research: Memory and Methodology in the Social Sciences." *International Journal of Social Research Methodology* 13, no. 1: 55–70.

Kleinman, Sherryl, and Martha A. Copp. 1993. *Emotions and Fieldwork*. New York: Sage.

Kolluoglu, Poyraz. 2020. "A 21st Century Repertoire: Affective and Urban Mobilization Dynamics of the Gezi Commune." *Interface* 12, no. 1: 437–63.

Leveille, John. 2017. *Searching for Marx in the Occupy Movement*. Lanham, MD: Lexington.

Lustiger-Thaler, Henri. 2014. "Occupying Human Values: Memory and the Future of Collective Action." In *Reimagining Social Movements: From Collectives to Individuals*, edited by Antimo L. Farro and Henri Lustiger-Thaler, 35–50. Farnham, UK: Ashgate.

Marx, Karl, and Friedrich Engels. 1981. *The Marx–Engels Correspondence: The Personal Letters, 1844–1877: A Selection*. Edited by Fritz Joachim Raddatz. London: Weidenfeld and Nicolson.

Özkırımlı, Umut. 2014. Introduction to *The Making of a Protest Movement in Turkey: #occupygezi*, edited by Umut Özkırımlı, 1–6. New York: Palgrave Macmillan.

Radstone, Susannah. 2016. *Memory and Methodology*. New York: Bloomsbury.

Roberts, Alasdair. 2012. "Why the Occupy Movement Failed." *Public Administration Review* 72, no. 5: 754–62.

Roediger, Henry L., and James V. Wertsch. 2008. "Creating a New Discipline of Memory Studies." *Memory Studies* 1, no. 1: 9–22.

Ross, Kristin. 2015. *Communal Luxury: The Political Imaginary of the Paris Commune*. London: Verso.

Seel, Benjamin. 2013. "Lady in the Red Dress and Her Dream of Turkish Rebirth." *Telegraph*, June 8. At http://www.telegraph.co.uk/news/worldnews/europe/turkey/10108014/Lady-in-the-Red-Dress-and-her-dream-of-a-Turkish-rebirth.html.

Shihade, Magid, Christina Flesher Fominaya, and Laurence Cox. 2012. "The Season of Revolution: The Arab Spring and European Mobilization." *Interface* 4, no. 1: 1–16.

Sitrin, Marina. 2006. *Horizontalism: Voices of Popular Power in Argentina.* Chico, CA: AK Press.

Taylor, Diana. 2003. *The Archive and the Repertoire: Performing Cultural Memory in the Americas.* Durham, NC: Duke Univ. Press.

Taylor, Verta. 1999. "Gender and Social Movements: Gender Process in Women's Self-Help Movements." *Gender and Society* 13, no. 1: 8–33.

Tugal, Cihan. 2014. "Gülenism: The Middle Way or Official Ideology?" In *The Making of a Protest Movement in Turkey: #occupygezi*, edited by Umut Özkırımlı, 50–76. New York: Palgrave Macmillan.

Turan, Ömer, and Burak Özçetin. 2017. "Football Fans and Contentious Politics: The Role of Çarşı in the Gezi Park Protests." *International Review for the Sociology of Sport* 54, no. 2: 199–217.

Velut, Jean-Baptiste. 2015. "Memory and Amnesia in the Occupy Wall Street Movement." In *Generations of Social Movements: Remembering the Left in the US and France*, edited by Hélène Le Dantec Lowry and Ambre Ivol, 37–50. London: Routledge.

White, Jenny B. 2003. "State Feminism, Modernization, and the Turkish Republican Woman." *NWSA Journal* 15, no. 3: 145–59.

14

Women Continue the Unfinished Project of Liberation in the MENA Region through Online Activism

Victoria Tahmasebi-Birgani

The significance of social media as a mode of organizing, mobilizing, and resisting authoritarianism and as a tool to bring about collective action was demonstrated during Iran's Green Movement of 2009 and the Arab uprisings known as the "Arab Spring" in 2011. During and after both of these events, it became evident that feminists and women activists are at the forefront of political struggles to bring about social and political change in the Middle East and North Africa (MENA), often risking their lives in the process. By incorporating digital technology as an integral component of their activism, these activists have built transnational solidarity and advocacy networks among women activists, public intellectuals, and academics. From taking advantage of information and communication technology applications to using online social networking sites to write political blogs, post on YouTube, and set up Facebook and Twitter accounts, these activists have utilized cyberspace to create vast online networks to connect, communicate, mobilize, and rally around different social, cultural, and political causes (Juris 2012; Lim 2012; Papacharissi 2010; Taylor 2014).

Social media (in particular Facebook and Twitter) were instrumental in informing Egyptians about the 2011 uprising and the gatherings in Tahrir Square and in shaping individual and collective decisions to join rallies and protests (Tufekci and Wilson 2012). The success of the Facebook campaign "We are all Khaled Said," created after twenty-eight-year-old Khaled Said was tortured to death by Egyptian police officers in June 2010, played a significant role in mobilizing Egyptian activists on the ground (Eaton 2013). Activists in Egypt, Bahrain, and Kuwait used social media to mobilize people, gather momentum for political movements, and

266

coordinate protest rallies. Social media are increasingly influencing the ways in which people in MENA and in the broader global community communicate and express their political will in the public sphere, turning ordinary people to citizen journalists (Khamis and Vaughn 2013; Lotan et al. 2011; Papacharissi and de Fatima Oliveira 2012). Social media were also instrumental in the Gezi Park protests in Istanbul, Turkey, in 2013; in the Occupy movements in Western countries in 2011–12; in student and environmental protests in Chile in 2011; in mass demonstrations against sexual harassment in Delhi in 2012; and in the Shahbag Square protests in Dhaka, Bangladesh, in 2013 (Eslen-Ziya 2013; Sorour and Dey 2014; Wall 2007)

Women's online activism not only continually builds on the achievements of popular uprisings in the region but also creatively expands on the meanings of democracy, gender equality, and justice to continue conversations on how social movements in the region need to incorporate women's demands in moving forward and building a stronger front against tyranny, oppression, and injustice. After the brutal suppression of popular revolt in the region, MENA activists continue the unfinished work of liberation, proving that MENA, far from being an exceptional case, is a dynamic and politically charged region marked by complex modes of struggle and resistance. To circumvent systematic repression, women activists have increasingly opted to create subaltern online public spheres to articulate their voices, to produce political contestation, and to influence social and political change in the MENA region. Recognizing the importance of social media as a critical tool for activism, MENA feminists and women activists have recently begun to use cyberspace to draw widespread attention to a number of urgent and significant causes, to connect with larger communities, to share information, to educate broader sets of communities about women's issues in the region, to build feminist subaltern communities, to build transnational advocacy networks, to create feminist online campaigns, to globalize their campaigns' goals and objectives, and to facilitate online political participation and engagement of marginalized groups in MENA, such as sexual minorities and young people. Women's groups in MENA have, further, succeeded in establishing networks of solidarity with women's organizations elsewhere (Sreberny 2015).

More importantly, these online public spheres have become a bridge between online and offline activism as well as between activists living inside the MENA countries and those living in diaspora outside the region. They contribute to creating what Clay Shirky (2009) calls a "shared awareness" and to producing "movement spillover." They provide an archive, a memory, and a repository of texts and audio-visual symbolic contents relating to protests, tactics, organizations, and ideas; they continue to effect change even after the fact—after the hashtag dies or the virtual community becomes inactive. In this way, the self-mediations of protesters and activists contribute to a global archive of protest artifacts and hence to ongoing collective action and liberatory projects.

In discussing specific successful online campaigns by MENA activists, this chapter argues that women in MENA countries are at the forefront of reconceptualizing and rewriting the unfinished project of the Arab Spring. Women's online networking plays a crucial role in facilitating the mobilization for and coordination of direct actions offline. And in doing so, it helps lower the cost and increases the efficiency of mobilization and coordination and enables on-the-spot or in-real-time communicative practices, which are essential in any activism. Further, online networks also help to distribute movement goals more easily by increasing the capacity to transmit text and image, and, finally, they help to facilitate internal debate among activists and ordinary women.

The chapter concludes that although sociopolitical change in the region cannot be downloaded, the evolution of women's activism from the streets to social media and back to the streets has now made the interplay between online and offline activism as well as the close working between the two spaces essential for any grassroots movement. The permanent nature of these artifacts enables the symbols embedded in these networks and spaces to be culturally transmitted, feeding offline struggles and contributing to a collective memory of protest. In this way, online activism transfers knowledge and influences future movements through what is called "movement spillover."

New Technologies and Social Activism: Historical and Theoretical Background

A strong body of scholarship has posed serious questions about the role of new technologies in political praxis, challenging the notion that online activism has the capacity to bring about real political change. Much of this research problematizes and makes crucial interventions into celebratory accounts of cyberactivism; the term *feel-good online activism* has been coined to draw attention to the limited scope of such political engagement (Gladwell 2010; Howard 2011; Morozov 2009b). Evgeny Morozov questions the political and social impact of online activism; his term *slacktivism* describes the limitations of replacing real-world, offline networking and activism with attempts to "click" our way to revolution (Morozov 2009a, 2009c, 2011; see also Van de Donk et al. 2004). Malcolm Gladwell (2010) poignantly challenges the effectiveness of online activism, underscoring the importance of mutual trust and concrete interaction in mobilizing and organizing for political change. Such indispensable forms of interaction, according to a number of studies, are more likely to be formed in physical social networks than on social networking sites (Diani 2000). Gilbert Achcar (2013) warns against the valorization of media and their role in the making of revolutions, and Summer Harlow and Dustin Harp (2012) note a tendency to overestimate the role of digital technologies in bringing about real political change. Lei Guo and Summer Harlow's (2014) study demonstrates that rather than offering a countersphere, social media such as YouTube often perpetuate the same biases found in mainstream media. Studies suggest that information technologies do not topple dictatorships but rather act as pressure tools, which may contribute to making authoritarian apparatuses vulnerable to grassroots demands (Gladwell 2010; Howard 2011).

Yet most feminist media scholars have a more optimistic view about the impact of social media on political activism. For example, Sahar Khamis and Amel Mili's collected volume *Arab Women's Activism and Socio-political Transformation* (2018) argues that in Arab countries there exists a complex relationship between women's online activism and sociopolitical transformation. Arab women's cyberactivism both activates and accelerates mass mobilization and plays the role of "catalyst" for sociopolitical change in those countries.

Other scholarly works have demonstrated that women activists use social media platforms for crucial political work, such as disseminating news about upcoming protests and rallies (Lotan et al. 2011), sustaining core networks of activists (Tufekci and Wilson 2012), fostering political discussions, and inspiring other activists as well as ordinary women to think about and reflect on the most important issues in their lives (Khamis and Vaugh 2011, 2013; Tahmasebi-Birgani 2017). Moreover, transnational feminist theorists have already begun to develop the interpretive tools to critically engage with the global networks created by diverse feminist movements and communities, to examine how women's online networks emerge, and to study the implications of these cybernetworks for solidarity movements among women and for the empowerment of women both individually and collectively (Blair, Gajjala, and Tulley 2009; Gajjala 2004; Stephan 2013). For example, research on both South Asian and African American women has produced concrete, situated knowledge about the strong feminist presence of members of these two communities on the net (Everett 2009; Gajjala 2001, 2004; Gajjala and Gajjala 2008). Other scholars have focused on the ways in which transnational women's online networks are used to inform social praxis (Blair, Gajjala, and Tulley 2009), advocate for gender equality in Latin America (Friedman 2005), promote women's empowerment in MENA (Radsch and Khamis 2013; Rivetti 2017, 2020), produce sites of feminist learning and pedagogy (Irving and English 2011), challenge mainstream public-policy decision making (Dingo 2008), fight online racism (Watkins, Gajjala, and Zhang 2012), challenge racial divides on the net (Wright 2005), deconstruct Orientalist representations of "Third World" women (Queen 2008), and mobilize for political change (Pierce 2010).

MENA Women: From Street Protests to Virtual Networking

Virtual spaces play an even more crucial role in MENA countries that take repressive measures against women and other minority groups (Abbasgholizadeh 2014; Akhavan 2014; Newsom and Lengel 2012; Skalli-Hanna 2006, 2010). This is true despite the fact that women's access to the internet in MENA continues to be determined by class, age, and regional differences (Schradie 2012). Social media platforms are all the more instrumental for feminists, women activists, and ordinary citizens who are often denied access to mainstream media and mainstream party politics (Papacharissi 2009). A recent body of research points to the various ways in which MENA women utilize social networking sites as new resources for social and political activism (Gheytanchi and Moghadam 2014; Khamis 2011; Khamis and Vaughn 2011, 2012; Radsch 2011, 2012a, 2012b; Stephan 2013).

For example, in one study that analyzes 220,000 Facebook posts and comments on three of the most popular MENA feminist Facebook pages, Ahmed al-Rawi (2014) concludes that social networking sites are instrumental in empowering MENA women to address, discuss, and challenge social and cultural taboos in their societies. In another study, Hande Eslen-Ziya (2013) shows that a Turkish women's online campaign was crucial in forcing the government of Turkey to drop antiabortion legislation. In response to rampant sexual harassment, Egyptian women activists created the HarassMap website (http://harassmap.org/en/), which operates in both English and Arabic, to monitor, control, and raise awareness about the sexual harassment of women in the streets of Egyptian cities. And, finally, LGBTQ+ people from MENA countries have created vast online networks to fight for their rights and to make the cause of sexual minority groups more visible. Some of the most horrific crimes against LGBTQ+ people in the region are broadcast by networks of citizen journalists who risk their lives to record and post videos online and to report these crimes to the world and to human rights international tribunals. The Facebook page and the website of the Iranian Railroad for Queer Refugees, a nonprofit organization, were created to help Iranian LGBTQ+ individuals connect with each other and thus to escape isolation inside the country. These online platforms have become a space wherein individuals speak about their experiences of persecution, discrimination, and marginalization. Individuals also post inspiring stories that speak to the resilience and strength of Iranian LGBTQ+ people. The Iranian Railroad for Queer Refugees also helps Iranian

LGBTQ+ refugees escape persecution by fleeing to a safe country. As Annabelle Sreberny (2015) argues, the spread of social media platforms in the region's native languages has had a decisive impact on the increase in women's and other minority groups' political participation.

Iranian women activists have a highly visible and increasingly significant presence on social media platforms (Yahyanejad and Gheytanchi 2012). The Iranian regime blocks social media such as Facebook, Twitter, and YouTube, so Iranians must bypass internet censorship and filtering by using virtual private networks. The exact number of Facebook users in Iran is thus unknown, but a recent study shows that, despite this filtering, 58 percent of Iranians are users (Knowles 2012). According to an interview with Mehdi Jafari, the chief of the Technology and Information and Cultural Organization for Students of the *Basij* (the Revolutionary Guard's volunteer militia) in 2011, the *Asr Iran* news website reported that there were about 17 million active Facebook users in Iran at the time (see Center for Human Rights in Iran 2015). The number has since then risen significantly. Iranian activists are increasingly using new services such as WhatsApp, Viber, and Telegram to send messages, spread news and information about events, and raise awareness about women's issues. Yet Facebook, even more than Twitter, continues to be the preferred platform for Iranian women activists and organizations. By allowing users to type in more than 140 characters in a single post, which is the current Twitter limit, Facebook offers them a way to participate in deeper and more meaningful conversations with one another. Further, the platform's interactive and multimedia capability provides women activists with an opportunity to debate and converse about women's issues with a larger audience. Finally, most of these women activists were forced into exile after the brutal crackdown of the Green Movement in 2009; they now run their Facebook campaigns from outside the country.

My Stealthy Freedom, one of the most visited and talked about Iranian women's Facebook campaigns, takes a stance against compulsory veiling in Iran. With more than 950,000 likes, this Facebook page has become one of the most visible online feminist campaigns in support of Iranian women's freedom to choose what they wear. Since its creation, the campaign has gained support from activists, grassroots organizations, and Western corporate media. The Facebook campaign was launched in 2014 by an Iranian journalist currently living in exile in the United Kingdom. In her initial message, Masih Alinejad invited Iranian women, especially those inside the country, to post selfies taken in public spaces without the headscarf. Even though being unveiled in public in Iran carries the risk of arrest, the payment of a monetary fine, acid attacks by vigilantes, and even public flogging in smaller cities, Iranian women have welcomed the opportunity to post unveiled pictures, videos, and personal stories from inside Iran—under their real names and, most of the time, with their faces revealed. Each of Alinejad's posts attracts thousands and sometimes tens of thousands of likes and generates long strings of comments and conversation. As such, the My Stealthy Freedom Facebook page is extremely active and lively; participants discuss a wide range of social, cultural, and political issues. One of the most important consequences of this Facebook page is that it has given Iranian women (and men, for that matter) a space to actively participate in ongoing evaluations and rearticulations of the politics of culture, gender identity, resistance, and activism. Therefore, although the page promotes a single-issue campaign, participants regularly locate and discuss Iran's compulsory veiling within the larger economic, social, and geopolitical context.

More importantly, by producing movement spillover, the My Stealthy Freedom page has become a bridge between online and offline activism as well as between activists inside Iran and those outside it (in the diaspora). One such spillover is the White Wednesday Campaign. In May 2017, Alinejad started this campaign by asking Iranian women to oppose the compulsory hijab by taking photos of themselves wearing a white scarf and posting them on the Facebook page as well as on Twitter. Using the hashtag #whitewednesdays, women started posting pictures and videos of themselves wearing white headscarves or pieces of white clothing as symbols of protest. Since then, hundreds of women have been arrested in the streets of Iran for wearing white scarves on Wednesdays. Owing to the state's crackdown of women in white, the campaign has now morphed into a guerilla performative tactic dubbed the "Girls of Enghelab (Revolution) Street," in which women use performative street art to show their objection to the compulsory hijab.

The use of this tactic began when in December 2017 a lone woman, Vida Movahedi, climbed a utility box on a busy street in Tehran, tied her hijab, a white headscarf, to a stick, and silently waved it to the crowd as a flag. She immediately became a symbol of Iranian women's defiance, and memes of her action spread online. Movahedi was immediately arrested, but several other women followed in her footsteps, standing on the same electrical post on the same street. In response, to prevent other women activists from standing there, the authorities altered the utility box to make it more difficult to stand on. But people went back and altered the altered box so that women could continue to climb on it. In addition, for several weeks police guarded the utility box, arresting any woman who got close it. Soon, other women took similar stands, climbing utility boxes and taking off their hijabs on different streets in different cities in Iran. The symbolism of the initial protests taking place on Revolution Street was not lost on those following the events.

Lessons Learned

Several distinct lessons emerge out of women's online activism in MENA, with significant implications for ongoing struggles toward a more democratic and inclusive future in the region as well as for transnational women's movements both online and offline. First, MENA women's online campaigns and activities promote a model of nonhierarchical, horizontal, networked activism, akin to the global Occupy movements. As noted earlier, scholars have debated the role of networked activism in promoting democracy and inclusivity. Manuel Castells, who coined the term *network society* (Castells 1996), has been optimistic about the liberating power of new communications technologies for ordinary people. However, two serious criticisms have been expressed regarding celebratory accounts of network activism. One criticism relates to the fact that online networking brings with it a measure of transparency, making it much easier for states to engage in surveillance of political activists. It is true that states not only exert censorship over internet and social networking sites whenever they have the chance but also monitor and put under surveillance the individuals who are active on these networks. In other words, censorship is meant to prevent activists from connecting and communicating with one other, and the same regimes use the transparency afforded by online networks to identify, arrest, and imprison activists and suppress dissent (as WikiLeaks and Edward Snowden have already revealed).

Nonetheless, this mode of activism is still relevant and particularly useful in countries run by authoritarian state apparatuses. Women activists continue to find new ways to circumvent censorship and better protect their identities, especially in countries with repressive regimes. Furthermore, nonvertical, decentralized, and multiple-user-generated activism allows the participation of actors who are geographically dispersed, spanning many national boundaries. Therefore, this form of activism can help save the lives of activists who would be more easily detected, identified, and arrested in a more centralized organizational structure. Further and more importantly, in a patriarchal culture where the (symbolic father) male leader often presides over micro and macro institutions, this nonhierarchical form of praxis could in the long run challenge rigid patriarchal frameworks of political activism still so prevalent in MENA countries. This decentralized and inclusive form of political dissent could help destabilize authoritarian structures and their patriarchal principles, which deeply inform and shape everyday cultural practices and the organizational orientation of political activism in MENA countries.

Another line of criticism argues that it is too optimistic to see all actors and all content produced on these networks as of equal value and as having equal impact.

Social actors enter these networks with unequal power and are positioned differently within the network and its constitutive nodes. In other words, online networks, even the most progressive ones, are already embedded in well-established hierarchies of power, which are implicitly recognized in real, offline social relations and then find expression online. Speakers are heard and issues become visible in ways that reflect the existence of a core elite, whose members act as gatekeepers within the online network (Hamdy and Gomaa 2012; Meraz and Papacharissi 2013). This gatekeeping results in the marginalization of some voices and the visibility and dominance of others. For example, many activists have criticized the My Stealthy Freedom Facebook campaign for its exclusive focus on compulsory veiling, which some argue is a concern of wealthy middle-class women living in large urban cities in Iran rather than of poor and lower-class rural women. These critics argue that compulsory veiling cannot be separated from other forms of surveillance over women's bodies and sexualities, nor can it be divorced from the socioeconomic marginalization of the millions of Iranian women who live in abject poverty—issues that the campaign ignores. The same criticism was previously applied to the mushrooming of online campaigns against the practice of female genital mutilation (mainly in East and West Africa) over the past few decades. The critics rightly argue that the practice of female genital mutilation cannot be singled out without considering the wider context of colonialism and economic exploitation of African countries.

Reflecting on anti-sexual-harassment campaigns in the context of Arab countries, in particular Egypt, Nadje al-Ali (2014) voices a similar concern. She rightly argues against focusing on women's sexual harassment without considering the role that colonialism, capitalism, structural adjustment, neoliberal policies, and the militarization of public spaces continue to play in perpetuating gender-based violence in the region. Ignoring this context also leads to essentialist representations of Muslim men as inherently violent and oppressive.

It is undeniable that gatekeeping is as rampant and widespread in online platforms as it is in offline social movements; it is systematic and built in. The same applies to online and offline women's movement in MENA. Often, the concerns and the issues of urban middle-class women occupy center stage at the expense of marginalizing the voices of working-class women, peasants, and women who belong to ethnic, linguistic, sexual, and religious minorities in the region. However, women who participate in activists' online networks and campaigns often bring their own concerns and issues to the discussion and creatively establish relationships between concerns that are seemingly unrelated. The long strings of posts, comments, debates, and conversations more often than not enable ordinary women to engage with complex issues and make connections between the concrete, everyday realities of their personal lives and the abstract articulations of social issues.

The second distinctive feature of MENA women's online activism is the role played by ordinary women in generating content on these networks. One aspect of user-generated content is the transformation of ordinary women into dissident journalists. Egyptian women's reports of sexual harassment and the details of their experiences are incorporated into a map on the HarassMap website, which in turn notifies other women of the exact location and the details of the harassment in real time. When the Iranian government banned the celebration of International Women's Day in 2016, ordinary women went to the streets to take selfies or recorded messages to post on the My Stealthy Freedom Facebook page for the whole world to see (see My Stealthy Freedom 1 n.d.). Many others, acting as photojournalists, posted images of graffiti on walls that commemorated International Women's Day (see My Stealthy Freedom 2 n.d.).

These acts of defiance allow women to engage with, challenge, and transgress boundaries drawn by the state apparatus and by long-standing patriarchal cultures and traditions. I do not desire to exaggerate the role of online activism in empowering MENA women. In fact, a substantial body of scholarly work suggests that the link between women's online presence and their political empowerment must be assessed with caution; the relationship is neither immediate nor automatic and, as discussed earlier, is mediated by a host of economic, social, and geopolitical considerations (Gladwell 2010; Howard 2011; Morozov 2009b). Nonetheless, by producing content and engaging with social, cultural, and political issues on activist social networks, MENA women are learning to use their own voices and to exercise their agency; they are learning to speak on their own terms, articulate their everyday experiences in their own words, and redefine the world based on what they, both individually and collectively, imagine a more egalitarian world could look like.

Conclusion

It is a serious misconception that after the brutal suppression of Iran's Green Movement in 2009 and the military coup in Egypt after the Arab Spring in 2011 social movements in the MENA region withered away. Far from being over, the popular uprisings in MENA countries continue to unfold in varied and multiple ways. Although people's physical presence in the form of street protests has subsided, political activists, social reformers, human rights advocates, and women's groups have continued their activism in virtual spaces and social networking sites. MENA women are at the forefront of the struggle for justice, equality, and democratization in all aspects of their lives. MENA women's online activism is but one example of such efforts.

Their online activism has enabled them to build extensive transnational advocacy networks as well as virtual "civil societies" for the exchange of ideas, the sharing of information, and the garnering of international grassroots support to reimagine and rebuild social movements in many countries. Replacing the "real" public squares, these virtual sites have become enabling feminist spaces that offer MENA activists a chance to identify, highlight, and examine the intersections of various patterns of inequalities and to form virtual debates and conversations around local, regional, and global issues.

References

Abbasgholizadeh, Mahboubeh. 2014. "'To Do Something We Are Unable to Do in Iran': Cyberspace, the Public Sphere, and the Iranian Women's Movement." *Signs* 39, no. 4: 831–40. doi:10.1086/675722.

Achcar, Gilbert. 2013. *The People Want: A Radical Exploration of the Arab Uprising.* Berkeley: Univ. of California Press.

Akhavan, Niki. 2014. *Electronic Iran: The Cultural Politics of an Online Evolution.* New Brunswick, NJ: Rutgers Univ. Press.

Al-Ali, Nadje. 2014. "Reflections on (Counter)Revolutionary Processes in Egypt." *Feminist Review* 106:122–28.

Blair, Kristine, Radhika Gajjala, and Christine Tulley. 2009. *Webbing Cyberfeminist Practice: Communities, Pedagogies, and Social Action.* Cresskill, NJ: Hampton.

Castells, Manuel. 1996. *The Rise of the Network Society.* Oxford: Blackwell.

Center for Human Rights in Iran. 2015. "Iranian Officials Re-affirm That Facebook Will Remain Completely Blocked in Iran." At https://www.iranhumanrights.org/2015/05 /officials-re-affirm-facebook-blocked/.

Diani, Mario. 2000. "Social Movement Networks Virtual and Real." *Information, Communication, & Society* 3, no. 3: 386–401.

Dingo, Rebecca. 2008. "Linking Transnational Logics: Feminist Rhetorical Analysis of Public Policy Networks." *College English* 70, no. 7: 490–505.

Eaton, Tim. 2013. "Internet Activism and the Egyptian Uprisings: Transforming Online Dissent into the Offline World." *Westminster Papers* 9, no. 2: 3–24. At https://doi.org /10.16997/wpcc.163.

Eslen-Ziya, Hande. 2013. "Social Media and Turkish Feminism: New Resources for Social Activism." *Feminist Media Studies* 13, no. 5: 860–70. doi:10.1080/14680777.2013 .838369.

Everett, Anna. 2009. *Digital Diaspora: A Race for Cyberspace.* Albany: State Univ. of New York Press.

Friedman, Elisabeth Jay. 2005. "The Reality of Virtual Reality: The Internet and Gender Equality Advocacy in Latin America." *Latin American Politics and Society* 47, no. 3: 1–34.

Gajjala, Radhika. 2001. "Studying Feminist E-Spaces: Introducing Transnational/Postcolonial Concerns." In *Technospaces: Inside the New Media*, edited by Sally Munt, 113–26. London: Continuum International.

———. 2004. *Cyber Selves: Feminist Ethnographies of South Asian Women*. Walnut Creek, CA: AltaMira.

Gajjala, Radhika, and Venkataramana Gajjala. 2008. *South Asian Technospaces*. New York: Peter Lang.

Gheytanchi, Elham, and Valentine N. Moghadam. 2014. "Women, Social Protests, and the New Media Activism in the Middle East and North Africa." *International Review of Modern Sociology* 40, no. 1: 1–26.

Gladwell, Malcolm. 2010. "Small Change: Why the Revolution Will Not Be Tweeted." *New Yorker*, Oct. 4. At http://www.newyorker.com/magazine/2010/10/04/small-change-malcolm-gladwell.

Guo, Lei, and Summer Harlow. 2014. "User-Generated Racism: An Analysis of Stereotypes of African Americans, Latinos, and Asians in YouTube Videos." *Howard Journal of Communications* 25, no. 3: 281–302. doi:10.1080/10646175.2014.925413.

Hamdy, Naila, and Ehab H. Gomaa. 2012. "Framing the Egyptian Uprising in Arabic Language Newspapers and Social Media." *Journal of Communication* 62, no. 2: 195–211. doi:10.1111/j.1460-2466.

Harlow, Summer, and Dustin Harp. 2012. "Collective Action on the Web." *Information, Communication, & Society* 15, no. 2: 196–216. doi:10.1080/1369118X.2011.591411.

Howard, Philip N. 2011. *The Digital Origins of Dictatorship and Democracy: Information Technology and Political Islam*. Oxford: Oxford Univ. Press.

Irving, Catherine J., and Leona M. English. 2011. "Community in Cyberspace: Gender, Social Movement Learning, and the Internet." *Adult Education Quarterly* 61, no. 3: 262–78.

Juris, Jeffrey. 2012. "Reflections on Occupy Everywhere: Social Media, Public Space, and the Emerging Logics of Aggregation." *American Ethnologist* 39, no. 2: 259–79.

Khamis, Sahar. 2011. "The Arab 'Feminist' Spring?" *Feminist Studies* 37, no. 3: 692–95.

Khamis, Sahar, and Amel Mili, eds. 2018. *Arab Women's Activism and Socio-political Transformation: Unfinished Gendered Revolutions*. Cham, Switzerland: Springer International.

Khamis, Sahar, and Kathryn Vaughn. 2011. "Cyberactivism in the Egyptian Revolution: How Civic Engagement and Citizen Journalism Tilted the Balance." *Arab Media & Society* 14, no. 3: 1–25.

———. 2012. "'We Are All Khaled Said': The Potentials and Limitations of Cyberactivism in Triggering Public Mobilization and Promoting Political Change." *Journal of Arab & Muslim Media Research* 4, nos. 2–3: 145–63.

————. 2013. "Cyberactivism in the Tunisian and Egyptian Revolutions: Potentials, Limitations, Overlaps, and Divergences." *Journal of African Media Studies* 5, no. 1: 69–86.

Knowles, Jamillah. 2012. "58% of Iranians Use Facebook despite Blocks and Censorship, Study Finds." *TNW*, Nov. 8. At http://thenextweb.com/me/2012/11/08/iranian-online -research-panel-releases-its-latest-study-into-attitudes-and-behaviours-online-inside -iran/.

Lim, Merlyna. 2012. "Clicks, Cabs, and Coffee Houses: Social Media and Oppositional Movements in Egypt, 2004–2011." *Journal of Communication* 62:231–34.

Lotan, Gilad Lotan, Erhardt Graeff, Mike Ananny, Devin Gaffney, Ian Pearce, and danah boyd. 2011. "The Revolutions Were Tweeted: Information Flows during the 2011 Tunisian and Egyptian Revolutions." *International Journal of Communication* 5. At http://ijoc.org/index.php/ijoc/article/view/1246.

Meraz, Sharon, and Zizi Papacharissi. 2013. "Networked Gatekeeping and Networked Framing on #Egypt." *International Journal of Press/Politics* 18, no. 2: 138–66. doi:10.1177/1940161212474472.

Morozov, Evgeny. 2009a. "Foreign Policy: Brave New World of Slacktivism." NPR, May 19. At http://www.npr.org/templates/story/story.php?storyId=104302141.

————. 2009b. "Iran: Downside to the 'Twitter Revolution.'" *Dissent* 56, no. 4: 10–14.

————. 2009c. "Texting toward Utopia: Does the Internet Spread Democracy?" *Boston Review*, Mar. 1. At http://bostonreview.net/evgeny-morozov-texting-toward-utopia -internet-democracy.

————. 2011. *The Net Delusion: The Dark Side of Internet Freedom.* New York: PublicAffairs.

My Stealthy Freedom 1. N.d. At https://www.facebook.com/stealthyfreedom/videos/134 0732662607491/. Accessed Mar. 16, 2016.

My Stealthy Freedom 2. N.d. At https://www.facebook.com/StealthyFreedom/photos/a.85 910222410387.1073741828.858832800797482/1341494252531332/?type=3&permPage =1. Accessed Mar. 16, 2016.

Newsom, Victoria A., and Lara Lengel. 2012. "Arab Women, Social Media, and the Arab Spring: Applying the Framework of Digital Reflexivity to Analyze Gender and Online Activism." *Journal of International Women's Studies* 13:31–45.

Papacharissi, Zizi. 2009. "The Citizen Is the Message: Alternative Modes of Civic Engagement." In *Journalism and Citizenship: New Agendas in Communication*, edited by Zizi Papacharissi, 29–43. New York: Routledge.

————. 2010. *A Private Sphere: Democracy in a Digital Age.* Cambridge: Polity.

Papacharissi, Zizi, and Maria de Fatima Oliveira. 2012. "Affective News and Networked Publics: The Rhythms of News Storytelling on #Egypt." *Journal of Communication* 62, no. 2: 266–82.

Pierce, Tess. 2010. "Singing at the Digital Well: Blogs as Cyberfeminist Sites of Resistance." *Feminist Formations* 22, no. 3: 196–209.

Queen, Mary. 2008. "Transnational Feminist Rhetorics in a Digital World." *College English* 70, no. 5: 471–89.

Radsch, Courtney. 2011. "Re-imagining Cleopatra: Gendering Cyberactivism in Egypt." Paper presented at the Middle East Studies Association (MESA) Annual Conference, Washington, DC, Dec. 1–4.

———. 2012a. "Arabic Twitter Stars Come Face-to-Face in Cairo." *Women's e-News*, Jan. 25. At http://womensenews.org/2012/01/arabic-twitter-stars-come-face-face-in-cairo/.

———. 2012b. "Unveiling the Revolutionaries: Women, Cyberactivism, and the Arab Uprisings." James A. Baker III Institute for Public Policy Research Paper, Rice Univ., May 17. At http://papers.ssrn.com/sol3/papers.cfm?abstract_id=2252556.

Radsch, Courtney C., and Sahar Khamis. 2013. "In Their Own Voice: Technologically Mediated Empowerment and Transformation among Young Arab Women." *Feminist Media Studies* 13, no. 5: 881–90.

Al-Rawi, Ahmed. 2014. "Framing the Online Women's Movements in the Arab World." *Information, Communication, & Society* 17, no. 9: 1147–61. doi:10.1080/1369118X .2014.889190.

Rivetti, Paola. 2017. "Political Activism in Iran: Strategies for Survival, Possibilities for Resistance, and Authoritarianism." *Democratization* 24, no. 6: 1178–94.

———. 2020. *Political Participation in Iran from Khatami to the Green Movement*. Cham, Switzerland: Springer International.

Schradie, Jen. 2012. "The Trend of Class, Race, and Ethnicity in Social Media Inequality: Who Still Can't Afford to Blog?" *Information, Communication, & Society* 15, no. 4: 555–71.

Shirky, Clay. 2009. *Here Comes Everybody: The Power of Organizing without Organizations*. New York: Penguin.

Skalli-Hanna, Loubna H. 2006. "Communicating Gender in the Public Sphere: Women and Information Technologies in the MENA." *Journal of Middle East Women's Studies* 2, no. 2: 35–59.

———. 2010. "New Modes of Communication: Youth, Women, and Web Representations in North Africa." In *Encyclopedia of Women & Islamic Cultures*, edited by Suad Joseph. Leiden, Netherlands: Brill Online. At https://referenceworks.brillonline.com /browse/encyclopedia-of-women-and-islamic-cultures.

Sorour, Karim, and Bidit Dey. 2014. "Energising the Political Movements in Developing Countries: The Role of Social Media." *Capital & Class* 38, no. 3: 508–15.

Sreberny, Annabelle. 2015. "Women's Digital Activism in a Changing Middle East." *International Journal of Middle East Studies* 47, no. 2: 357–61. doi:10.1017/S002074 3815000112.

Stephan, Rita. 2013. "Creating Solidarity in Cyberspace." *Journal of Middle East Women's Studies* 9, no. 1: 81–109.

Tahmasebi-Birgani, Victoria. 2017. "Social Media as a Site of Transformative Politics and Political Dissent: Iranian Women's Online Contestations." In *Iran's Struggles for Social Justice: Economics, Agency, Justice, and Activism*, edited by Peyman Vahabzadeh, 181–98. New York: Palgrave MacMillan.

Taylor, Astra. 2014. *The People's Platform: Taking Back Power and Culture in the Digital Age*. New York: Metropolitan Books.

Tufekci, Zeynep, and Christopher Wilson. 2012. "Social Media and the Decision to Participate in Political Protest: Observations from Tahrir Square." *Journal of Communication* 62, no. 2: 363–79.

Van de Donk, Wim, Brian D. Loader, Paul G. Nixon, and Dieter Rucht. 2004. *Cyberprotest: New Media, Citizens, and Social Movements*. London: Routledge.

Wall, Melissa A. 2007. "Social Movements and Email: Expressions of Online Identity in the Globalization Protests." *New Media & Society* 9, no. 2: 258–77.

Watkins, Sean, Radhika Gajjala, and Yahui Zhang. 2012. "Home of Hope: Voicings, Whiteness, and the Technological Gaze." *Journal of Communication Inquiry* 36, no. 3: 202–21.

Wright, Michelle M. 2005. "Finding a Place in Cyberspace: Black Women, Technology, and Identity." *Frontiers* 26, no. 1: 48–59.

Yahyanejad, Mehdi, and Elham Gheytanchi. 2012. "Social Media, Dissent, and Iran's Green Movement." In *Liberation Technology: Social Media and the Struggle for Democracy*, edited by Larry Diamond and Marc F. Plattner, 139–53. Baltimore, MD: Johns Hopkins Univ. Press.

15

Women's Engagement in the Tunisian Revolution

Nermin Allam

In her dramaturgic account of the Arab Spring, Tawakkul Karman, the Yemeni activist and Nobel laureate, emphasized women's commitment to collective social justice during the episodes of protests that swept the Middle East and North Africa (MENA) in 2010–11. In the early days following the uprisings, Karman was widely described in media and popular accounts as the "mother of the revolution" and came to represent the face of women in the uprisings that led to the toppling of long despotic regimes in Tunisia, Egypt, Yemen, and Libya. In a conversation we had in 2012, Karman stressed the importance and significance of uniting protestors' demands to communicate power and solidarity and warned against the dangers of raising group-specific demands during contention.[1] Her view about what constitutes a "winning" collective-action frame is deeply rooted and ingrained in our modern and present history. In Tunisia, women's engagement in the Jasmine Revolution mirrored this ideal of unity, solidarity, and cohesion. In the early days of the revolution, little was said about women's specific rights, and the women's collective-action frame did not explicitly incorporate demands for women's rights and gender equality.

Studies on collective-action frames examine the strategic interpretations of issues offered by frames that are intended to mobilize people to act and join collective action (Kuumba 2001; McAdam 1988; Noonan 1995). Neil J. Smelser (1971) argues that although grievances are significant elements in originating collective action, they will not lead to participation until they are perceived. Smelser's perspective corresponds to David A. Snow and Robert Benford's views that participants in collective actions are not "structurally guaranteed"; rather, they cluster around master collective-action frames (Benford 1993, 1997; Snow and Benford

---

1. Tawakkul Karman, Yemeni activist and Noble laureate (2011), interview by the author, Edmonton, Canada, Nov. 2012, in Arabic, translated by the author.

1988, 1992; Snow et al. 1986; Snow, Soule, and Kriesi 2004). At the most basic
level, a frame identifies a problem that is social or political in nature, the parties
responsible for causing the problem, and a solution for it (Gamson 1975; Snow and
Benford 1988, 1992). Frames of collective action, in this sense, redefine a status quo
that is perceived as ranging from "unfortunate but perhaps tolerable" to "unjust
and immoral" (Tarrow 1998) and thus mobilize participants to join repertoires
of contention. To attract large participation, frames need to widely resonate with
the different segments of society. Frames are thus often built from old and new
symbols, incorporating new but also old understandings and ideas about politics,
activism, and mobilization.[2]

In this chapter, I focus on women's collective-action frame in the 2010–11
Tunisian revolution that led to the ousting of the country's president, Zine El
Abidine Ben Ali, who had been in that office since 1987. I specifically investigate
women's framing during the early cycles of protests in late 2010 and early 2011.
The overarching objective igniting this study is to understand why gender issues
were largely absent from women's framing of their participation in the early phase
of protests and the impact of this framing on their experience. I argue that the
absence of gender issues from women's framing needs to be situated within the
context of Tunisia's past and present politics. Underpinning this argument is a
view of the women's collective frame as situated within the context of complex
structures and relations in given times and places. In my own work on women's
engagement in the Egyptian uprising in 2011, I investigated the centrality of the
broad citizen frame in framing women's political activism during protests (Allam
2017). Like their Tunisian counterparts, Egyptian women were influenced in their
collective-action framing by their prior relations with the regime and shaped by
the general aura of equality and solidarity that marked the initial phase of the
uprising. This chapter expands and extends this analysis to the case of Tunisia and
thus further refutes misconceptions about women in the Middle East and their
exercise of agency.

Structures, critical scholars hold, both constrain and enable action and change
(Foucault 1980; Giddens 1979). In line with feminists and postcolonial scholars, I
further argue that within the context of the MENA region, the relation between
structure and agency is often ambiguous, multifaceted, and complex (Abu-Lughod
1990; Ahmed 2011; Mahmood 2005; Mohanty 1984). I build on Nancy Fraser's
astute critique and avoid either exaggerating the structural constraints so much

---

2. This discussion is given in greater detail in my book *Women and the Egyptian Revolution*
(2017).

that we "deny women any agency" or portraying women's agency "so glowingly that the power of subordination evaporates" (1992, 17). Rather, the analysis I present here elucidates the power of the structure in shaping women's collective-action frame while emphasizing women's agency in negotiating power hierarchies and gender structures. The chapter thus not only documents women's accounts but also situates their experiences within the broader historical and sociopolitical landscape of Tunisia.

Toward this end, the chapter adopts a twofold approach. In the first section, I interrogate the agenda of women's rights in Tunisia under the two regimes in power before the revolution. My aim is to emphasize the ways in which Ben Ali's policies toward and, before him, Habib Bourguiba's reforms regarding women were developed under what I term a framework of *deliberate civic muddle*. Under this civic muddle, the regime appeared ostensibly sensitive to women's issues and gender equality even while it steadily chipped away at the democratic rights of the Tunisian people. The implication of this civic muddle was distancing the discourse of women's rights from its grassroots base and moving it toward the regime in power. I build on this analysis to highlight the importance of state policies and former relations with the regime in shaping women's collective-action frame, particularly at times of political change. Based on my work on women's engagement in the Egyptian uprising of 2011 as well as on other feminists' contribution to framing theory (Abdulhadi 1998; Allam 2017; Kuumba 2001, 2002; Noonan 1995), I proceed by interrogating the character of women's collective-action frame at the time of the revolution. I argue that female protestors framed their participation in demonstrations in light of their relations to the broader contention at play and conventional politics. As a result, they indeed demanded change, but they also accommodated inherited frames, symbols, and repertoires. I build on this analysis to highlight the resonance of women's collective-action frame at the initial phase of protests and situate it within women's groups' past relations with the Ben Ali regime and women's subjective experiences of solidarity and equality during antiregime demonstrations.

To illuminate women's experience and collective-action frame in the Tunisian revolution, I gathered data from seventeen semistructured interviews with protestors, activists, and nongovernment organization leaders. I conducted the interviews mostly in Arabic between February and March 2016 and translated them into English after that. I conducted most of the personal interviews in Tunis, the capital of Tunisia.[3] In the attempt to empirically investigate how women negotiate

---

3. I interviewed Karman in 2012 as part of my doctoral dissertation project.

new and old symbols in framing their participation in collective action, I analyzed data from the interviews using critical discourse analysis, which entails a close and multilayered reading of participants' accounts.

In this close look at women's engagement in the revolution, women are brought to the center of analysis, and their voices are reclaimed. The analysis contributes to expanding debates on women's participation in national struggles in the MENA region beyond reductionist accounts that view their engagement as misguided or passive. This nuanced narrative recovers women's voices in the writing of Tunisia's modern history and opens up new ways of understanding the Tunisian revolution. There exists an important academic literature that examines the Tunisian revolution from a gender perspective (for example, al-Ali 2012; Charrad and Zarrugh 2014, 2020; Johansson-Nogués 2013; Khalil 2015; Olimat 2013; Sadiki 2014). This chapter builds on and contributes to this body of literature. The study also extends framing theory to new and non-Western episodes of contention and incorporates gender structures in its analysis. It elaborates how women's collective-action frame is both historically and politically embedded and how the effects of contentious politics in an authoritarian context go well beyond political outcomes.

A State of Civic Muddle:
Women and the State in Pre-revolution Tunisia

In the Arab and Muslim world, Tunisia has been recognized as one of the most progressive states when it comes to gender equality. Since the 1950s, Tunisian regimes implemented gender legislations that expanded women' rights in several areas. In this section, I briefly survey some of these key reforms and problematize their functions. My aim is to highlight the ways in which these reforms aimed at modernizing the Tunisian society but without democratizing it. The analysis underscores the effects of state policies and former relations with the regime in shaping women's collective-action frame at times of political change. It also highlights the implication of women's rights discourse prior to the Jasmine Revolution on women's engagement in the revolution.

Bourguiba's reforms and Ben Ali's policies toward women were developed in an authoritarian and antidemocratic framework. This civic muddle was deliberate, I argue, as each regime often used women's rights agenda to appeal to a Western audience and thus to offer "an alibi" (Zlitni and Touati 2012, 46) to evade its human rights violations against the Islamist opposition, whom the regime often portrayed as an antifeminist threat to women's rights. The effect of this state of deliberate civic muddle was the tension between the legal advancement in women's rights and the wider persistent socioeconomic inequality and political oppression in the country.

Advancements in legal equality is evident in the promulgation of the Tunisian Code du statute personnel (Code of Personal Status, CPS) in 1956 and the reforms of the citizenship law in the 1990s. Scholars view these two developments as key in advancing women's rights in Tunisia (Charrad 2001, 2007; Khalil 2014; L. Labidi 2007; Murphy 2003). President Habib Bourguiba introduced the CPS in the mid-1950s at the time of the formation of a national state in the aftermath of independence from French colonial rule. The CPS brought major changes that transformed family laws and expanded women's rights in Tunisia (Charrad 2001; "Code du statut personnel—Tunisie" 1957; Curtiss 1993; "The Tunisian Code of Personal Status" 1957). The most popular aspect of the CPS was the outright abolition of polygamy. On the issue of divorce, the CPS introduced judicial intervention, eliminated the husband's right to repudiate his wife, and allowed women to file for divorce. The code also established the principle of alimony, reformed custody, and protected women's rights to education.

The CPS also took a major step toward reinterpreting shari'a and the Qur'an (Honwana 2013). This reinterpretation, Bourguiba often stressed, did not challenge religion. Rather, it was based on liberal *ijtihad* (independent reasoning) and imbued with the contributions of Taher Haddad,[4] the reformist Islamic scholar.[5] Notwithstanding Bourguiba's effort to link the CPS to the principles of Islam, the code caused an outcry from traditionalists and theologians at home and abroad. Bourguiba, one of my participants recalled, was often described by many Arab leaders and in many Islamic societies as an atheist leader who was leading a nation of atheists because of his secularist policies.[6] Underpinning this statement is the view that Bourguiba's project clashed with religion. Augustin Jomier (2011), however, refutes this view in his analysis of the place of religion in Bourguiba's reform project, which, he argues, was instead a takeover of religion by the state aimed at reducing the power of the ulama and weakening Islamists' opposition.

4. In 1930, Taher Haddad published his infamous book *Amra'tna fi al-shari'a wa al-mogtama'* (Our Woman [*sic*] in the Shari'a and Society), where he criticized the absence of education for girls, condemned polygamy, and called for equal inheritance. His work was based on a reinterpretation of the Qur'an; however, it was highly condemned at the time of its publication.

5. Hela Limame, project coordinator at the Association tunisienne de lutte contre la violence, phone interview by the author, Feb. 2016, originally in Arabic, translated by the author.

6. Interviewee 4, phone interview by the author, Feb. 2016. All numbered interviews were originally conducted in Arabic and then translated into English by the author.

A second important wave of reforms in women's legal status took place in 1993 under President Zine El Abidine Ben Ali. The new reforms changed the conditions for the transmission of Tunisian citizenship, as stated in the Code de nationalité tunisienne (Code of Tunisian Nationality, 1963, amended 1984). Under the new reform, Tunisian women could pass their nationality to children born abroad, regardless of the nationality of the child's father. Unlike in the reforms of 1956, women's groups played a greater role in pushing the new wave of reform (Charrad 2001, 2007). Although women have always been active in the Tunisian society and political landscape, it was only toward the end of the 1980s and the beginning of the 1990s that the women's movement in Tunisia became increasingly active and vocal—but still within the limitations imposed by the regime (Gilman 2007; Khalil 2014; L. Labidi 2007). During this period, a number of women's associations—for example, the Association des femmes tunisiennes pour la recherche sur le développement (Association of Tunisian Women for Research and Development) and the Association tunisienne des femmes démocrates (Tunisian Association of Democratic Women)—were allowed to exist and function in society.

Although the women I interviewed represent a wide range of ideological perspectives, they all equivocally supported the reforms of the 1950s and 1990s. They, however, were astute in pinpointing the regime's political agenda and the strategic function underpinning these reforms as well as the reforms' implications on both the agenda and the function of the women's movement in Tunisia.

Several of my interviewees explained how the advanced legal status of women was instrumental for the construction of the modern national Tunisian state under President Bourguiba.[7] It defined the contours of Bourguiba's nationalist project and placed it in contrast to patriarchal tribal traditions. Mounira Charrad (2009) rightly describes the CPS as part of Bourguiba's reformist political project that aimed at delegitimizing kin groupings, where women often had inferior status to men, rather than as part of a vision of the inherent value of gender equality and women's rights.

Bourguiba's project, I would add, was an attempt to modernize the face of the society without actually reforming or democratizing its institutions. Although my participants often described Bourguiba's reform with a great sense of pride and patriotism, they were quick to acknowledge the authoritarian character of

7. Limame interview, Feb. 2016; Hedia Bel Haj Youssef, documentation officer and Gender Based Violence Programme coordinator, Center of Arab Woman for Training and Research (CAWTAR), phone interview by the author, Mar. 2016, originally in Arabic, translated by the author.

his regime.[8] Indeed, Bourguiba ruled with sweeping powers; under his regime, civil liberties were constricted, media were heavily censored, and opponents were frequently imprisoned (Sassoon 2016). The modernization project Bourguiba carried out in Tunisia was thus distanced or, more accurately, divorced from democracy. Tunisia is not an exception in this regard in either the MENA context or the global context; in Latin America also, modernization projects are often divorced from democratization (Brand 1998; Hatem 1992; Murphy 2003; Noonan 1995; Sadiki 2002).

Under Ben Ali, the agenda of women's rights continued to play an important role in the regime's policies. The regime used reforms in women's rights to polish its image, consolidate its power, and appeal to Western donors. For instance, several scholars argue that Leila Trabelsi, the First Lady of Tunisia in Ben Ali's administration, verbally championed women's causes only to secure a leading role among Arab First Ladies (Brand, Kaki, and Stacher 2011; see also El-Masri 2015). Trabelsi's commitment to women's rights, a number of my participants held, was merely rhetorical.[9] In an article on the First Ladies in MENA, Laurie Brand, Rym Kaki, and Joshua Stacher (2011) reveal how Trabelsi was deeply complicit with the oppressive regime and how her leadership reflected the regime's authoritarian character. Indeed, Trabelsi and her family came to be known as the "Mafia family" in Tunisia in reference to their repression of both women and men activists who exposed the family's corruption.

Ben Ali's regime, several scholars further argue, opened a space for women to mobilize and form civil society associations merely to weaken the Islamists' influence (Gilman 2007; Khalil 2014; L. Labidi 2007; Marks 2013; El-Masri 2015; Murphy 2003; Zlitni and Touati 2012). It mobilized and co-opted women's groups under the banner of defending the CPS in the face of a growing conservative Islamist movement. Given that some members of the Islamist movement have occasionally challenged the code, the regime used the Islamists' stance to portray the whole movement as an antifeminist threat to the CPS code. A similar trend often took place and continues to take place in other MENA societies. In *Seeking Legitimacy: Why Arab Autocracies Adopt Women's Rights* (2019), Aili Mari Tripp eloquently explains why and how autocratic regimes adopted women's rights reforms in Algeria, Morocco, and Tunisia and compares them to their Middle Eastern counterparts. She highlights the symbolic and instrumental functions

8. Interviewees 12, 13, and 14, interviewed by the author, Mar. 2016, Tunis, Tunisia; interviewee 17, interviewed by the author, Mar. 2016, Edmonton, Canada.

9. Interviewees 13, 14, and 17.

of women's rights reforms across different political projects. Autocratic regimes in the Maghreb countries adopted women's rights reform as part of their political strategies to counter extremist Islamist trends in their societies (2019, 24), to distinguish themselves from the Islamist opposition in politics (5), and to portray their societies as modern and thus to appeal to a Western audience.

The instrumentalization of women's rights organizations and the feminist movement had mixed implications for the movement and its grassroots base in Tunisia (al-Kkly 2014; Khalil 2014; L. Labidi 2007; Marks 2013; El-Masri 2015; Murphy 2003). The process, Lilia Labidi (2007) highlights, succeeded in opening a space for women's mobilization and activism, but that space also had strict limits. Among these limitations, Emma C. Murphy (2003) contends, was the absence of effective independent feminist movements through which women could challenge the authoritarian structure of Ben Ali's government (see also Khalil 2014, 2015; Marks 2013). Furthermore, independent feminists who resisted co-optation and exposed human rights violations carried out by the state, such as Khadija Arfaoui, Radhia Nasraoui, and Sihem Bensedrine, faced persecution and imprisonment (K. Labidi 2010; Marks 2013).

The regime's ostensible preferential treatment of state-sponsored feminists, Abdel Salam al-Kkly (2014) further argues in his analysis of women's political engagement in Tunisia, had negative implications in the struggle for women's rights. It contributed to constructing an arbitrary distinction in the eyes of the public between women's struggle for gender equality and the larger population's struggle for political and socioeconomic equality. It is important to reiterate that the regime's preferential treatment of certain feminists was only a facade, lacking the real gender equality that feminist and postcolonial scholars have rightly emphasized to be central in any project for social justice and human rights.

The negative image of women's groups under Ben Ali's regime was further perpetuated, several participants argue, by the "exclusionary"[10] character of some of these groups. In her study of the women's movement in Tunisia, Maria Marks (2013) echoes a similar view. According to her, these organizations failed in gaining a wider constituency, and their work remained limited to legal change. One of my participants, a film director who produced an acclaimed documentary on women's rights in rural Tunisia, emphasized the ways in which these organizations were sometimes distanced from the experiences and needs of poor women and of women from different ideological backgrounds.[11] For instance, she described

10. Interviewee 11, interviewed by the author, Mar. 2016, Tunis, Tunisia.
11. Interviewee 1, Skype interview by the author, Feb. 2016.

how for many decades secular feminists dominated and restricted the discourse of women's rights in these groups. According to her, although these groups did offer services and support to conservative Muslim women, they failed to incorporate these women's religious views and conceptualization of women's rights. That is, the organizations were not often sensitive to women's various modalities of agency, their intersectional positionalities, and their diverse gendered experiences that disrupt the modern/traditional and secular/religious dichotomy.

My point is not to assess the work of these organizations; rather, I aim to draw attention to the historical, structural, and institutional limitations that shape and restrict the discourse of women's rights and the framing of feminist activism in an authoritarian context. The influence of these limitations does not completely cease to exist at moments of upheaval and political openings. In their study of historical and modern movements, Charles Tilly and Sidney Tarrow (2007) observe that although opportunities signaled to "some" are also available to "many," the different sectors within movements experience opportunities differently (see also McAdam, Tarrow, and Tilly 2001; Tarrow 1998, 77; Tilly 1978). Participants in the same movement experience opportunities differently based on a number of factors, salient among which is their prior relations with the regime in question. In the context of Tunisia, the close association between women's rights and the regime, scholars demonstrate, had negative implications for women's issues at the time of regime change and political transformation (Khalil 2014; Marks 2013).

The absence of complete autonomy for feminist groups and the place of gender in nationalist-related projects in Tunisia had an important influence on women's collective-action frame. For women, participating in the revolution was conditioned on rejecting and distancing themselves from the regime's projects and agendas—including its women's rights discourse. In the early phase of the Tunisian revolution, women thus participated and framed their demands as citizens of Tunisia rather than as women with gender-specific demands.

Women's Collective-Action Frame

A collective-action frame defines the motivations, grievances, and demands of the movement's members as well as their identity (Gamson 1975; Givan, Roberts, and Soule 2010; Snow and Benford 1988, 1992). A frame, David Snow and Robert Benford describe, is an "interpretive schemata" that simplifies and condenses "the world out there by selectively punctuating and encoding objects, situations, events, experiences, and sequences of actions within one's present or past environment" (1992, 137). Frames thus mobilize participation in collective action by providing the meaning, rationale, and incentive for action and activism.

At times of collective action, the citizen frame is among the popular frames adopted by different groups, including women, across different societies and particularly in the Middle East (Allam 2017). During my interviews, female protestors and activists described how they participated as the *sha'b*, the citizens/people, of Tunisia rather than as the women of Tunisia.[12] The category of *sha'b*, the Tunisian scholar Nadia Marzouki (2011) explains, was part and parcel of the collective cri de coeur and central to the success of the mobilization. That is not to say that the category of the *sha'b* is irreconcilable with the category of women. Rather, it was the reference point for many groups—including women—in the revolution because it signified inclusiveness and consensus among participants.

Women demonstrated, chanted the revolution's slogan, "Shogl, hurriya, wa-karama wataniyah" (Bread, freedom, and national dignity), and called for Ben Ali to *dégagé* (leave). That is, women called for the rights of the society as a whole; they did not restrict themselves to gender-specific demands. This long-standing commitment to the rights of the "society as a whole" (Cooke 1995, 21, quoted in Khalil 2014, 188) is the subject of several studies on women's engagement in the Tunisian revolution (Honwana 2013; Khalil 2014; Tchaïcha and Arfaoui 2012; Zlitni and Touati 2012). In her study of women's participation in the revolution and the transitional period, Andrea Khalil emphasizes the prevalence of this sentiment among participants. Building on her interviews with female protestors, she describes how participants often stressed that their activism was motivated by a concern for the freedom of all citizens and not just of women (2014, 188–89). This sentiment, she adds, was shared by women from both secularist and religious grounds (188).

Women's collective-action frame, I argue, thus aligned with the revolution's master frame of citizenship, given the latter's broad and inclusive character in terms of the number of themes and ideas incorporated and articulated in it. Social movement scholars define a "master frame" as a generic type of collective-action frame that is wider in scope and influence (Snow and Benford 1992; see also Oliver and Johnston 2000). In Tunisia, the frame was sufficiently inclusive that different groups—including women—could relate to it and adopt it.

Indeed, during my interviews, participants often emphasized the ways in which the citizen frame resonated with their personal, everyday experiences as Tunisian youth.[13] They explained how youth, regardless of their gender, were among the primarily marginalized groups under Ben Ali. "We are a destitute

---

12. Interviewees 12, 13, and 14.

13. Interviewee 3, phone interview by the author, Feb. 2016; interviewee 4; interviewees 6 and 8, phone interviews by the author, Mar. 2016; interviewees 11, 13, and 14.

generation,"[14] one of my participants described. Although their parents' generation suffered from political oppression, she explained, the young generation under Ben Ali suffered from political, economic, *and* intellectual impoverishment.

Ben Ali's regime deliberately maintained a flawed educational system, several of my participants argued, to maintain its grip on power and weaken any potential opposition.[15] As one of my participants described, it was an effective strategy "to circumscribe potential, to-be political activist."[16] Flawed education resulted in what several of my participants called "an intellectual desertification" among youth.[17] The reference here is to the absence of quality education for and critical thinking among youth. Despite the regime's policies attempt to sustain a sort of "political and social coma,"[18] Tunisians joined the revolution and challenged the state's oppressive and corrupt policies that created mass unemployment, criminalization of opposition and dissent, disparities between Tunisia's coastal and interior regions, and a stagnant social and political situation (Guessoumi and Judy 2012; Honwana 2013; Sadiki 2014).

Tunisian citizens, both men and women, suffered from the implications of these policies; they shared the same grievances and thus gathered around the same demand: "Ash-sha'b yurid isqat an-nizam" (The people want the fall of the regime). That is not to say that women did not have gender-specific grievances under the Ben Ali regime, but as social movement scholars attest, participants in a social movement learn which values and demands divide them as well as what unites them and choose to emphasize the latter and gloss over the former (Tarrow 1998, 122). This approach ensures that the movement's framing will resonate with the diverse experiences and grievances of the wider population.

The absence of gender from women's framing of their demands in the Tunisian revolution, I hold, was not a sign of an absent or passive (feminist) agency. It was a function of frame resonance. Participants in social movements seek to adopt a highly resonant frame that can be interpreted broadly so as to garner wider support and participation (Gamson 1995, 90; Hunt, Benford, and Snow 1992; Snow and Benford 1988). During the initial phase of the Tunisian uprising, different participants, including Tunisian women, framed their participation around their citizenship to gain attention and ultimately to secure the support of bystanders. As I have argued elsewhere, this strategy can limit the establishment of feminist

---

14. Interviewee 11.

15. Interviewee 11; interviewee 15, interviewed by the author, Mar. 2016, Tunis, Tunisia.

16. Interviewee 13.

17. Interviewees 11, 13, and 17.

18. Interviewee 5, phone interview by the author, Feb. 2016.

networks and consciousness (see Allam 2017). It is, however, popular in framing women's political participation in the Middle East and beyond because of its ability to resonate with wider masses and diverse groups.

Frame resonance is particularly significant, I hold, in the absence of leadership. In the absence of leadership in the Tunisian revolution, the citizen frame created a repertoire of interpretations, cross-movement networking, and unity among different groups. Scholars within the social movement tradition show that frames built around strong ties do much of the work that would normally fall to organizations (McAdam, Tarrow, and Tilly 2001; Tarrow 1998; Tilly 1997). This is particularly important in the context of authoritarian systems, where, Valerie Bunce (1991) elaborates, the greatest strength of rather weak movements is that they have a great deal in common.

Frame resonance is tied not only to a particular sociohistorical context but also to the immediate context of collective action and to the participants' subjective experience of it (Allam 2017). Frame analysts describe framing as an emergent and context-specific social process (Gamson 1995, 90; McAdam, McCarthy, and Zald 1996, 6; Snow and Benford 1988, 199). It is guided by the larger political culture or public discourse within which contention develops (Gamson 1988, 221–22, and 1992). Framing theorists further maintain that the construction of frames in collective action is "situationally sensitive" (Benford and Hunt 1992; Gamson 1995, 90; Klandermans and Staggenborg 2002; McAdam, McCarthy, and Zald 1996, 6; Snow and Benford 1988; Tarrow 1992, 190–91). That is, it is "keyed to interactive processes, and occurs in a recursive relationship with the dynamics of collective action" and the larger cycles of protest (Steinberg 1998, 846; see also Hunt, Benford, and Snow 1994, 191–92 as well as Klandermans and Staggenborg 2002).[19]

The widespread solidarity and equality that characterized the interactions among participants in the Jasmine Revolution, I argue, explain in part why women actively utilized the citizen frame in defining their participation. Sentiments of equality, solidarity, and oneness that often mark initial phases of protests across different societies, I argue, influence participants' framing of their demands. The public space during the Tunisian revolution, one of my participants emphasized, transformed into "an open space for all."[20] "All were welcome in the demonstrations,"[21] a member of the queer community recounted, emphasizing how even members of the LGBTQ+ community felt safe participating in the

19. For further discussion, please see my detailed analysis in Allam 2017.
20. Interviewee 4.
21. Interviewee 3.

revolution. The same sentiment was often echoed in reports and media coverage of women's engagement, which emphasized the absence of social differences and the prevalence of solidarity across protestors (Centre for Research, Studies, Documentation, and Information on Women 2013; *France 24* 2012; see also Honwana 2013 and Khalil 2014).

In a report titled *Tonisiates* (Tunisian Women) published by the Centre for Research, Studies, Documentation, and Information on Women (CREDIF), participants echoed this sentiment, emphasizing the spirit of solidarity that marked the twenty-eight days of the revolution. Through researching and documenting the role of women in Tunisian society and politics, CREDIF aims to promote gender-sensitive approaches to economic and political development in the country. Among the projects it has carried out is a report that would bring together women's stories and accounts of the Jasmine Revolution and the transitional period. Female protestors interviewed as part of this archival project describe the early antigovernment demonstrations, in contrast to the postrevolution period (CREDIF 2013). In my study of women's experiences in the January 25 uprising in Egypt in 2011, participants described a similar experience, wherein differences, including gender differences, seemed suspended during the eighteen-day uprising (Allam 2017).

The powerful sentiment of equality experienced among the crowds has been the subject of sociological and psychological research. In his book *Crowds and Power* (1960), Elias Canetti challenges the early representations of a crowd by theorists Gustave Le Bon, Gabriel Tarde, and others as inherently irrational and dangerous. Canetti unpacks the dynamics of the crowd and emphasizes instead that in a crowd "all are equal; no distinctions count, not even that of sex" (15). He adds that equality within a crowd is

> absolute and indisputable and never questioned by the crowd itself. It is of fundamental importance and one might even define a crowd as a state of absolute equality. A head is a head, an arm is an arm, and differences between individual heads and arms are irrelevant. It is for the sake of this equality that people become a crowd and they need to overlook anything which might detract from it. All demands for justice and all theories of equality ultimately derive their energy from the actual experience of equality familiar to anyone who has been part of a crowd. (29)

Female protestors who participated among the crowds in the Tunisian revolution often recount how they experienced this equality. These women's subjective experience of solidarity and equality, I argue, contributed to framing their participation around their identity as Tunisian. The absence of gender issues from their framing of their participation is thus not a sign of coercion or of the absence of agency. Several of my female participants contended that they did not think that they were giving up their demands and rights as women.[22] The unity over demands is not to be understood as an abandonment of specific demands.

The emphasis on the larger community, shared experiences, and common grievances, I argue, was central for constructing a resonant frame in the Tunisian revolution. Constructing a resonant frame is significant to communicate power and encourage the mobilization of different groups (Tarrow 1998, 2012; Tilly 1997). The frame resonated with different groups—including women—given their past experiences with the regime in addition to their subjective experiences of equality and solidarity during the twenty-eight-day revolution. My point is that in the case of the Tunisian revolution, women's collective-action frame was the product of deliberate and organic processes. Participants aimed to construct a resonant frame at the intersection of different groups' demands and the wider cultural disposition in order to garner support and encourage broad mobilization (Tarrow 1998). However, as the situation changed, and gender inequalities resurfaced, women put forward gender-equality demands at the center of their framing. For example, they fiercely and successfully fought against a controversial article in the draft of the new Constitution in 2012 that defined women as "complementary" rather than equal to men. In response, women protested in large numbers, voicing their demands for gender equality and chanting, "Women are complete, not complements" (Ghacibeh 2012, quoted in Charrad and Zarrugh 2020, 85).

In the period immediately following the revolution, Soukeina Bouraoui, the executive director of the Center of Arab Women for Training and Research, described how the number of women's rights groups and organizations tremendously increased across Tunisia.[23] These organizations disrupted the secular/religious dichotomy as their members came from diverse ideological backgrounds. Their greatest success was to mobilize women of all backgrounds to defend their interests, Bouraoui stressed. Indeed, women's groups succeeded in curtailing attempts to weaken the principles of human rights in the new Tunisian Constitution, as is evident in the various drafts that have surfaced since 2011 (Marks 2013; El-Masri 2015).

The presence of these organizations, explained Khadija Arfaoui, a feminist researcher and former member of the Tunisian Association of Democratic Women, attests that women's rights were present in the revolutionary momentum,

22. Interviewees 8, 11, 12, and 13.

23. Soukeina Bouraoui, executive director of CAWTAR, interviewed by the author, Mar. 2016, Tunis, Tunisia, originally in Arabic, translated by the author.

even if they were absent at the revolutionary moment.[24] My conversation with Dr. Arfaoui as well as with the other participants in my fieldwork left me thinking about revolutionary moments and revolutionary momentums. I began to question the differences between the two concepts, the two points of time, and the implications of looking at women's rights at each. I am not suggesting here that women were less feminist or less agentic during the twenty-eight-day demonstrations than they were in the postrevolutionary period. My point is that the women's collective-action frame cannot be analyzed in isolation; it should be understood in relation to the complex context of broader structures in given moments, situations, and places.

Conclusion

Feminist scholars have long emphasized the importance of reclaiming women's voices and documenting their experiences during political struggles (Khalil 2015; Khamis and Mili 2018; Olimat 2013; Stephan and Charrad 2020; among others). Aware that the omission of women's voices from history has implications for their present struggles, in this chapter I analyzed women's engagement during the Tunisian revolution of 2010–11. The analysis captured women's experience and situated their collective-action frame within the historical, political, and socioeconomic flows and trajectories in Tunisia.

Building on framing theory, I interrogated the character of Tunisian women's collective-action frame at the time of the revolution to draw linkage between past and present politics in Tunisia. Women's activism, I argued, does not occur in a vacuum; it needs to be examined in relation to the governing processes, regime policies, gender institutions, and symbols of a particular society. These factors affect women's ability to participate in politics and in activism as well as shape women's interests at the time of contention and regime change. In the case of Tunisia, women subscribed to the citizen frame, a frame that is popular during times of contentions, because this framing resonated with both women's and other groups' past experiences with the regime. The citizen frame, I argued, created a repertoire of interpretations, cross-movement networking, and unity among different groups in the Tunisian revolution.

The absence of gender issues from women's framing of their participation is thus not a sign of coercion, nor does it reflect the absence of agency. Their framing

---

24. Khadija Arfaoui, feminist researcher and former member of the Tunisian Association of Democratic Women, Skype interview by the author, Mar. 2016, originally in Arabic, translated by the author.

strategy attempted to secure frame resonance across a wider audience. It was also a function of women's groups' relations with the prior regimes and women's subjective experiences of equality and solidarity during the twenty-eight days of the revolution. The analysis presented in this chapter encourages us to avoid viewing women's interests, strategies, and identities as constant; rather, they shift and change at the intersection of and in response to conventional and contentious politics. A situated analysis promises to broaden our understandings of women's interests and mobilization under different political and historical trajectories.

References

Abdulhadi, Rabab. 1998. "The Palestinian Women's Autonomous Movement: Emergence, Dynamics, and Challenges." *Gender and Society* 12, no. 6: 649–73.

Abu-Lughod, Lila. 1990. "The Romance of Resistance: Tracing Transformations of Power through Bedouin Women." *American Ethnologist* 17, no. 1: 41–55.

Ahmed, Leila. 2011. *A Quiet Revolution: The Veil's Resurgence, from the Middle East to America.* New Haven, CT: Yale Univ. Press.

Al-Ali, Nadje. 2012. "Gendering the Arab Spring." *Middle East Journal of Culture & Communication* 5, no. 1: 26–31. doi:10.1163/187398612X624346.

Allam, Nermin. 2017. *Women and the Egyptian Revolution: Engagement and Activism during the 2011 Arab Uprisings.* Cambridge: Cambridge Univ. Press.

Benford, Robert D. 1993. "'You Could Be the Hundredth Monkey': Collective Action Frames and Vocabularies of Motive within the Nuclear Disarmament Movement." *Sociological Quarterly* 34, no. 2: 195–216.

———. 1997. "An Insider's Critique of the Social Movement Framing Perspective." *Sociological Inquiry* 67, no. 4: 409–30.

Benford, Robert D., and Scott A. Hunt. 1992. "Dramaturgy and Social Movements: The Social Construction and Communication of Power." *Sociological Inquiry* 62, no. 1: 36–55.

Brand, Laurie A. 1998. *Women, the State, and Political Liberalization: Middle Eastern and North African Experiences.* New York: Columbia Univ. Press.

Brand, Laurie A., Rym Kaki, and Joshua Stacher. 2011. "First Ladies as Focal Points for Discontent." *Foreign Policy,* Feb. 16. At https://foreignpolicy.com/2011/02/16/first-ladies-as-focal-points-for-discontent/.

Bunce, Valerie. 1991. "Democracy, Stalinism, and the Management of Uncertainty." In *Democracy and Political Transformation: Theories and East-Central European Realities,* edited by Gyorgy Szoboszlai, 138–64. Budapest: Hungarian Political Science Association.

Canetti, Elias. 1960. *Crowds and Power.* Translated by Carol Stewart. New York: Seabury.

Centre for Research, Studies, Documentation, and Information on Women (CREDIF). 2013. *Tonisiates* (Tunisian women). Tunis, Tunisia: CREDIF.

Charrad, Mounira. 2001. *States and Women's Rights: The Making of Postcolonial Tunisia, Algeria, and Morocco.* Berkeley: Univ. of California Press.

———. 2007. "Tunisia at the Forefront of the Arab World: Two Waves of Gender Legislation." *Washington & Lee Law Review* 64, no. 4: 1513–27.

———. 2009. "Kinship, Islam, or Oil: Culprits of Gender Inequality?" *Politics & Gender* 5, no. 4: 546–53. doi:10.1017/S1743923X09990353.

Charrad, Mounira M., and Amina Zarrugh. 2014. "Equal or Complementary? Women in the New Tunisian Constitution after the Arab Spring." *Journal of North African Studies* 19, no. 2: 230–43. doi:10.1080/13629387.2013.857276.

———. 2020. "'Women Are Complete, Not Complements': Terminology in the Writing of the New Constitution of Tunisia." In *Women Rising: In and beyond the Arab Spring*, edited by Rita Stephan and Mounira M. Charrad, 85–95. New York: New York Univ. Press.

"Code de nationalité tunisienne." 1963. At http://www.e-justice.tn/fileadmin/fichiers_site_francais/codes_juridiques/Code_de_la_nationalite_tunisienne.pdf.

"Code du statut personnel—Tunisie." 1957. At http://www.jurisitetunisie.com/tunisie/codes/csp/Csp1010.htm.

Cooke, Miriam. 1995. "Arab Women Arab Wars." *Cultural Critique*, no. 29: 5–29.

Curtiss, Richard H. 1993. "Women's Rights: An Affair of State for Tunisia." *Washington Report on Middle East Affairs*, Sept.–Oct., 33–37.

Foucault, Michel. 1980. *Power/Knowledge: Selected Interviews and Other Writings, 1972–1977.* Translated by Colin Gordon. New York: Vintage.

France 24. 2012. "The Unfinished Revolution of Tunisia's Women." Mar. 7. At http://www.france24.com/en/20120307-tunisia-unfinished-revolution-international-women-day-rights-islamist.

Fraser, Nancy. 1992. Introduction to *Revaluing French Feminism: Critical Essays on Difference, Agency, and Culture*, edited by Nancy Fraser and Sandra Lee Bartky, 1–17. Bloomington: Indiana Univ. Press.

Gamson, William A. 1975. *The Strategy of Social Protest.* Homewood, IL: Dorsey Press.

———. 1988. "Political Discourse and Collective Action." In *From Structure to Action: Comparing Social Movement Research across Cultures*, edited by Bert Klandermans and Hanspeter Kriesi, 219–44. Greenwich, CT: JAI Press.

———. 1992. "The Social Psychology of Collective Action." In *Frontiers in Social Movement Theory*, edited by Aldon D. Morris and Carol McClurg Mueller, 53–76. New Haven, CT: Yale Univ. Press.

———. 1995. "Constructing Social Protest." In *Social Movements and Culture*, edited by Hank Johnston and Bert Klandermans, 85–106. Minneapolis: Univ. of Minnesota Press.

Ghacibeh, Greta. 2012. "Tunisian Town Hall on Women's Rights." *American Abroad Media*, Sept. 6. At http://www.americaabroadmedia.org.

Giddens, Anthony. 1979. *Central Problems in Social Theory: Action, Structure, and Contradiction in Social Analysis.* London: Macmillan.

Gilman, Sarah E. 2007. "Feminist Organizing in Tunisia: Negotiating Transnational Linkages and the State." In *From Patriarchy to Empowerment: Women's Participation, Movements, and Rights in the Middle East, North Africa, and South Asia*, edited by Valentine M. Mogahdam, 97–119. Syracuse, NY: Syracuse Univ. Press.

Givan, Rebecca Kolins, Kenneth M. Roberts, and Sarah Anne Soule. 2010. *The Diffusion of Social Movements: Actors, Mechanisms, and Political Effects.* Cambridge: Cambridge Univ. Press.

Guessoumi, Mouldi, and R. A. Judy. 2012. "The Grammars of the Tunisian Revolution." *boundary 2* 39, no. 1: 17–42. doi:10.1215/01903659-1506227.

Hatem, Mervat F. 1992. "Economic and Political Liberation in Egypt and the Demise of State Feminism." *International Journal of Middle East Studies* 24, no. 2: 231–51.

Honwana, Alcinda. 2013. *Youth and Revolution in Tunisia.* London: Zed Books.

Hunt, Scott A., Robert D. Benford, and David A. Snow. 1994. "Identity Fields: Framing Processes and the Social Construction of Movement Identities." In *New Social Movements: From Ideology to Identity*, edited by Enrique Laraña, Hank Johnston, and Joseph R. Gusfield, 185–208. Philadelphia: Temple Univ. Press.

Johansson-Nogués, Elisabeth. 2013. "Gendering the Arab Spring? Rights and (In)Security of Tunisian, Egyptian, and Libyan Women." *Security Dialogue* 44, nos. 5–6: 393–409. doi:10.1177/0967010613499784.

Jomier, Augustin. 2011. "Secularism and State Feminism: Tunisia's Smoke and Mirrors." Translated by John Zvesper. *Books and Ideas*, Nov. 29. At http://www.booksandideas.net/Secularism-and-State-Feminism.html.

Khalil, Andrea. 2014. "Tunisia's Women: Partners in Revolution." *Journal of North African Studies* 19, no. 2: 186–99. doi:10.1080/13629387.2013.870424.

———. 2015. *Gender, Women, and the Arab Spring.* London: Routledge.

Khamis, Sahar, and Amel Mili, eds. 2018. *Arab Women's Activism and Socio-political Transformation: Unfinished Gendered Revolutions.* Cham, Switzerland: Springer Nature for Palgrave Macmillan.

Al-Kkly, Abdel Salam. 2014. "Al Mara' al Tunisia kabl al-sorah wa-ba'daha" (Tunisian women before and after the revolution). *Astrolabe*, n.d. Formerly at http://bit.ly/1pKEKyJ.

Klandermans, Bert, and Suzanne Staggenborg, eds. 2002. *Methods of Social Movement Research.* Minneapolis: Univ. of Minnesota Press.

Kuumba, M. Bahati. 2001. *Gender and Social Movements.* Lanham, MD: AltaMira Press.

———. 2002. "'You've Struck a Rock': Comparing Gender, Social Movements, and Transformation in the United States and South Africa." *Gender and Society* 16, no. 4: 504–23.

Labidi, Kamel. 2010. "Tunisia Is Backtracking on Women's Rights." *Guardian*, Aug. 25. At http://www.theguardian.com/commentisfree/libertycentral/2010/aug/25/tunisia-backtracking-womens-rights.

Labidi, Lilia. 2007. "The Nature of Transnational Alliances in Women's Associations in the Maghreb: The Case of AFTURD and ATFD in Tunisia." *Journal of Middle East Women's Studies* 3, no. 1: 6–34. doi:10.2979/mew.2007.3.1.6.

Mahmood, Saba. 2005. *Politics of Piety: The Islamic Revival and the Feminist Subject.* Princeton, NJ: Princeton Univ. Press.

Marks, Monica. 2013. "Women's Rights before and after the Revolution." In *The Making of the Tunisian Revolution: Contexts, Architects, Prospects*, edited by Nouri Gana, 224–51. Edinburgh: Edinburgh Univ. Press.

Marzouki, Nadia. 2011. "From People to Citizens in Tunisia." *Middle East Report* 259 (Summer). At https://merip.org/2011/06/from-people-to-citizens-in-tunisia/.

El-Masri, Samar. 2015. "Tunisian Women at a Crossroads: Co-optation or Autonomy?" *Middle East Policy* 22, no. 2: 125–44. doi:10.1111/mepo.12133.

McAdam, Doug. 1988. *Freedom Summer.* New York: Oxford Univ. Press.

McAdam, Doug, John D. McCarthy, and Mayer N. Zald. 1996. *Comparative Perspectives on Social Movements: Political Opportunities, Mobilizing Structures, and Cultural Framings.* Cambridge: Cambridge Univ. Press.

McAdam, Doug, Sidney G. Tarrow, and Charles Tilly. 2001. *Dynamics of Contention.* Cambridge: Cambridge Univ. Press.

Mohanty, Chandra Talpade. 1984. "Under Western Eyes: Feminist Scholarship and Colonial Discourses." *boundary 2* 12–13, no. 3: 333–58.

Murphy, Emma C. 2003. "Women in Tunisia: Between State Feminism and Economic Reform." In *Women and Globalization in the Arab Middle East: Gender, Economy, and Society*, edited by Eleanor Abdella Doumato and Marsha Pripstein Posusney, 169–94. Boulder, CO: Lynne Rienner.

Noonan, Rita K. 1995. "Women against the State: Political Opportunities and Collective Action Frames in Chile's Transition to Democracy." *Sociological Forum* 10, no. 1: 81–111.

Olimat, Muhamad. 2013. *Arab Spring and Arab Women.* London: Routledge.

Oliver, Pamela E., and Hank Johnston. 2000. "What a Good Idea! Ideologies and Frames in Social Movement Research." *Mobilization* 5, no. 1: 37–54.

Sadiki, Larbi. 2002. "Bin Ali's Tunisia: Democracy by Non-democratic Means." *British Journal of Middle Eastern Studies* 29, no. 1: 57–78. doi:10.1080/13530190220124061.

———, ed. 2014. *Routledge Handbook of the Arab Spring: Rethinking Democratization.* London: Routledge.

Sassoon, Joseph. 2016. *Anatomy of Authoritarianism in the Arab Republics.* Cambridge: Cambridge Univ. Press.

Smelser, Neil J. 1971. *Theory of Collective Behavior.* New York: Free Press.

Snow, David A., and Robert D. Benford. 1988. "Ideology, Frame Resonance, and Participant Mobilization." *International Social Movement Research* 1, no. 1: 197–217.

———. 1992. "Masters Frame and Cycles of Protest." In *Frontiers in Social Movement Theory*, edited by Aldon D. Morris and Carol McClurg Mueller, 133–56. New Haven, CT: Yale Univ. Press.

Snow, David A., E. Burke Rochford, Steven K. Worden, and Robert D. Benford. 1986. "Frame Alignment Processes, Micromobilization, and Movement Participation." *American Sociological Review* 51, no. 4: 464–81. doi:10.2307/2095581.

Snow, David A., Sarah A. Soule, and Hanspeter Kriesi, eds. 2004. *The Blackwell Companion to Social Movements*. Oxford: Wiley-Blackwell.

Steinberg, Marc W. 1998. "Tilting the Frame: Considerations on Collective Action Framing from a Discursive Turn." *Theory and Society* 27, no. 6: 845–72.

Stephan, Rita, and Mounira M. Charrad, eds. 2020. *Women Rising: In and beyond the Arab Spring*. New York: New York Univ. Press.

Tarrow, Sidney G. 1992. "Mentalities, Political Cultures, and Collective Action Frames: Constructing Meaning through Action." In *Frontiers in Social Movement Theory*, edited by Aldon D. Morris and Carol McClurg Mueller, 174–202. New Haven, CT: Yale Univ. Press.

———. 1998. *Power in Movement: Social Movements and Contentious Politics*. Cambridge: Cambridge Univ. Press.

———. 2012. *Strangers at the Gates: Movements and States in Contentious Politics*. Cambridge: Cambridge Univ. Press.

Tchaïcha, Jane D., and Khedija Arfaoui. 2012. "Tunisian Women in the Twenty-First Century: Past Achievements and Present Uncertainties in the Wake of the Jasmine Revolution." *Journal of North African Studies* 17, no. 2: 215–38.

Tilly, Charles. 1978. *From Mobilization to Revolution*. New York: Random House.

———. 1997. "Parliamentarization of Popular Contention in Great Britain, 1758–1834." *Theory and Society* 26, nos. 2–3: 245–73.

Tilly, Charles, and Sidney G. Tarrow. 2007. *Contentious Politics*. Boulder, CO: Paradigm.

Tripp, Aili Mari. 2019. *Seeking Legitimacy: Why Arab Autocracies Adopt Women's Rights*. Cambridge: Cambridge Univ. Press.

"The Tunisian Code of Personal Status (Majallat al-Ahw al al-Shakhsiy Ah)." 1957. Translated by George N. Sfeir. *Middle East Journal* 11, no. 3: 309–18.

Zlitni, Sami, and Zeineb Touati. 2012. "Social Networks and Women's Mobilization in Tunisia." *Journal of International Women's Studies* 13, no. 5: 46–58.

16

The Egyptian Uprising and Sexual Violence

Mark Muhannad Ayyash

In his work on the Arab Spring and the question of postcoloniality, Hamid Dabashi (2012) argues that the Egyptian uprising and the Arab Spring in general signal the beginning of the end for postcoloniality as a historic trauma, a system and regime of authoritarian postcolonial rule that never challenged the colonial system of power but simply built on and exacerbated it. Dabashi does not downplay the entrenchment and persistence of postcolonial authoritarian rule; he rather points out that the uprising, in its demand not just to overthrow Hosni Mubarak but to overthrow the regime, changed the language of politics in the region. In their actions and words, the people of the region were creating a new public, both conceptually and spatially, and reshaping all political and social relations in the process. Race, class, and gender relations, for example, cannot escape the effects of this new public space, this new language that treats these differences not as fixed and separate positions speaking to one another across an abyss but rather as relational points that are discovering the intricate complexities of their connectivity (Dabashi 2012, 171–202).

In this chapter, I focus on the *persistence* of postcoloniality and how postcolonial power countered the uprising's efforts to reimagine and transform the structure of the social-political relationship. I argue that the main difficulty of the Egyptian uprising—what remains unfinished in its revolutionary project and potential—is that the movement never managed to make central the question of the sexual contract during the revolutionary moment. The authoritarian military regime was able to exploit this failure and through it to reentrench its postcolonial power.

My understanding of the sexual contract stems from the work of Veena Das (2007). In her discussion on the figure of the "abducted woman" during the partition of India in 1947, Das shows how state formation was founded on a story of abduction and recovery of women during the violence of the partition. She argues that a social contract in which men formed the political sphere had as its counter-part a sexual contract through which women were forced into the domestic sphere, where the "right" kind of men (i.e., "protectors of women from lustful men") would be produced for the political sphere (19–22, 33). The figure of the abducted woman emerged in nationalist state discourse as constitutive of a sexual contract that then allowed for the institution of a masculine social contract: both contracts were part of the state's inaugural moment (Das 2007, 179). Das's theoretical artic-ulation of the relationship between the social (social roles, norms, beliefs, civil organizations, and so on), and the political (government, political parties, police, military, the judiciary, and so on) in the state's inauguration opens the analysis to the underlying structure that forms this relationship and posits the social and the political as two separate and even oppositional spheres. The underlying sexual contract ascribes gender roles to each sphere, prohibiting women from the politi-cal and restricting their roles in the social, which serves to maintain the separation of the social and the political. For Das, the social-political order certainly hides this underlying structure, even from itself (particularly through the discourse of "protecting women from lustful men"), which is all the more reason why social scientists should focus on the formation and operation of the sexual contract in their study of the postcolonial state's inauguration or, as in the case of Egypt, its reinauguration or reentrenchment.

It was through sexual violence and the "virginity tests" that the Egyptian mil-itary regime was able to (re)assert a sexual contract and its postcolonial authori-tarian power in response to the uprising, which highlights that the persistence of postcoloniality is perhaps secured on the difficulty of destroying the sexual con-tract. This sexual contract has long served in Egypt to secure and maintain the gendered division of the social and the political. As Jihan Zakarriya puts it, "Suc-cessive patriarchal political systems in Egypt sustain and practice gender-based violence and sexual prejudices against women as a means of fostering their polit-ical gains and the socio-economic hierarchy" (2014, 47). Crucially, the women's struggle in Egypt has revealed this sexual contract as colonial and neocolonial in its foundation. In their resistance to British colonialism at the beginning of the twentieth century, "revolutionaries and social leaders considered that any social or political reform has to be accompanied by a systematic restructuring of women's conditions on both the social and the political levels" (Moussawi and Koujok 2019, 43). Ever since then, the struggle for women's social and political rights has had a continuing presence in all struggles against political repression and authoritarian regimes in Egypt and across the Middle East and North Africa (MENA) (Mous-sawi and Koujok 2019). Certainly, there are important shifts and transformations in the framings, techniques, and positionalities of the women's struggle throughout its long history, but the point I want to emphasize here is that the struggle has always understood the separation between the social and the political as part and parcel of the colonial project, and therefore revolutionaries sought to move across the two spheres and reconnect them in their actions and framings for social and political change.

As the work of the famous Egyptian writer and activist Nawal El Saadawi shows, the links between colonial history, imperialism (or neocolonialism), patriarchy, economic exploitation in modern colonial global capitalism, and religious fundamentalisms (across religions) must always be foregrounded (El Saadawi 2005, 21–23; see also Jilani 2021). Against these obstacles, women's struggles throughout their history in Egypt have understood the critical significance of unity, of a radical transformation of both social and political spheres, and, indeed, of how we understand the interconnectedness and interdependency of the social-political relationship (El Saadawi 1993). This element of the women's struggle in Egypt was very much operative in the Egyptian uprising.

In this chapter, then, gender relations and the sexual contract are not theorized or understood as just one issue among many others that the uprising rearticulated, highlighted, and/or advanced: indeed, "gender issues took center stage in the sociopolitical transformations and debates that arose in the context of the Arab Spring uprisings" (Khamis and Mili 2018b, 2). Moreover, this center staging occurred across the social-political divide as revolutionaries "were determined to merge the struggle for equal citizenship and full participation in the political arena with that for greater gender equality in the social arena" (Khamis and Mili 2018b, 3). Therefore, I argue that gender-power relations point toward the core problem of postcoloniality and the major difficulty the uprising faced: overcoming a decisive separation between the social and the political that was introduced in and through colonial regimes of domination (Ayyash 2017).

This difficulty was not lost on some of the activist groups involved in the uprising. The April 6 Youth Movement, in which women played a critical role (Hafez 2014a, 89; Khamis and Mili 2018b, 5), and materials produced by a group of feminist activists, Nazra for Feminist Studies, provide windows into the workings of the sexual contract in the Egyptian revolutionary and postrevolutionary moments. Even though these two groups (among others) never managed to shape the movement as a struggle against gender-power relations, it is important to understand how they perceived the stakes of this struggle. I begin with how activists, in particular those of the April 6 Youth Movement, attempted to rethink the social-political relationship and sought to create it anew.

Mona el-Ghobashy (2011) argues that three mobilizing structures or sectors were operative in the Egyptian uprising of January 2011: workplace, neighborhood, and association. Each had its own dynamics and mobilizing techniques, but the important point is that all three built bridges across ideological divides despite the differences in the contents of their claims. The three sectors managed to link and unite in a diffuse manner that was very threatening to the Mubarak regime, which, despite its best efforts, could not divide and conquer the various groups in these sectors. One of these groups was the April 6 Youth Movement, which played an important role in mobilizing the massive demonstrations on January 25, 2011.[1]

Central to April 6's message was its notion of freedom. On the surface, this notion of freedom seems abstract and unattainable, but its appeal is based precisely on its universality. In the April 6 discourse was a notion of freedom so broad that it became not only easily relatable across Egyptian society but also easily communicable across cultures and nation-states: not just freedom from authoritarian rule, torture, death, and poverty but also a freedom for self-rule, for collectively benefiting from the created wealth of the nation and a freedom that is an assertion of the people's willpower over the power of tyranny (April 6 Youth Movement 2011f, 2011g). On a fundamental level, April 6's was not a political notion of freedom but a social one. It certainly made political and economic promises, but they were promises that the movement could not possibly achieve or deliver. However, the social collectivity that this freedom created and in which it operated was precisely what made the diffuse unity of the uprising possible in the first place. That is, not only did this notion of freedom claim the desired collectivity, but it also in fact created a social collectivity that was observable in the actions of the activists and people in the streets of Cairo and beyond.

In a sense, this freedom was not April 6's own to formulate and spread; rather, it became palpable only in everyday practices, actions, and words. If April 6's ideas and tactics introduced freedom as a universality, they could do so only because of the actions and beliefs and cries of the thousands of Egyptians who largely had no political or social movement affiliations. Street cleaning, health and education services, distribution of food and drink, street art, poetry readings, collective prayers and the human chains that surrounded and protected them, the formal and informal discussions, the building of shelters in Tahrir Square—all of these actions and more were part of the emerging social collectivity that spread across Egypt. The protestors' ability to build their desired Egypt, a free Egypt, became possible,

1. See Abdul-Magd 2012 for an overview of some of the Western-mediated myths of the Egyptian revolution. For a useful overview of the social, political, and economic conditions and processes that sparked and facilitated the Arab uprisings, see Gelvin 2012.

became a lived experience, in this moment of social freedom within the social realm. All of the Mubarak regime's efforts to break this social collectivity, to separate the various groups, failed one after the other, and this failure can be explained by the people's formation of a new social-political relationship. Although on a fundamental level this notion of freedom was a social one, it operated across both the social and the political realms. This can be seen, briefly, across three analytical dimensions that I have theorized elsewhere (Ayyash 2017, 1205–7): communication, membership, and participation in rule.

First, the protestors' collectivity fed and kept feeding on a new free Egypt that was communicated in words and actions across Egypt by anyone and everyone as well as with such speed and intensity that it staved off separation of groups that might have occurred through power relationships and hierarchical lines of communication (Telmissany 2014, 40–41). Because the message and notion of freedom were not anyone's to own or deliver, the collectivity truly emerged from, of, and for the people. Simultaneously, the protestors engaged in heated and important debates between the different groups (on economic systems, the role of religion, public civility, etc.) on and off the streets, maintaining a sense of difference within the collectivity. Avoiding hierarchical lines of communication allowed the protestors to avoid making a distinction between the social (concerning the basic necessities of life, such as food, shelter, etc.) and the political (concerning constitutions, governance, etc.). The two spheres became indistinguishable with respect to the goal and project of Egyptian liberation and freedom.

Second, all Egyptians were more or less included in the uprising, regardless of their ideological or political beliefs and affiliations and even if briefly they avoided the dynamic of one group possibly coming to overpower all others (Singerman 2013; Telmissany 2014, 40–41). To be a member of the uprising, one merely had to be present on the streets. There were certainly boundaries of membership, evident in the highly nationalistic character of the uprising, but they were not overly rigid boundaries of membership. The protestors welcomed any and all non-Egyptian support and presence on the streets (from activists to media) and, indeed, drew inspiration, tactics, and strategies from a wide variety of international and transnational sources (from Tunisia to Serbia) (Gelvin 2012, 53–55). This combination of acceptance of all within certain nonrigid and ever-shifting boundaries allowed the uprising to avoid the dangers of separation (i.e., it did not matter who you were or where you were from; so long as you contributed in any way, you were a member of the uprising) and to avoid the dangers of a unidirectional relationship within the Egyptian sociopolity, wherein certain groups were included in the membership but without having any real voice or place within the membership. Membership could thus operate openly and transparently across the social and the political.

Finally, there was total participation[2]—anyone could start a discussion group, for example—but it was understood that no one individual or group was exempt from doing any given task, including those that might have been considered menial. That the organizers and the loosely called "leadership" would undertake all required activities on and off the street displayed a mode of rule where no task was deemed so menial that it was ejected from the realm of worthy tasks. The interconnection of the parts and the whole was so apparent that one's mere presence on the streets became part and parcel of the dawn of a new Egypt. Not only did sweeping the streets, for example, not carry a stigma whereby the one who did it would occupy a lower position within the division of labor, but the task itself also became the embodiment of the highest ideals and causes. Rule itself—where everyone participated in ruling and in being ruled, where the small act of cleaning a street was indistinguishable from the larger goal of a free Egypt—became at one and the same time freedom.

It is precisely in this free, open, transgressive operation across the social-political, reimagining the relationship and creating it anew, that the uprising's promise and indeed major achievement can be seen (Telmissany 2014, 44–45).[3] But it is also here that the uprising's major difficulties can be spotted, which manifested themselves in greater scope in the postrevolutionary moment. As May Telmissany puts it, two opposite utopian projects were at play here: "One is looking backwards to the past and imposing it on the present, the transcendental utopia [e.g., the Islamists and the military regime]; and the other one imagines the present and the future in terms of a fundamental transformation of the social and political order, the revolutionary utopia [e.g., April 6]" (2014, 38).

Most significantly, then, this opposition can also be observed in the struggle among feminists, the military, and the Muslim Brotherhood. Many analysts and commentators focus on the rift between feminists and the Muslim Brotherhood, and although it is an important rift and requires analytical attention (Moussawi and Koujok 2019), the confrontation between feminist groups and the military is the primary contention that exhibited the disintegration of the social collectivity well before the constitutional debate with the Muslim Brotherhood.

2. Participation does not necessarily mean presence in the streets and squares of Egypt. Many people were not able to participate outside the home, which was especially the case for many women. Yet it would be a mistake to overlook these women and cast them as nonparticipants; on the contrary, they were active in myriad and often unseen affective ways (Winegar 2012).

3. Khalid Amine offers a similar argument that focuses on the element of "revolutionary-becoming" and emphasizes the long-term processual character of the uprising, which was exemplified, for Amine, in theatrical performances across the region (2013, 100).

I cannot generalize about all feminist groups and activists,[4] but it is fair to argue that Nazra for Feminist Studies provides a window into the dynamics of disintegration that I am interested in examining. Nazra identifies itself as "a group that aims to build an Egyptian feminist movement, believing that feminism and gender are political and social issues affecting freedom and development in all societies."[5] This group of women and men strive to educate the public on gender and feminist issues and to make these issues part of everyday discussions, debates, and vocabularies. Their activities cut across all sectors, such as the production of sociological knowledge on gender issues, support for female political figures and human rights defenders (see Nazra for Feminist Studies 2012b), the creation of art that speaks to gender issues, the education of youth, and the litigation of court cases on gender issues. Nazra also documents human rights abuses and violations of women and supports all and any group that combats these crimes in general but gender-based crimes in particular. Two of the more heinous crimes that target women specifically are sexual violence and the "virginity tests." Both crimes were regular features of the Mubarak regime and the military regime that assumed power between Mubarak's resignation and Mohamed Morsi's election, the Supreme Council of the Armed Forces (SCAF), headed by Field Marshal Abdel Fattah al-Sisi (Kurtz 2015, 345). Nazra rightly does not explain away these crimes by attributing them to a few "rogue" officers or soldiers but rather makes clear in its statements that these crimes "will not stop until militarism is dismantled in Egypt" (Nazra for Feminist Studies 2011c). The "virginity tests" were well organized by SCAF and were meant to oppress, humiliate, and punish women so as to discourage all women from protesting the authoritarian military rule (Singerman 2013).

Nazra (along with other organizations and groups) points out how SCAF continued to systematically function on the former regime's laws and methods for suppressing demonstrations and dissent in general: SCAF indoctrinated and trained its soldiers to physically abuse and kill demonstrators without regard to human rights or life; it used emergency laws in its formulation of tactics and policies; it used armed criminals in civilian clothes to attack peaceful protestors; and it refused to seriously investigate crimes committed against protestors in general and women in particular (Johansson-Nogués 2013, 400).[6] The military's

4. For an overview of feminist thought and activism in Egypt during the twentieth and twenty-first centuries as well as a discussion of some of the various feminist/women's groups and organizations that participated in the uprising, see Middleton-Detzner et al. 2015, 330–36, and Zakarriya 2014.

5. Quoted from Nazra's website at http://nazra.org/en/about-us.

6. For examples, see Nazra for Feminist Studies 2011a and 2012a.

repeated and systematic targeting of activists and defenders of women's human rights "include[d] arbitrary detention, beatings and kicks, at times with military boots, dragging, attempted choking, sexual harassment including attempts to strip women, rape threats during detention, insults of a sexual nature" (Nazra for Feminist Studies 2011b). This strategy of separating the protestors along gender lines shows precisely how SCAF aimed to reestablish its postcolonial authority through brutal forms of gendered separation and the fermentation of divisions (Hafez 2014a, 91).

Nazra was not blind to these tactics and strategies, not only the separation of men and women but also the separation of the protestors along sectarian and religious lines.[7] Nazra rejected the idea that so-called sectarian violence required the state to act as the "guardian" of women against the chaos and uninhibited violence committed by religious fundamentalists. Its members understood that the state's mode of narrating sectarian violence was the same in structure as the state's narration of "protecting women from lustful men" on the streets of Egypt.[8] They articulate this point when discussing the violent attacks against human rights defenders of Coptic Christians on October 9, 2011, which left twenty-five people dead and three hundred injured. SCAF was quick to paint these events as clashes between Muslims and Christians and as interference by the proverbial "foreign elements," while ignoring the crucial role the military forces themselves played in these violent events, which was evident in testimonies of eyewitnesses and television cameras. SCAF simply continued the Mubarak regime's policy of exacerbating the problem of sectarianism and using it to create more separation and violence within Egyptian society in order to place itself in the only position to deal with this sectarian violence and to protect people from it (see Nazra for Feminist Studies 2011d).

The experiences of several organizations and political movements within Egypt support this observation. April 6 and other groups, for example, sought to create and indeed did create joint demonstrations of solidarity between Christians and Muslims who decried and opposed sectarian violence. The authorities actively opposed such solidarity initiatives and movements. That the authorities, according

7. This can also be seen in some of April 6's somewhat desperate calls to Egyptians not to let themselves be distracted by the authorities' tactics to divide and separate them under the guise of maintaining "security." Activists astutely drew a direct link between a divided Egyptian population and the failure of the uprising very early on in this process. See, for example, April 6 Youth Movement 2011e.

8. This is the main reason why I focus on the rift between feminists and the military as opposed to the rift between feminists and the Muslim Brotherhood.

to April 6, continuously showed their willingness to work with and support armed criminals and Islamist fundamentalists but never committed their resources and support to groups such as Nazra speaks to the point that the authorities wanted to exacerbate sectarianism (see April 6 Youth Movement 2011a, 2011b, 2011c). For Nazra, this issue of sectarianism follows the same grammar of gendered divisions. The marked feature of a postcolonial authority—that is, what shows it is following the colonial logic—is that it exists on the basis of stark and volatile divisions and separations within the sociopolity and, indeed, cannot exist otherwise (see Ahmad [1980] 2006, 129–30, 140).

Postcolonial authority cannot exist on the basis of an open and free debate between differing viewpoints. I am not referring here to the tired and scripted public "debates" that we might find today in the mainstream media and official political arenas of Canada and the United States. I am referring, rather, to unscripted debate or, better yet, Gadamerian dialogue, where the dialogue unfolds so as to reach into the heart of the subject matter at hand and follows the subject's different dimensions irrespective of the interlocutors' intentions or, to a certain extent, their interests. We can see glimpses of this kind of dialogue emerging in the public arena during the revolutionary and postrevolutionary moments: a thoughtful, incise, respectful, yet highly critical analysis by Nazra challenging the Muslim Brotherhood on the rights of women (Emam 2012); public discussions among diverse groups on the meanings of liberty, freedom, democracy; a plethora of new social media outlets and voices discussing and arguing over issues of taxation, everyday social interactions, constitutional rights, civil associations, civil society, public transportation, respectful social behavior, religious ceremonies, public holidays, the economy, and so on; public art from graffiti to music to poetry readings that challenged and critiqued social mores and norms; an April 6 campaign that encouraged all Egyptians to "write your constitution" (electronically or orally or graphically) and to participate fully in the construction of this crucial document (April 6 Youth Movement 2011d).

This is not a romanticized view of such activities, nor is it an overestimation of their value and "originality" (a troublesome word regardless of the context). Rather, these activities' value becomes clear when they are counterposed to the constitutional debates that firmly gripped Egypt after the Muslim Brotherhood won the elections. Despite the efforts of activist groups such as Nazra and April 6, the Muslim Brotherhood not only monopolized the debate over the Constitution but also actively excluded various groups from the writing of it under President Mohammad Morsi in 2012. Nazra specifically points out the exclusion of women from the constitutional debates and the predictable exclusion of women from the public sphere in the written Constitution (a claim supported in Maya

Morsy's [2014] study of this issue). It was as if women had not even participated in the uprising (Middleton-Detzner et al. 2015, 337–38; Nazra for Feminist Studies 2013a), so they responded in the only appropriate manner: they went back to the streets to affirm their rights and ownership of their past, present, and future.

Massive protests and demonstrations in the early summer of 2013 backed the army in its removal of Morsi and the Muslim Brotherhood. While many activists and protestors celebrated the removal of the Muslim Brotherhood, and, of course, while many other Egyptians who voted for Morsi mourned and rejected this turn of events (and were consequently violently attacked and suppressed by SCAF), groups such as Nazra supported the army in the actual ouster but were extremely wary of the direction in which the army was heading. They could already see that the army was making superficial promises and engaging in empty rhetoric, particularly on women's issues. Because Nazra and April 6 were all too aware of the military's involvement in violence against women, its sustained tactics and strategies to oust women from the political sphere and limit their roles in the social sphere—that is, because they understood that SCAF sought to reactivate the sexual contract—they could already observe in the summer of 2013, perhaps more so than other groups, that the army was beginning to reentrench itself as the postcolonial authority (see Nazra for Feminist Studies 2013b). They were well placed to observe this trend because of their attentiveness to the workings of the patriarchal masculine spaces (whether Islamist, secular, or military) that dominate Egyptian public life and continuously regulate, suppress, and oppress women's bodies within that space (Hafez 2014b, 182–84).

In addition to the virginity tests, Nazra documents some of the cases of rape and sexual assault and harassment that took place in the vicinity of Tahrir Square during various periods of protest (see Nazra for Feminist Studies 2012c). For the members of Nazra, these "mob"[9] attacks against women were indicative of deep social problems regarding gender and gender-based violence—problems that, of course, had preceded the uprisings.[10] The powerful testimonies[11] of women who

9. Nadje al-Ali points out some of the pitfalls of utilizing the rhetoric of "male mob violence," particularly in how this rhetoric hides the political economy of gender-based violence as well as the sociopolitical organization of such attacks and reduces the matter to "Arab culture" or to the "uncontrollable Arab man," thus reproducing Orientalist discourse (2014, 122–25). It is important to add that activists have made some progress in changing and shaping public discourse on the issue of sexual harassment (Eltantawy 2018; Langohr 2015).

10. These problems are of course not unique to Egyptian society or to the Arab world, as some Orientalists would like us to believe.

11. See, for an example, Nazra for Feminist Studies 2013c.

have experienced such attacks provide a penetrating critique of the social and political dimensions of Egyptian society and make apparent the urgent necessity of directly facing and tackling gender and feminist issues on both the social level and the political level. In other words, power works on multiple levels to discourage women from fully participating in the social and political spheres (al-Ali 2014, 126–27). *And the form of division inscribed into these gender-power relations always already lends itself to a postcolonial authority that cannot exist without separation*: it is in this sense that the sexual contract, insofar as it separates the social and the political as opposing spheres, underpins the postcolonial authoritarian regime.

The fissure between the social and the political was already underway in Tahrir Square during the uprising, and it took the form (among others) of gender-power relationships, of the (re)formation of a sexual contract. Activists, women and men, observed this fissure and responded as best they could by forming security checkpoints, human chains, and educational workshops on gender relations. They perhaps instinctively understood the stakes of this fissure. SCAF also perhaps instinctively understood the stakes and quickly employed tactics and strategies to widen the fissure, to destroy the bridge that was being built across it, and in doing so began in earnest the most effective counterrevolutionary battle: a strategy that first and foremost concerned the reestablishment of the social-political division as a firm and decisive opposition through gender-power relations.

The failures in the Egyptian uprising can be found not in the fact that there were competing and differing ideologies and political affiliations within the movement. It is not simply the case that these different groups could create and sustain a unity within the revolutionary moment only because their common enemy, Mubarak, was the greater evil or that the unity shattered after the removal of this enemy or that their competition with each other separated all the different groups in a battle that served none of them at the end. This is not a case of the movement not being able to maintain a fidelity to the initial ethos of the uprising (à la Badiou 2012). The main difficulty of the uprising was that the movement as a whole, outside of groups such as Nazra and April 6, never fully saw their actions and proclamations as being fundamentally an effort to bridge the social-political divide, the underlying structure of which is the sexual contract. Even though some groups and activists managed to successfully accomplish this feat in so many innovative ways, the inability to firmly establish this accomplishment across the movement as a whole and then transpose it into the postrevolutionary moment led to the failures of the constitutional debates and the consequent reentrenchment of the postcolonial authority. The social and the political were allowed to maintain their oppositional divide, and in this fissure the military was able to reassert itself, thus highlighting that the persistence of postcoloniality is secured not on its own ideological ground but on the difficulty of thinking and living a new social-political relation. The latter task must begin with a reconfiguration of gender relations and the dismantling of the sexual contract.

Conclusion

Sahar Khamis and Amel Mili contend that a "reason for the prominence of gender issues in the midst of the Arab Spring or Arab Awakening movements is the crossover from the political to the social realm, and vice versa, as illustrated by the myriad of overlapping issues and intersecting activities which Arab women took part in, and across these two domains simultaneously" (2018b, 3). As the revolutionaries, in particular women, cut across the social-political divide, they were incisively attacking the core structure of postcolonial authoritarian power: the separation of the social and the political. The failure of this latest attempt to cut across the divide means that these gendered revolutions are unfinished. There are numerous reasons for this latest failure (without of course overlooking the gains); most prominent perhaps is the revolutionaries' inability to trickle down ideas from more or less elite urban spaces to the masses (Khamis and Mili 2018a, 245–51). Such analysis is critical for the next round of revolutionary upheaval, and activists, civil society organizations, and movements need to critically reflect on lessons learned from the uprisings with the goal of improvement "the next time" in mind. But I want to emphasize here in the conclusion that the difficulties that revolutionaries face are not just restricted to Egyptian or Arab Muslim sociopolitics. Rather, these obstacles and problems are rooted in the colonial, neocolonial, and postcolonial construction of the social-political as an oppositional structure throughout the world.

Much of Euro-American political and public discourse centers the failures of the Egyptian uprisings around the idea that "Arab and Muslim culture" is incapable of building, securing, and cementing democracy, freedom, and gender equality. This chapter shows, however, that what Egyptians face as a major obstacle is not any sort of cultural exceptionality but, indeed, a postcolonial authority that thrives on a colonial sexual contract—a system of rule and power that is salient around the world. The appearance of sexual violence in the uprisings was *not* simply a manifestation of Arab or Muslim culture but rather of the colonial sexual contract that the postcolonial authoritarian regime used to reentrench the social-political relationship as oppositional. The challenge that the revolutionaries faced and continue to face today is nothing short of a radical and major transformation of the social-political relationship that has been constructed and cemented through centuries of colonial modernity.

In my previous theorization of that relationship, I asked: "Does the challenge of decolonial struggles concern not 'democratization' but rather the radical transformation of fundamental conceptions of the social-political?" (Ayyash 2017, 1207). The challenge of dismantling the sexual contract is not unique to the Egyptian context, but it is bigger than the challenge as manifested in Euro-American states and societies precisely because of the colonial and imperial power practiced by those very same states and societies in Egypt and other parts of the MENA region. The burden that these revolutionaries must bear is none other than building a new decolonial world that destroys the logics, systems, structures, cultures, economics, politics, and worldviews of colonial modernity. In this enormous task, the solution cannot be to mimic Euro-American states and societies that were only—could only be—constructed as "democratic" and "free" by their colonial, neocolonial, and settler-colonial destruction of societies across the globe. These Euro-American states and the colonial global system are part of the problem that is to be overcome if the next generation of Egyptian and other revolutionaries are to successfully destroy the sexual contract and inaugurate a new decolonial society and politics.

References

Abul-Magd, Zeinab. 2012. "Occupying Tahrir Square: The Myths and the Realities of the Egyptian Revolution." *South Atlantic Quarterly* 111, no. 3: 565–72.

Ahmad, Eqbal. [1980] 2006. "Postcolonial Systems of Power." In *The Selected Writings of Eqbal Ahmad*, edited by Carollee Bengelsdorf, Margaret Cerullo, and Yogesh Chandrani, 128–41. New York: Columbia Univ. Press.

Al-Ali, Nadje. 2014. "Open Space Reflections on (Counter)Revolutionary Processes in Egypt." *Feminist Review* 106:122–28.

Amine, Khalid. 2013. "Re-enacting Revolution and the New Public Sphere in Tunisia, Egypt, and Morocco." *Theatre Research International* 38, no. 2: 87–103.

April 6 Youth Movement. 2011a. "April 6 and Baradei Campaign Sponsor Popular Reconciliation and National Unity March in Imbaba Denouncing Sectarian Tribulations." May 10. At http://6april.org/english/modules/news/article.php?storyid=54.

———. 2011b. "April 6 Statement Concerning the Horrific Sectarian Events at Imbaba." May 10. At http://6april.org/english/modules/news/article.php?storyid=56.

———. 2011c. "April 6 Youth Form Committee to Protest Imbaba Churches." May 9. At http://6april.org/english/modules/news/article.php?storyid=52.

———. 2011d. "April 6 Youth Launch 'Write Your Constitution' Campaign for Discussion." June 13. At http://6april.org/english/modules/news/article.php?storyid=81.

———. 2011e. "The Reasons Why We Must Continue Our Revolution." Mar. 7. At http://6april.org/english/modules/news/article.php?storyid=30.

———. 2011f. "Tunisia Flying towards Freedom." Jan. 15. At http://6april.org/English/.

———. 2011g. "Why Are We Participating in the 'Second Uprising-Friday 27/5'?" May 24. At http://6april.org/english/.

Ayyash, Mark Muhannad. 2017. "Rethinking the Social-Political through Ibn Khaldûn and Aristotle." *Interventions* 19, no. 8: 1193–209.

Badiou, Alain. 2012. *The Rebirth of History: Times of Riots and Uprisings*. New York: Verso.

Dabashi, Hamid. 2012. *The Arab Spring: The End of Postcolonialism*. New York: Zed.

Das, Veena. 2007. *Life and Words: Violence and the Descent into the Ordinary*. Berkeley: Univ. of California Press.

Eltantawy, Nahed. 2018. "'I Am Untouchable!' Egyptian Women's War against Sexual Harassment." In *Arab Women's Activism and Socio-political Transformation: Unfinished Gendered Revolutions*, edited by Sahar Khamis and Amel Mili, 131–48. Cham, Switzerland: Springer International for Palgrave Macmillan.

Emam, Fatma. 2012. "Critical Review." Nazra for Feminist Studies, Feb. 25. At http://nazra.org/en/2012/02/critical-review-statements-manal-abul-hassan.

Gelvin, James L. 2012. *The Arab Uprisings: What Everyone Needs to Know*. New York: Oxford Univ. Press.

El-Ghobashy, Mona. 2011. "The Praxis of the Egyptian Revolution." *Middle East Research and Information Project* 41 (Spring). At http://www.merip.org/mer/mer258/praxis-egyptian-revolution.

Hafez, Sherine. 2014a. "Gender and Citizenship Center Stage: Sondra Hale's Legacy and Egypt's Ongoing Revolution." *Journal of Middle East Women's Studies* 10, no. 1: 82–104.

———. 2014b. "The Revolution Shall Not Pass through Women's Bodies: Egypt, Uprising, and Gender Politics." *Journal of North African Studies* 19, no. 2: 172–85.

Jilani, Sarah. 2021. "The Pioneering Anticolonial Feminism of Nawal El Saadawi (1931–2021)." *Art Review*, Mar. 30. At https://artreview.com/the-pioneering-anti-colonial-feminism-of-nawal-el-saadawi-1931-2021/.

Johansson-Nogués, Elisabeth. 2013. "Gendering the Arab Spring? Rights and (In)Security of Tunisian, Egyptian, and Libyan Women." *Security Dialogue* 44, nos. 5–6: 393–409.

Khamis, Sahar, and Amel Mili. 2018a. "Concluding Remarks: What's Next?" In *Arab Women's Activism and Socio-political Transformation: Unfinished Gendered Revolutions*, edited by Sahar Khamis and Amel Mili, 241–52. Cham, Switzerland: Springer International for Palgrave Macmillan.

———. 2018b. "Introductory Themes." In *Arab Women's Activism and Socio-political Transformation: Unfinished Gendered Revolutions*, edited by Sahar Khamis and Amel Mili, 1–23. Cham, Switzerland: Springer International for Palgrave Macmillan.

Kurtz, Mariam M. 2015. "The Egyptian Revolution Empowers Women." In *Women, War, and Violence: Topography, Resistance, and Hope*, vol. 1, edited by Mariam M. Kurtz and Lester R. Kurtz, 343–48. Santa Barbara, CA: Praeger.

Langohr, Vickie. 2015. "Women's Rights Movements during Political Transitions: Activism against Public Sexual Violence in Egypt." *International Journal of Middle East Studies* 47:131–35.

Middleton-Detzner, Althea M., Jillian M. Slutzker, Samuel F. Chapple-Sokol, and Sana A. Mahmood. 2015. "Women and the Egyptian Revolution: A Dream Deferred?" In *Women, War, and Violence: Topography, Resistance, and Hope*, vol. 1, edited by Mariam M. Kurtz and Lester R. Kurtz, 325–42. Santa Barbara, CA: Praeger.

Morsy, Maya. 2014. "Egyptian Women and the 25th of January Revolution: Presence and Absence." *Journal of North African Studies* 19, no. 2: 211–29.

Moussawi, Fatima, and Samira Koujok. 2019. "The Political Participation of Women in the Arab World: Mapping the Movement, Experiences, and Challenges Facing Arab Women from the Beginning of the Twentieth Century until the Post–Arab Uprisings Era: Expectations, Paths, and Outcomes." In *Women, Civil Society, and Policy Change in the Arab World*, edited by Nasser Yassin and Robert Hoppe, 33–61. Cham, Switzerland: Springer Nature for Palgrave Macmillan.

Nazra for Feminist Studies. 2011a. "Army Shootings against Civilians a Dangerous Precedent for Which There Must Be Accountability." Apr. 10. At http://nazra.org/en/2011/04/army-shootings-against-civilians-dangerous-precedent-which-there-must-be-accountability.

———. 2011b. "Continued Militarization." Dec. 18. At http://nazra.org/en/2011/12/continued-militarization-increased-violence-against-women-human-rights-defenders.

———. 2011c. "During the Celebration of the International Day on Women Human Rights Defenders." Dec. 11. At http://nazra.org/en/2011/12/women-activists-are-still-being-pushed-away-public-sphere-authorities.

———. 2011d. "Maspero: State Incitement of Sectarian Violence and Policy of Extrajudicial Killings." Oct. 16. At http://nazra.org/en/2011/10/maspero-state-incitement-sectarian-violence-and-policy-extrajudicial-killings.

———. 2012a. "Abbasiya Events a Continuation of SCAF's Systematic Violations of Human Rights in the Transitional Period." May 7. At http://nazra.org/en/2012/05/abbasiya-events-continuation-scaf%E2%80%99s-systematic-violations-human-rights-transitional-period.

———. 2012b. *Manual on Women Human Rights Defenders*. Apr. 30. At http://nazra.org/en/2012/04/manual-women-human-rights-defenders.

———. 2012c. "Testimonies on the Recent Sexual Assaults on Tahrir Square Vicinity." June 13. At http://nazra.org/en/2012/06/testimonies-recent-sexual-assaults-tahrir-square-vicinity.

———. 2013a. "Analytical Paper: The Right of Women to Public Political Space." July 28. At http://nazra.org/en/2013/07/analytical-paper-right-women-public-political-space.

———. 2013b. "Exclusion of Women in the Political Process and the Constitutional Declaration Should be Treated Immediately." July 12. At http://nazra.org/en/2013/07/exclusion-women-political-process-and-constitutional-declaration-should-be-treated.

———. 2013c. "Testimony from a Survival of Gang Rape on Tahrir Square Vicinity." Jan. 26. At http://nazra.org/en/2013/01/testimony-survival-gang-rape-tahrir-square-vicinity.

El Saadawi, Nawal. 1993. "Women's Resistance in the Arab World and in Egypt." In *Women in the Middle East: Perceptions, Realities, and Struggles for Liberation*, edited by Haleh Afshar, 139–45. London: Palgrave Macmillan.

———. 2005. "Imperialism and Sex in Africa." In *Female Circumcision and the Politics of Knowledge: African Women in Imperialist Discourses*, edited by Obioma Nnaemeka, 21–27. London: Praeger.

Singerman, Diane. 2013. "Youth, Gender, and Dignity in the Egyptian Uprising." *Journal of Middle East Women's Studies* 9, no. 3: 1–27.

Telmissany, May. 2014. "The Utopian and Dystopian Functions of Tahrir Square." *Postcolonial Studies* 17, no. 1: 36–46.

Winegar, Jessica. 2012. "The Privilege of Revolution: Gender, Class, Space, and Affect in Egypt." *American Ethnologist* 39, no. 1: 67–70.

Zakarriya, Jihan. 2014. "Sexuality, Religion, and Nationalism: A Contrapuntal Reading of the History of Female Activism and Political Change in Egypt." *Journal of International Women's Studies* 16, no. 1: 47–61.

Afterword

A Personal Retrospection on the Aborted Spring and Islamic Exceptionalism

Khaled Abou El Fadl

For so many in the Middle East and North Africa (MENA) region, the series of events that unfolded roughly from the end of 2010 to the end of 2011 was nothing short of thrilling and even ecstatic. It is important to remember that the story began when a street vendor named Mohamed Bouazizi in the city of Sidi Bouzid, Tunisia, was purportedly slapped on the face by a policewoman. Like many unlicensed street vendors, Bouazizi had spent his life enduring the twin indignities of poverty and being hounded by officers who are accustomed to humiliating and mistreating disempowered citizens. Feeling degraded and despondent, Bouazizi did something relatively uncommon in the Arab world. In a public act of self-immolation, he set himself on fire in an open square, and this was the spark that ignited the Tunisian revolution—also known as Thawrat al-Bouazizi, which literally means the "Bouazizi Uprising" (Zemni 2015, 77). Likewise, the protests and uprisings in Egypt were partially incited by the brutal beating to death of a young man named Khaled Said, who had uncovered and filmed unlawful drug-trafficking activities by a few police officers. His death led to the formation of the "We are all Khaled Said" opposition movement and in due time to the adoption of the same motto as an archetypal slogan in the Egyptian revolution (see Ghabra 2015, 199–214; Ketchley 2017; Marfleet 2016).

Many imbued the series of uprisings that spread across the Arab world in 2011 with a variety of competing interpretations and meanings, some more flattering or outlandish than others. But it was indisputable that the uprisings that covered the span of Tunisia, Egypt, Libya, Syria, Yemen, Bahrain, Jordan, Algeria, Morocco, Sudan, Oman, Iraq, and Kuwait—and even Saudi Arabia for a short time—came as a sign of some type of awakening or pulse of a new emerging life (Ramadan 2012). Although the expression "Arab Spring" was coined in the West, many commentators in the Middle East gleefully and gratefully adopted it. It did seem like the dawn of a new age. In the early stages of each uprising, demonstrators emphasized their rejection of violence and their insistence on the right to peacefully protest by repeating "silmiyya, silmiyya" (peaceful, peaceful) (Abou El Fadl 2015). The rallying cries of *silmiyya* must have challenged and irked all the Western Islamophobic pundits, who are accustomed to pontificating about jihad and the proclivity of the Muslim mind toward violence and militancy. Not only this, but in nearly all of the protests one heard the same demands being repeated again and again—*hurriyya* (liberty), *karama insaniyya* (human dignity), and a protest against poverty articulated in a single word: *'ish* (bread) (Abou El Fadl 2015, 253–60). In nearly all of the protests, women participated in great numbers (Cooke 2016), and in most cases the demonstrators seemed at least for a while to have overcome ethnic, sectarian, and religious divides; it also appeared that they asserted their demands on behalf of a citizenry reclaiming its right to citizenhood within the framework of the modern nation-state.

Like so many other Arabs watching these events, I was glued to my television screen, anxiously anticipating the reactions and counterreactions and mining every possible bit of credible data that could be uncovered from a network of academics, journalists, politicians, and activists. Anxiety turned to shock, disbelief, and even exuberance as we witnessed a number of the oldest despots and firmly anchored dictatorships in the region succumb and seemingly fall. I am not ashamed to admit that on the day that Hosni Mubarak fell, I shed tears of happiness because I could not have ever imagined that I would live to see the day that the Mubarak family would no longer be in power.

It is difficult to explain the sense of excitement and hopefulness that enthralled the hearts and minds of so many during the revolutions of the Arab Spring. The Arab Spring ignited the dream that had lain dormant since the age of colonialism: that the Arabs exercise a level of autonomy over their own affairs, that they elect their leaders and hold them accountable, and that they cease to be simply the passive recipients of whatever history dictates. Arabs have for long ached to shape and craft their destinies while taking ownership of their own history. But now, in light of the ignoble fate of the Arab Spring, it is exceedingly difficult to recall, let alone write about, the thrill and infectious optimism that enraptured so many in the early days of the demonstrations.

Indeed, now that the revolutions have been subverted and the possibilities of change have been thoroughly squashed (Abou El Fadl 2015, 258), it is equally difficult to acknowledge the sense of loss and the bitter dreariness that at the present haunt one's mind. The somber and often mournful sentiments of which I speak are not just over the loss of what appeared to be a historic opportunity for fundamental and essential progress but, more importantly, over the enormous sacrifices made by countless Arabs who were killed, maimed, imprisoned, or tortured in the course of the forgone Spring. Carrying the burden of knowing the intimate details of the involvement of perhaps too many people and the stories of their untold suffering, and having lost so many friends who sacrificed their lives for the sake of a better future, I suffered a massive heart attack shortly after the coup in Egypt in July 2013. The moment the military launched its coup, the Arab Spring and all the dreams it had engendered became an aborted project. I could very clearly see that the coup in Egypt meant that the old order represented by Saudi Arabia, the United Arab Emirates (UAE), the Mubarak regime, Jordan, and Kuwait—this old order with all its corruption and draconian tyranny—had succeeded in breaking the back of the revolution and that democracy had once again become a very distant fantasy in the Arab world as well as perhaps in the entire MENA region (Fraihat 2016; Hellyer 2016; Marfleet 2016).

All too often, those living in the West fail to appreciate or even to imagine the sheer magnitude of the sacrifices made by so many in the Arab world in pursuit of the dream of liberty, dignity, and justice. The fact that these causes are so broad as to encompass a sweeping variety of ideological orientations ranging from the far left to the far right and from the staunchly secularist to the conservatively Islamist does not in any way lessen or take away from the enormity and sanctity of the sacrifices made. As a matter of conviction and faith, I have always believed that the rights of human beings do not expand and shrink in proportion to the danger or risk their ideas and actions may pose. In other words, a saint and a criminal have the same human rights; we do not treat them differently because they are entitled to different rights. We treat them differently despite their equal rights, and we do so because the criminal presumably has violated the rights of others; thus, an affirmation and restoration of the principle of equal rights are made necessary. The images of women, children, and men murdered and tortured as they attempted to demand their most basic right to living with dignity and honor free from the degradations of despotism and corruption haunt my conscience and being. As painful as these images are, they are also profoundly humbling. Therefore, despite the melancholia and gloom and, of course, the heart attack and other ailments, there remains no choice but to bear witness and testify.

As an Arab Muslim academic who immigrated to the United States in the 1980s, I often found myself in a position of having to narrate myself—as in bearing witness by testifying to one's own experiences in life—to a Western audience that is simultaneously eager to understand but uncomfortably distant and aloof. With the rise of Islamophobia and intellectualized racism and bigotry in the West, narrating the self has become for an Arab Muslim not just humbling but rather debasing and at times ignominious (see Abou El Fadl 2014, 151–182; Ali et al. 2011; Ernst 2013; Lean 2012; Sheehi 2011). It is debasing because one's testimony is suspect simply on the grounds that one is a Muslim and an Arab, and it is ignominious in that one becomes like the prototypical native informant who, knowingly or not, colludes with the powerful against the disempowered and therefore, intentionally or not, collaborates in his or her own debasement. With this said, though, my personal narrative is in so many ways unremarkable and indistinguishable from the narratives of numerous Arab Muslims. Like so many, I was driven out of my homeland because of the abysmal status of human rights in Egypt. In Egypt, as in all the countries of the Arab Spring, human beings have no rights. Whatever rights people are allowed to enjoy are as if a gratuity bestowed by the benevolent despotic state that has the power to do what it wills, with whomever it wills, and whenever it wills.

As a child, I was weaned on the sour taste of political oppression. My father was a political prisoner in one of Gamal Abdel Nasser's prisons, and we grew up painfully aware of the effects of torture upon him. As a child, I would hear and at times read memoires about the indescribable torments that political prisoners in Egypt had to endure. After being imprisoned for a year, during which he was repeatedly tortured, my father was forced to flee Egypt, and at one point he and his children (me and my siblings) were stripped of Egyptian citizenship. Through benevolence or corruption or a mixture of both, we were able to obtain Jordanian passports so that we did not join the Palestinians in the ignoble status of being without citizenship. Our Egyptian citizenship was eventually restored, but by then I was grown up enough to become painfully aware of our status as guests in Kuwait. I grew up there with the perpetual fear that at any time if I had the displeasure of picking a fight with the wrong Kuwaiti, or if I voiced an undesirable opinion, I could be deported from Kuwait without haste. Even more terrifying was the possibility of a sufficiently influential Kuwaiti claiming that they heard me insult the emir (the prince of Kuwait) or the ruling family—an accusation that could lead to being tortured, imprisoned, and, if one was lucky, deported. Even a traffic violation was a terrifying possibility because it would bring one in contact with the local police and their whimsies. Kuwaiti police treated people according to an unofficial class system based on nationality, not financial status. Fellow Arabs, unless from another Persian Gulf oil-producing country, were not treated well but ultimately fared a little better than people from South Asia. First-class treatment was reserved for people from the West as long as they looked white; so, for instance, an Egyptian or Palestinian holding US citizenship would still be treated with the whimsical arrogance reserved for fellow Arabs.

My more personal brushes with autocratic power occurred when as a young man in my late teens I started publishing short stories and poetry. I cannot remember the number of times I was warned by teachers and others about the political messages contained within my prose. But I think it was my regular attendance at Islamic circles of learning (known as the *halaqa*s) that led to the most agonizing and traumatic encounters with the autocratic state's whimsical powers. I got to experience firsthand the horror of being entirely at the will and whim of a state that is dedicated to the thorough dehumanization and extinction of its perceived potential enemies. This state, however, considers an enemy to be any person who might question the legitimacy of power that is yielded without limits, constraints, or principles. In other words, any person who perceives of his or her relationship to the state in terms of a citizenry and its public servants instead of in terms of ruling masters and their obsequious servants becomes a potential enemy of the state.

After torture, a person's bonds to society and community become severely strained because, if nothing else, the survivor is forced to go through the agonizing process of rehumanizing after becoming thoroughly dehumanized. Many never succeed in restoring their shattered sense of being, and the consequences are often disastrous both for the survivors and for society. Like so many before and after me, I could not rebuild my broken self in Egypt, where all sanctities were violated and all social bonds had become deconstructed. I often wondered what would have become of this shattered and alienated self if I had not been able to reach the safe haven of the United States, where I struggled to reclaim and heal the fragments of humanity that remained within. Sadly, the fates of my friends and others who remained trapped within the authority of the state that persecuted them were invariably tragic.

In the United States, I threw myself into the cathartic work of human rights advocacy and service. I worked on more cases of detainees, refugees, asylees, displaced persons, and other victims of human abuse than I can possibly remember. I also worked with many prominent American and international human rights nongovernmental organizations on cases all over the Muslim and Arab worlds. Again, there was nothing atypical in someone with my background launching himself in human rights work to make sense of a world in which very few beings can be said to actually possess inviolable rights. My experience, however, was atypical only in one regard: I worked from a distinctly religious and, more specifically, Islamic perspective in the culture of human rights advocacy, which tends to be areligious and markedly secular. For me, thinking through the theological and philosophical consequences of reconciling the Islamic tradition to the human rights tradition became a lifetime endeavor. The anchoring point for me always was the fact that in my view there could be no greater heresy or blasphemy than what I had experienced in Egypt. One of the foundational dogmas of Islam is that God dignified and honored human beings, and so they cannot be rightfully robbed of this dignity. Moreover, only God may demand submission of people, but in Islamic dogma submission to God means freedom from submission to anyone but God. For the past fifty years or more, Arab states—whether pronouncedly secular or ostensibly Islamic—have consistently usurped God's authority and demanded absolute submission from their citizens (see Diamond and Plattner 2014; Heydemann 2017; Karakoç 2015). In the damp, dark, bloodied cells of Cairo's political prisons, where the echoes of the screams of agony never stop, I heard officers tell their prisoners: "If Allah came down from the heavens to help you, we would throw Him in the cell right next to you, and you would hear His screams of agony!" To pretend that human rights are not needed to restrain the mad powers of the modern state is an indulgence of sheer foolishness!

There are thousands, if not millions, of personal narratives of physical abuse and oppression in the Arab world like mine and much worse. Of course, it is naive to think that the success of the Arab revolutions would have meant an end to all human rights abuses or an immediate transformation of the political system or the civic order necessary for upholding and promoting human rights. However, such a success, as incomplete and misguided as it would have been, would certainly be a step toward the dialectical negotiation of a constitutional and democratic order that synthesizes inherited cultural and religious values with contemporary values of self-rule, autonomy, and immunities or protections that are held against the state. Most critically, the success of the Arab Spring would have meant a break with the repetitive ruinous and crippling cycle that has plagued the Arab states since colonialism.

Colonial powers in the Middle East realized that every substantial resistance movement against foreign domination was Islamically motivated and driven. From Napoleon's invasion of Egypt in 1798 on, colonial powers found that Islam was utilized, especially by Sufi orders, as a powerful motivational and organizational force in movements of cultural and military resistance. Not surprisingly, as a result, colonial powers developed a rather contradictory and derogatory discourse. On the one hand, Islam was cast as the source of Oriental despotism because of its political quietism. On the other hand, it was depicted as a militant and radicalizing faith that led to political instability. Colonial countries played a critical role in educating the elites of Middle Eastern states to the extent that, for instance, the British insisted the sons of the khedives and later on of the kings of Egypt receive their primary educations in England. Other than the cultural literary elite, colonial powers exercised a profound influence on the militaries of most

Arab countries. After abolishing the domestic military systems of the colonialized countries, colonial powers built new military organizations that, although often nationalistic, were organized, trained, and supplied by their former colonial masters. Colonial powers finally formally withdrew from the occupied territories, but not before creating client states that were heavily dependent on their former colonial masters militarily, financially, epistemologically, and culturally (Abou El Fadl 2013; Abul-Magd 2017). The elites of these client states, including their militaries, Western-modeled judiciaries, and police forces, were and continue to be thoroughly alienated from their native intellectual and epistemological heritage. In all cases, a paradigm was set in motion that continues to hold sway today. The colonizers considered themselves trustees charged with the obligation of civilizing the uncivilized, and the subsequent native rulers applied the same logic but saw themselves as bearers of the burden of development and modernization of a backward and reactionary people. The irony is that in all the Arab republics, the state persistently pushes the argument that whatever autocratic and repressive measures it takes are necessary to prepare society for eventual democracy. Every single republican Arab state has been purportedly preparing its society for democracy for the past seventy years (Bolme 2015)!

Part and parcel of the state's purported efforts to achieve development and modernization was for it to take control of the institutions of faith and thus to shape and define civil religion. Whether ruling through a theocracy or some form of purported republican system of governance, Arab rulers inherited the colonial attitude of visceral fear of Islamic activism unless it is strictly controlled by the state (Abou El Fadl 2014, 203–14). Historically, this attitude has led to nationalizing all Islamic institutions that at one time were part of civil society as independent private charitable endowments and to marshaling them in the state's service (Abou El Fadl 2014, 304–5). The emergence of expressions of Islamicity or Islamically inspired activism outside the officially constructed civil religion, such as the circles of learning that I attended, is often met with brutal savagery.

Since the advent of colonialism and beyond, Arab Muslims have been confronted by stark choices—either they are secularists in the sense of excluding religion from the public sphere, or they must accede to the civil Islam as constructed and controlled by the state's apparatus. This polarized and exclusionist stasis has compelled the production of numerous religiously inspired movements that range from the traditional conservative to the liberal reformist. To one degree or another, all these homegrown movements have tried to reclaim an original and native form of Islam that does not pander to the interests of neocolonial Western states or to the interests of the national petty autocrats of the Arab world. The postcolonial autocratic Arab states' response has consistently been the same: brutal repression of anything it cannot control and dominate. The game changer in this equation was the aggressive intervention of Saudi-sponsored Wahhabi Islam, which, rich in petrodollars, managed to co-opt much of the traditional fundamentalist Islamic movement and in doing so reoriented its priorities from challenges to unjust power to indulgences in sectarianism, patriarchy, and orthoproxy (Abou El Fadl 2005 and 2014, 215–70).

The Arab Spring did nothing short of threaten this entire empire of corrupt power by ripping Islamicity out of the hands of the state, including the Saudi Wahhabi state, and restoring it to the public space, where it would have to negotiate its place unaided and unmolested by the hands of the autocratic state. I recall that shortly after the start of the Tahrir Square demonstrations, I was sent a copy of a decisively resolute Saudi fatwa advising all Muslims who demonstrate against the holders of power or who join any purported revolution that they were buying a permanent place in hellfire. The urgent and desperate tone of the Saudi fatwa betrayed to me the sense of shock at the fact that the petrodollars had failed to contain the situation, in Egypt in particular, and the sense of desperation at the mere prospect of a radical renegotiation of an Islamicity in the absence of a brutally repressive state, such as Mubarak's and others like it. At the time, I responded to the fatwa by arguing that it had no sound basis in Islamic jurisprudence and that it was strictly a political and not a legal fatwa. Perhaps the Saudis' anxiety only escalated when they found that during the Arab Spring very few people were in the mood to listen to their dutifully malleable and pliant jurists.

However, the Saudis had learned well from their colonial masters: if people demand power to the people, then put together a coup! The national military can repress people to death while claiming to hold power on behalf of and in protection of the people! The magic of the national military is that anyone that opposes it risks appearing as if they have no regard for national security and that they are unpatriotic. Hence, in the name of patriotism and fighting terrorism, Abdel Fattah El Sisi of Egypt and Bashar al-Assad of Syria have slaughtered thousands and will slaughter thousands more. Having secured a coup in Egypt, Saudi Arabia and its allies were now ready to move against the revolutions in Libya, Yemen, and Tunisia.

Most of the Western world stood silent and impervious to the atrocities committed by the coup in Egypt, by the Saudis in Bahrain, by the Egyptians and Emiratis in Libya, and by the Saudis and Emiratis in Yemen (see Aras and Falk 2015; Sager 2014). In the name of the war on terror, the Trump administration continued to unleash a frenzy of violence in Afghanistan, Iraq, Yemen, Libya, Syria, Somalia, and Niger. And in the name of fighting Islamism and preempting the revolutionary zeal of Islamists, human rights violations escalated to unprecedented levels not only in the Arab world but also against Muslims in China, India, and Myanmar. I, like so many intellectuals before me, am left puzzled: Is Israel the only democracy (if it can be called such) that the West and their Arab allies are willing to support or even allow to exist in the Middle East? Is any compromised solution possible that does not involve the slaughter and torture of a group and the suppression of an entire civilizational heritage? After the sacrifices and horrendous sufferings by the beleaguered people of the entire MENA region, is it possible to conceive of a more dignified future? I believe that when all is said and done, the unfinished social movements of the MENA region are quintessentially and fundamentally about identity and human dignity.

The worst thing for an intellectual is to suspect that his entire life's work has been for naught. For so many Muslim intellectuals from the so-called subaltern world, our words pale in contrast to the enormity of the power structures and privileges that we try to challenge. As the fate of the journalist Jamal Khashoggi and so many like him remind us, the price of speaking out is often so very high. Personally, for all the writings I churned out on the Arab Spring, especially on Egypt, I now find myself where my father was more than fifty years ago. I am unable to visit Egypt or even go to pilgrimage in Mecca because of the horrors of the persecution that would inevitably await me. I have not been able to attend the funerals of loved ones who were murdered in Egypt or visit age-old friends who have been sentenced to ridiculous prison terms simply for expressing their opinions on a Twitter or Facebook account or for holding a sign while silently demonstrating. Perhaps history will put those who committed true crimes against humanity where they belong and grant those who rose up against tyrants their rightful place. Perhaps. But believing this will happen requires a leap of faith—a leap of faith that is persistently undermined and frustrated by the continued surreptitious racism of Islamophobia and exceptionalism.

I must admit that I grow weary of responding to Islamophobia and arguments about Islamic exceptionalism. Both Islamophobia and Islamic exceptionalism are ideological stances with a horrible pedigree rooted in the White Man's Burden and colonialism (Abou El Fadl 2014, 125–35). It is true that one must be alert to the particularism and integrity of each culture, and one must also respect the right to be different. But even the most intellectualized arguments cannot be separated from the power dynamics that inspire, legitimate, and revive them. Islamophobia and arguments touting Islamic exceptionalism have without exception been marshalled in the service of despotism, oppression, and injustice. To my knowledge, the "clash of civilizations" thesis and the argument for Islamic exceptionalism have never been invoked in the context of privileging Muslims with morally praiseworthy values (Abou El Fadl 2014, 183). They are invariably invoked in the context of privileging Muslims with Oriental despotism, oppression, injustice, patriarchy, and inequality—in short, with barbarism. The idea that natives are barbaric and are incapable of civilization is at least as old as colonialism, and as an epistemic attitude and vision it has always been animated by racism, ethnocentrism, and religious bigotry. Against statist arguments that serve to legitimate oppressive power structures, it is imperative that we insist on critical honesty in interrogating the epistemic vision that animates such arguments, and we have every right to be deeply skeptical of any vision that consistently places a people in a subordinate and inferior position.

In my view, the intellectual vision that one beholds is ultimately a product of personal experience. This is precisely why I chose to provide a retrospective to the learned articles by eminent scholars in this volume by sharing my own personal experiences in response to the Arab Spring, a pivotal event in the modern history of the entire MENA region. The chapters in this book have already vetted out the incoherence of the arguments in support of Islamic exceptionalism, but in sharing my personal experience I hope to emphasize that there is one simple core issue for so many Muslims in the modern age: dignity. In the modern age, dignity is not possible without basic, fundamental, and inherent human rights. Numerous theological and philosophical challenges confront Muslims in developing a human rights commitment anchored in the epistemologies of the modern age (Abou El Fadl 2003). However, such a commitment and the parallel epistemological awareness it mandates are not possible without the personal experiences that evolve in a democratic practice. Put simply, as long as Muslims continue to theorize about democracy without practicing it, there will be little progress, and this is precisely why the aborted Arab Spring was such a huge loss.

I do hope that Mojtaba Mahdavi is correct in his assessment that the social movements of the MENA region have not exhausted their momentum. The challenge is that there are no inevitabilities in history, and whether the region moves toward democracy or something else depends on numerous internal and external factors that are impossible to predict. For instance, it is highly unlikely that the Islamic State would have ever emerged had it not been for the US invasion of Iraq and the unprincipled, undisciplined, and asymmetrical so-called war on terror. Purportedly, the United States has military troops in Egypt, Lebanon, Syria, Jordan, Iraq, Saudi Arabia, Kuwait, UAE, Qatar, Bahrain, Oman, and Turkey. Other Western countries such as Britain, France, and Italy are involved in the region through their own proxy allies. It is naive to think that the persistent military interventions in the region do not have a radicalizing and polarizing impact that consistently impedes progress toward democracy. I agree with Tariq Ali that there has been a virtual recolonization of the Arab world, and in my view this process of recolonization consistently robs the Indigenous population of the right to self-determination. It is rather incredulous that many analysts pretend that the garish military interventions in Near Eastern countries, the arming of various warring sectarian groups, and the exploitative policies pursued through proxy dictators do not radicalize and polarize the politics of the region. The election of Donald Trump as well as his pathological hostility toward Iran, his unbridled and unprincipled support of Israel's brutal occupation of Palestine, and his support of brutal dictatorships in Egypt, Saudi Arabia, UAE, and Bahrain have had an undeniable corrupting impact on any social momentums toward democracy.

Mahdavi and others argue that many social movements in the MENA region no longer ascribe to an Islamist paradigm that seeks to establish an Islamic state. Rather, the prevailing paradigm among social movements in the MENA region is post-Islamist. According to Mahdavi, post-Islamism is "a notion referring to a profound discursive and sociohistorical transformation in MENA and other Muslim-majority societies wherein neither the hegemonic universalism of colonial modernity nor a supposed cultural essentialism/particularism of Islamism captures the complexity of the region" (introduction). Mahdavi explains further that "a post-Islamist polity is not a caliphate; it is a modern civil/*urfi* democracy attentive to local culture and values, including those of Islam. Post-Islamism is a grassroots discourse—a 'universalism from below' that synthesizes the global and local paradigms of social justice, freedom, human rights, and Islamic values. It is a glocal paradigm" (introduction, citations omitted). I agree with Mahdavi that numerous sociocultural transformations in the MENA region have led to the sound deconstruction of the legitimacy of the theocratic state, in which the government rules and legislates in God's name. I also agree that the idea of an Islamic state is a postcolonial invention that does not have sound justification in the Islamic tradition.

The irony is that after the Arab Spring, what emerged as the sworn enemies of so-called political Islam and of Islamist or post-Islamist movements are countries such as the UAE and Saudi Arabia. Theologically, both countries fully embrace and continue to support what is known as the Jami-Salafi or al-Madkhaliyya al-Jamiyya Salafi creed.[1] This creed emphasizes blind obedience to rulers as one of God's solemn laws and condemns democracy as a heresy. According to this creed, even if the ruler commands the subjects to commit a sin, or even if the ruler openly violates God's laws, the ruler is owed nothing but absolute and

1. The name "Madkhaliyya" refers to this creed's founder, Rabi' ibn Hadi al-Madkhali, who promotes Salafi quietism. His teachings can be accessed through a dedicated website at http://rabee.net/ar/. For a study of Salafism in Saudi Arabia, see, for example, Lacroix 2011. For the typology of Salafism, see Hegghammer 2009, 244, and Wiktorowitcz 2006.

unquestioning obedience. In some of the more infamous fatawa of this creed, even if the ruler fornicates on public television every day, or if the ruler murders one-third of a country's population, nevertheless disobedience or rebellion remains the gravest sin (Abou El Fadl 2018). Like the theology of al-Qaeda and the Islamic State, the Jami-Salafi creed is an offshoot of Wahhabism. Like traditional Wahhabism, it is decisively anti-Shi'ite, anti-Sufi, and antidemocratic, but unlike Wahhabism it is strictly politically quietist. But Jami-Salafism is not an otherworldly theology that emphasizes mysticism or strict piety, and it is not necessarily apolitical. Paradoxically, Jami-Salafism enthusiastically supported the coup in Egypt and has been among the strongest supporters of Sisi's despotic government. It fair to say that Jami-Salafism is identical to traditional Wahhabism except that it considers criticizing or disobeying the ruler to be the gravest sin against God (Bozeid 2012).

Not surprisingly, Jami-Salafism has been opportunistically convenient for authoritarian secular regimes in the Middle East. More importantly, under the leadership of Mohammed bin Salmanal Saud, Saudi Arabia has recently withdrawn its support of traditional Wahhabism and imprisoned hundreds of Wahhabi ulama who opposed or simply refused to support Jami-Salafism. Saudi Arabia is currently funding and supporting Jami-Salafism as the only legitimate and orthodox version of Sunni Islam. Although it would not be accurate to claim that the governments of Egypt and the UAE have propagated Jami-Salafism, as the Saudi government has done, both governments have become sworn enemies of so-called political Islam and have enthusiastically endorsed Jami-Salafism as an acceptable alternative.

Like the Islamophobes in the West, the governments of Saudi Arabia, the UAE, Egypt, and Bahrain make no distinction between the Muslim Brotherhood of Egypt and the Nahda (Renaissance) Party in Tunisia (Abou El Fadl 2017; Qandil 2018). Likewise, these states do not distinguish among political Islam, Islamism, and post-Islamism. The only form of Islamism they are willing either to tolerate or to endorse is Jami-Salafism. But despite Saudi Arabia's best efforts and significant resources, I doubt whether Jami-Salafism will catch on and become to any extent as significant a movement as traditional Wahhabism. Having said this, however, one cannot ignore the fact that in the Sunni world Jami-Salafism has the power of oil money behind it. Nevertheless, it is important to point out that Jami-Salafism rejects the establishment of a caliphate, would welcome the creation of an Islamic state but does not seek it, accepts the legitimacy of secular governments as God's will but is morally opposed to democratic governance, and espouses absolute and unconditional obedience to the Guardian of the Holy Sites—in other words, the rulers of Saudi Arabia. Jami-Salafism is thoroughly modern in the sense that it has adapted Islamic theology to the demands of the secular nation-state but has done so in the most opportunistic fashion. It is also glocal in the sense that it adapts global and international products to local and particularized demands but, again, does so in the most politically opportunistic fashion. Jami-Salafism considers the legalization of something formerly forbidden—such as music and women driving cars—to be theologically acceptable because it is part of God's will, the part that is contingent on the will of the ruler, whether this ruler is secularly or religiously inspired.

My point in emphasizing the role of the Saudi-backed Jami-Salafism is to pose the following question: Is Jami-Salafism post-Islamist? My goal is not to challenge the concept of post-Islamism but to emphasize that whether we designate a movement as Islamist or post-Islamist does not seem to me to be the material issue. The material issue is expressed in one word: *democracy*. The issue is whether a movement, Islamist or post-Islamist, accepts that people have basic inalienable rights, that people have a right to elect their governments and hold these governments accountable, and that a movement accepts the basic and fundamental proposition that the primary role of a government is to represent the will of the people and not the will of any other power, including God. This does not mean the complete exclusion of God's law from the public space within a polity, but there are two important qualifiers. One, people must be free to accept or reject most laws that claim to be rooted in the divine will; and, two, it is critical to differentiate between divine laws that overlap with universal natural laws and those that do not. Natural laws, like overlapping basic and fundamental divine laws—such as the prohibitions against murder, punishment without due process, or torture—are moral and legal norms that are beyond majoritarian desires. Of course, the issue of precisely which divine laws overlap with universal natural law and thus may be considered fundamental and invariable human norms or just cogens is a complex question that warrants separate treatment (Abou El Fadl 2014, 291).

Since the break of modernity, the logic of exceptionalism has always incited Western policy makers, at the very least, to distrust the emergence of innate and umbilical democratic and constitutional movements in the Muslim world. Practically, this has meant that native homegrown Islamic movements that aspire toward democracy and constitutionalism are forced to contend not only with local national despots but also very often with the foreign powers that back up and support these despots. The history of colonialism and postcolonialism is replete with truly ignoble examples in which Western powers, especially the United States, Britain, and France, helped abort homegrown Muslim democratic movements. Unfortunately, as noted earlier, the distrust of Islam and anything Islamic is deeply rooted in European and American histories, and the logic of Islamic exceptionalism only legitimates, bolsters, and empowers this distrust, very often with horrendously tragic consequences. The problem with the logic of Islamic exceptionalism is that very often it ignores the fact that dignity is an inherent and fundamental human right and that in the contemporary age democracy and constitutionalism are indispensable instrumentalities for upholding and safeguarding the right to human dignity. How to precisely reconcile between Islamic theology and law, on the one hand, and the instrumentalities of democracy and constitutionalism, on the other, must be left up to Muslims. But as long as Islamic theology and law remain a source of political and cultural dread, a proverbial boogeyman, for both the West and secular Muslims, I fear that the entire MENA region will remain locked in an endless cycle of despotism, exclusion, violence, and human suffering.

References

Abou El Fadl, Khaled. 2003. "The Human Rights Commitment in Modern Islam." In *Human Rights and Responsibilities in the World Religions*, edited by Joseph Runzo, Nancy M. Martin, and Arvind Sharma, 301–64. London: Oneworld.

———. 2005. *The Great Theft: Wrestling Islam from Extremists*. New York: HarperOne.

———. 2013. "The Praetorian State in the Arab Spring." *University of Pennsylvania Journal of International Law* 34, no. 2: 305–14.

———. 2014. *Reasoning with God: Reclaiming Shari'ah in the Modern Age*. Lanham, MD: Rowman & Littlefield.

———. 2015. "Failure of a Revolution: The Military, Secular Intelligentsia, and Religion in Egypt's Pseudo-Secular State." In *Routledge Handbook of the Arab Spring: Rethinking Democratization*, edited by Larbi Sadiki, 253–60. London: Routledge.

———. 2017. "Who's Afraid of the Muslim Brotherhood? How Hatred of Islam Is Corrupting the American Soul." *ABC Religion & Ethics*, Jan. 18. At https://www.abc.net.au/religion/whos-afraid-of-the-muslim-brotherhood-how-hatred-of-islam-is-cor/10096150.

———. 2018. "Saudi Arabia Is Misusing Mecca." *New York Times*, Nov. 12. At https://www.nytimes.com/2018/11/12/opinion/saudi-arabia-mbs-grandmosque-mecca-politics.html.

Abul-Magd, Zeinab. 2017. *Militarizing the Nation, the Army, Business, and the Revolution in Egypt*. New York: Columbia Univ. Press.

Ali, Wajahat, Eli Clifton, Matthew Duss, Lee Fang, Scott Keyes, and Faiz Shakir. 2011. *Fear, Inc.: The Roots of the Islamophobia Network in America*. Washington, DC: Center for American Progress.

Aras, Bülent, and Richard Falk. 2015. "Authoritarian 'Geopolitics' of Survival in the Arab Spring." *Third World Quarterly* 36, no. 2: 322–36.

Bolme, Selin M. 2015. "The Roots of Authoritarianism in the Middle East." In *Authoritarianism in the Middle East: Before and after the Arab Spring*, edited by Jülide Karakoç, 7–37. New York: Palgrave Macmillan.

Bozeid, Bomadyan. 2012. "Al-Jamiyya wa al-Usul al-Wahabiyya." In *Al-Salafiyya al-jamiyya: 'Aqidat al-ta'a wa tabdi' al-mukhtalif*, edited by al-Mesbar, 175–93. Dubai, United Arab Emirates: al-Mesbar.

Cooke, Miriam. 2016. "Women and the Arab Spring: A Transnational, Feminist Revolution." In *Women's Movement in Post-"Arab Spring" North Africa*, edited by Fatima Sadiqi, 31–44. New York: Palgrave Macmillan.

Diamond, Larry, and Marc F. Plattner, eds. 2014. *Democratization and Authoritarianism in the Arab World*. Baltimore, MD: Johns Hopkins Univ. Press.

Ernst, Carl W. 2013. *Islamophobia in America: The Anatomy of Intolerance*. New York: Palgrave Macmillan.

Fraihat, Ibrahim. 2016. *Unfinished Revolutions: Yemen, Libya, and Tunisia after the Arab Spring*. New Haven, CT: Yale Univ. Press.

Ghabra, Shafeeq. 2015. "The Egyptian Revolution: Causes and Dynamics." In *Routledge Handbook of the Arab Spring: Rethinking Democratization*, edited by Larbi Sadiki, 199–214. London: Routledge.

Hegghammer, Thomas. 2009. "Jihadi–Salafis or Revolutionaries? On Religion and Politics in the Study of Militant Islamism." In *Global Salafism: Islam's New Religious Movement*, edited by Roel Meijer, 244–66. New York: Columbia Univ. Press.

Hellyer, H. A. 2016. *A Revolution Undone: Egypt's Road beyond Revolt*. New York: Oxford Univ. Press.

Heydemann, Steven. 2017. *Upgrading Authoritarianism in the Arab World*. Washington, DC: Brookings Institution Press, Oct. 15.

Karakoç, Jülide, ed. 2015. *Authoritarianism in the Middle East: Before and after the Arab Uprisings*. New York: Palgrave Macmillan.

Ketchley, Neil. 2017. *Egypt in a Time of Revolution: Contentious Politics and the Arab Spring*. Cambridge: Cambridge Univ. Press.

Lacroix, Stephane. 2011. *Awakening Islam: The Politics of Religious Dissent in Contemporary Saudi Arabia*. Cambridge, MA: Harvard Univ. Press.

Lean, Nathan. 2012. *The Islamophobia Industry: How the Right Manufactures Fear of Muslims*. London: Pluto.

Marfleet, Philip. 2016. *Egypt: Contested Revolution*. London: Pluto Press.

Qandil, Mohamed Mokhtar. 2018. *The Muslim Brotherhood and Saudi Arabia: From Then to Now*. Washington, DC: Washington Institute, May 18. At https://www.washington institute.org/fikraforum/view/the-muslim-brotherhood-and-saudi-arabia-from-then -to-now.

Ramadan, Tariq. 2012. *Islam and the Arab Awakening*. New York: Oxford Univ. Press.

Sager, Abdul Aziz. 2014. "Challenging Time for Saudi Foreign Policy." *Arab News*, Jan. 23.

Sheehi, Stephen. 2011. *Islamophobia: The Ideological Campaign against Muslims*. Atlanta, GA: Clarity.

Wiktorowicz, Quintan. 2006. "Anatomy of Salafi Movement." *Studies in Conflict and Terrorism* 29, no. 3: 207–39.

Zemni, Sami. 2015. "The Roots of the Tunisian Revolution: Elements of a Political Sociology." In *Routledge Handbook of the Arab Spring: Rethinking Democratization*, edited by Larbi Sadiki, 77–88. London: Routledge.

Contributor
Biographies

Index

Contributor Biographies

Contributor biographies listed in order of appearance in this volume.

John L. Esposito (jle2@georgetown.edu) is University Professor of religion and international affairs and of Islamic studies at Georgetown University. He is founding director of the Alwaleed Center for Muslim–Christian Understanding and the Bridge Initiative: Protecting Pluralism—Ending Islamophobia at the Walsh School of Foreign Service. Esposito's more than fifty-five books include *Shariah: What Everyone Needs to Know* (with Natana Delong-Bas, 2018), *Religion and Violence* (2016), *Islam and Democracy after the Arab Spring* (with John O. Voll and Tamara Sonn, 2015), *The Future of Islam* (2013), *What Everyone Needs to Know about Islam* (2011), *Islamophobia: The Challenge of Pluralism in the 21st Century* (2011), and *Who Speaks for Islam? What a Billion Muslims Really Think* (with Dalia Mogahed, 2008). Esposito's books and articles have been translated into more than fifty languages.

Mojtaba Mahdavi (mojtaba.mahdavi@ualberta.ca) is professor of political science and chair in Islamic studies of the Edmonton Council of Muslim Communities at the University of Alberta. He is the author and editor of numerous works on post-Islamism, contemporary social movements, democratization in the Middle East and North Africa, postrevolutionary Iran, and modern Islamic political thought. He is the coeditor of *Rethinking China, the Middle East, and Asia in a "Multiplex World"* (with Tugrul Keskin, 2022) and *Towards the Dignity of Difference? Neither "End of History" nor "Clash of Civilizations"* (with W. Andy Knight, 2012). He served as the guest editor for the special issues "The Many Faces of Contemporary Post-Islamism" of the *Journal of Religions* (2021) and "Contemporary Social Movements in the Middle East and Beyond" of the *Sociology of Islam* (2014).

Peyman Vahabzadeh (peymanv@uvic.ca) is professor of sociology at the University of Victoria. He is the author and editor of nine books, including *The Art of Defiance: Dissident Culture and Militant Resistance in 1970s Iran* (2022), *Crossing Borders: Essays in Honour of Ian H. Angus* (with Samir Gandesha, 2020), *Violence and Nonviolence: Conceptual Excursions into Phantom Opposites* (2019), *A Rebel's Journey: Mostafa Sho'aiyan and Revolutionary Theory in Iran* (2019), *Iran's Struggles for Social Justice: Economics, Agency,*

Justice, Activism (2017), and *A Guerrilla Odyssey: Modernization, Secularism, Democracy, and Fadai Discourse of National Liberation in Iran, 1971–1979* (2010). Vahabzadeh has also authored eight books of poetry, fiction, literary criticism, and memories in Persian. His research has appeared in English, Persian, Spanish, German, Kurdish, and French.

Abigail B. Bakan (abigail.bakan@utoronto.ca) is professor in the Department of Social Justice Education (SJE) at Ontario Institute for Studies in Education and cross-appointed to the Department of Political Science. Her research is in the area of antioppression politics, with a focus on the intersections of gender, race, class, political economy, and citizenship. Her current research funded by the Social Sciences and Humanities Research Council (with Yasmeen Abu-Laban) addresses United Nations world conferences and declarations regarding antioppression and human rights. Her publications include *Israel, Palestine, and the Politics of Race: Exploring Identity and Power in a Global Context* (with Yasmeen Abu-Laban, 2020) and *Theorizing Anti-racism: Linkages in Marxism and Critical Race Theories* (coedited with Enakshi Dua, 2014). Her articles have appeared in *Race and Class*, *Social Identities*, *Rethinking Marxism*, *Politikon*, *Socialist Studies*, *Atlantis*, *Signs*, the *Canadian Journal of Law and Society*, and *Studies in Political Economy*.

Yasmeen Abu-Laban (yasmeen@ualberta.ca) is professor and Canada Research Chair in the politics of citizenship and human rights in the Department of Political Science at the University of Alberta. She is also a fellow at the Canadian Institute for Advanced Research. Her published research addresses ethnic and gender politics, nationalism, globalization and processes of racialization, immigration policies and politics, surveillance and border control, as well as multiculturalism and antiracism. She served as president of the Canadian Political Science Association in 2016–17 and as vice president of the International Political Science Association in 2018–21. She has coauthored and edited five books, including *Israel, Palestine, and the Politics of Race: Exploring Identity and Power in a Global Context* (with Abigail B. Bakan, 2020). She has also written more than one hundred journal articles and book chapters.

Navid Pourmokhtari (npourmok@ualberta.ca) holds a PhD in political science from the University of Alberta. His research interests lie in the areas of international relations, comparative politics, revolutionary movements, peace studies, and international security studies. His most recent publications have appeared in *Third World Quarterly*, *International Sociology*, *Jadaliyya*, the *Journal of Legal Pluralism and Critical Social Analysis*, and *Foucault Studies*. He is the author of *Iran's Green Movement: Everyday Resistance, Political Contestation, and Social Mobilization* (2021).

Juan Cole (jrcole@umich.edu) is a public intellectual, prominent blogger and essayist, and the Richard P. Mitchell Collegiate Professor of History at the University of Michigan. He has published in the areas of modern and contemporary history of the Middle East and

South Asia, intellectual and cultural history, and religion of Asia and Middle East. He is the author and editor of several books, including *Peace Movements in Islam: History, Religion, and Politics* (2021), *The Rubaiyat of Omar Khayyam: A New Translation with Historical Afterword* (2020), *Muhammad: Prophet of Peace amid the Clash of Empires* (2018), *Global Connections: Politics, Exchange, and Social Life in World History*, 2 vols. (2015), and *The New Arabs: How the Millennial Generation Is Changing the Middle East* (2014). He is also the author of many journal articles and book chapters.

Mariam Georgis (mariam.georgis@umanitoba.ca) is a Social Sciences and Humanities Research Council postdoctoral fellow in the Department of Political Studies and in Mamawipawin: Centre for Indigenous Governance and Community Based Research at the University of Manitoba. She is the coauthor of "Indigenising International Relations: Insights from Centring Indigeneity in Canada and Iraq" in *Millennium: Journal of International Studies* (with Nicole V. T. Lugosi-Schimpf) and "Violence on Iraqi Bodies: Decolonising Economic Sanctions in Security Studies" in *Third World Quarterly* (with Riva Gewarges), among other journal articles and book chapters.

Tariq Ali is a political activist, writer, journalist, historian, filmmaker, and public intellectual. He is a member of the editorial committee of the *New Left Review* and *Sin Permiso* and contributes to the *Guardian*, *Counter Punch*, and the *London Review of Books*. He has written more than two dozen books on world history and politics, including *Winston Churchill: His Times, His Crimes* (2022), *The Extreme Centre: A Warning* (2015), *The Obama Syndrome* (2010), *The Duel* (2008), *Conversations with Edward Said* (2005), *The Clash of Fundamentalisms: Crusades, Jihads, and Modernity* (2002), as well as five novels in his Islam Quintet series and scripts for the stage and screen.

Bessma Momani (bmomani@uwaterloo.ca) is full professor of political science and assistant vice president, research and international, in the Office of Research at the University of Waterloo. She is also a senior fellow at the Centre for International Governance and Innovation and a nonresident fellow at the Gulf States Institute in Washington, DC. She was also a nonresident senior fellow at the Brookings Institution. Momani is currently a governor on the International Development Research Council and formerly was on the National Security Transparency Advisory Group to advise the deputy minister of public safety and other government officials on improving the transparency of Canada's national security and intelligence departments and agencies. She has authored and coedited twelve books and more than eighty scholarly and peer-reviewed journal articles and book chapters that examine international affairs, diversity and inclusion, Middle East affairs, and the global economy. Her latest publications include *Middle Power in the Middle East* (coedited with Thomas Juneau, 2022), *What's Wrong with the IMF and How to Fix It* (with Mark R. Hibben, 2017), and *Arab Dawn: Arab Youth and the Demographic Dividend They Will Bring* (2015).

Melissa Finn (melissa.l.finn@gmail.com) is a research associate in the Department of Political Science at the University of Waterloo and the Balsillie School of International Affairs in Waterloo, Canada. She is the coauthor of multiple journal articles and chapters on citizenship, transnationalism, and youth political participation. She is the author *Al-Qaeda and Sacrifice: Martyrdom, War, and Politics* (2012).

Michael Frishkopf (michaelf@ualberta.ca) is professor of music at the University of Alberta, adjunct professor of medicine and dentistry, director of the Canadian Centre for Ethnomusicology, and adjunct professor in the Faculty of Communication and Cultural Studies at the University for Development Studies in Ghana. His research, including fieldwork in Egypt and Ghana, includes music and Islam, music and architecture, music and development, music and global health, soundscape therapy, digital repositories, virtual reality, artificial intelligence and machine learning, and social network analysis. He is the author and editor of numerous articles, chapters, and books, including *Music, Sound, and Architecture in Islam* (2018) and *Music and Media in the Arab World* (2010); a selected list of his publications is available at http://frishkopf.org. In 2011, he launched the documentary project *Songs of the New Arab Revolutions.*

Guilnard Moufarrej (moufarre@usna.edu) is associate professor in the Languages and Cultures Department at the United States Naval Academy and visiting scholar at the Institute of Music Research at the University of Wuerzburg, Germany. She is an ethnomusicologist specializing in Arab music and cultures in the Arab world and the diaspora. Her research areas include music and social protest; music and liturgy in the Eastern churches; music and forced migration; music and emotion; music and identity; and the role of music in foreign-language acquisition. She has published articles in the *Yearbook for Traditional Music, al-Masaq Journal*, and *al-ʿArabiyya Journal*, among others. Her forthcoming essay "Protest Songs, Social Media, and the Exploitation of Syrian Children" discusses the use of Syrian children in music and social media as a propaganda tool during the recent war in Syria. Her current project focuses on music, trauma, and community building among Syrian refugees in Germany.

George Mürer (gmurer@gradcenter.cuny.edu) is an ethnomusicologist and filmmaker with interests in Iran, Kurdistan, Central Asia, North Africa, and the Indian Ocean region. His doctoral work was on music and cultural performance among Baloch communities in the eastern Arabian Peninsula, and he has recently published articles devoted to aspects of this research in journals and edited volumes. He recently guest coedited a themed issue of *World of Music* (new series) on the topic "New Contours in Kurdish Music Research." He is completing a feature-length documentary on the professional circuits of young Kurdish wedding musicians and the subcultural dimensions to the aesthetics of electrification as well as working on a book project related to his doctoral research. Of late, he has been teaching at Hunter College, Brooklyn College, and Columbia University.

Carolyn Ramzy (carolyn.ramzy@carleton.ca) is associate professor of sociology and anthropology cross-appointed with music at Carleton University. She is an ethnomusicologist who focuses on Egyptian Christian popular music in Egypt and a growing diaspora in the United States and Canada. She is interested in how Orthodox music culture shapes the Coptic community's gendered subjectivities and the use of virtual technologies to challenge traditional understanding of (holy) belonging, sexuality, and faith. Her work has appeared in the *Journal of Canadian Society for Coptic Studies*, *Music & Politics*, *The Oxford Handbook of Musical Repatriation* (2019), and the *International Journal of Middle East Studies*, among other publications.

Jonathan Shannon (jshanno@hunter.cuny.edu) is professor of anthropology at Hunter College and a member of the doctoral faculties in music and anthropology at the Graduate Center of the City University of New York. His research and writing focus on aesthetics and music performance in the Mediterranean and Arab world, with a special focus on Syria, Morocco, and Spain. His current research investigates the dynamics of collective memory and musical performance among migrant Syrian musicians in Turkey and across Europe. He is the author of numerous articles and three books, including *Performing al-Andalus: Music and Nostalgia across the Mediterranean* (2015), *A Wintry Day in Damascus: Syrian Stories* (2012), and *Among the Jasmine Trees: Music and Modernity in Contemporary Syria* (2006).

Nermeen Youssef (nermeen@ualberta.ca) received her PhD in pharmacology from the University of Alberta and BS in pharmacy from Cairo University. Having always had a keen interest in the space where science, politics, and art intersect, she founded the Egyptian Film Festival in Edmonton and serves as a board member for Alberta's LitFest and Broad View International Film Festival in parallel to being a health-policy adviser for the provincial government.

Iman Mersal (iman.mersal@ualberta.ca) is a poet and associate professor in the Department of Modern Languages and Cultural Studies at the University of Alberta. Her writing has appeared in *Blackbird*, the *American Poetry Review*, *Parnassus*, *New York Review of Books*, *Paris Review*, the *Nation*, and the *New Republic*. She has read at numerous poetry festivals around the world, including the London Poetry Parnassus, billed as the biggest gathering of poets in world history, where she represented Egypt. Selected poems from Mersal's oeuvre have been translated into numerous languages, including English, French, German, Spanish, Dutch, Macedonian, Hindi, and Italian. *These Are Not Oranges, My Love*, a selection of Mersal's work translated into English by Khaled Mattawa was published in 2008, and a collection entitled *The Threshold*, translated into English by Robyn Creswell, was published in 2022. She is the recipient of the 2021 Sheikh Zayed Book Award in Literature for her creative nonfiction work *Fee athar Enayat al-Zayyat* (In the footsteps of Enayat al-Zayyat, 2019).

Ramin Jahanbegloo (ramin495@yahoo.com) is a public intellectual and currently vice dean and head of the Center for Mahatma Gandhi Studies at Jindal Global University, India. He formerly taught in the University of Toronto's Department of Political Science, served as the head of the Department of Contemporary Studies at the Cultural Research Centre in Tehran, and was Rajni Kothari Professor of Democracy at the Centre for the Study of Developing Societies in New Delhi, India. He has published many books, journal articles, and book chapters in English, French, and Persian on modernity, nonviolence, and cultural dialogue. His books include *Mahatma Gandhi: A Nonviolent Perspective on Peace* (2021), *Nonviolent Resistance as a Philosophy of Life* (2021), *Mapping the Role of Intellectuals in Iranian Modern and Contemporary History* (2021), *The Passion of Politics: Conversations with Contemporary American Political Philosophers Gene Sharp, Andrew Arato, and Michael* Walzer (2020), *The Gandhian Moment* (2013), *The Spirit of India* (2008), *India Revisited: Conversations on Contemporary India* (2007), *The Clash of Intolerances* (2007), and *Iran: Between Tradition and Modernity* (2004).

Roozbeh Safshekan (roozbeh.safshekan@ualberta.ca) received his PhD in political science from the University of Alberta and was a postdoctoral fellow at MIT. His research interests include cyberpolitics, international relations theory, and comparative social movements. His publications include two book chapters, "The Revolutionary Guard in Iranian Domestic and Foreign Power Politics" (with Farzan Sabet, 2019) and "An Unfinished Odyssey: The Iranian Student Movement's Struggles for Social Justice" (2017), as well as two journal articles, "Iran and the Global Politics of Internet Governance" (2017) and "The Matrix of Communication in Social Movements: A Comparison of the 1979 Revolution and 2009 Green Movement in Iran" (2014).

Paul S. Rowe (Paul.Rowe@twu.ca) is professor and coordinator of political and international studies at Trinity Western University. His research focuses on the politics of Christian minority communities in Middle Eastern states. He is the editor of *Routledge Handbook of Minorities in the Middle East* (2019) and the author of *Religion and Global Politics* (2012). His recent publications include "The Church and the Street: Copts and Interest Representation from Mubarak to Sisi" (*Religion, State, and Society*, 2020) and "The Open Sanctuary: Palestinian Christian Civil Society Organizations and the Survival of the Christian Minority in Israel–Palestine" (*Journal of Church and State*, 2017).

amina wadud (awadud@sksm.edu) is a visiting professor at the National Islamic University Sunan Kalijaga in Yogyakarta, Indonesia, and the Indonesian Consortium for Religious Studies at Gadja Mada University in Yogyakarta, Indonesia. She is also a visiting researcher at Starr King School for the Ministry in Oakland, California. amina wadud is the author of *Inside the Gender Jihad: Women's Reform in Islam* (2013) and *Quran and Women: Rereading the Sacred Text from a Women's Perspective* ([1992] 1999). She is founder of Queer Islamic Studies and Theology (QIST1.com), an online collaboration to resume the studies of sexuality as part of Islamic Studies. Mother of five, nana of six, she is best known as the Lady Imam. She currently resides in Indonesia.

Poyraz Kolluoglu (poyraz@hotmail.com) is assistant professor at Istanbul Aydin University, Turkey. His research interests and publications include gender and development, social and cultural anthropology, theories of nationalism, social movements, popular culture, and Turkish studies.

Victoria Tahmasebi-Birgani (v.birgani@utoronto.ca) is associate professor of women, gender, and sexuality studies in the Department of Historical Studies at the University of Toronto–Mississauga and in the Women and Gender Studies Institute at the University of Toronto. She is the author of *Emmanuel Levinas and the Politics of Non-violence* (2014). Her research and publications encompass feminist theories in relation to continental and transnational contexts, critical theories of women's movements in the Middle East, digital activism, gender and ethics of nonviolence, and contemporary history of social and political thought.

Nermin Allam (nermin.allam@rutgers.edu) is assistant professor of politics at Rutgers University–Newark. Before joining Rutgers, Allam held a Social Sciences and Humanities Research Council of Canada postdoctoral fellowship at Princeton University. She works on social movements, gender politics, Middle Eastern and North African studies, and political Islam. She is the coeditor of *Gulf Cooperation Council Culture and Identities in the New Millennium: Resilience, Transformation, (Re)Creation, and Diffusion* (with Magdalena Karolak, 2020) and the author of *Women and the Egyptian Revolution: Engagement and Activism during the 2011 Arab Uprisings* (2017).

Mark Muhannad Ayyash (mayyash@mtroyal.ca) was born and raised in Silwan, al-Quds (Jerusalem), before immigrating to Canada, where he is now a professor of sociology at Mount Royal University. He is the author of *A Hermeneutics of Violence: A Four-Dimensional Conception* (2019). He has published several academic articles on topics such as political violence, vaccine apartheid, exiling writing, the social-political relationship, and Palestinian decolonial movements in journals such as *Distinktion*, *Interventions*, *European Journal of International Relations*, *Comparative Studies of South Asia, Africa, and the Middle East*, and *European Journal of Social Theory*. He also is the author of multiple book chapters and coeditor of *Protests and Generations: Legacies and Emergences in the Middle East, North Africa, and the Mediterranean* (2020). He writes opinion pieces for al Jazeera, the *Baffler*, *Middle East Eye*, *Mondoweiss*, and the *Breach*, among other news sites and publications. He is currently writing a book on settler colonial and decolonial sovereignties in Palestine/Israel.

Khaled Abou El Fadl (ABOUELFA@law.ucla.edu) is the Omar and Azmeralda Alfi Distinguished Professor of Law at the University of California, Los Angeles (UCLA), School of

Law and the founder of the Institute of Advanced Usuli Studies (the "Usuli Institute"). He was also formerly the chair of the Islamic Studies Interdepartmental Program at UCLA. He is the author of numerous books and articles on various topics in Islam and Islamic law. His books include *The Prophet's Pulpit: Commentaries on the State of Islam* (2022), *Reasoning with God: Reclaiming Shari'ah in the Modern Age* (2014), *The Great Theft: Wrestling Islam from the Extremists* (2005); *Speaking in God's Name: Islamic Law, Authority, and Women* (2001), *Rebellion and Violence in Islamic Law* (2001), *Islam and the Challenge of Democracy* (2004), *The Place of Tolerance in Islam* (2002), *The Search for Beauty in Islam: A Conference of the Books* (2006), as well as *And God Knows the Soldiers: The Authoritative and Authoritarian in Islamic Discourses* (2001). He received the American Academy of Religion Martin E. Marty Award for the Public Understanding of Religion in 2020 and the University of Oslo Human Rights Award, the Leo and the Lisl Eitinger Prize in 2007.

Index

CPSIA information can be obtained
at www.ICGtesting.com
Printed in the USA
LVHW011200230623
750603LV00009B/72

9 780815 637929